W9-AQK-568

Better Homes and Gardens®

ENCYCLOPEDIA
of
COOKING

Volume 20

Tempt appetites with the wonderful aroma of homemade bread baked in the oven. This version, Three-Flour Bread, is prepared with all-purpose, whole wheat, and rye flours.

On the cover: For a truly elegant dinner, feature Standing Rib Roast surrounded by crisp and puffy Individual Yorkshire Puddings, which are baked separately in custard cups.

BETTER HOMES AND GARDENS BOOKS
NEW YORK • DES MOINES

© Meredith Corporation, 1970, 1971, 1973. All Rights Reserved.
Printed in the United States of America.
Special Edition. First Printing.
Library of Congress Catalog Card Number: 73-83173
SBN: 696-02040-8

WHEAT—The grain of a widely produced cereal grass. Wheat has been so basic to man's diet that it is called the "staff of life," and the term "daily bread" (made from wheat) symbolizes life's necessities.

Wheat shares honors only with rice as the leading food for the world's population. In the United States, Europe, and western Asia wheat is the predominant cereal grain. Only in the Orient and in Africa is rice more prominent.

Exactly where wheat originated is uncertain because wheat does not preserve well for archaeological purposes. Wheat is thought to be from the area considered the birthplace of mankind, southwestern Asia. It was used for food thousands of years ago, and there are records that reveal that the Chinese honored cereals in ceremonies as early as 2800 B.C.

Ancient tribes probably came across wheat in their wanderings. Finding the seeds good to eat, they returned to the wheat fields year after year. In time, they found that the grain could be stored and used both as food during the winter and as seed in the spring. As man began to fashion shelter so that he could stay near his crops, the land best suited to crop growth attracted settlers, who joined together in communities for mutual protection. In this way, wheat cultivation contributed greatly to civilization.

Neolithic man developed tools for wheat cultivation. He used a pointed stick for a plow and a crude sickle for harvesting. Even today, in some of the less developed areas of the world, similar tools are used for harvesting the crops.

Primitive man saw the relationship of wheat to life and incorporated wheat into his religion. The Egyptians believed that the goddess, Isis, discovered wheat in the country now called Lebanon.

The ancient Greeks worshiped Demeter, the grain goddess. The corresponding figure among Roman deities was Ceres, whose name evolved into "cereal." Unlike other gods, who, according to legend, could be arbitrary and cruel, Demeter was a provident, kind figure. She was worshiped not in the bloody sacrifices that were made to other gods, but in humble acts—petitions for a bountiful harvest.

Wheat has played a major role in shaping world history. "The first word in war is spoken by guns, but the last word has always been spoken by bread," said former President Herbert Hoover, who served as Chief of the American Relief Administration after World War I. History offers numerous examples to support his statement. For example, Napoleon's armies advanced so rapidly into Russia that food supplies were left far behind. The Russians destroyed food as they retreated, so when the tide of war turned, the French could not get any food.

Wheat is not native to North America. The Spaniards introduced wheat to Mexico in the 1500s, and British colonists brought wheat to America in 1607.

The development of wheat as a crop is an important chapter in the history of the American colonies. During the early years of colonial America, New Jersey, Pennsylvania, and Maryland were called the "bread colonies" because the people there were able to produce wheat beyond their own needs and export to their neighbors.

As the frontier moved west, so did the center of wheat production. Wheat was a good crop for pioneers. It requires less manpower per acre produced than most other grains, and it has comparatively good keeping qualities. Also, the frontier provided the wide stretches of land needed for wheat cultivation. These factors and the immense popularity of wheat foods made wheat a leading crop.

The outcome of the American Civil War has been described as a victory of bread over cotton. In the North enough wheat was grown to feed the Union army and the civilians. The South's principal product, cotton, could not be eaten.

Wheat classifications: There are many varieties of wheat, each named according to the morphology of the grain, plus the area where it is grown and its intended use. Wheat belongs to the genus *Triticum*, which includes several species, among them being common or bread wheat. Wheat varieties are divided into "hard" and "soft" varieties. Hard wheat contains a stronger quality gluten (elastic protein substance) than do the soft wheat

varieties. The varieties can be further divided into winter and spring wheats, based on planting times. In mild climates, such as that found in the Middle Great Plains, wheat is planted in the fall. It is called "winter wheat" and reaches maturity in June and July. In the states farther north, wheat is planted after the threat of frost is past and is called "spring wheat."

The major classes of wheat are hard red spring, hard red winter, durum, soft red winter, white, and red durum. The hard spring and winter wheats are used for bread flour; durum wheat, for pasta products; and soft red winter and white wheat, for pastry flour. Red durum is used for livestock feed.

In the United States, Kansas has been the leading producer of wheat in most of the years of the twentieth century. North Dakota has been on occasion a leading producer, but normally Kansas grows between one-sixth to one-fourth of the nation's total wheat crop.

How wheat is grown: In appearance the plant is slender and golden-colored, and is usually two to four feet high, but it can reach seven feet high. The kernels of the wheat plant are produced in spikes at the head of the stem. The head has four to ten rows of two to over ten kernels.

The wheat kernel is made up of three parts: endosperm, bran, and germ. The endosperm is the starchy interior which makes up about 83 percent of the kernel. Most of the protein in wheat is in the endosperm. The bran is the outer coat, which accounts for 14½ percent of the kernel. The bran is rich in the B vitamins, especially niacin. The germ is the embryo or sprouting section, making up 2½ percent of the kernel. It is usually separated from the rest of the kernel because its fat content limits the keeping qualities. The germ is especially high in thiamine.

How wheat is harvested and processed: Today's child may be confused by references to haystacks, such as the one that cradled "Little Boy Blue." Although once familiar on the rural landscape, they left when modern farm machinery arrived.

In 1831 Cyrus McCormick first demonstrated his mechanical reaper. Since that time, farm machinery has reduced the time required to harvest wheat.

After harvest, grain is stored by the farmer for later sale or is shipped to elevators. At the elevator, a sample of grain is taken from each load and a price is set according to the grade, weight, protein content, and moisture content. Market conditions also affect price. From the country elevator, wheat is shipped to larger storage facilities, either at mills or in silolike bins of a terminal elevator.

At the mill, wheat is made into flour. There are four steps to milling flour: cleaning, tempering, grinding, and post treating. During cleaning, the grain is separated from foreign material and each kernel is scoured clean. Tempering involves adding moisture, which helps separate the outer coatings of bran from the endosperm. During the grinding step, the wheat flows through metal corrugated rollers to give what millers call "the first break." The bran is removed and particles are sized and graded. The grinding continues until the endosperm is freed as much as possible from the bran and germ. The post treatment, depending on the future use of the flour may include blending, maturing, enriching, bleaching.

Parts of the wheat kernel

1   Endosperm

2   Bran

3   Germ

Delicately spiced nut bread

Sandwich slices of Whole Wheat Nut Bread → together with cream cheese, then cut in triangles, or serve thin slices with butter.

Nutritional value: The major wheat food in the United States is baked bread. About 98 percent of the products from commercial bakers are made of white flour, which is made from the endosperm (the natural nutrients of the bran and germ have been removed). The endosperm contains protein, the B vitamins, and carbohydrate.

To compensate for this lack of nutrients, enrichment of the bread is now required in many of the states and in Puerto Rico. In actual practice, all family flours are enriched as is much of the commercially baked standard white bread.

Enrichment first came about as a result of surveys taken during the 1930s, which showed that poor diets were widespread. During the Second World War, concern for improving nutrition grew. The **National Nutrition Conference for Defense** in 1941 set up standards for the enrichment of bread and flour with thiamine, riboflavin, niacin, and iron. Flour products were chosen for enrichment because the members of the conference felt that these products were the ones in most use.

Wheat is also used for breakfast cereals, of which the nutritional value varies with the processing. Look on the package label for specific nutrition information.

Products from wheat: Wheat that is milled into flour is used at home in two ways: as flour and as commercially baked products. Packaged flour includes both all-purpose and cake flour, which are available in most supermarkets. Whole wheat flour is also available, but it is not as widely used as the all-purpose type.

Gluten, a protein in flour, gives baked goods structure. The gluten in all-purpose flour is stronger and more elastic than that in cake flour, making all-purpose flour suitable for breads. The gluten that is present in cake flour produces baked products that are tender.

Flour is also used in prepared mixes for cakes, breads, rolls, cookies, and pancakes. These packaged products account for a high percentage of the flour that is milled and used in the home. The forerunner of mixes is self-rising flour, which millers created by adding a leavening agent and salt to flour.

In addition to its use in baked products, flour is also used as a thickener in cooking. For example, soups, sauces, and gravies are often thickened with flour.

Because of flour's many uses, most homemakers have all-purpose flour on hand at all times. Some homemakers also keep cake flour for use in delicately structured cakes. However, flour does not keep well indefinitely. Use it within a year of purchase. A covered container or canister in a cool place is best for storage.

Most of the flour produced in the United States is used by the commercial bakers. It reaches the table in the form of breads, rolls, cookies, crackers, cakes, and pastries. Snack foods made from flour are also becoming very popular.

Wheat also appears in cereal boxes in a wide array of forms: puffed wheat, wheat flakes, bran flakes, and shredded wheat are just a few. These cereals are ready to eat without further cooking.

Other wheat cereals need to be cooked before eating. Those served hot include wheat meal, malted breakfast food, and farina. Rolled wheat is also available either as a breakfast food or as an ingredient in baked products. Breakfast foods can be shelf-stored, but they should be used within three months of purchase.

Other wheat products that are available in addition to flour, mixes, commercially baked products, and cereals include bulgur, pasta products, and wheat germ.

Bulgur is one of the oldest forms of wheat. It is enjoying renewed popularity and is usually served as a meat accompaniment. Its taste is similar to that of wild rice. Bulgur is wheat that has been parboiled, dried, and partially debranned.

The pasta products include macaroni, spaghetti, noodles, and the many variations of each. Pasta foods made from durum wheat are excellent in color, flavor, and in holding shape when cooked.

Wheat germ is the germ section of the kernel, which has been separated from the endosperm and bran in milling. Processed wheat germ can be added to breakfast cereals or used in baked goods for added flavor and nutrition. (See *Cereal, Durum Wheat, Flour, Grain, Macaroni* for additional information.)

Wheat Bread

Flavored with shredded wheat cereal—

>   2 packages active dry yeast
> 4¾ to 5 cups sifted all-purpose
>   flour
> 2¼ cups milk
> ⅓ cup honey
> ¼ cup butter or margarine
>   1 teaspoon salt
>   • • •
> 1½ cups crushed shredded wheat
>   cereal (3 large biscuits)

In large mixer bowl combine yeast and *2 cups* of the flour. Heat the milk, honey, butter, and salt just till warm, stirring occasionally to melt butter. Stir the wheat cereal into milk; add to dry mixture in mixing bowl. Beat at low speed with electric mixer for ½ minute, scraping sides of bowl constantly. Beat 3 minutes at high speed. By hand, stir in enough of remaining flour to make a moderately stiff dough. Turn out on lightly floured surface; knead till smooth and satiny, 5 to 8 minutes.

Shape into ball; place in greased bowl, turning once to grease surface. Cover; let rise in warm place till double, about 1 hour. Punch down. Cut into 2 portions. Shape in smooth ball; cover and let rest 10 minutes. Shape into 2 loaves. Place in 2 greased 8½x4½x2⅝-inch loaf pans. Cover and let rise till double, 30 to 45 minutes. Bake at 375° till done, about 40 to 45 minutes. Cover loosely with foil during the last 20 minutes if the loaves brown too quickly. Makes 2 loaves.

Curried Wheat Snacks

> 6 tablespoons butter or margarine
> ½ to 1 teaspoon curry powder
> ¼ teaspoon onion salt
> ⅛ teaspoon ground ginger
> 3 cups spoon-sized shredded wheat
>   biscuits

Melt butter in large skillet. Blend in seasonings. Add shredded wheat and toss to coat with butter. Heat about 5 minutes over low heat, stirring frequently. Drain on paper toweling. Serve warm. (Or reheat in oven just before serving.) Makes 3 cups.

Three-Flour Bread

Pictured on page 2434—

>   2 packages active dry yeast
> 1½ cups whole wheat flour
> ½ cup rye flour
> 3¼ to 3½ cups sifted all-purpose
>   flour
>   2 cups milk
> ½ cup brown sugar
>   3 tablespoons shortening
>   2 tablespoons granulated sugar
>   1 tablespoon salt

Combine yeast, whole wheat flour, rye flour, and *1 cup* of the all-purpose flour in a large mixer bowl. Heat together milk, brown sugar, shortening, granulated sugar, and salt just till warm. Add to dry mixture. Beat at low speed of electric mixer for ½ minute, scraping bowl constantly. Beat 3 minutes at high speed. Stir in enough of the remaining all-purpose flour to make a moderately stiff dough. Turn out onto floured surface; knead 8 to 10 minutes.

Place in greased bowl, turning once. Cover; let rise till double, 1½ hours. Punch down; let rest 10 minutes. Shape into 2 loaves; place in 2 greased 8½x4½x2½-inch loaf dishes. Let rise till double, 45 to 60 minutes. Bake at 375° till done, about 40 minutes. Makes 2.

Quickly turn ready-to-eat breakfast cereal into Curried Wheat Snacks, a sophisticated tidbit that is served while it is still warm.

Whole Wheat Nut Bread

A spicy quick bread—

    1 cup sifted all-purpose flour
    2 teaspoons baking powder
    ½ teaspoon ground cinnamon
    ¼ teaspoon salt
    ¼ teaspoon ground nutmeg
    ¼ teaspoon ground allspice
    ½ cup whole wheat flour
        •   •   •
    ¼ cup butter or margarine
    ¾ cup sugar
    2 eggs
    ⅔ cup milk
    ½ teaspoon vanilla
    ½ cup chopped walnuts

Sift together the all-purpose flour, baking powder, cinnamon, salt, nutmeg, and allspice. Stir in the whole wheat flour.

Cream together the butter or margarine and sugar. Add eggs, one at a time, beating well after each addition. Add dry ingredients to creamed mixture alternately with milk and vanilla. Beat smooth after each addition. Stir in the chopped walnuts. Turn into a greased 8½x4½x2⅝-inch loaf pan. Bake at 350° till loaf tests done, 50 to 55 minutes. Cool 10 minutes. Remove from pan. Makes 1 loaf.

WHEY *(hwā, wā)*—The thin, watery liquid part of milk that is left after the curds have formed, as when milk is curdled for making cheese. Whey, as well as the curd, is used in making some kinds of cheeses.

WHIP—1. To beat air into a food, such as egg whites or cream, lightening its texture and increasing its volume. 2. An alternate name for a whisk, which is often used in the whipping process. 3. A light dessert that is made fluffy and delicate by adding beaten cream or egg whites or by beating a gelatin mixture before it is completely set. The dessert is frequently flavored with fruit pulp, such as prunes or plums, or with other ingredients, such as chocolate and/or nuts. Whips are light desserts, making them a perfect ending for a hearty meal. (See *Dessert, Whisk* for additional information.)

Chocolate–Pecan Whip

    1 envelope unflavored gelatin
        (1 tablespoon)
    ¼ cup sugar
        Dash salt
    2 egg yolks
    1½ cups milk
    1 teaspoon vanilla
    2 egg whites
    ¼ cup sugar
    1 cup whipping cream
    ½ cup semisweet chocolate pieces
    ¼ cup broken pecans

In saucepan thoroughly mix gelatin, ¼ cup sugar, and salt. Beat together egg yolks and milk; stir into gelatin mixture. Cook and stir over low heat till slightly thickened. Add vanilla; chill till partially set.

Beat egg whites till soft peaks form. Gradually add ¼ cup sugar, beating till stiff peaks form; fold into gelatin mixture.

Whip the cream. Reserve *half* of the whipped cream and a few chocolate pieces for garnish; set aside. Chop remaining chocolate pieces. Fold remaining whipped cream, chopped chocolate, and the nuts into gelatin mixture. Spoon into dessert dishes; chill. Garnish with reserved chocolate and whipped cream, and additional pecans, if desired. Makes 6 to 8 servings.

Chilled Prune Whip

    1½ cups whole prunes
    1½ cups water
    3 egg whites
    ¼ teaspoon salt
    ⅓ cup sugar
    2 tablespoons lemon juice
    ¼ cup chopped pecans

In saucepan combine prunes and water; bring to boiling. Cover and simmer 10 minutes; allow to cool in liquid. Drain. With kitchen shears, snip prunes from pits in small pieces; set aside. In large mixer bowl beat egg whites with salt till soft peaks form. Gradually add sugar, beating till stiff peaks form. In small mixer bowl combine prunes and lemon juice; beat till well blended. Fold into egg whites; fold in nuts. Spoon the mixture into dessert dishes; chill. Makes 6 to 8 servings.

Plum Whip

  1 envelope unflavored gelatin
      (1 tablespoon)
¼ cup cold water
  1 7¾-ounce jar strained plums
      (junior food)
10 drops red food coloring
  1 tablespoon lemon juice
¾ cup milk
  2 egg whites
  3 tablespoons sugar
½ cup frozen whipped dessert
      topping, thawed

Soften gelatin in cold water. Heat strained plums in a saucepan till boiling. Add softened gelatin, food coloring, and lemon juice. Stir till gelatin dissolves. Add milk. Cool till partially thickened. Beat egg whites till soft peaks form; gradually add sugar and beat till stiff peaks form. Add plum mixture gradually and beat till fluffy. Fold in the thawed dessert topping. Spoon into sherbet glasses. Chill thoroughly. Before serving, top with additional thawed whipped dessert topping, if desired. Makes 6 to 8 servings.

WHIPPED TOPPING—A fluffy nondairy product used to garnish desserts. Some toppings are used also as an ingredient in desserts or salads for volume and flavor.

Various forms of whipped toppings are available on the market. One type comes frozen in covered bowls, needing only to be thawed before use. Another topping that comes frozen needs to be thawed and whipped before it is used. Pressurized containers of whipped dessert topping are also available and are ready for use. In addition, you'll find dessert topping mixes on the supermarket shelf. These can be made into whipped toppings by adding liquid and beating, following the directions on the package label.

A light, refreshing dessert

Plum Whip, which gets its delicate color and flavor from a jar of junior food, is sure to be a favorite with the adults, too.

Whipped cream adds richness and a light texture to Lemon Frost Pie. To serve, spoon fresh Blueberry Sauce over wedges of the pie.

WHIPPING CREAM—A milk product containing a minimum of 30 percent milk fat that can be whipped until fluffy, thickened, and doubled in volume. It is also called heavy cream or heavy whipping cream if it has more than the minimum amount of milk fat.

There are specified amounts of milk fat for whipping cream. Light whipping cream must contain 30 to 36 percent, while heavy cream or heavy whipping cream must contain at least 36 percent.

Whipping cream adds calories and a small amount of vitamin A to the diet. One tablespoon of light whipping cream has 45 calories; heavy cream, 52 calories.

The uses of whipping cream are numerous. It's a favorite dessert topper, plain or flavored, and it is also used as an ingredient in chilled and frozen desserts, supplying both volume and richness. Whipped cream and nuts on an ice cream sundae add a special note. Whipping cream is also used in other dishes, such as vegetables. (See also *Cream*.)

Volcano Potatoes

    4 or 5 medium potatoes, peeled
      Milk
    ½ cup whipping cream
    2 ounces sharp process American
      cheese, shredded (½ cup)

Cook potatoes till tender; drain and mash. Season with salt and pepper. Whip potatoes with enough hot milk (about ¾ cup) to make fluffy. Pile into greased 8-inch round baking dish, mounding into volcano shape. Make a crater in center. Whip cream; fold in cheese. Pour over potatoes. Bake at 350° till lightly browned, about 20 minutes. Serves 6.

Whipping cream know-how

● Whipping cream doubles in volume when whipped; thus, one cup of cream will yield about two cups of whipped cream. Do not overwhip the cream or it may turn to butter.

● Use chilled cream that is at least 24 hours old. If the cream is too warm, it won't whip.

● For best volume, don't try to whip more than two cups of cream at a time.

● A chilled bowl, preferably with sloping sides and deep enough to allow the cream to double, is the best container to use.

● Use chilled beaters of an electric mixer or a chilled rotary beater to rapidly whip the cream until it mounds and holds shape.

● To sweeten whipped cream, add two to four tablespoons of sugar per cup of unwhipped cream after the whipping process is almost completed. If sugar is added too soon, the volume and stiffness of the final product will be decreased. A small amount of vanilla can be added for extra flavor.

● To freeze mounds of whipped cream for a dessert topper, whip cream and add sugar and flavoring, if desired. Drop from spoon into mounds on waxed paper-lined baking sheet. Freeze till mounds are firm. Place in freezer container; seal, label, and freeze. Store in freezer up to three months. When ready to use, place frozen mounds on servings of dessert. Let stand at room temperature about 20 minutes.

Lemon Frost Pie

    1 cup sifted all-purpose flour
    ½ cup butter or margarine
    2 tablespoons sugar
    ¼ teaspoon salt
        • • •
    2 egg whites
    ⅔ cup sugar
    2 teaspoons grated lemon peel
    ¼ cup lemon juice
    5 drops yellow food coloring
    1 cup whipping cream
        Blueberry Sauce

Mix flour, butter, 2 tablespoons sugar, and salt till crumbly. Place ⅓ cup crumb mixture in baking dish; press remaining into greased and floured 9-inch pie plate. Bake both at 375° for 12 to 15 minutes; cool. Combine egg whites, ⅔ cup sugar, lemon peel and juice, and food coloring; beat to stiff peaks. Whip cream; fold into lemon mixture. Turn into pie shell; top with crumbs. Chill or freeze.

Serve with *Blueberry Sauce:* Combine ⅔ cup sugar, 1 tablespoon cornstarch, and dash salt. Add ⅔ cup water. Cook and stir till thick; cook 2 minutes more. Add 2 cups fresh blueberries; return to boiling. Chill.

WHISK—1. A utensil made of wire loops fastened to a handle, designed for beating foods till frothy or fluffy. Whisks range in size from a tiny one suitable for beating one egg to large balloon-shaped whisks for beating doughs. Whisks are also called whips. **2.** To beat or whip foods, such as cream or eggs, till frothy.

WHISKEY, WHISKY—A spirit distilled from the fermented mash of a grain. According to United States regulations, whiskey must be distilled at less than 190 proof, be diluted to a strength of from 80 to 110 proof, and be aged in charred oak barrels. The word whiskey is a derivation of a Celtic word meaning "water of life." Irish and Americans prefer the first spelling; Scottish and Canadians, the latter.

Both Ireland and Scotland are closely allied to the evolution of whiskey. In fact, both countries still vie for the claim to whiskey's origin. In the United States, too, whiskeymaking was initiated by the colonists of Irish and Scottish descent who first operated pot stills for their personal consumption shortly after the American Revolution.

Growth of whiskey production in the United States was a logical result of America winning its independence. After the Revolution, the import duty placed on molasses made rum, once the most important colonial spirit, unprofitable if not almost impossible to produce. Whiskey stills increased particularly in areas of Maryland, Virginia, and the Carolinas where the grains used for whiskey were readily available to anyone who wanted them and at a reasonable price.

As Irish and Scottish pioneers settled farther west into western Pennsylvania, Kentucky, and Tennessee, they found that whiskey production was even more economically necessary. The equivalent of 24 bushels of grain in the form of whiskey could be transported to eastern markets as opposed to only 4 bushels of actual grain. The distillery, first a family then a community project, gradually became an extremely large commercial venture. In less than twenty years after the first distillery was established near Pittsburgh, Pennsylvania, thousands of other distilleries were in operation.

Whiskey production up to this time was not governmentally regulated. But in 1791, when the value of the dollar plummeted, a tax was imposed on whiskey. The distillers' opposition that followed, now called the Whiskey Rebellion, even required the use of military force. Although the tax was repealed in 1802, a whiskey tax was soon here to stay.

How whiskey is produced: All whiskies are based on the general procedures of fermentation and distillation. Many different kinds of whiskies are made simply by varying the grain used or by adding a unique stage of production.

First, the fermenting mixture called the mash is prepared by mixing the dried, crushed grain with hot water. Next, the yeast is added by either the sour or sweet mash methods. For a sour mash, a portion of a previous fermentation is added to

the fresh mash. For a sweet mash, only new yeast-starter is used. Fermentation continues for several days.

When the fermented liquid, now known as "low wine" or "distillers' beer," has reached the proper stage, the mixture is pumped into the stills where distillation occurs. The whiskey is distilled one or more times, depending on the type. After distillation, the alcoholic content is reduced by adding water and the liquid is placed in charred oak barrels to age.

Types of whiskies: There are many kinds of whiskies sold in the United States. Some are labeled (and their production controlled) by the country in which the whiskies are distilled. The other types are designated by the grain content.

Bourbon whiskey is the only spirit that was first made in the United States. Bourbon must contain at least 51 percent corn, be distilled at not more than 160° proof, and be aged in new charred oak barrels. It has a full-bodied, sweet flavor.

Canadian whisky is produced in Canada principally from corn, but it also contains some rye, barley, and wheat. The mash is distilled off at a high proof and is filtered before bottling. A minimum of two years aging is required in either new or used barrels. Canadian whisky has a characteristic light, slightly sweet flavor.

Irish whiskey, the product of Ireland, consists mainly of malted plus sprouted barley. Wheat, oats, and a little rye may also be included. Distillation is carried out at a low proof, often as many as three times. The Irish whiskey available in American markets is usually seven or more years old. The liquor has full, smooth body and malt flavor.

Scotch whisky comes from Scotland and is made from peat-dried, malted barley that has been fermented and distilled then blended with a corn-rye whiskey. The barley whiskey is distilled off at 140 proof; the corn-rye whiskey, at 180 proof. The Scotch whisky sold in the United States has been aged over four years. It is light-bodied and has a smoky flavor.

Straight whiskey is legally defined as being distilled at no higher than 160 proof, aged in new charred oak barrels at least two years, reduced to not less than 80 proof in strength, and containing no additives other than water. A straight whiskey has full flavor, body, and aroma. The dominant grain used in the mash (over 51 percent) determines the name of the whiskey—straight Bourbon whiskey if corn; straight rye whiskey if rye; straight wheat whiskey if wheat; straight malt whiskey if barley malt; and straight rye malt whiskey if rye malt. Straight corn whiskey, however, must be distilled from a mash containing at least 80 percent corn. Tennessee whiskey must be produced in the state of Tennessee from at least 51 percent corn. Blended straight whiskey consists of straight whiskies taken from different distilling periods and from different distilleries.

Blended whiskey is a mixture of whiskey and neutral spirits (a liquor of 190 proof or more). At least 20 percent of a blended whiskey must consist of the grain whiskey. Because of the neutral spirits concentration, blended whiskies are naturally lighter in flavor and body than are straight whiskies. Most whiskey sold in the United States is blended.

How to use: Whiskies are used widely in beverages and find lesser use in cooked foods. Some people insist that whiskey is best when consumed straight. Others prefer it on the rocks or with water. Others prefer soda mixtures and cocktail blends such as sours, Manhattans, mint juleps, old-fashioneds, or highballs. When you prepare a soup or a dessert topping try using a whiskey to accent the flavor. Fruit flavors are also complemented with the addition of small amounts of whiskey. (See also *Wines and Spirits*.)

Whiskey Sour

½ jigger fresh lemon or lime juice
2 jiggers Bourbon, Scotch, or rye
1 teaspoon confectioners' sugar
3 or 4 ice cubes

Combine all ingredients. Shake well. Strain into a glass. If desired, trim with a lemon slice and maraschino cherry. Makes 1 drink.

WHITEFISH—A saltwater or freshwater fish related to the salmon and trout. A few are found along California's coast, but the majority are found in the colder waters of North America, Europe, and Asia. Those sold in America come from the Great Lakes, Minnesota, and Canada.

Whitefish have green and silvery coloring, large scales, a small mouth with no teeth, and a forked tail fin. These fish average between two and four pounds.

The whole fish and fillets are sold fresh and frozen. Smoked whitefish and roe are also available. The flesh of the whitefish can be cooked by baking, broiling, frying, boiling, or steaming.

Whitefish's nutritional value consists of protein, minerals, and B vitamins. There are about 155 calories in an uncooked piece measuring 3x3x⅞ inches (about 3½ ounces). A 3½-ounce serving of whitefish when stuffed and baked has 215 calories. (See also *Fish*.)

WHITE PEPPER—A light-colored spice made from the berries of a vine called *Piper nigrum*. White pepper is made from the same berries as black pepper, but it has a more subtle flavor and a pale yellow or gray appearance. The white spice is made from mature berries, whereas black pepper is made from immature ones.

In making white pepper, the berries are soaked in water to loosen the outside skin. The skin is rubbed off and the cores, or white peppercorns, are sun-dried. If the pepper is to be ground, this is the next step in production.

White pepper is widely used in Europe as a seasoning. In the United States it is used most often in recipes such as cream sauces and salad dressings, when the dark specks of black pepper are not wanted. White pepper can be substituted for black pepper. (See also *Pepper*.)

WHITE SAUCE—A basic sauce prepared with butter or margarine, flour, milk, cream, or white stock. The sauce is prepared by melting the butter, then blending in flour and seasonings. Liquid is added and the mixture is stirred till thickened and bubbly.

Prepare white sauce in varying thicknesses, according to your needs. For example, use thin white sauce in soups and creamed vegetables, and medium white sauce in scalloped and creamed dishes. Make thick white sauce for croquettes and soufflés. (See also *Sauce*.)

White Sauce

Thin:
- 1 tablespoon butter or margarine
- 1 tablespoon all-purpose flour
- ¼ teaspoon salt
- 1 cup milk

Medium:
- 2 tablespoons butter or margarine
- 2 tablespoons all-purpose flour
- ¼ teaspoon salt
- 1 cup milk

Thick:
- 3 tablespoons butter or margarine
- ¼ cup all-purpose flour
- ¼ teaspoon salt
- 1 cup milk

In a heavy saucepan melt butter or margarine over low heat. Blend in flour, salt, and dash white pepper. Stir till bubbly. Add milk all at once. Cook quickly, stirring constantly till mixture thickens and bubbles. Makes 1 cup.

How to repair white sauce

If white sauce cooks too long, it may become thick and the butter will separate out. To repair the sauce, stir in a little more milk. Then, cook the mixture quickly, stirring constantly, until the sauce bubbles.

WHITE WINE—An almost white to deep gold, dry or sweet wine that is made either by using white grapes or by fermenting purple grapes without skins and seeds.

White wine production usually is more exacting than that for red wines. Controls maintain the color and flavor balance. White wines are usually aged less and reach maturity sooner than red wines.

The largest class of white wines is dinner or table wines, such as Rhine, chablis, or sauterne, and those named for the grape varieties from which they are principally made, such as Riesling, Pinot Chardonnay, and Sauvignon Blanc.

Serve white dinner wines at about 50° and use to complement light-flavored foods, such as poultry, fish, and shellfish. (See also *Wines and Spirits*.)

WHITING—A lean, saltwater fish of the cod family. Other names include silver hake, kingfish, and frostfish. The whiting lives along the New England and English coasts. It has a long, slender body colored brown or green and silver. Identifying lateral lines run the length of the fish. The size can reach as much as 30 inches in length and five pounds in weight.

Whiting sold on the market weigh one to four pounds and usually measure about 12 inches long. They come dressed, drawn, filleted, or in portions, and may be frozen, fresh, or smoked. Boil, steam, or fry this firm, white, tender fish. If butter or shortening is added, broil or bake the fish. (See also *Fish*.)

WHOLE WHEAT—The entire wheat kernel with only the harsh outer hull removed. Because the whole kernel is used, whole wheat products contain the nutrients of the whole grain, including the B vitamins, protein, and minerals. Since the germ is included, whole wheat, and the flour ground from it, does not have the keeping quality of white flour. Buy whole wheat products in small quantities and use up your supply quickly. Whole wheat is also used in cereals. (See *Cereal*, *Wheat* for additional information.)

WHORTLEBERRY (*hwûr' tuhl ber' ē, wur'-*) —An edible, dark blue to black berry, similar in size to a black currant, found growing in England, northern Europe, and Asia. The sweet flavor of whortleberries is enjoyed fresh during July and August, or in preserves during the off-season. They taste like huckleberries.

WIENER (*wē' nuhr*)—Another name for a frankfurter. (See also *Frankfurter*.)

WIENER SCHNITZEL (*vē' nuhr shnit' suhl*) —A Viennese main dish prepared with veal cutlets, which are breaded, then sautéed in shortening. The name is derived from the German word *schnitzel*, which means a slice of meat or a cutlet. When a fried egg tops the cooked cutlet, you have *Wiener Schnitzel à la Holstein*. The dish is often served with lemon wedges. (See also *Viennese Cookery*.)

Wiener Schnitzel

1½ pounds veal cutlets, ½ inch thick
¼ cup all-purpose flour
1 teaspoon salt
¼ teaspoon pepper
1 beaten egg
1 tablespoon milk
1 cup fine dry bread crumbs
¼ cup salad oil
Lemon wedges

Cut meat into 4 pieces; pound ¼ to ⅛ inch thick. Cut small slits around edges to prevent curling. Coat meat with flour seasoned with salt and pepper. Combine egg and milk. Dip floured cutlets in egg mixture, then in bread crumbs. Cook the meat in hot oil till tender, 2 to 3 minutes on each side. Serve with lemon wedges. Makes 4 servings.

Wiener Schnitzel à la Holstein: Prepare Wiener Schnitzel. In skillet, fry 4 eggs in butter till whites are set. Add 1 tablespoon water. Cover; cook till eggs are done. Place one cooked egg on each veal cutlet. Sprinkle with snipped parsley, if desired.

WILD GAME—A wild animal or bird that is taken for food. (See also *Game*.)

WILD MARJORAM—An alternate name for the herb, oregano. (See also *Oregano*.)

WILD RICE—The seed of an annual marsh grass. The name "wild rice" is only partly accurate. This rice does grow wild along the shallows of lakes, in streams, and in swampy places, but it is not related to the oriental grain that has been called rice for many centuries.

Wild rice, a native of North America, was once an important food for the American Indians. They introduced it to French explorers, who agreed that it was delectable. The French named it wild oats.

Today, about three million pounds of wild rice are harvested yearly in the United States and Canada, with about 60 percent coming from Minnesota.

Wild rice is self-sowing and reaches a height of four to eight feet. The plant has flat, spreading leaves and bears a large cluster of seeds. The grain of wild rice is slender, round, and two to three times longer than white rice. It is dark brown in color and chewy when cooked. Wild rice is somewhat nutlike in flavor.

The industrial revolution has had very little effect on wild rice production. The grain still is harvested from boats, similar to the way it was done before the Europeans came to the New World.

Harvesting wild rice consists of freeing the seeds from the plant. The stalks are bent over the boat and the heads of the plants are knocked with a club that looks like an oversized drumstick. The ripe rice falls into the boat while the unripened grains remain on the head of the plant. For this reason, harvesting is done three to four times to get all the ripened rice. Only about 25 percent of the crop is taken; the remainder falls back into the water for reseeding and food for wildlife. However, there are specific regulations set up regarding harvesting. These include size of boat, size of the club used for knocking off the ripened rice, who can harvest the crop, and harvesting times.

The American Indians dried wild rice, then placed it in a hole in the ground that had been lined with animal skins. In order to loosen the hulls, the Indians stamped on the grains. The rice was then transferred to a blanket and tossed up in the air to separate it from the loosened hulls. Today, most rice is harvested and then sold to processors who use machinery to complete the parching, hulling, winnowing, cleaning, and grading.

Wild rice makes about the same contribution to the diet as do other whole grains. It supplies some carbohydrate, calcium, iron, protein, and the B vitamins.

Wild rice is sold as either plain wild rice or wild rice mixed with long-grain white rice. The price of wild rice is high because only 25 percent of the crop is taken and because 100 pounds of the green rice produces 40 pounds of rice suitable for sale. However, the appeal to gourmet tastes makes it worth the extra cost. Wild rice mixed with white rice costs less and contributes much of the eating enjoyment of the unmixed product.

If wild rice is not to be used immediately, it is best to transfer it to a container with a tight-fitting cover.

Unlike regular white rice, wild rice needs to be rinsed before using. Place the amount to be cooked in a pan of warm water, stir, then drain and remove any particles that float to the top. This should be done twice, followed by a rinsing in a strainer. One cup of uncooked wild rice yields three to four cups cooked rice.

Cooked wild rice is used as an accompaniment for game and poultry. It is often used in a stuffing, cooked with other ingredients and used as a main dish, topped with butter, or served with a sauce.

Wild Rice and Mushrooms

Drain one 3-ounce can broiled, sliced mushrooms, reserving liquid. Mix one 10½-ounce can condensed beef broth, mushroom liquid, and enough water to make 2 cups. Add 2 medium onions, finely chopped; bring to boiling. Add ½ cup rinsed wild rice. Reduce heat; simmer, covered, for 20 minutes. Add 1 cup long-grain rice. Return to boil. Reduce heat; simmer, covered, 20 minutes longer. Add mushrooms and 2 tablespoons butter. Heat. Add 2 tablespoons snipped parsley. Serves 6 to 8.

Wild Rice Stuffing

Cook one 6-ounce package long-grain and wild rice mix according to package directions. Cool the rice. Stir in ½ cup chopped celery; one 5-ounce can water chestnuts, drained and sliced; one 3-ounce can chopped mushrooms, drained; ¼ cup butter, melted; and 1 tablespoon soy sauce. Makes about 4 cups stuffing or enough for 4 Cornish game hens.

WINES AND SPIRITS

*A clear and concise primer to help you choose,
use, and enjoy alcoholic beverages.*

Much mystery surrounds the words wines and spirits. Together they conjure up a picture of liquids in dusty bottles and sparkling glasses. Encompassing these liquids are centuries of traditions regarding production, use, and selection in concert with such words as bouquet, body, and flambé.

But there need be nothing mysterious or earthshaking about wines and spirits if you know a little about them. You will have the delightful experience of knowing that you can break the rules, have fun drinking the beverage you like, and use it to best advantage in foods.

The essence of all wines and spirits is fermentation, the frothy interaction of sugar and yeast. Simply said, this wonder of nature changes sugar to alcohol.

Producing alcohol that is not only potable but that tastes and looks good, however, is more complex than this, for an alcoholic product is influenced by the nature of the food used for fermentation as well as by the way it is fermented. Grapes, for example, include sugar and water plus other constituents such as acids, cellulose, and essential oils. Likewise, fermentation is a combination of reactions that change the substances in the juice. These changes give each alcoholic beverage its color, flavor, and bouquet.

How the liquid is fermented and subsequently handled differentiates wines from spirits. A wine is made by fermenting a

fruit, vegetable, or herb juice. When the word wine is used by itself, it is commonly held to mean grape wine. Wines made from other fruits carry the name of the fruit, for example, apple wine and cherry wine. A spirit, on the other hand, is a highly alcoholic liquid that has been distilled from juice containing alcohol.

Only in fairly recent times has it been understood how foods are transformed into wines and spirits, but the making of alcoholic beverages dates back to ancient times. Winemaking is by far the oldest of the two techniques. Although distillation was known by some early civilizations, it took some time before the process was used for making alcoholic spirits.

Wines

Although wine was made in China prior to 2000 B.C., the early winemaking that most influenced the Western world began in the "cradle of civilization," the Middle East. Vineyards abounded in Egypt, Palestine, and Persia. A 30,000 gallon winery was located at Gibeon, near Jerusalem, until the city's destruction in 600 B.C.

The history of winemaking coincides with the development of great civilizations. Both the Greeks and Romans worshiped a god of wine. Following the conquest of Gaul, the Romans pursued grape cultivation and winemaking throughout their empire. By the fifteenth century, Europe had become the foremost wine-producing region in the world.

European settlers brought their knowledge of growing grapes and making wine to the Western Hemisphere. Even though native American grapes were already growing profusely on the new land, the colonists began importing cuttings from

A connoisseur's touch

← Cooking with wines and spirits adds gourmet flavor to Snow-Capped Pâté, Scallopine Burgers, Bourbon Balls, and Orange-Rum Cake.

the European vines. Attempts to grow European vines on the East Coast were unsuccessful, but fruitful results were immediate in Mexico and California.

During the 1800s, United States' wine production became commercial in nature, but its growth was soon interrupted. First, a severe predator of grapevines, Phylloxera, infested and almost destroyed the vineyards. Then, in 1920, the United States government's move to prohibit alcohol greatly curtailed wine production.

Following the repeal of Prohibition, there was a quick revival of wineries that produced quality wines. Today, the demand for good wines continues to increase—so much so, in fact, that the United States has become one of the ten largest wine-producing countries.

How wine is produced: Successful wine-making is more than simply letting grapes ferment naturally. Rather, it is a combination of growing quality grapes and caring for the must (pressed grape juice) daily as it ferments and ages.

Since a wine is only as good as the grapes from which it is made, grape cultivation (viticulture) is a vital step in winemaking. Harvesting the grapes at just the right time is one of the most critical steps. As the grapes mature, they are regularly tested for sugar and acid content. A higher sugar concentration is desired for grapes used in making sweet wines than for those used for dry wines.

The science of winemaking (enology) takes over after the grapes are picked. For a white wine, either white grapes are used or the juice of red grapes is expressed and separated from the skins and seeds. If a rosé (pink) or red wine is desired, the juice, skins, and seeds of red grapes ferment together for a time.

Although grape skins are covered with wild yeasts that can initiate fermentation naturally, most winemakers kill the wild yeasts and add special yeast cultures for better control. If a dry wine is desired (one without residual sugar), fermentation continues to completion. (The maximum alcoholic content this wine can attain is about 14 percent.) If a partially or fully sweet wine is desired,

however, fermentation is halted by either adding brandy, using small amounts of a sterilizing substance, filtering, or other means. Addition of brandy often increases the alcoholic content up to 21 percent.

When fermentation has subsided, the wine is still not at its best. Aging in wood (letting the wine rest) permits the characteristic flavor, body, and bouquet to develop. White wines generally age in less time than do the red ones.

Bottling of the wine follows. In the bottle, the flavor and bouquet continue to develop. Wine is the only beverage that changes once it is bottled.

To produce a sparkling, effervescent wine, a dry wine is subjected to a second fermentation in sealed containers prior to the final bottling. When fermentation is complete, the yeast sediment is removed and the wine is bottled.

Wine vinegar, a by-product of wine, is made by introducing acetic acid bacteria to a dry red, rosé, or white wine for a second fermentation. Sometimes, the wine is additionally flavored with herbs such as tarragon.

Classes of wines: For clarification, wines often are categorized into five classes: appetizer, red dinner, white dinner, dessert, and sparkling. Each class name describes the general character or use of the wines within the class.

Appetizer or aperitif denotes wines that are preferred for before-meal or cocktail consumption. In most cases, the dry wines are preferred over the sweet ones. The most well-known appetizer wines are Sherry and Vermouth, but another group, the natural or flavored wines, is rapidly gaining popularity.

Dinner (table) wines are, quite naturally, those customarily served with the main course of the meal. Red dinner wines such as red Burgundies, Clarets, and red Chiantis are predominantly dry and rich in taste and sometimes carry a tartness or astringency. The flavor diversity of white dinner wines encompasses very dry and tart to sweet and full-bodied wines. Some of the popular types of white dinner wines are Chablis, Rhine wines, white Burgundies, drier Sauternes, and

white Chiantis. Pink Rosé wines, ranging in flavor from sweet to slightly astringent, also fall under the dinner wine category.

Dessert wines, the sweetest and fullest-flavored wines, are served at the last course of the meal. Well-known types include Ports, Muscatels, Tokays, sweet Sherries, and sweeter Sauternes.

Sparkling wines, because of their versatility, taste equally good before, during, or at the end of a meal. The traditional sparkling wines are Champagne and Sparkling Burgundy. Cold Duck is the newest of the sparkling wines.

European wines: The Europeans were the first to perfect winemaking techniques. The people of France, Germany, Italy, and Portugal made the earliest con-tributions. The wines that they developed are the ones that winemakers throughout the world try to equal or excel.

French wines—Four principal regions produce the French wines that have given this country its reputation: Bordeaux, Burgundy, Champagne, and Alsace. Red Clarets, always-sweet Sauternes, and white Graves wines are produced in and around Bordeaux. Red, white, and sparkling Burgundy wines are produced in the region of Burgundy. From the Champagne region come the sparkling white wines of the same name. Alsace produces the Rhine wines of France such as Riesling and Traminer.

German wines—The best-known German wines are white, made from Riesling grapes, and come from two sectors, the

Tantalize thirsty friends with these drinks. For wine enthusiasts, try Tomato-Vermouth Cocktail, Rosé Frappé, or Summer Sangria (see *Sangria*). Lime Fizz appeals to liqueur lovers.

		Wine Chart		
Class	Wine family	Varietal wines in family	Serving temperature	Best with
Appetizer	Sherry (dry) Vermouth Flavored wines		Cool room temperature (60° to 70°) *or* chilled (45° to 55°)	All appetizer foods—canapés, hors d'oeuvres, soups, dips
Red Dinner Wines	Burgundy (red) Claret (Bordeaux) Chianti (red) Rosé	Pinot Noir, Gamay Cabernet Sauvignon, Zinfandel Grignolino	Cool room temperature (60° to 70°) *except* for Rosé Chilled (45° to 50°)	Hearty foods—all red meats including beef, veal, pork, game; cheese, egg, and pasta dishes
White Dinner Wines	Chablis (White Burgundy) Rhine Sauterne (dry) Chianti (white)	Pinot Chardonnay, Folle Blanche Riesling, Sylvaner, Traminer Semillon, Sauvignon Blanc	Chilled (45° to 50°)	Light foods—poultry, fish and shellfish, veal
Dessert Wines	Port Tokay Muscatel Sauterne (sweet) Sherry (sweet)		Cool room temperature (60° to 70°)	All desserts—fruits, nuts, cakes, dessert cheeses
Sparkling Wines	Champagne Sparkling Burgundy Sparkling Rosé Cold Duck		Chilled (40° to 45°)	All foods and occasions

Rhine and Moselle valleys. Rhine wines (Hock wines) may be dry or sweet, and light-bodied or full-bodied. Moselle wines are dry and lighter than are Rhine wines.

Italian wines—Italy is the home of some delicious wines that have won world acclaim. From the Piedmont region come the greatest Italian wines: heavy, red Barolo and Barbaresco, and somewhat sweet, sparkling Asti spumanti. From Tuscany comes Chianti in its traditional straw-covered flasks.

Spanish wines—In Spain as in Italy, many wines are produced. Dry to sweet Sherry must come from the Jerez region. Montilla is dry, sherrylike wine made outside of the Jerez region. The red, white, and rosé Rioja wines of northern Spain are among the top table wines.

Portuguese wines—Although most Portuguese wines are better known locally, three wine families have gained world prominence—Port, Madeira, and Rosé. Port, a dessert wine, must be produced within the Douro region. Madeira wine, also a dessert wine, gets its name from its homeland, the Portuguese-owned island of Madeira. Portuguese Rose wines are often sold in earthenware bottles.

United States-produced wines: America's wineries market generic, varietal, and proprietary wines. The federal government and, in some cases, the state governments strictly control the production, naming, and selling of these wines. Generally, the wines are categorized into two major geographical divisions: Californian wines and American wines (wines produced in any other state).

Californian wines—Eighty percent of America's wines are produced in California. Because of climatic conditions unique to California, virtually every European grape variety can be successfully cultivated there. Thus, California offers a large number of wines.

American wines—About 11 percent of the United States' wines are produced in the northern New York area known as the Finger Lakes region. The remaining nine percent come from many other states such as Ohio and Michigan. Eastern wineries rely mainly on the native

How wines are named

The name of a wine can be recognized as falling into one of the three main categories: generic, varietal, or proprietary.

The generic wine names usually are the oldest and most well-known ones. These names frequently, but not always, identify the European region, commune, city, or vineyard where the wines were first made.

Generic Name	Geographical Origin
Burgundy	Burgundy region of France
Port	City of Oporto, Portugal
Claret	Bordeaux region of France
Sherry	City of Jerez, Spain

Wines with characteristics similar to these Old World wines but made in other parts of the world may also be given generic names. The generic name must be accompanied by the place where the wine was made.

Generic Name	Wine Name With Origin
Sherry	California Sherry
Champagne	New York Champagne
Chablis	American Chablis

Varietal naming, a second method of naming wines, is particularly popular in the United States. The name of a varietal wine identifies the major grape variety (by United States law, at least 51 percent) that is used in making the wine. Some varietal wines are blends of several grape varieties, with one grape variety predominating; others are made from only one grape variety. Quite often, a varietal wine will have appearance and taste characteristics similar to those of a wine that is generically named.

Generic	Varietal Counterpart
Claret	Cabernet Sauvignon, Zinfandel
Rhine	Riesling, Sylvaner
Chablis	Pinot Chardonnay, Pinot Blanc

The proprietary name, a third type of wine nomenclature, often is given to a special wine that has unique character and is made by only one vintner or winery. Rubion, Paisano, Capella, Vins da Tovora, and Emerald Dry are examples of such names.

American grapes and their hybrids, such as Delaware, Duchess, and Niagara, for the varietal and generic wines.

How to select wines: What kind, how much, and what quality are three questions you need to answer before you buy wine. If you're new to the wine world, a wine label will help you quite a lot. The label not only indicates the brand name and descriptive name of the wine but also its origin and vintner, alcoholic content, net contents, and sometimes vintage year and how the wine is best used.

The statement of origin and vintner indicates where and by whom the wine was made. The origin may be very general (American Sherry) or be more specific, naming the state or region where the wine originated. The vintner's name and address must always be stated. "Estate bottled" may be used when the bottler produced wine from grapes grown in vineyards that are in the vicinity of the winery and are owned or controlled by the bottler. When three-fourths of the wine is produced by the vintner, it may be labeled "produced and bottled by" or "bottled at the winery." The phrase "made by" may indicate that the wine was bottled from a blend of wines made by more than one vintner.

The alcoholic content (always given by volume, never by proof) must be labeled on any wine containing 14 percent or more alcohol. If it has less than 14 percent alcohol, the wine must be denoted as "dinner," "light," or "table" wine *or* the alcoholic content must be stated.

The most common bottle size for United States' wines (regardless of the shape) is the fifth. This has a net content of four-fifths quart or 25.6 ounces. Smaller and larger bottles are also available as needed. To judge how much wine you need, see the box on page 2456.

Appetizer openers

← Cranberry-Wine Hors d'Oeuvres, cubes of ham, chicken, and turkey that have simmered in a wine sauce, are for company.

A vintage year is rarely designated on United States' wines since the quality of the wines is consistent year after year. But all United States' wines so designated must have been produced within the specified year. European wine quality fluctuates more widely. Most of the vintage-dated European wines consist of wine produced in that year, although a small amount of wine produced in other than the vintage year may be included.

Last but not least, the label may indicate wine classification. Although this is not mandatory, wineries include the class, and often how to use the wine, as a guide to selection for consumers.

There are several points to consider when selecting a quality wine. A brand that has been produced for many years is probably one you can rely on. And, in general, the more specific the wine name, the better the quality. A domestic wine named Riesling, for instance, is produced under more rigid controls than the generic one called Rhine wine. The bottler's statement, "estate bottled," is a more exact designation of the wine's source than "produced by" and "made by."

How to store wines: Since wine continues to change after it is bottled, it is necessary to know a few storage guidelines to keep wine at its best.

Unopened corked bottles of wine should be stored on their sides, away from sunlight, at a constant temperature (ideally 55° to 60° and not over 70°), and free from vibrations. This permits the wine to age without spoiling. Screwcap bottles may be stored upright or on their sides.

You don't need an involved setup to meet wine storage needs. A wine rack as simple as a wine packing case placed on its side and located in a quiet place will do. If possible, arrange the bottles in the rack so that the less-stable wines are kept the coolest: sparkling and white dinner wines on the bottom, rosé and red table wines in the middle, and appetizer and dessert wines on top.

Storage for partially used bottles of wine is quite a separate story. Opened wines with over 14 percent alcohol may be refrigerator stored for weeks. However,

because of the lower alcoholic content, dinner wines are more perishable when opened. Refrigerate the unused portion of dinner wines, tightly sealed, and use the remainder within a week to 10 days.

Sparkling wines are best served immediately after opening. If you have some left over, store it well-stoppered in the refrigerator and use in a day or two.

Unused portions of dinner or sparkling wine are not a loss. Besides being good beverages to accompany the meal, they are ideal for many cooking uses.

How to use wines: Although it's common knowledge that wines can be used as beverages or as ingredients in a wide variety of prepared foods, there are still many questions that arise concerning their use. At the outset, one thing must be clear. The guidelines that are given here are merely suggestions; they are not hard-and-fast rules. Wines are made to be enjoyed, and their use need not be tangled in a myriad of formalities.

As a beverage — You can serve wine as a beverage before, during, or after any meal course. Some of the suggested rules of etiquette used for selecting, opening, serving, and drinking wine follow.

First, there are guidelines that help in selecting the right wine for a certain course or a particular food. As with appetizer foods, appetizer wines are chosen to stimulate the appetite for the remaining courses of the meal. In this same light, sweet wines, like cakes and pies, are recommended for dessert.

Red and white dinner wines complement different types of foods. Usually robust, red wines pair well with hearty foods like beef, pork, cheese, and pasta dishes. The delicate white dinner wines, on the other hand, enhance subtly flavored foods — poultry, fish, or veal, for example — without overpowering the entrée.

Rosé and sparkling wines are enjoyed at all occasions by themselves or with any food. (For more specific wine-food pairing, see chart on page 2452.)

How Much Wine To Buy

The amounts of wine you need to buy are based on the average size of each wine serving. In the case of dinner and sparkling wines, the average serving is 4 to 6 ounces. For appetizer and dessert wines, figure on 2 to 2½ ounces per serving.

Bottle size	Fluid ounces	Number of servings	
		Dinner and sparkling wines	Appetizer and dessert wines
Split (2/5 pint)	6.4	2	2-3
Tenth (4/5 pint)	12.8	2-3	5-6
Pint	16	3-4	6-7
Fifth (4/5 quart)	25.6	4-6	10-12
Quart	32	5-8	12-16
Half gallon	64	10-16	25-32
Gallon	128	21-32	51-64

As with wine selection, recommendations for wine serving temperatures are helpful for the novice wine drinker. Most white and rosé wines are prechilled to between 45° and 50°, and sparkling wines are best even colder, 40° to 45°. Except for dry Sherry and dry Vermouth, which are chilled (45° to 55°) or served on the rocks, appetizer, dessert, and red dinner wines, for the most part, are served at a cool room temperature (60° to 70°). Red dinner wines are often opened about an hour before serving to allow the bouquet to develop more fully. Other wines are not opened until just before they are served.

Although there are many types of wineglasses, some with specific uses, the most important part is the wine, not the glass. The 8- to 10-ounce all-purpose wineglass that is clear, stemmed, and tulip-shaped is a good investment for multiple-use drinking. If you wish to add to your selection of glasses, the 6-ounce tulip glass is popular for appetizer and dessert wines. The tall, slender tulip or stemmed, saucerlike glass is good for sparkling wines.

Placement of wineglasses at the table is very simple: the wineglass is placed to the right and slightly ahead of the water glass. If there are to be two wines at the meal, place the glasses side-by-side or one in front of the other.

The proper use of a good corkscrew permits easy opening of a still wine bottle with a cork closure. For a still wine, cut the seal about ¼ inch below the bottle lip, remove the upper portion of the seal, then wipe the lip with a napkin. Insert the corkscrew. Giving a slight twist to the corkscrew as you begin to pull, remove the cork. Again using a napkin, wipe the inside of the bottle neck to remove any bits of remaining cork.

Uncorking sparkling wines requires care to prevent the cork from bursting out unexpectedly. First, cut the seal about 1½ inches down and remove the upper portion. Then, remove the wire hood by unwinding the loop. Keep your thumb on top of the cork as much as possible. With one hand holding the bottom portion of the bottle, grasp the cork with the other hand, keeping your thumb securely over the top of the cork. Angle the bottle to 45° (cork pointed away from you and anyone else) and begin twisting the bottle while holding the cork in a fixed position. As you twist, the internal bottle pressure will help push out the cork. Be sure to hold onto the cork as it leaves the bottle. If the cork doesn't come out, press the cork gently from side to side as you twist. Pour into glasses immediately.

When serving wine, make sure that the glasses are clean—completely dry and free of any film, lint, or water spots. The host first pours some wine into his glass and samples it. (In this way, he gets any pieces of cork, and an unpleasant wine can be detected.) After approving the wine, he pours the guests' glasses, filling a third to half full. Pour sparkling wine until the foam reaches the rim, then fill two-thirds to three-fourths full.

Tasting wine means taking in its color and bouquet, as well as its flavor. First, look at it for color, then sniff the bouquet. Take a sip and swirl the wine to the back of your tongue (that's where many taste buds are located). Hold it there a few seconds before swallowing. You will soon be using such descriptive words as fragrant, dry, sweet, and delicate to describe the taste sensations.

In addition to being served alone, wine also is used as an ingredient in mixed drinks and punches. Wines are well suited to this use since they contribute flavor and often color. They blend well with all kinds of fruit juices, carbonated beverages, sherbets, and ice creams.

Drier drinks such as Tomato-Vermouth Cocktail and Rosé Frappé are appetite stimulants. Sweeter versions such as Sherried Chocolate Frappé better fit into the refreshment and dessert uses.

Tomato-Vermouth Cocktail

    2 cups tomato juice, chilled
    ½ cup dry vermouth
    1 tablespoon lemon juice
      Ice

Combine all ingredients in shaker or screw-top jar; adjust lid. Shake well and chill. Serve in small glasses with ice. Serves 4.

Burgundy and Sherry work together to flavor the meat for Beef à la Wellington. Liverwurst and pastry layers enwrap the beef.

Rosé Frappé

    1 fifth rosé wine
    1 6-ounce can frozen lemonade
        concentrate, thawed
    ¾ cup water

Stir together wine, lemonade concentrate, and water. Pour over crushed ice in sherbets to serve. Makes 8 servings.

Sherried Chocolate Frappé

    2 cups milk
    ⅓ cup chocolate syrup
    ⅓ cup cream sherry
    1 pint vanilla ice cream
        •   •   •
    Ground cinnamon

Combine milk, chocolate syrup, and sherry. Spoon ice cream into 4 tall glasses; pour chocolate mixture over. Muddle mixture slightly; sprinkle with cinnamon. Makes 4 servings.

Punches take on a special entertaining light when sparked with wine. Burgundy helps to give Ruby Wine Punch its color.

Ruby Wine Punch

    ¾ cup water
    ¾ cup sugar
    6 inches stick cinnamon
    1 teaspoon whole cloves
        Dash salt
    2 cups red Burgundy, chilled
    1 32-ounce bottle cranberry-
        apple juice, chilled

In saucepan combine first 5 ingredients; bring to boil. Reduce heat; simmer 10 minutes. Strain; chill liquid. Combine with wine and fruit juice. Makes 12 to 14 four-ounce servings.

As an ingredient—Probably no other food is more closely linked with gourmet cooking than is wine. A few dashes of wine added to an appetizer, entrée, or dessert seem to transform the food magically into a connoisseur's delight. Because wine can change the nature of a food dramatically, one might also think that it requires the hand of an adept cook. Yet, because of wine's versatility, nothing is easier than cooking with wine. In most cases, wines can be used interchangeably in foods. Furthermore, the flavors of most foods are enhanced by wine.

Just as with using herbs and spices, there are general suggestions that help you get the most enjoyment from seasoning foods with wines. But let your imagination be the most influential guide. For example, when a recipe calls for water, milk, or bouillon, consider substituting some wine for a portion of the liquid. If you've tried a recipe once with Sherry, the next time give it a different flavor twist by using Sauterne or another type of white wine. Instead of using red Burgundy, utilize another red wine or even a white or rosé wine. Each time you'll have created a new combination.

Although any sound wine can be used for cooking, a good wine with full body and distinctive flavor imparts the best

cooking qualities. If you have some wine left from a meal or if you will be serving the wine at the meal to come, it's logical to use a little of it to flavor the food.

A wine designated as a "cooking wine" can be used equally well. The wine label will specify whether or not salt has been added to the wine. The seasoning level of the food may need to be adjusted when using a "salted" cooking wine.

Always use wine sparingly in food—you can always add more if it's needed. For best results, allow the natural flavor of the food to predominate.

Wine charts, besides being beverage guidelines, also are helpful when you cook with wine. For example, red dinner wines are more often used in hearty entrées; white dinner wines, in delicate-flavored entrées; and dessert wines, in dessert foods. Except when poured over fruit for an appetizer or dessert, sparkling wines do not serve a purpose in cooking since they lose one of their appeals, the effervescence.

Appetizer uses for wines encompass soups, canapés, dips, and hors d'oeuvres. Dry wine used in cheese fondue is a tradition. Onion soup takes on a new flair with a little white wine. Meat cube hors d'oeuvres boast a cranberry-wine sauce.

Onion-Wine Soup

In saucepan cook 3 medium onions, thinly sliced, in ¼ cup butter or margarine till lightly browned. Add two 10½-ounce cans *condensed* chicken broth, 1⅓ cups water, and ½ cup dry white wine; heat. Ladle into soup bowls. Sprinkle 8 toasted French bread slices with grated Parmesan cheese; float atop soup. Pass additional cheese, if desired. Makes 8 servings.

Cranberry-Wine Hors d'Oeuvres

    1 cup sugar
    ¾ cup water
    2 cups fresh cranberries
    ¼ cup dry white wine
    ¼ cup catsup
      Fully cooked ham, chicken, and
        turkey, cubed

In large saucepan combine sugar and water. Heat to boiling, stirring till sugar dissolves. Boil 5 minutes. Add cranberries; cook till skins pop, 5 minutes. Remove from heat. Stir in wine and catsup. Pour into small blazer pan of chafing dish; place meat in sauce. Keep warm over hot water (bain-marie). Spear with cocktail picks. Makes 2 cups sauce.

Wine gives gourmet flavor to meats and fishes of all kinds. As when drinking wines, red wines are often teamed with red meats and white wines with white meats. With fish, shellfish, and game meats, wine subdues intense flavors.

Beef à la Wellington

    1 cup red Burgundy
    1 cup dry sherry
    1 onion, quartered
    2 bay leaves
    1 3-pound eye of round beef roast
    2 cups sifted all-purpose flour
    ⅔ cup shortening
    1 4¾-ounce can liverwurst spread
    1 slightly beaten egg
    3 tablespoons all-purpose flour

Combine the first 4 ingredients. Place meat in pan; pour marinade over. Cover; refrigerate overnight. Remove meat from marinade, reserving ¼ cup for gravy. Roast meat on rack in shallow roasting pan at 425° till meat thermometer registers 130°, about 1¼ hours. Reserve drippings. Cool the meat.

Sift together 2 cups flour and ½ teaspoon salt; cut in shortening till coarse crumbs. Gradually add ⅓ to ½ cup cold water, tossing with fork till dampened. Form into ball. Roll to 12x11-inch rectangle; spread with liverwurst to within ½ inch of edges. Place meat, top side down, in center of pastry. Draw up long sides to overlap. Brush with egg to seal. Trim ends; fold up and brush with more egg to seal.

Place on greased baking sheet, seam side down. Brush with remaining egg. Bake at 425° for 30 to 35 minutes. Heat ¾ cup water with drippings. Blend together the 3 tablespoons flour and ½ cup cold water; add to pan with marinade. Cook, stirring constantly, till bubbly. Season to taste. Serves 8 to 12.

Wine flavor in a main dish comes from using the wine as a marinade, a basting sauce, or in a sauce. A marinade serves a dual purpose—it adds flavor and helps to tenderize less-tender cuts of meat.

Beef with Wine Sauce

    1 pound ground beef
    ½ cup rosé wine
    1½ teaspoons cornstarch
    1 tablespoon lemon juice
    ¼ cup orange marmalade

Form meat into 4 patties about ¾ inch thick. Sprinkle with salt. Broil 3 to 4 inches from heat for 6 minutes. Turn; broil 4 minutes longer or to desired degree of doneness.

Meanwhile, in small saucepan blend wine with cornstarch. Stir in lemon juice and marmalade. Cook, stirring constantly, till mixture thickens and bubbles. To serve, garnish patties with orange slices, if desired. Spoon wine sauce atop. Makes 4 servings.

Scallopine Burgers

    1½ pounds ground veal
    1 cup soft bread crumbs
    1 beaten egg
    2 tablespoons milk
    ¼ cup all-purpose flour
    ¼ cup salad oil
    1 8-ounce can tomato sauce
    1 3-ounce can chopped mushrooms,
        undrained
    ¼ cup dry white wine
    1 tablespoon finely snipped
        parsley
    ¼ teaspoon dried oregano leaves,
        crushed
    Hot cooked noodles
    Grated Parmesan cheese

Combine veal, crumbs, egg, milk, ½ teaspoon salt, and dash pepper; shape into 6 patties. Coat lightly with ¼ cup all-purpose flour. Brown in hot oil in skillet. Drain off excess fat. Combine tomato sauce, undrained mushrooms, wine, parsley, and oregano; pour over meat. Cover; simmer 20 to 25 minutes. Serve on noodles; sprinkle with cheese. Serves 6.

Vegetables and salads take on elegance with the addition of wine, too. Add wine to a cream sauce for vegetables and to the gelatin for molded salads or to creamy salad dressings for tossed salads. Use white wines for light-colored gelatins, red wines for red-colored gelatins. Use wine vinegar in place of cider vinegar to create flavorful salad dressings.

Orange-Port Mold

    2 3-ounce packages black cherry-
        flavored gelatin
    1½ cups boiling water
    3 oranges
    1 cup port
    1 cup orange juice

Dissolve cherry gelatin in the boiling water. Peel oranges; section each, reserving juice, and cut up pulp. Add enough water to reserved juice to make ½ cup liquid. Stir into dissolved gelatin along with wine and the additional 1 cup orange juice. Chill gelatin mixture till partially set. Fold in cut-up oranges; pour mixture into a 6½-cup ring mold. Chill till firm; unmold and fill center of ring with lettuce, if desired. Makes 8 to 10 servings.

To round out the recipe uses for wines, there is nothing more glamorous than wine-flavored desserts. Fruit compotes, dessert sauces, pies, and cakes become sophisticated food fare when spiced with an interesting wine.

Hot Fruit Compote

    1 16-ounce package dried prunes
    1⅓ cups dried apricots
    1 13½-ounce can pineapple chunks,
        undrained (1⅔ cups)
    1 21-ounce can cherry pie filling
    2 cups water
    ¼ cup dry white wine

Arrange first three fruits in 9x9x2-inch baking dish. Combine pie filling, water, and wine; pour over fruit. Cover; bake at 350° for 1½ hours. Serve warm. Makes 8 servings.

Spirits

Fermented liquids have been distilled since before the Christian Era. The early Chinese distilled a spirit from rice beer. East Indians distilled fermented sugarcane and rice as early as 800 B.C.

The development of distilled spirits in Europe and the United States was influenced mostly by the Celts of Great Britain and by the Arabs of the Middle East. The Celts distilled the first whiskey-like liquor, which they called *uisgebaugh* (water of life). As the civilization of Great Britain progressed, this spirit evolved into the Scotch and Irish whiskies. Although the Arabs could not distill alcohol because of religious beliefs, they did coin the word alcohol and become proficient in the distillation of flower fragrances for perfumes. The Spanish adapted this process to the distillation of grape wine.

In Europe, the interest in drinking spirits developed during medieval times. France imposed heavy taxes, determined by volume, on exported wines. To reduce the tax and also to save on shipping costs, winegrowers began distilling wine into brandy. When imported, the alcohol was to be diluted to its original state. Instead, the distilled product was soon recognized as being palatable itself.

Rum and later grain spirits were the most-consumed spirits in early America. It became more economical to ship grain grown in western Pennsylvania and Kentucky as spirits than as fresh grains. Distilleries sprang up on many farms.

Besides the traditional grain whiskies, one new type, named Bourbon after the Kentucky county where it was first made, was developed by an inventive distiller. The demand for Bourbon and other Kentucky whiskies sparked the growth of a new industry. Today, Kentucky distills 70 percent of American-produced spirits.

How spirits are produced: The distillation of alcohol from a fermented liquid (called the mash) is based on the fact that alcohol boils at a lower temperature than water (about 175° versus 212°). Wines, sugarcane, molasses, and grains are some of the raw materials used for the mash.

What is "proof?"

In times past, the strength of a liquor was determined by mixing equal portions of the liquor with gunpowder and igniting them. If the gunpowder did not burn, the spirit was too weak. If the flame was overly bright, the spirit was too strong. A spirit that created an even, blue flame, however, was said to have been "proved."

Today, the strength of a distilled alcohol is called its proof. Each degree of proof is equivalent to a half-percent of alcohol. Thus, a spirit that is labeled 160 proof consists of 80 percent alcohol.

When the liquid is heated to around 200° (boiling), the alcohol vaporizes; the water is left behind. This vapor is condensed in a closed container. It is now a highly alcoholic liquid—a spirit.

In theory, if all the alcohol is separated, the liquid will be completely pure—200 proof, colorless, odorless, and tasteless. In actuality, however, the purest spirits available, called neutral spirits, are distilled at 190 proof.

The apparatus used in the production of spirits is commonly referred to as a still. There are two kinds of stills—the older (but still used) is the batch still; the newer is called a continuous still. Although the batch still frequently produces a more flavorful product, distillation must be repeated two or three times to achieve the desired purity and alcoholic strength. The continuous still, on the other hand, requires no redistillation.

If the fermented liquid is distilled to less than 190 proof (which is most often the case), other substances in the liquid rise off with the alcohol. These elements, known as congeners, are the flavor components that develop during the aging process of a liquor. When aged in wood, the congeners create the characteristic appearance, aroma, and taste of the particular spirit. The lower the proof at which a spirit is distilled, the more congeners that are present in the alcohol and the more character the spirit has.

Not all of the spirits attain their flavors and appearances by wood-aging. Some, such as gin, are simply neutral spirits that have been distilled with flavoring components such as herbs.

After the desired aging has taken place, the spirit is bottled. Once it is in sealed glass containers, the spirit no longer changes in character.

Types of spirits: Varying the kind of fermented liquid used as well as the aging, flavoring, and blending techniques enables the production of many different spirits. The wide variety available suit the wide range of taste preferences.

Brandy is usually the distilled product of grape wine, but it may also be the distillate of other fruit wines. Except for grape brandy, the fruits from which the brandies are made (apple, cherry, for example) must be specified on the labels.

Liquors labeled "fruit-flavored" brandies, common to United States' markets, are not true fruit brandies. In reality, they are liqueurs consisting of grape brandy to which fruit flavors have been infused and sugar syrup added.

Gin is based on diluted neutral spirits that are distilled and sometimes redistilled in the presence of flavoring components. The traditional but not the only flavoring ingredient is juniper berries. Most gin is unaged, which results in a clear, colorless spirit.

Liqueur, also called cordial, is the family name for certain sweet, after-dinner spirits. Usually based on either neutral spirits or brandy, liqueurs are flavored by infusing or distilling the flavoring agents (plant flowers, roots, seeds, fruits, and the like) with the spirits.

Rum is distilled from sugarcane or molasses mash. For the most part, the dark rums are aged longer and have more intense flavor than the light rums.

Blazing entrée

← Warmed brandy provides the glowing flame for the pineapple- and apricot-sauced breasts of chicken in delicious Chicken Fantasia.

Tequila, Mexico's national drink, is a colorless spirit distilled from the fermented mash of the maguey plant.

Vodka has the least identifiable flavor of any spirit because it is simply diluted neutral spirits. No flavorings are added. Although often thought to be a potato distillate, vodka is more often distilled from grain or any inexpensive food.

Whiskey, although basically a grain distillate, comes in assorted types, depending on where, from what, and how it is made. All whiskies are aged in wood, usually oak. Scotch, Irish, and Canadian whiskies are made in the countries for which they are named. Each has a unique flavor—smoky, full-bodied, and light-bodied respectively. Of the many United States whiskies, the most all-American is Bourbon, made mainly from corn.

How to select and store spirits: When selecting spirits, purchase according to its intended use or your personal brand preferences. The superior-quality spirits are enjoyed by most people when they are consumed straight, over ice, or in cocktails of low dilution. For punches and more diluted cocktails, a less-expensive spirit usually suits the purpose adequately. Because production costs are passed on to the consumer, price is usually the best indication of quality.

Spirits are most often sold in fifths and quarts, but half-pints and pints are suitable for small use. Half-gallons are economical buys for large parties.

Because spirits are stable once they are bottled, most of them can be shelf stored for long periods. However, opened bottles of liqueurs lose their flavor power with storage. Pints of liqueurs are frequently most practical for home use.

How to use spirits: Spirits are America's traditional ingredients for cocktails and other alcoholic beverages, but they can also add new dimensions to prepared dishes. Using these beverage and cooking techniques will help you to develop a method of creating flavorful foods.

As a beverage—Efficient mixing and serving of spiritous beverages is one of the marks of a good host or hostess. First,

master the drinks you and your friends like best, then add a new drink to your repertoire from time to time. To make flavorful drinks you need the proper supplies: spirits and nonalcoholic accompaniments, bar supplies, and glassware.

The supply of spirits and drink accompaniments that you need depends on what drinks you plan to serve. Carbonated beverages such as club soda, ginger ale, and quinine water are common mixers. When fruit juices are needed for drinks, juice squeezed from fresh fruits imparts the best flavor. You may also need bitters and garnishes such as orange or lemon slices, maraschino cherries, and cocktail olives and onions. Since alcohol and icy liquids are poor solvents for sugar, fine granulated sugar (not confectioners') or a simple syrup are used for sweetening.

Simple Syrup

Combine equal amounts of sugar and water. Boil for 5 minutes. Store in a covered jar in the refrigerator until it is needed.

For bar equipment you can make use of kitchen items that you already own, but you will also need some special tools. Kitchen supplies that move to the bar include bottle openers, corkscrew, paring knife, juice strainer, ice cube cracker, ice crusher, ice bucket, and tongs. You'll probably also want coasters, straws, and cocktail napkins. Special bar supplies that you may have to purchase are the bar spoon, jigger-pony measure, bar strainer, and a mixer-shaker or blender.

Mixed drinks look best in specially designed glassware. Stemmed 4- to 6-ounce cocktail glasses are ideal for the ice cold but iceless cocktails. Stemless old-fashioned glasses with 7- to 8-ounce capacity are best for on-the-rocks drinks. The all-purpose wineglass can be used for any of the sours, Bloody Marys, or other medium-sized drinks. Tall highball glasses (8 to 12 ounces) are for large drinks such as highballs and Collins. And for liqueurs, the ¾- to 1-ounce cordial glasses are most appropriate.

Common bar measurements

1 wineglass equals 4 ounces
1 jigger equals 1½ ounces or 3 tablespoons
1 pony equals 1 ounce
1 ounce equals 2 tablespoons
1 dash equals 1/16 teaspoon
Juice of 1 lime is about 1 tablespoon
Juice of 1 lemon is about 3 tablespoons
1 bar spoon equals 1 teaspoon or 1/8 ounce

For good-tasting drinks, accurate measuring of ingredients is most important. Icing the drink without overdiluting it is equally vital. When you mix the ingredients, remember the following tips:

1. Prechill all of the ingredients and the glasses ahead of time.

2. The more ice used in the shaker, the faster the cooling of the liquid and the less the dilution of the beverage.

3. Do not overstir or overshake. This mistake results in excess dilution.

4. For faster chilling of on-the-rocks drinks, always use cracked ice.

5. If you use a blender for mixing, prechill the blender container and blend the ingredients for only a few seconds.

6. Before serving, add an appealing garnish if one suits the drink.

Warren's Glugg

Serve the punch informally right from the kettle—

Combine 2 quarts apple juice; ½ pound light raisins; 3 sticks cinnamon, broken; 1 tablespoon whole cloves; 4 cardamom buds;* and dash ground nutmeg. Let mixture stand for 12 to 24 hours. Before serving, pour the mixture into a kettle and bring to boiling; reduce heat and simmer for 30 minutes. Add 1½ oranges, sliced and quartered; heat through. Add 1 fifth dark rum and 1 fifth brandy. Serve mixture immediately from kettle; keep warm over low heat. Makes about 24 punch-cup servings.

*Use seeds only from cardamom buds; shell and crush the seeds between two tablespoons or in a mortar and pestle. Steep the crushed seeds in 2 or 3 tablespoons boiling water.

Tonic

Use gin, vodka, or Tequila—

Combine juice and rind of ¼ lime, 1 jigger gin, vodka, *or* Tequila (1½ ounces), and ice cubes in tall glass. Fill with tonic water. Stir.

As an ingredient—Since the function of a spirit as an ingredient is to flavor food, it is important to know how to use it and pair it with different foods.

Because excess alcohol imparts harsh flavor, moderation is the foremost guide to adding spirits to foods. Uncooked dishes rapidly take on the alcohol undertones. For cooked dishes, heat the mixture until the alcohol evaporates. The remaining spirit flavor should enhance but not overpower the flavor of the food.

For great drama, flame the added spirits. First, the spirit must have a sufficient concentration of alcohol. Spirits higher than 70 proof are best. If you use a liquor of low proof, add some vodka or brandy to increase the alcoholic strength. Next, place the liquor in a small saucepan and warm slowly till the alcohol begins to vaporize. Do not overheat. At the table, ignite the warmed alcohol (either in the saucepan or poured into a ladle), using a

Irish Coffee Pie (see *Pie* for recipe) is a dessert rendition of the famed beverage. The coffee- and whiskey-flavored filling is garnished with whipped cream and shaved chocolate.

safety match, and pour the flaming liquid over the dish. Allow the fire to burn out naturally. Although the technique appears to require a deft hand, you, too, can easily master this cooking art.

Banana-Raspberry Flambé

1 10-ounce package frozen
   raspberries, thawed
6 tablespoons orange liqueur
2 tablespoons granulated sugar
3 tablespoons butter or margarine
1 tablespoon brown sugar
6 medium bananas, sliced

Banana-Raspberry Flambé features an orange liqueur-sparked fruit sauce that is flamed and spooned over scoops of ice cream.

Combine raspberries, 2 *tablespoons* liqueur, and granulated sugar in blender container. Cover; blend till smooth. Sieve. In blazer pan of chafing dish melt butter; add brown sugar. When sugar is dissolved, add bananas. Cook 2 to 3 minutes. Add raspberry mixture to bananas; heat through. Heat remaining liqueur in ladle or small saucepan; flame and pour over fruits. Serve over ice cream. Makes 4 cups.

The pairing of spirits with food follows that for wines—full-bodied spirits season hearty foods well, while light-bodied spirits team better with delicate foods. Because of its lack of flavor, vodka does not serve a special cooking purpose.

Brandy sparks appetizer dips and spreads, meaty main dishes, coffee-flavored foods, puddings, cakes, and ice cream sauces. Fruit-flavored brandies are naturals with many fruit dishes.

Snow-Capped Pâté

½ cup chopped onion
1 small clove garlic, crushed
¼ cup butter or margarine
1 pound fresh or frozen chicken
   livers, thawed
2 teaspoons all-purpose flour
¼ teaspoon salt
¼ teaspoon dried thyme leaves,
   crushed
   Dash pepper
4 teaspoons brandy
2 3-ounce packages cream cheese,
   cubed and softened
3 tablespoons milk
¼ cup snipped parsley
½ cup chopped pecans

Cook onion and garlic in butter till tender. Add livers; cook, covered, 7 to 8 minutes. Stir in flour, salt, thyme, and pepper. Add brandy; cook and stir 1 minute. Transfer to blender container. Cover; blend smooth. (When necessary, use rubber spatula to scrape down sides.) Mold in small greased bowl; chill.

Unmold. Add cream cheese and milk to blender container. Cover; blend smooth. Spread over mold. Chill till serving time. Sprinkle parsley and nuts atop pâté. Serve with crackers.

Chicken Fantasia

6 small chicken breasts, boned
    and skinned (about 2½ pounds)
6 thin slices boiled ham
2 tablespoons butter or margarine
½ cup apricot preserves
2 tablespoons vinegar
½ teaspoon salt
½ teaspoon dry mustard
1 8¾-ounce can pineapple tidbits
2 tablespoons cornstarch
¼ cup brandy

Place chicken, boned side up, on cutting board. Pound to make cutlets ¼ inch thick. Place a ham slice on each cutlet; tuck in sides and roll up jelly-roll fashion. Skewer or tie. In large skillet slowly brown chicken in butter. Stir in ⅔ cup water, preserves, vinegar, salt, and mustard. Cook, covered, 20 minutes.

Drain pineapple, reserving syrup. Blend cornstarch and reserved syrup. Stir cornstarch mixture and pineapple tidbits into sauce in skillet. Cook, uncovered, till chicken is tender, 15 minutes, turning chicken rolls once.

At serving time, transfer chicken to blazer pan of chafing dish; garnish with canned apricot halves, if desired. Place over chafing dish burner. Pour sauce into heatproof dish. In small saucepan warm brandy; at table pour brandy over sauce. Ignite immediately; spoon flaming sauce over chicken. Makes 6 servings.

Hamburger Steak Diane

1½ pounds ground round or sirloin
1 teaspoon dry mustard
2 tablespoons butter or margarine
1 to 2 tablespoons lemon juice
1 tablespoon snipped parsley
½ teaspoon Worcestershire sauce
¼ cup brandy

Combine meat, mustard, 1 teaspoon salt, and dash pepper; mix well. Shape into 5 patties, ½ inch thick. Melt butter in blazer pan of chafing dish over direct heat. Cook 2 minutes on each side; remove. To blazer pan add lemon juice, parsley, and Worcestershire; bring to boiling. Reduce heat. In saucepan heat brandy over very low heat. Pour brandy over sauce; ignite. Serve at once over meat. Serves 5.

Bourbon adds a different touch to barbecue sauces and chocolate desserts. Bourbon Balls are a good confection.

Bourbon Balls

60 vanilla wafers
½ cup walnuts
1 cup sifted confectioners' sugar
2 tablespoons unsweetened cocoa
    powder
¼ cup bourbon
¼ cup light corn syrup
    Granulated sugar

Break 6 wafers into blender; blend to fine crumbs. Repeat. Put nuts in blender; blend till chopped. Add to crumbs. Combine confectioners' sugar, cocoa, and crumbs. Stir in bourbon and corn syrup. If necessary, add 1¼ teaspoons water so that mixture will shape. Form into ¾-inch balls. Roll in granulated sugar. Store in covered container. Makes 48.

Rum is one of the best seasonings for use in tropical foods such as chocolate, coffee, pineapple, and citrus fruits.

Orange-Rum Cake

2 17-ounce packages pound
    cake mix
2 tablespoons shredded orange
    peel
2 teaspoons shredded lemon peel
1 cup sugar
1 cup orange juice
3 tablespoons lemon juice
2 tablespoons rum

Prepare cake mixes together according to package directions, adding fruit peel. Turn into greased and lightly floured 10-inch tube pan. Bake at 350° till done, 1 to 1¼ hours. Cool 10 minutes; remove from pan. Cool 20 minutes.

Place on serving plate. Using long-tined fork or skewer, punch holes in top of cake at 1-inch intervals. Combine remaining ingredients; bring to boiling. Spoon *very slowly* over cake, *a small amount at a time*, allowing cake to absorb sauce. Continue till syrup is used. Chill.

Probably the most versatile spirits for ingredient uses are the liqueurs with their vast range of flavors. Their intenseness again implies sparing use. Ideas for using liqueurs include spooning them as is over ice cream, sherbet, or fruit, or adding them to dessert sauces or dessert soufflés. Liqueurs, such as orange- and mint-flavored ones, also enhance duck, pork, lamb, and fish entrées when the sweetness of the liqueur is tempered by the addition of a little lemon juice.

Orange–Date Medley

Almond topping adds crunch—

    5 oranges, peeled and sectioned
    1 cup sliced, pitted dates
    1 cup orange juice
    2 tablespoons orange liqueur
    ¼ cup toasted, slivered almonds

Place orange sections and dates in 10x6x1½-inch baking dish. Combine orange juice and orange liqueur; pour over fruit. Bake, covered, at 350° till heated through, about 30 minutes. Sprinkle almonds over top. Serves 6.

Lime Fizz

Prechill glasses in the freezer—

    ¼ cup frozen limeade concentrate,
        thawed
    3 ounces gin (2 jiggers)
    2 teaspoons fine granulated sugar
    2 teaspoons white crème de
        menthe
    1 drop green food coloring
    2 cups crushed ice
    1 7-ounce bottle carbonated
        water, chilled
    Fresh mint leaves

In blender container combine limeade concentrate, gin, sugar, white crème de menthe, green food coloring, and ice; blend for a few seconds. Divide mixture evenly into two highball glasses. Fill with carbonated water. Stir gently with up-and-down motion. Trim with fresh mint leaves. Makes 2 servings.

WINTERGREEN—The aromatic flavor born by the leaves of an evergreen herb that is distributed widely in northern woods. The bright red berries are often called checkerberries and can be eaten.

Fresh wintergreen cannot be obtained unless you know where to gather it, but oil of wintergreen, an aromatic, volatile oil, is available at pharmacies for use in making candies and confections. The oil is potent, so a few drops are sufficient to carry the flavor through an entire batch of candy. (See also *Flavoring.*)

WINTER SQUASH—Any fully mature squash variety with a hard rind and seeds. The best-known varieties of winter squash are acorn, banana, butternut, delicious, hubbard, and turban squash.

In addition to being packed with vitamin A, these dark yellow vegetables also contribute a fair amount of the B vitamin riboflavin. One-half cup of baked winter squash provides about 65 calories.

Although there is a wide color and shape differential between varieties, in general, purchase winter squash that have hard rinds and good variety color and shape, and that are heavy for their size. Most winter squash are marketed during fall and winter, but their storage stability enables year-round availability. If stored in a cool, dry area, winter squash will maintain their quality for several months. Handle gently to prevent bruising or damaging, as decay will set in.

Unlike summer squash, the rinds and seeds of winter squash are not usually eaten. Bake small varieties whole or cut in half and bake with seasoned butter or a meat or vegetable stuffing. For large squash, cut in cubes or serving-sized pieces before cooking. (See also *Squash.*)

WIRE WHIP—Another name for the utensil called a whisk. (See also *Whisk.*)

WITLOOF CHICORY *(wit' lōf)*—An alternate name for the vegetable Belgian Endive. (See also *Belgian Endive.*)

WOK—An iron, aluminum, or copper cooking pan of Chinese origin having a round bottom, sloping sides, and one or more

Try your hand at oriental cookery and prepare the main dish in a wok—a round, basin-shaped cooking pan of Chinese origin.

handles. Some woks have two handles, while others have one long handle, similar to that found on a frying pan. Modern versions usually are sold in a metal stand, which allows the pan to sit on the range without tipping. Pan sizes range from 10 inches to over 24 inches. The larger sizes are used mainly by restaurants.

The wok is used for stir-frying, braising, and stewing oriental dishes. Because of its shape, sauces or oil, if used, drains to the center where the heat is concentrated. Thus, quick cooking and constant stirring or tossing are necessary. It is an easy pan to keep clean because there are no corners in which the food can lodge. The wok should be seasoned before using. (See also *Oriental Cookery*.)

WON TON—The name of the Chinese filled dumpling. It is made of noodle dough with a meat, seafood, or vegetable filling, somewhat like a tiny ravioli. Won ton are served in broth for a soup, or they can be simmered in boiling water, fried, and served with a sauce. Won ton wrappers can be purchased in some specialty stores.

WOODRUFF—A perennial, wild herb. The leaves are long, oval, and deep green; the flowers are white. The dried leaves have a sweet aroma. Other names for this herb are sweet woodruff and waldmeister.

The most popular use of woodruff is to flavor the German punch, May wine. Woodruff also adds flavor to candies, punches, fruit cups, and other beverages.

WORCESTERSHIRE SAUCE *(wŏŏs' tuhr shēr,' -shuhr)*—A piquant brown liquid seasoning sauce that takes its name from Worcester, England, where it was first prepared commercially many years ago. Its ancestry, however, dates back to ancient India and to the Romans.

Worcestershire is commercially prepared by secret formula from soy sauce, anchovies, onions, tamarinds, garlic, vinegar, molasses, sugar, salt, and spices. It's a sauce for meats, but it is also used in sauces, soups, and casseroles.

Cheeseburger Pie

Combine 1 pound ground beef; ½ cup evaporated milk; ½ cup catsup; ⅓ cup fine dry bread crumbs; ¼ cup chopped onion; ¾ teaspoon salt; ½ teaspoon dried oregano leaves, crushed; and ⅛ teaspoon pepper. Prepare pastry for one-crust 8-inch pie (see *Pastry* for recipe). Line pie plate with pastry and fill with meat mixture. Bake at 350° for 35 to 40 minutes. Toss 4 ounces process American cheese, shredded (1 cup), with 1 teaspoon Worcestershire sauce. Sprinkle atop pie. Bake 10 minutes longer. Remove from oven; let stand 10 minutes before serving. Makes 6 servings.

WORMWOOD—A bitter herb used in making absinthe, a potent liqueur. The plant is native to Europe and northern Asia. Because absinthe made with wormwood is thought to have harmful effects on the nervous system, absinthe is outlawed in many countries, including the United States. Absinthe is still made in Spain.

WURST *(wûrst, wŏŏrst)*—The German word for sausage. The word is used alone or in a combined type name, such as liverwurst.

X-Y

XERES *(hā' rās)*—The French word for sherry wine, derived from Jerez, the name of the Spanish town where the wine originated.

YAM—1. A starchy root vegetable of the *Dioscorea* genus that is common to tropical regions. 2. The name given to a moist-fleshed sweet potato.

The true *Dioscorea* yams have been a staple food of Central and South America for centuries. When Columbus and his fellow explorers landed at Haiti in 1492, they were given yams to eat by the natives. Later, African slaves from Senegal that were brought to the West Indies named these vegetables *nyami*, their word for "to eat." Yams were then taken back to Africa and cultivated there.

There are hundreds of varieties of true yams found and used abundantly in the southern regions of the Western Hemisphere. Some are immense, growing 7 to 8 feet in length and weighing over 100 pounds; others, called yampees, are smaller than a potato. In texture, they may be coarse, dry, and mealy; fine and tender; and crisp or mushy. Flavor varies.

True yams are seen in our country only as oddities, but in the tropics they are enjoyed in many dishes. Yams can be prepared in a variety of ways—baking, boiling, steaming, or frying.

The vegetables labeled yams in the supermarkets, on the other hand, are a type of sweet potato. They have brown skins with orange to pinkish orange overcasts and golden orange flesh that is sweet and syrupy when cooked. Louisiana and Florida are the primary producers of this vegetable. (See also *Sweet Potato*.)

YEAST—Microscopic, one-celled living plants. Yeast converts carbohydrates into alcohol and carbon dioxide gas; this process is known as fermentation.

Certain types of yeasts are used to bring about alcoholic fermentation in the production of wine and champagne and in the brewing of beer. Other yeasts provide leavening in raised bread products, resulting in a light, porous structure. Another type of yeast, brewers' yeast, is a dried yeast that is available in tablet or powdered form. It is consumed for its nutritional value.

Yeast is the earliest known leavening agent. It was used by the Egyptians for making beer and bread about 2000 B.C. The ancient Egyptians noted that when their bread dough was set aside, the mixture puffed up and soured—improving the flavor. Unknown to them, yeast plants from the air settled on the dough and grew into the dough. With this newly discovered bread product, the Egyptians

invented an oven in which to bake the puffy bread. They also noticed that a piece of the dough from a previous batch could be used to leaven the next freshly made batch of dough. In this way, the first leavened sour dough bread came into being. However, it wasn't until the late nineteenth century that the details of yeast chemistry were discovered.

From this early method of leavening bread, a much more satisfactory way was discovered to grow the yeast for bread-making. At one time, yeast was grown on mashes used in brewing beer. In the late eighteenth century, an Englishman discovered how to compress yeast.

Years later, in 1868, an American, Charles Fleischmann, introduced an improved yeast that was pressed into cakes. This made it possible for breadmaking to be carried out commercially on a large scale. In the years that followed, yeasts were improved by dehydration, forming another product called active dry yeast. This dry form originally was made for the military so that fresh bread could be made on the battlefield. Later improvements of active dry yeast included finer granules, which make for easier blending of the yeast with other ingredients.

Certain conditions are necessary for good yeast growth. Yeast grows best at warm temperatures—80° to 90° F. With temperatures that are higher than this, there is a possibility of killing the yeast. At lower temperatures, the action of the yeast is slowed down.

Yeast also needs carbohydrates, such as sugar, and moisture to live and bring about the fermentation action. During

Choose from an assortment of breads leavened with yeast. They include Refrigerated Herb Rolls, round Sweet Banana Bread, Cream of Potato Soup Bread, Two-Tone Bread, Cheese Braid.

fermentation, the enzymes present in the yeast break down the carbohydrate in the warm, moist dough, producing bubbles of carbon dioxide gas. These gas bubbles are trapped in the dough as the bread bakes. Alcohol that forms during fermentation is driven off during baking.

Yeast products available to homemakers for baking purposes include compressed cakes and active dry yeast. Both of these yeasts are alive in their packages; however, the active dry yeast is in a resting stage until suspended in warm liquid. It should be dissolved in warm water or mixed with part of the flour.

Active dry yeast and compressed yeast can be substituted for one another since one cake of compressed yeast equals one package or about two teaspoons active dry yeast. Follow label or recipe directions for the method of dissolving and incorporating the type of yeast being used.

Compressed yeast is a mixture of yeast and a small amount of starch. It is perishable and must be kept under refrigeration. If you question whether the yeast is still usable, crumble it between your fingers. If it crumbles easily, it is still good. It is desirable to dissolve compressed yeast in lukewarm water (about 85° F).

The more popular type of yeast used by homemakers for baking bread is the active dry yeast, which is sold in moisture-proof, airtight packages or vacuum-packed jars. It can be stored on the shelf in a cool place for several months. Be sure to use the yeast before the expiration date stamped on the package. To lengthen the storage time of active dry yeast, store it in the refrigerator.

There are several methods of adding yeast to the other ingredients when making bread products. The most recent technique involves combining active dry yeast with a portion of the flour. The liquid and some of the other ingredients are heated together and added to the dry mixture. Then, the eggs are added. An electric mixer is used to beat the dough at this stage, then the remaining flour is stirred in by hand.

Another mixing method that is used quite often calls for dissolving the yeast in either warm or lukewarm water. Then, the dissolved yeast is added to other combined ingredients and all of the flour is stirred in by hand.

Yeast is used to leaven many bread products, from plain white bread to coffee cakes. Rolls are another popular yeast bread. (See *Bread, Leavening Agent* for additional information.)

Two-Tone Bread

    2 packages active dry yeast
5¼ to 5½ cups sifted all-purpose
        flour
    3 cups milk
    ⅓ cup sugar
    ⅓ cup shortening
    1 tablespoon salt
    3 tablespoons dark molasses
2¼ cups whole wheat flour

In large mixer bowl combine the 2 packages yeast and *3 cups* of the all-purpose flour. Heat together milk, sugar, shortening, and salt just till warm, stirring occasionally to melt shortening. Add to dry ingredients in mixer bowl. Beat at low speed of electric mixer for ½ minute, scraping sides of bowl constantly. Beat 3 minutes at high speed.

Divide dough in half. To one half, stir in enough of the remaining all-purpose flour to make a moderately stiff dough. Turn onto lightly floured surface and knead till smooth and elastic, 5 to 8 minutes. Place in well-greased bowl, turning once to grease surface; set aside. To remaining dough, stir in molasses and whole wheat flour. Turn onto lightly floured surface. Knead till smooth and elastic, 5 to 8 minutes, kneading in enough additional all-purpose flour (about 3 tablespoons) to form a moderately stiff dough. Place in well-greased bowl, turning once to grease surface. Let both doughs rise till double, about 1 to 1¼ hours. Punch down. Cover the dough and let it rest on a lightly floured surface 10 minutes.

Roll out *half* the light dough and *half* the dark dough, each to a 12x8-inch rectangle. Place dark dough atop light dough; roll up tightly, beginning at short side. Repeat with remaining doughs. Place in 2 greased 8½x4½x 2½-inch loaf dishes. Cover and let rise till double, 45 to 60 minutes. Bake at 375° till done, 30 to 35 minutes. Makes 2 loaves.

Cream of Potato Soup Bread

    2 packages active dry yeast
5½ to 6 cups sifted all-purpose
      flour
1½ cups milk
    2 tablespoons butter or margarine
    2 tablespoons sugar
    2 teaspoons salt
    1 10½-ounce can condensed cream
      of potato soup

Combine yeast and *2½ cups* of the flour. Heat together milk, butter, sugar, and salt just till warm, stirring occasionally to melt butter. Add to dry ingredients in mixer bowl; add potato soup. Beat at low speed of electric mixer for ½ minute, scraping sides of bowl. Beat 3 minutes at high speed. By hand, stir in enough of remaining flour to make a moderately stiff dough. Turn onto lightly floured surface. Knead till smooth, 5 to 8 minutes. Place in greased bowl, turning once. Cover; let rise till double, 50 to 60 minutes. Punch down. Cover; let rest for 10 minutes.

Divide dough in half; shape into two loaves. Place in two greased 8½x4½x2½-inch loaf dishes. Let rise till double, 25 to 30 minutes. Bake at 400° for 25 to 30 minutes. Makes 2.

Cheese Braid

Combine 1 package active dry yeast and 2 cups sifted all-purpose flour. Heat together 1½ cups milk, 2 tablespoons sugar, and 1½ teaspoons salt just till warm. Add to dry ingredients. Add 1 egg and 8 ounces process pimiento cheese, shredded (2 cups). Beat at low speed of electric mixer for ½ minute, scraping sides of bowl. Beat 3 minutes at high speed. By hand, stir in 2½ to 3 cups sifted all-purpose flour, enough to make a stiff dough. Turn onto lightly floured surface. Knead till smooth, 8 to 10 minutes. Place in greased bowl, turning once to grease surface. Cover; let rise till double, about 1½ hours. Punch down.

Divide dough in six pieces. Cover; let rest 10 minutes. Roll each piece into rope 15 inches long. On greased baking sheets, shape into 2 braids, using 3 ropes of dough for each loaf. Cover; let rise till almost double, 35 to 45 minutes. Bake at 375° for 15 to 20 minutes. Brush with melted butter. Makes 2 braids.

Sweet Banana Bread

Combine 2 packages active dry yeast and 2 cups sifted all-purpose flour. Heat together ¾ cup milk, ½ cup butter, ½ cup sugar, and 1 teaspoon salt just till warm, stirring occasionally to melt butter. Add to dry ingredients. Add 2 eggs and 2 ripe bananas, mashed (1 cup). Beat at low speed of electric mixer for ½ minute, scraping sides of bowl. Beat 3 minutes at high speed. By hand, stir in 3½ to 4 cups sifted all-purpose flour, enough to make a moderately stiff dough. Turn onto lightly floured surface. Knead till smooth, 5 to 8 minutes. Place in greased bowl, turning once. Cover; let rise till double, about 1 hour. Punch down. Let rest 10 minutes.

Divide dough in half. Shape into 2 round loaves; place on greased baking sheets. Make vertical cuts about ⅛ inch deep around each loaf at ¾-inch intervals.

Slightly beat 1 egg white with 1 teaspoon water. Brush over entire surface of loaves. Let rise again till double, 30 to 45 minutes. Bake at 400° for 30 minutes. Makes 2 loaves.

Refrigerated Herb Rolls

    1 package active dry yeast
3¼ to 3½ cups sifted all-purpose
      flour
    2 teaspoons celery seed
    1 teaspoon dried thyme leaves,
      crushed
1¼ cups milk
    ¼ cup shortening
    ¼ cup sugar
    1 egg

Combine yeast, *1½ cups* of the flour, celery seed, and thyme. Heat together milk, shortening, sugar, and 1 teaspoon salt just till warm. Add to dry mixture in mixing bowl; add egg. Beat at low speed of electric mixer for ½ minute, scraping sides of bowl constantly. Beat 3 minutes at high speed. By hand, stir in enough of the remaining flour to make a moderately soft dough. Place in greased bowl, turning once. Cover; chill at least 2 hours.

Shape into 18 cloverleaf rolls: Place three 1¼-inch balls in greased muffin pans. Brush with melted butter. Let rise till double, about 1 hour. Bake at 400° for 12 to 15 minutes.

Orange-Butter Coffee Cake

    2 packages active dry yeast
    ½ cup warm water
    ¼ cup granulated sugar
    2 eggs
    ½ cup dairy sour cream
    6 tablespoons butter or margarine,
        melted
    1 teaspoon salt
    3¾ cups sifted all-purpose flour
    ⅔ cup granulated sugar
    1 cup flaked coconut, toasted
    2 tablespoons shredded orange peel
    2 tablespoons butter or margarine,
        melted
    1 cup sifted confectioners' sugar
    3 to 4 teaspoons orange juice

Soften yeast in the warm water. In mixing bowl combine ¼ cup sugar, eggs, sour cream, 6 tablespoons melted butter, and salt. Stir in softened yeast. Gradually add enough of the flour to form a moderately stiff dough, beating well. Cover; let rise in warm place till double, about 45 minutes.

Combine ⅔ cup sugar, coconut, and orange peel. Knead dough a few strokes on well-floured surface. Roll *half* the dough to a 12x8-inch rectangle. Brush with *1 tablespoon* of the melted butter. Sprinkle with *½ cup* of the coconut mixture. Roll up, starting with long side. Cut into twelve 1-inch slices. Place, cut side down, in greased 9x1½-inch round baking pan. Repeat shaping with remaining dough, butter, and another ½ cup coconut mixture. Let rise in warm place till light, 30 to 45 minutes. Sprinkle rolls with remaining coconut mixture. Bake at 350° till light golden brown, about 30 minutes. Remove from pans and cool right side up. Combine confectioners' sugar and orange juice. Drizzle over cooled coffee cakes. Makes 2 coffee cakes.

YELLOW PERCH—A freshwater fish of the perch family that is found mainly in the Great Lakes area. Commercially, it is a very important food fish with a sweet and firm flesh. (See also *Perch.*)

YERBA MATE *(yar' buh)*—Another name for the tealike beverage, maté, popular in South America. (See also *Maté.*)

YOGURT, YOGHURT, YOGHOURT *(yō' guhrt)*—A fermented, custardlike milk product having a tangy flavor. In the United States, yogurt is prepared from fresh, partially skimmed, cow's milk. In some countries, it is made from the milk of sheep, goats, or water buffalo.

The origin of yogurt dates back several thousand years to countries in the Middle East. The nomads of early times are thought to have carried yogurt in goatskins on their long journeys through the deserts. They discovered that this cultured, semisolid milk was safe to eat even after several days in the hot sun.

Although yogurt was a familiar food to people of other countries, it was not until the early twentieth century that the culture used in making yogurt was isolated. Dr. Illya Metchnikoff, who was Louis Pasteur's successor as director of the Pasteur Institute, was responsible for isolating the culture from Bulgarian yogurt. He named the culture *Bacillus bulgaricus.* For his work on yogurt, he received a Nobel Prize. Around 1940, commercial production of yogurt in America began.

The commercial method for preparing yogurt is to inoculate fresh, pasteurized, partially condensed milk with a culture that is taken from a previous batch of yogurt. The milk is usually partially skimmed, and nonfat dry milk solids are added. At this point, the milk is incubated for several hours at 105° to 115° until a curd forms. Flavorings are often added.

Yogurt is related to dairy sour cream because both are cultured dairy products. However, yogurt has fewer calories. One cup of plain yogurt made from skim milk has 125 to 150 calories, while one cup of dairy sour cream contains about 485 calories. The same amount of cream-style cottage cheese has 240 to 260 calories. The fruit-flavored yogurts contain more calories, averaging around 350 per cup, and they have sugar added.

Yogurt contains the same nutrients as does the milk from which it is made, making it a good source of calcium. In addition, it is easily digested by the body, and the lactic acid in yogurt aids in the digestion of other foods.

Since yogurt is a perishable dairy product, store it in the refrigerator as soon as possible after purchase.

Yogurt is gaining in popularity as a dairy product, especially since the introduction of the flavored varieties. People are discovering that plain and flavored yogurts are not only nutritious but they have a delicious flavor.

Plain yogurt can be substituted for dairy sour cream in many recipes, giving a more tangy flavor to the product. Like dairy sour cream, yogurt needs low cooking temperatures and a short heating period so that it doesn't separate. To prevent yogurt from separating during cooking, stabilize it with flour or cornstarch. Another tip to prevent yogurt from breaking down is to gently fold it in rather than vigorously stirring it.

Use yogurt as a sauce for vegetables, and in dips, spreads, salad dressings, casseroles and other main dishes, pies, and other desserts. Both plain and flavored yogurts are also delicious to eat as is without added ingredients.

Fruit Galaxy Salad

A low-calorie recipe—

    1 8-ounce can dietetic-pack
         pineapple tidbits
    1 tablespoon cornstarch
    2 tablespoons lemon juice
       Noncaloric liquid sweetener
         equal to ¼ cup sugar
    ½ cup plain yogurt
    1 cup sliced, fresh peaches
    1 cup diced, unpeeled apple
    ½ cup diced, fresh pear
    ½ cup sliced banana
    ½ cup halved, seedless green
         grapes

Drain pineapple tidbits, reserving ½ cup juice. In 1½-quart saucepan gradually stir pineapple juice into cornstarch. Stir in lemon juice and sweetener. Cook and stir over medium heat till thickened and bubbly; cool. Fold in yogurt, then pineapple, peaches, apple, pear, banana, and grapes. Chill salad for several hours before serving. Makes 8 servings.

Honeydew Stack-Up

Cut 1 honeydew melon into six ½-inch thick slices. Peel and remove seeds. Place each melon slice on lettuce-lined plate. Top with one 16-ounce can pitted, dark sweet cherries, drained and halved; and 6 peaches, sliced. Serve with *Blue Cheese Dressing:* Stir together ⅓ cup plain yogurt and 1 tablespoon sugar till blended. Then, stir in 2 tablespoons crumbled blue cheese. Makes 6 servings.

Yogurt Salad Dressing

    1 cup plain yogurt
    2 teaspoons milk
    1 teaspoon lemon juice
    ¼ teaspoon garlic salt
    ¼ teaspoon onion salt
       Dash dried rosemary leaves,
         crushed

Combine all ingredients; chill. Makes 1 cup.

Seasonal fresh fruits topped with yogurt and blue cheese dressing make Honeydew Stack-Up a great-tasting, low-calorie salad.

Cheese-Topped Pears

½ cup plain yogurt
¼ cup cream-style cottage cheese
2 tablespoons mayonnaise or
   salad dressing
1 tablespoon blue cheese
1 29-ounce can pear halves,
   drained and chilled

Blend together first 4 ingredients. To serve, spoon a little cheese mixture over center of each pear half. Makes ¾ cup dressing.

Strawberry Yogurt Medley

2 medium bananas, sliced
   Lemon juice
2 cups fresh strawberries, halved
2 medium oranges, peeled and
   sectioned
   • • •
½ cup strawberry yogurt
1 4-ounce package whipped cream
   cheese
2 tablespoons sugar

Dip bananas in lemon juice. Combine strawberries, orange sections, and bananas; chill. Stir yogurt into cream cheese; add sugar. Arrange fruit in compote; spoon on yogurt mixture. Or stir topping into fruit and serve in lettuce cups. Makes 4 to 6 servings.

Pineapple-Orange Yogurt Dip

1 8-ounce carton orange yogurt
   (1 cup)
⅓ cup chopped, fresh pineapple
2 tablespoons brown sugar
   Fresh pineapple cubes
   Whole fresh strawberries

Combine yogurt, chopped fresh pineapple, and brown sugar. Chill to blend flavors. To serve, dip pineapple cubes and strawberries in yogurt dip. Makes 1⅓ cups dip.

YOM KIPPUR *(yôm kip′ uhr)*—The Jewish high holy day, also called the Day of Atonement. It is a day of fasting (abstinence from food and drink), which follows the holidays of Rosh Hashanah.

The final meal eaten before sundown on the eve of Yom Kippur is a substantial one at which bland foods are served to prevent thirst during the following day of fast. (See also *Jewish Cookery*.)

YORKSHIRE PUDDING *(yôrk′ sher, -shuhr)* —A favorite English, breadlike accompaniment traditionally served with roast beef. The pan of Yorkshire pudding was originally set under the meat roasting over an open fire. Baked in this way, it caught the meat drippings.

Contrary to its name, Yorkshire pudding is not a pudding as such. The batter is similar to a popover batter, and it is sometimes poured over the meat drippings in the roasting pan. Then, it's baked and cut into squares. However, Yorkshire pudding is easily baked and attractively served as individual portions, using custard cups. (See also *English Cookery*.)

Individual Yorkshire Puddings

2 eggs
1 cup milk
1 cup sifted all-purpose flour
1 tablespoon salad oil
   Beef drippings (about ¼ cup)

Place eggs in mixing bowl. Add milk, flour, and ½ teaspoon salt. Beat 1½ minutes with rotary or electric beater. Add salad oil and beat ½ minute longer. With some of the beef drippings, grease 6 to 8 custard cups. Place about 1 teaspoon additional drippings in each cup. Fill cups half full with batter. Bake at 475° for 15 minutes. Reduce heat to 350° and bake till browned and firm, about 25 minutes longer. Serve them piping hot with roast beef and gravy, or eat them as popovers. Makes 6 to 8 puddings.

Company-best dinner

Surround a Standing Rib Roast (see *Beef* for → recipe) with Individual Yorkshire Puddings, which are baked in custard cups.

Z

ZABAGLIONE *(zä′ buhl yō′ nē)*—An Italian dessert consisting of a foamy egg custard flavored with sugar and wine (usually Marsala). Constant beating over hot water enables the custard to become thick and frothy. The dessert is usually served in individual glasses, although it is sometimes used as a sauce. The French version of zabaglione is called sabayon.

Easy Zabaglione

This simplified version is uncooked—

> 1 3¾-ounce package vanilla
>   whipped dessert mix
> 1 egg
> ¼ cup sugar
> ⅓ cup dry sherry

In a small, deep bowl thoroughly blend vanilla whipped dessert mix and ½ cup water. Whip at highest speed of electric mixer for 1 minute. (Mixture will be quite thick.) Add ¾ cup water. Whip at high speed till mixture thickens, about 4 minutes; set the mixture aside.

Beat egg till thick and lemon-colored, 3 to 5 minutes. Gradually add sugar, beating till mixture is very thick. Blend egg mixture and wine into whipped dessert mix. Chill at least 1 hour. Before serving, stir till smooth. Serve over chilled fresh or canned fruit. Serves 8.

ZEST—1. The thin, bright-colored outer portion of orange, lemon, or lime peel. This part, rich in the flavor of the fruit oils, is used for grated peel. 2. The oil extracted from this outer peel.

ZINFANDEL—1. A grape variety grown primarily in California. 2. The name of a red wine made from these grapes.

This grape variety and wine hold an aura of mystery since it is not known where the grapes themselves or the name they were given originated. However, zinfandel grapes and wine are almost exclusively produced in California. The fruity, spicy, and zesty wine is of the claret type. (See also *Wines and Spirits.*)

ZITI *(zē′ tē)*—A large, smooth, tubular macaroni with a diameter of one-fourth to one-half inch. (See also *Macaroni.*)

ZUCCHINI SQUASH—A summer squash variety of Italian origin. Other names for this squash include Italian marrow, Italian squash, baby marrow, and courgette. Zucchini have an almost straight, cylindrical shape that gradually enlarges toward the base. The rind is a deep green with pale yellow spots that almost group in stripes. Although zucchini can grow quite large, they are preferred for eating when about five to seven inches long.

Nutritional value: From a half-cup serving of cooked zucchini comes a wide assortment of valuable nutrients: a good amount of vitamin C; fair amounts of vitamin A and the B vitamin niacin; lesser levels of other vitamins and minerals; and approximately 15 calories.

How to select and store: Fresh zucchini are available in largest quantities during the summer. Choose squash that are heavy for their size, have glossy, deep green rinds, and are relatively small and straight. Large zucchini are less tender and flavorful than are the small ones.

At home, use zucchini squash as soon as possible. If zucchini must be held a few days before use, store them in the refrigerated vegetable keeper.

How to prepare: Zucchini is one of the most versatile squash varieties since it is tender enough to serve raw or cooked. Either way, the skin is left on. For added attractiveness, the rind may be scored lengthwise with fork tines.

Zucchini flavor and texture are preferred when cooked to the crisp-tender stage. Cook sliced or cubed zucchini in boiling, salted water for 8 to 15 minutes. Or slice and fry it in butter for 5 minutes, covered, then about 5 additional minutes, uncovered. Bake zucchini half shells.

How to use: In the uncooked state, serve zucchini as a dipper for dips and dunks or as an ingredient in tossed salads. For a buffet, surround a mound of potato salad with sliced zucchini, tomato wedges, and asparagus spears.

Cooked zucchini is attractive when baked "on the half shell" or when sliced and dressed with a clear or creamy sauce. Because of its mild flavor, zucchini blends well with tomatoes, cheese, onion, eggs, and various seasonings such as garlic and herbs. It's fun and easy to prepare this squash because it has so many uses and cooks so quickly. (See also *Squash.*)

Zucchini Parmesan

    3 cups thinly sliced zucchini
        squash
    2 tablespoons butter or margarine
    ½ teaspoon salt
      Dash pepper
        • • •
    2 tablespoons grated Parmesan
        cheese

Cook zucchini, covered, with butter, salt, and pepper in skillet over low heat for 5 minutes. Uncover and cook, turning slices, for 5 minutes more. Sprinkle with cheese. Serves 4.

Zucchini Half-Shells

    6 small zucchini squash
        • • •
    ¼ cup butter or margarine
    1 tablespoon grated onion
    1 beef bouillon cube, crushed
    2 tablespoons water

Trim ends from zucchini; cut in half lengthwise. Melt butter in large skillet; add onion and bouillon cube. Add zucchini halves, cut side down, and cook till golden. Turn; add water. Cover and cook over low heat about 10 minutes more. Makes 5 or 6 servings.

Easy Zabaglione, a modernized variation of the Italian dessert, blankets a fruit cup. Another time, use it as a cake sauce.

Spanish Zucchini

Uses popular ingredients of Spain—

1½ teaspoons salt
½ teaspoon chili powder
Dash pepper

• • •

4 pork chops, cut ½ inch thick
½ cup uncooked long-grain rice
1 29-ounce can tomatoes
½ cup chopped green pepper
½ cup chopped onion
½ cup chopped, pitted ripe olives
1 tablespoon sugar
2 cups thinly sliced, unpeeled zucchini squash

• • •

¼ cup grated Parmesan cheese

Mix salt, chili powder, and pepper. Trim fat from pork chops and heat trimmings in skillet until 2 tablespoons fat accumulate. Remove trimmings and brown the chops; season with *1 teaspoon* of the chili mixture. Drain off fat. Add rice, tomatoes, green pepper, onion, olives, and sugar. Border with zucchini; sprinkle all with remaining chili mixture.

Cover; cook, stirring occasionally, till pork is done, about 1 hour. Top with Parmesan cheese; cover skillet to melt cheese. Serves 4.

Spanish Zucchini, a meal-in-one dish, offers chili-spiced pork chops cooked with rice, zucchini, and assorted vegetables.

ZUBROVKA, ZUBROWKA (*zōō brōōf' kä*) —A Polish vodka flavored with the bitter-tasting grass of the same name. The grass gives this liquor a light goldish green cast. A wisp of the dried grass is included in every bottle. (See also *Vodka*.)

ZUPPA INGLESE (*zōō' puh in glā' zā*) —A dessert made with cake, rum, and a filling. Translated, it means English soup, but in reality it's an Italian dessert. Like English Trifle, it consists of rum-soaked sponge cake layered with custard or whipped cream. Candied fruit often acts as a garnish for this dessert.

ZWIEBACK (*zwī' bak,' -bäk'*) —A specially formulated slice of slightly sweetened hard bread. The German word *zwei-bachen*, which gives the bread its name, means twice-baked.

The bread dough for zwieback is usually flavored lightly with lemon and cinnamon. The baked loaves are cooled, cut into slices, then oven-toasted at a low temperature until dried and golden brown.

Zwieback is an old-fashioned food for babies, given to them to exercise their gums when cutting teeth. Soaked in hot milk, it's good for convalescents.

Zwieback Meatballs

Combine 1 beaten egg, ⅓ cup milk, ½ cup crushed zwieback (4 to 5 slices), 1 tablespoon finely chopped onion, ½ teaspoon salt, ¼ teaspoon ground nutmeg, and dash pepper. Add 1 pound ground beef; mix well. Shape mixture into 20 meatballs. In skillet brown meatballs with 1 tablespoon hot shortening. Remove meatballs from skillet; discard the drippings.

Dissolve 1 beef bouillon cube in ¾ cup boiling water. Blend 2 tablespoons all-purpose flour with ¼ cup cold water. In skillet stir flour mixture into bouillon. Cook and stir till mixture is thickened and bubbly. Return the meatballs to skillet. Cover the mixture and simmer 20 minutes. Makes 4 or 5 servings.

ZWIEBEL—The German word for onions. The word is used in the names of some recipes containing onions.

INDEX

The index on the following pages has been designed to make it easy for you, the busy homemaker, to find the specific recipe you are searching for. Each recipe in the 20 volumes is listed not only by its title, but is also listed by its major category where appropriate, such as casserole, cookie, beverage, salad, dessert, or type of meat. Where necessary, the recipe is listed again by its major ingredient.

For example, Crisp Pecan Slices is listed under the first word in its title, *Crisp*. It's also listed under the nut, *Pecan*. If there were any other major ingredients listed in the title, it would be listed there too. This recipe is a cookie, so you'll find it in the general category *Cookie*. Because the recipes are cross-referred in this manner, you should be able to quickly and easily find just what you want.

To help you still further, some of the major categories, such as *Bread, Casserole*, and *Salad* are further divided into smaller groups for ease in finding a particular recipe quickly. As examples, you will find the *Bread* category divided into convenience, quick, and yeast; the *Cas-*serole category divided into main dish and vegetable; and the *Salad* category divided into fruit, main dish, and vegetable.

There are also special categories for *Foreign Cookery* and *Regional Cookery*. You will find all kinds of favorites, from regional Jambalaya to a foreign favorite, Pfeffernuesse. In addition, listed under *Menus* are all the menu plans—breakfast, brunch, dinner, low calorie, lunch, supper, and other occasions—contained in the 20 volumes of the encyclopedia.

The index also contains all of the major articles presented in the encyclopedia. These are listed in all capital letters.

The numbers at the end of each listing will make the index easy for you to use. As an example, Beef Burgundy is listed on 3·310. The **3** in heavy type indicates that the recipe is located in volume 3, and the 310 in light type designates the page number in that volume. When the reference listing reads **PEACH** . . . . . . **13**·1599-1608, this means that it is a major article and that you will find information on this subject from page 1599 through page 1608.

Reference to Charts and Tips

Almonds, Easy Ways to Blanch . . **1**·36
Almonds, Ways to Roast or Toast . . . . **1**·37
Altitude Corrections
  Candy . . . . **3**·375
  Canning . . . . **4**·391
  High Altitude Cake Baking . **9**·1147
Angel Food Cakes Fail, Why . . . . **1**·52
Apples and Their Uses . . . . . **1**·80, 81

Bar Measurements, Common . . . . **20**·2464
Basic Four Food Groups . . . . **12**·1485
Beef
  Roasting Chart . . . . **2**·192
  Storage, Maximum Time for . . **2**·193
Beverage Cups and Glasses . . . . **2**·216
Blender Tips . . . . **2**·237

Caloric Needs, Determining **11**·1318
Candied Flowers . . . . **3**·368
Candy, Temperatures and Tests for . . . . **3**·375
Cereal Terms to Know . . . . **4**·441

Cheese, Classification of Natural . . . . **4**·459
Cheese, Know Your . . . . **4**·457
Chicken, How Much, to Buy for a Serving . . . . **4**·479
Chicken Roasting Chart . . . . **4**·479
Chinese Cooking Methods . . **12**·1526
Chopsticks, How to Use . . . . **12**·1527
Citrus Fruit, How to Section . . . . **5**·545
Clams, Opening . . . . **5**·554
Coconut, How to Tint or Toast . . **5**·568
Coffee, How to Make . . . . **5**·575
Cold Cuts Identification . . . **5**·589-590
Container Sizes, Common . . . . . **4**·389
Cookie Mailing Tips . . . . **5**·603
Cornish Game Hens, How to Roast . . . . **5**·636
Crowd, Guide to Shopping for a . . . . **15**·1815
Custard Substitutions . . . . **6**·721
Cutting Bride's Cake . . . . **3**·285

Dried Fruit, How to Cook . . . . . . **7**·802
Duck, Roasting Chart for . . . . . . **7**·812

Egg Grades . . . . **7**·832
Eggs, Using Frozen . . . . **7**·833
Equipment, Basic Kitchen . . . . . . **7**·859
Evaporated Milk, How to Whip . **7**·862

Fire Building (Barbecue) . . . **2**·146-148
Fish
  Barbecue Tips . . . . **7**·895
  Carving . . . . **7**·892
  Fat and Calorie Content of . . . **7**·886
  How Much, to Buy . . . . **7**·888
  Market Forms of . . . . **7**·887
Food Regulations, United States . . . . . . **19**·2336-2341
Freezing
  Cooked Foods . . . . **8**·947-949
  Dairy Products . . . . **8**·943
  Fish . . . . **8**·943
  Fruit . . . . **8**·941
  Headspaces for . . . . **8**·940
  Meat . . . . **8**·943
  Pies . . . . **14**·1678
  Poultry . . . . **8**·943
  Shellfish . . . . **8**·943

Freezing *continued*
  Vegetables ....**8**·945
  Wrapping Food for ....**8**·939
Frostings Fail, Why Cooked ....**8**·969
Fruit
  Canning ....**4**·393
  Color-Bright ....**8**·983
  Combination Guide .....**15**·1916
  Guide to Buying Fresh ..**8**·981-982
  Guide to Storing Fresh ....**8**·985
  Sources of Vitamins A and C .**8**·980
  -Syrup Proportions ....**8**·942
Fudge Failures,
  How to Rescue ....**8**·997

Game Birds,
  Roasting Chart for ....**8**·1004
Gelatin Techniques, Basic ...**8**·1019
Gelatin Terms to Know ......**8**·1017
Goose Roasting Chart ....**9**·1039
Grape Varieties, Popular ....**9**·1047
Ground Beef Patties, Cooking **9**·1084
Guinea Hens, How to Roast ..**9**·1096

Ham
  Facts at a Glance ....**9**·1105
  Glazing ....**9**·1110
  Roasting Chart ....**9**·1109
  Scoring ....**9**·1110
Hamburgers, Tips for Making .**9**·1122
Honey Substitution Guide ...**9**·1151

Ice Ring ....**15**·1806

Jelly, Causes of Poor Products **10**·1210
Jelly Doesn't Gel, If Your ...**10**·1211

Lamb
  Chop Broiling Chart .....**10**·1255
  Roasting Chart ....**10**·1254
Leftovers, Tips for Storing ...**10**·1270
Lobster, How to Eat ....**11**·1311
Lunch Box Menus ....**11**·1329

Macaroni Vocabulary ......**11**·1335
Mayonnaise Fails, If ....**11**·1362
Meal Planning Chart ..**11**·1366-1367
Measure Fats and Oils, How to .**7**·867
Measuring ....**11**·1369
Meat
  Bone Identification Chart,
    Basic ....**11**·1373
  Bone Shapes Indicate
    Cooking Methods .....**11**·1373
  Canning ....**4**·394
  Carving ....**4**·415-416
  Roasting Chart .....**11**·1378-1379
Meat Loaf Shaping Made Easy **9**·1082
Melons, Know Your ....**11**·1395
Mushroom Equivalents .....**12**·1448

Noodle Know-How ....**12**·1466
Nuts, Buying Guide for .....**12**·1475
Nutrition ....**12**·1484-1486
  (See also entries for *Carbohydrate*
  4·406; *Fat* **7**·866-867; *Meal
  Planning* **11**·1365-1368; *Mineral*
  12·1419; *Protein* **14**·1789; *Vitamin*
  19·2400-2402.)

Olive Sizes, Ripe ....**12**·1496
Oven Temperatures ....**13**·1539
Oysters, Grades of ....**13**·1544

Pancakes Hot, Keeping ....**13**·1552
Pans, Guide for Buying ....**14**·1763
Parsley, To Snip ....**13**·1572
Pasta Hints ....**13**·1579
Pastry
  Decorative Trims ...**13**·1583-1584
  Lattice Tops ....**10**·1264-1265
  Problems, Common .....**13**·1585
Peaches to Buy, How Many
  Fresh ....**13**·1601
Peach Pointers ....**13**·1602
Pears, Purchasing ....**13**·1621
Pear Varieties, Favorite .....**13**·1620
Pheasant, How to Roast ....**13**·1654
Pickle Pointers ....**13**·1656
Pie Cues ....**14**·1672
Pineapple Styles to know ...**14**·1687
Plums are Ripe, How to Tell
  When ....**14**·1704
Popcorn Pointers ....**14**·1716
Popovers "Pop," Secrets for
  Making ....**14**·1718
Pork Roasting Chart ....**14**·1729
Pork to Buy, How Much ....**14**·1728
Poultry
  How Much Stuffing ......**18**·2183
  How to Cut Up ....**14**·1770
  Mounting, Correctly on the
    Spit ....**15**·1892-1893
  Roasting Chart ....**14**·1774
  Storage Time for ....**14**·1771
Prune Arithmetic ....**14**·1791

Quail, How to Roast ....**15**·1811
Quick Breads, Standard
  Proportions in ....**3**·272

Raisins, Easy Ways to Chop
  and Grind ....**15**·1833
Raisins, Ways to Plump .....**15**·1832
Rice to Cook, How Much ...**15**·1866

Salad
  Success Tips ....**15**·1911
  Tossed, Combination
    Guide ....**15**·1912-1913
  Tossing Tips ....**15**·1910

Salad Dressing
  Dictionary ....**16**·1929
  Tips ....**16**·1924
  Using Herbs and Spices ..**16**·1930
Sandwich Tips, Party ....**16**·1956
Sandwich, Ways to Cut a ...**16**·1948
Sauces, Know Your Classic .**16**·1964
Sauce Success Tips ....**16**·1966
Sausage Chart ....**16**·1980-1981
Season a Griddle, How to ....**9**·1075
Seasoning Guide
  Herbs, for ....**9**·1140
  Meat ....**11**·1380
  Spices, for ....**17**·2109
  Vegetables, for ....**19**·2380
Seasoning Iron Utensils ....**10**·1191
Seasonings, When to Add ...**16**·2015
Sesame Seed, Toasting .....**16**·2018
Shellfish, How Much to Buy .**16**·2029
Shortened Cakes Fail, Why ....**3**·343
Shrimp You Need,
  Determining How Much .**17**·2054
Soup Garnishes ....**17**·2087
Steaks Come from, Where ..**17**·2141
Substitutions, Emergency ...**18**·2192
Sugar Syrups ....**18**·2227

Tea, How to Make ....**18**·2257
Timesaving Tips ....**15**·1822
Turkey
  Carving ....**4**·417
  How to Mount, on Spit ...**19**·2311
  Tests for Doneness ....**19**·2310

Variety Meats, Basic
  Directions for ....**19**·2349
Vegetable
  Canning ....**4**·396-397
  Cooking Fresh .....**19**·2376-2378
  Guide to
    Buying Fresh ....**19**·2370-2371
  Guide to
    Storing Fresh ....**19**·2372-2373
  Nutrition Summary ......**19**·2369
Vitamins, More About ......**19**·2401

Walnut Halves, Perfect .....**19**·2415
Whipping Cream
  Know-How ....**20**·2442
White Sauce, How to Repair **20**·2445
Wine
  Chart ....**20**·2452
  How, are Named ....**20**·2453
  How Much, to Buy ......**20**·2456

Yield
  Canned Fruit ....**4**·392
  Canned Vegetable ....**4**·398
  Frozen Fruit ....**8**·942
  Frozen Vegetable ....**8**·944

Recipe Index

A

Abacus Ribs .... **10**·1227

Acorn Squash
Apple-Filled .... **17**·2135
Applesauce, and .... **1**·19
Baked .... **1**·19
Chips .... **17**·2136
Delight .... **17**·2136
Elegante .... **1**·20
Fruit-Filled .... **1**·19
Glazed, with Onions .... **1**·20
Nutmeg Whipped .... **1**·21
Pineapple .... **1**·20
Rings, Glazed .... **1**·21
Sausage, and .... **1**·19
Sausage-Stuffed .... **18**·2190
Skillet, Ham- .... **1**·21
Stuffed .... **1**·20
Aebleskiver (Danish
Doughnuts) .... **16**·2004
After Dinner Mocha .... **4**·506
Airy Cheese Rolls .... **4**·464
Aladdin's Salad Bowl ...... **16**·1933
Allemande Sauce .... **1**·32
Almendrado .... **1**·34

Almond
Almendrado .... **1**·34
Balls, Cherry- .... **5**·531
Balls, No-Bake .... **19**·2347
Brittle, Quick .... **3**·380
Brittle Torte .... **17**·2118
Butter Crunch .... **1**·38
Cake, Regal .... **1**·37
Caramels .... **18**·2199
Chicken .... **2**·138
Chiffon Roll, Peachy- .... **10**·1218
Chocolate Cake .... **1**·38
Coffee Cake, Apricot- ..... **5**·583
Coffee Roll .... **5**·337
Coffee Tortoni .... **5**·577
Cookies, Chinese .... **12**·1529
Cream Filling .... **6**·692
Crescent Rolls .... **3**·271
Deviled .... **1**·74
Filling ...... **5**·610; **1**·41; **16**·2002
Flip-Top Cake .... **1**·38
Fudge Delight .... **8**·1000
Glazed .... **9**·1035
Horns .... **1**·41
Ice Cream, Chocolate- ... **10**·1171
Ice Cream, Maple- ...... **10**·1174
Ice Cream, Peach- .... **1**·40

Almond *continued*
Paste Frosting .... **3**·348
-Peach Torte .... **13**·1608
Peas and .... **4**·499
Sauce, Shrimp- .... **15**·1825
Velvet, Choco- .... **19**·2390

Amandine
Asparagus .... **1**·114
Green Beans .... **1**·44
Pompano .... **14**·1714
Turkey, on Toast .... **1**·44
Amber Tea Delight .... **18**·2257

Ambrosia .... **1**·45
Baked .... **6**·762
Crepes .... **17**·2162
Delight .... **11**·1326
Fluffy .... **1**·45
Fresh Fruit .... **1**·44
Green and Gold .... **9**·1051
Potato Bake .... **5**·547

American
Chop Suey .... **2**·181
Glögg, -Style .... **9**·1036
Hot Mulled Apple
Cider .... **5**·536
Pizza .... **7**·869
Anadama Bread .... **1**·46

Anchovy
Butter Sauce .... **1**·47
Dip .... **1**·47
Salad .... **1**·47
Salad, Italian .... **9**·1072
Angel Cheesecake .... **4**·465

Angel Food Cake
Angel Berry Cake .... **3**·339
Angel Cake .... **1**·50
Angel Loaf Cake .... **1**·52
Cherry Angel Roll .... **1**·53
Chocolate Angel Cake ..... **1**·50
Chocolate Ripple Cake ..... **1**·53
Easy Daffodil Cake .... **6**·731
Lemonade Angel Dessert ... **1**·52
Lemon Glow Angel
Cake .... **3**·338
Neapolitan Cake .... **3**·340
Orange Sunshine Cake .... **3**·339
Raspberry Angel Dessert ... **1**·50
Angels on Horseback .... **1**·56
Angel Sweets .... **3**·382

Anise
Butter, -Flavored .... **1**·58
Loaf, Glazed .... **1**·56
-Sugar Cookies .... **19**·2347
Antipasto .... **1**·60
Antipasto Sandwich .... **1**·59

APPETIZER .... **1**·62-77
(See also *Canapé, Dip, Pâté,
Spread.*)
Angels on Horseback .... **1**·56
Antipasto Sandwich .... **1**·59
Artichoke-Ham Bites ...... **9**·1113
Banana-Berry Cup .... **8**·987
Barquette of Tiny Shrimp . **16**·2022
Bite-Sized Chicken Puffs .. **18**·2261
Blueberry-Honeydew Cup .. **8**·987
Blue Cheese Bites .... **2**·247
Breakfast Cocktail Deluxe **13**·1561
Cantaloupe Especiale ...... **8**·987
Cantaloupe Mist .... **4**·400
Cantaloupe Supreme ...... **8**·987
Caviar Appetizers .... **4**·435
Caviar-Stuffed Eggs .... **4**·436
Cheese Mousse .... **1**·70
Cheese-Stuffed Mushrooms ..**5**·558
Chicken-Sesame Balls .... **16**·2018
Clams Casino .... **15**·1877
Cocktail Wieners .... **8**·933
Crab Cocktail .... **1**·62
Crab-Stuffed Mushrooms ....**6**·652
Crab-Swiss Bites .... **16**·2034
Cranberry-Sauced Bites .. **19**·2315
Cranberry-Wine
hors d'oeuvres .... **20**·2459
Curried Wheat Snacks ... **20**·2439
Deviled Almonds .... **1**·74
Dilled Vegetable Sticks ... **19**·2381
Dilly Brussels Sprouts ...... **3**·301
Dipper's Drumsticks .... **4**·482
Fancy Franks .... **1**·75
French Cheese Pastries ..... **8**·958
French-Fried Camembert ... **8**·954
French Onion Pie .... **14**·1669

Fresh Fruit Aloha .... **17**·2167
Fruit Cup Combinations .... **8**·984
Fruit Cup Tower .... **8**·987
Fruit Sparkle Cup .... **9**·1047
Glazed Sausage Bites .... **1**·75
Gourmet Shrimp .... **17**·2058
Grapefruit-Crab Cocktail .. **9**·1053
Green and Gold Compote **11**·1319
Ham-Pretzel Teasers ..... **14**·1785
Herbed Cocktail .... **2**·217
Holiday Cocktail Deluxe . **14**·1713
Individual Antipasto .... **1**·59
Italian Gnocchi .... **9**·1038
Juices .... **2**·218
Leek Lorraine .... **10**·1269

Appetizer *continued*

Mapled Appetizers .... **9**·1072
Marinated Artichoke Hearts ... **1**·59
Marinated Artichokes .... **1**·108
Marinated Beef Strips .... **1**·72
Marinated Sprouts .... **11**·1318
Melon Cocktail .... **8**·987
Mexican Tostadas .... **1**·77
Mushroom Cocktail ..... **12**·1450
Noodle Nibbles .... **5**·521
Olive-Cheese Snacks .... **12**·1496
1-2-3 Fruit Cup .... **5**·563
Oyster Cocktail .... **13**·1544
Oysters on the Half Shell . **13**·1544
Oysters Rockefeller ...... **13**·1547
Parmesan Nibble Mix .... **14**·1785
Parmesan-Rice Squares .. **13**·1571
Party Potato Chips .... **1**·75
Peanut-Cheese Straws .... **4**·468
Pickled Mushrooms ..... **12**·1451
Pickled Onions .... **12**·1507
Pickled Shrimp .... **16**·1931
Pie .... **1**·76
Pineapple Cocktail .... **5**·563
Plum-Glazed Franks .... **1**·75
Plump Prunes .... **1**·66
Po Po .... **9**·1135
Prosciutto and Artichokes . **14**·1788
Rainbow Melon Julep .... **1**·73
Raspberry-Nectarine
  Cocktail .... **8**·987
Sassy Franks .... **10**·1214
Scallops and Bacon ...... **16**·1991
Scramble .... **4**·443
Shrimp-Cheese Turnovers ... **6**·675
Shrimp Cocktail .... **5**·563
Shrimp in Beer .... **2**·202
Shrimp in Jackets .... **1**·75
Skewer Dogs .... **2**·153
Snappy Cheese Appetizers .... **1**·73
Snowcap Cherry Nibbles .... **2**·224
Spiced Citrus Appetizer
  Cup .... **5**·544
Spicy Oranges 'n Prunes .. **14**·1792
Strawberry Starter .... **8**·987
Stuffed Celery .... **16**·2006
Stuffed Edam .... **7**·829
Stuffed Mushrooms .... **1**·64
Summer Fruit Cocktail ...... **5**·562
Sweet-and-Sour Surprises .... **4**·446
Swiss and Frank Spirals ..... **8**·937
Teriyaki Meatballs .... **1**·64
Teriyaki Miniatures .... **9**·1087
Tomato Refresher .... **11**·1319
Tomato Zip .... **5**·563
Tropic Isle Appetizer .... **2**·232
Tuna Rounds .... **7**·876
Turkey Cocktail .... **19**·2315
Turkey in Sour Cream .... **19**·2315
Two-Tone Cocktail .... **2**·217

Appetizer *continued*

Vegetable Cocktail Soup . **18**·2282
Walnut Snack .... **19**·2416
Welcome Wafers .... **1**·72

APPLE .... **1**·79-96
-Apricot Pie .... **14**·1671
-Avocado Ring .... **1**·122
Bean Bake .... **2**·172
-Beef Patties .... **2**·188
Blush .... **1**·92
Butter .... **1**·91
Butter Betty .... **2**·213
Butter Cake .... **1**·91
-Buttered Pork Loin ...... **14**·1734
Cake, Harvest .... **3**·348
Cake, Upside-Down .... **3**·345
Caramel .... **1**·85
Cheese Bake, Creamy ...... **1**·93
Cheese-Stuffed .... **1**·85
Cider, American Hot
  Mulled .... **5**·536
Cider, Ham Baked in ...... **8**·996
Cider Snap .... **5**·536
Cinnamon .... **8**·907
Cinnamon Crunch .... **1**·96
-Cinnamon Sauce .... **10**·1180
-Cot Cooler .... **12**·1459
Crisp .... **1**·89
Crisp, Mincemeat- ...... **12**·1419
Crumb Pie .... **1**·87
Custard Pie .... **1**·88
Dumplings .... **1**·89
Dumplings, Basic .... **7**·819
Dumplings, Quick .... **15**·1845
Eggnog .... **19**·2347
-Filled Oatmeal Cookies .. **12**·1489
-Filled Squash .... **17**·2135
Filling .... **5**·559
Filling, Cranberry- .... **7**·882
Franks, Glazed, and ...... **8**·936
Fritters .... **8**·965
Frost .... **2**·222
Frosting .... **3**·348
Glaze .... **3**·267
Glaze, Crab .... **6**·654
Glaze, Ham with Crab ... **13**·1662
-Grapefruit Molds ...... **9**·1054
-Ham Bake, Carrot- .... **1**·86
Ham Salad, and .... **9**·1113
-Honey Tea .... **2**·222
Jelly, Cinnamon- .... **10**·1211
Jelly, Mint- .... **12**·1423

Apple *continued*

-Lime Cooler .... **1**·92
Maple Baked .... **1**·87
-Melon Toss .... **11**·1395
-Mint Jelly .... **10**·1213
-Oatmeal Cookies .... **1**·89
Onion Bake, and .... **12**·1509
Onions, Liver with, and .. **19**·2350
-Orange Brownies .... **5**·605
-Orange Toss .... **1**·85
Pancakes .... **13**·1554
Pandowdy .... **13**·1559
Parfaits, Big .... **1**·96
-Peach Conserve .... **1**·85
Pheasant with .... **8**·1005
-Pickle Relish .... **15**·1856
Pie, Custard-Sauced
  Deep-Dish .... **6**·747
Pie, Deep-Dish .... **14**·1671
Pie, European .... **14**·1675
Pie, 1-2-3 .... **15**·1797
Pie, Perfect .... **1**·87
Pie, Tart and Saucy ...... **12**·1484
Pie, Topsy-Turvy .... **1**·87
Pinwheels, Quick .... **5**·582
-Raisin Cake .... **13**·1630
Raisin-Filled .... **12**·1411
-Raisin Loaves .... **3**·267
-Raisin Pie .... **1**·88
Relish, Curried .... **1**·93
Rings, Cinnamon .... **1**·94
Rings, Panned .... **3**·360
Ring, Sweet .... **1**·83
Ring Waldorf .... **1**·86
Salad, Cinnamon- ...... **15**·1842
Salad, Lemon .... **1**·85
Salad, Swiss .... **17**·2093
Salad, Tropical .... **19**·2419
Sandwich, Camembert- ..... **3**·360
-Sauced Potato Cakes .... **13**·1556
Sausage-Stuffed .... **1**·86
Sautéed .... **8**·1005
Skillet, Beet and .... **2**·208
Snow Salad .... **1**·85
Spicy Baked .... **1**·83
Spicy Cinnamon, in Foil .... **8**·919
Spicy Fruit Puffs .... **1**·83
Strudel .... **17**·2175
Strudel, Quick .... **17**·2176
Tarts, Cran- .... **18**·2251
Toddy, Hot .... **8**·995
Torte, Date .... **1**·93
Toss, Turkey- .... **19**·2321
Tuna Toss .... **1**·86
Turkey Sandwiches .... **1**·87
Waffles, Fresh .... **3**·273
Waldorf, Date- .... **15**·1917
-Walnut Cobbler .... **7**·863
Whirls, Caramel- .... **15**·1844
Wrap, Sausage- .... **3**·363

Applesauce ....1·94
  Bread, Spiced .... **16**·1933
  Brownies, Diamond ....1·96
  Cake ....1·95
  Crisp, Quick ....1·94
  Doughnuts ....1·96
  -Fig Loaf ....7·871
  Meat Loaf ....1·96
  -Peach Salad .... **13**·1603
  Pudding .... **15**·1796
  Puffs .... **15**·1800
  Squash and ....1·19

Apricot
  -Almond Coffee
    Cake ....5·583
  Apple-Cot Cooler .... **12**·1459
  Bowl, Prune and .... **14**·1792
  Bran Bread ....2·256
  Bubble Balls ....7·881
  -Buttermilk Pie ....3·320
  Cake, Coconut ....1·100
  Cake, Crunchy ....3·350
  -Cherry Sauce .... **10**·1180
  Chiffon Pie ....1·102
  -Coconut Ring ....5·568
  Cream, Molded .... **19**·2346
  Crepes, Ham- ....6·693
  Dressing .... **16**·1929
  Foldovers ....8·920
  Freeze, Orange- ....1·101
  Glaze .... **16**·1988
  -Grapefruit Ice .... **9**·1057
  -Ham Patties .... **14**·1782
  Ladder Loaf ....1·101
  Loaf, Pork- .... **11**·1307
  Mold, Spicy ....5·557
  Mold, Tangerine .... **18**·2245
  Pastries, Quick .... **17**·2095
  Peach-Cot Cherry
    Bake ....8·991
  Pickled .... **15**·1856
  Pie, Apple- .... **14**·1671
  Pie, Banana- ....6·679
  Pie, Fresh ....1·100
  -Pineapple Jam .... **10**·1202
  Ring, Orange- .....2·240; **5**·546
  Salad, Cranberry- ....6·666
  Sauce ....6·693
  Sauce, Golden ....6·767
  Sauce, Squab with .... 8·1004
  -Scotch Cobbler ....6·756
  Shake .... **12**·1417
  Soufflé, Easy ....1·101
  Split-Ups ....7·793
  Squares, Bran ....3·300
  Stuffed Chops ....1·99
  -Sweet Potatoes .... **18**·2213
  Swizzle ....2·232
  Syrup, Maple- .... **11**·1348

Apricot *continued*
  Topped Coffee Bread .... **19**·2421
  -Topped Veal Loaf .... **19**·2365
  Torte, Frozen ....8·976
Armenian Marinade .... **11**·1352
Armenian Shish Kabobs .... **10**·1227

Artichoke
  Bake, Crab- ....1·109
  Casings, Filled ....1·109
  Crab Rémoulade, and ... **15**·1858
  -Grapefruit Salad .... **9**·1057
  -Ham Bites .... **9**·1113
  Heart Salad ....1·108
  Lamb-Stuffed ....1·107
  Luncheon Salad, Crab- ......6·653
  Marinated ....1·108
  Marinated, Hearts ....1·59
  Parsley-Chive Dip for ....1·108
  Pickled, Hearts .... **13**·1661
  Prosciutto and .... **14**·1788
  Velvet ....1·108

Asparagus
  Amandine ....1·114
  Blankets, in ....1·113
  Broil, Ham- .... **18**·2223
  Casserole ....1·113
  -Cheese Soup .... **10**·1160
  Cheese, with .... **19**·2387
  Fold-Overs ....1·64
  Oriental ....1·111
  Salad, Molded ....1·114
  Soup, Cheesy- .... **17**·2088
  Soup, Chilled ....1·114
  -Tomato Salad ....1·114
  Toss ....1·114
  Two-Cheese Sauce, with ....7·863

Aspic
  Brussels Sprouts in ....3·302
  Cabbage .... **11**·1321
  Crab-Tomato ....6·653
  Creamy ....1·116
  Soufflé, Tomato ....7·862
  Sunshine ....1·116
  Tomato-Celery ....1·116
  Turkey Aspic Salad ..... **19**·2320
Austrian Cabbage Salad ......4·405
Austrian Linzer Cookies .... **10**·1206

Avocado
  Boats, Bean and .... **15**·1914
  Bowl, Spinach- .... **17**·2112
  Chilled Avo-Mato
    Soup .... **17**·2087
  -Citrus Salad ....1·122
  Clam-Guacamole Dip ... **10**·1275
  Cocktail Spread ....1·121
  Crab-Stuffed ....1·122

Avocado *continued*
  -Cream
    Dressing ..... **17**·2093; **19**·2427
  Deviled Guacamole ...... **9**·1093
  Dressing ....1·122
  Fruit Freeze ....1·121
  Guacamole .... **9**·1093
  Mex-acado Sauce ....1·15
  Mold, Cranberry- ....6·664
  Mold, Salmon- .... **16**·1939
  Open-Facers .... **15**·1824
  Ring, Apple- ....1·122
  Ring, Shrimp in .... **15**·1919
  Salad, Endive- ....7·852
  Shrimp Rémoulade, with ....1·123
  Toss, Orange- ....1·122

B

Baba au Orange ....1·125
Baba au Rhum ....1·124
Bacardi Cocktail ....1·126

Bacon
  Bake, Yankee ....5·637
  -Bean Bake, Canadian ......3·365
  Big Boys ....1·128
  -Blue Dip .... **13**·1640
  Broiled ....1·128
  Burgers, Mushroom- .... **9**·1070
  -Chive Corn Muffins ....5·637
  Crisps ....1·128
  Eggs, Scalloped, and ..... **16**·1993
  -Flavored Beans .... **19**·2385
  Fried ....1·128
  -Hominy Scramble .... **9**·1149
  Lettuce, and
    Tomato Salad .... **18**·2277
  Liver Bake, and .... **11**·1307
  -Macaroni Bake ....1·127
  Mixed Grill .... **10**·1232
  Oriental ....2·180
  Oven-Baked ....1·128
  Potatoes, Blue Cheese- ... **14**·1748
  Roast Canadian ....3·365
  Roll-Ups, Easy-Do ....3·271
  Rounds, Crab Meat- ....3·366
  Sandwich, Peanut Butter- . **15**·1803
  Scallops and .... **16**·1991
  Spoon Bread .... **15**·1852
  Stack-Ups, Canadian .... **1**·127
  Waffles .... **19**·2432

Baked
  Acorn Squash ....1·19
  Alaska ....2·134
  Ambrosia ....6·762
  Banana Squash ....2·143
  Bean Pie .... **19**·2388

Baked *continued*
Caramel Custard . . . . **6·**724
Chocolate Custard . . . . **19·**2345
Chutney Pears . . . . **5·**535
Crimson Pears . . . . **13·**1619
Custard . . . . **6·**724
Custard (low calorie) . . . . . **11·**1323
Deviled Tomatoes . . . .**7·**771
Eggplant . . . .**7·**849
Fish Fillets . . . .**7·**889
Indian Pudding . . . . **10·**1188
Liver and Rice . . . . **16·**1998
Liver Pâté . . . .**8·**956
Lobster Savannah . . . . **11·**1311
Orange Cups . . . . **11·**1327
Pears Elegante . . . . **13·**1622
Potato Toppers . . . . **14·**1747
Prune Whip . . . . **17·**2151
Rice . . . .**4·**428
Rice Pudding . . . . **15·**1869
Spaghetti . . . . **17·**2100
-Stuffed Potatoes . . . . **11·**1326
Tomatoes . . . . **18·**2279
Turkey Fondue . . . . **19·**2317
Baking Powder Biscuits . . . .**2·**229
Baklava . . . . **12·**1458

Banana
Ambrosia Ring . . . .**2·**141
-Apricot Pie . . . .**6·**679
aux Fruits . . . . **16·**1973
-Berry Cup . . . .**8·**987
Bran Muffins . . . .**9·**1045
Bread, Cranberry- . . . .**6·**663
Bread, Jeweled . . . .**7·**879
Bread, Sweet . . . . **20·**2473
-Brittle Dessert . . . . **13·**1613
Burgers . . . .**2·**142
Butter . . . .**3·**315
Cake . . . .**8·**914
Cheesecake, Chilled . . . . . **15·**1847
-Cheese Dressing . . . . **16·**1926
Coffee Bread . . . .**5·**584
Cream Pie . . . .**2·**142
Foster . . . .**2·**142
Fritters . . . .**2·**141
Honey-Baked . . . .**9·**1035
Ice Cream . . . .**2·**140
Ice, Strawberry- . . . . **17·**2170
Island Nut . . . .**9·**1136
Milk Shake . . . .**17·**2063
Mold, Honey- . . . .**7·**863
Mold, Strawberry- . . . .**2·**141
Nectar, in . . . .**9·**1136
Nut-Crusted . . . .**2·**141
Pecan Crunch . . . .**2·**142
Pisang Goreng . . . . **14·**1694
-Raspberry Flambé . . . . . . **20·**2466
Shake, Strawberry- . . . . . . **12·**1417
Shortcake, Cranberry- . . . .**6·**664

Banana *continued*
Split Pie . . . .**6·**768
Splits, Broiler . . . .**2·**140
Split, Top . . . . **10·**1185
-Strawberry Freeze . . . . . . **17·**2168
Syrup, Honey- . . . .**9·**1152
Waffles . . . . **19·**2407
Banbury Tarts . . . .**2·**143

BARBECUE . . . .**2·**145-159
Abacus Ribs . . . . **10·**1227
Appetizer Skewer Dogs . . . . .**2·**153
Apple-Buttered Pork Loin . **14·**1734
Armenian Shish Kabobs . . **10·**1227
Bass Steaks . . . . **16·**2013
Bean Bake . . . .**2·**174
Bean Soup . . . . **18·**2282
Beef and Beans in Foil . . . . .**9·**1085
Beef and Fruit Kabobs . . . . .**9·**1145
Beef Angus Kabobs . . . . . . **10·**1225
Beef Claret . . . .**5·**555
Beef Dinner in Foil . . . .**8·**916
Beer-Sauced Burgers . . . .**2·**203
Blue Cheese Burgers . . . .**2·**248
Blue Cheese Dogs . . . .**2·**248
Bologna Burgers . . . .**2·**155
Breads . . . .**2·**159
Broccoli in Foil . . . .**3·**293
Broiled Salmon
Epicurean . . . . **15·**1891
Broilers, Honey . . . .**4·**481
Brookside Fried Trout . . . . **18·**2298
Burger Mountains . . . .**9·**1124
Butterfly Leg of Lamb . . . . . .**2·**154
Cake Kabobs . . . .**2·**152
Campfire Pot Roast . . . .**1·**43
Campfire Spaghetti . . . .**3·**363
Campsite Stew . . . .**3·**363
Caper Burgers . . . .**4·**401
Caraway Chicken Halves . . . .**4·**406
Charcoaled Salmon Steaks . . .**7·**895
Cheese-Topped Tomatoes . . .**4·**464
Cheesy Corned Beef
Sandwiches . . . . **13·**1662
Chicken . . . .**4·**481
Chicken-in-the-Garden . . . . .**8·**918
Chinese Smoked Ribs . . . . **12·**1531
Chuck Roast . . . . **11·**1354
Chuck Steak, Lemon- . . . . . .**2·**197
Corned Beef and Cabbage
Bundles . . . .**2·**158
Cornish Game Hens on a
Spit . . . . **14·**1771

Barbecue *continued*
Easy Onion Bread . . . .**2·**159
Fiesta Beef Kabobs . . . . . . **10·**1225
Fisherman's Luck . . . .**9·**1100
Foiled Potatoes . . . .**8·**919
Foiled Vegetables . . . .**8·**919
Frankrauts . . . . **16·**1975
Fresh Corn on the Cob . . . **15·**1874
Frosted Luncheon Meat . . . **11·**1330
Fruit-Turkey Kabobs . . . .**8·**990
Gingered Ham Slice . . . . . **17·**2109
Gourmet Tenderloin on a
Spit . . . .**2·**158
Grilled-Broiled Cornish
Game Hens . . . .**5·**634
Grilled Garlic Slices . . . .**2·**159
Grilled Halibut . . . .**9·**1101
Grilled Ham Slice . . . . **10·**1214
Grilled Perch with Parsley
Sauce . . . . **13·**1648
Grilled Rib Eye Roast . . . . **15·**1894
Grilled Salmon Steaks . . . . **16·**1939
Grilled Sausage Treats . . . . .**9·**1075
Grilled Tomatoes . . . .**9·**1075
Grilled Turkey Pieces . . . .**2·**155
Grilled Vegetables in Foil . . . .**2·**159
Ham and Fruit Kabobs . . . . **9·**1111
Ham Steak . . . .**9·**1111
Ham with Crab Apple
Glaze . . . . **13·**1662
Hawaiian Ham Slices . . . . . **9·**1113
Herbed Steak Broil . . . . . . **16·**1932
Hibachi Totem Poles . . . . . .**9·**1145
Hickory Brisket Slices . . . . . .**3·**287
Hickory Fish Bake . . . .**9·**1146
Hickory Lamb Kabobs . . . **10·**1261
Hickory Smoked Turkey . . . .**2·**151
Hilo Franks . . . . **15·**1854
Hobo Rice . . . .**2·**159
Horseradish-Stuffed Rib
Roast . . . . **15·**1874
Indian-Style Corn on the
Cob . . . .**2·**159
Individual Clambake . . . .**5·**550
Island Teriyaki . . . .**2·**153
Kau Kau Kabobs . . . . **16·**2044
Kowloon Duckling . . . .**2·**150
Lamb and Frank Burgers . . **11·**1379
Lamb Kabobs . . . .**2·**152
Lamb Racks with Herb
Jackets . . . .**2·**157
Lamb Shanks . . . .**10·**1258
Lamb Shanks, Armenian-
Italian . . . . **16·**2024
Luau Ribs . . . . **17·**2104
Mandarin Dinner . . . . **10·**1227
Marinated Beef Cubes . . . . **16·**2045
Marinated Hickory Steaks . **9·**1146
Meatball . . . .**2·**152
Midas Meat Loaf . . . . **11·**1386

Barbecue *continued*

Minted Leg of Lamb on a
Spit . . . . **12**·1423
Mushroom-Bacon
Burgers . . . . **9**·1070
Nutty Pups . . . . **8**·934
Onion-Cheese Loaf . . . . **3**·267
Onion Potatoes . . . . **13**·1662
Orange-Glazed Grilled
Chuck . . . . **11**·1354
Orange-Pork Curry . . . . **2**·157
Outdoor Burgers . . . . **2**·155
Over-the-Coals Lobster
Tails . . . . **16**·2033
Peanut Buttered Pork . . . . **13**·1615
Pineapple Spareribs . . . . . **10**·1234
Pineapple-Stuffed Cornish
Hens . . . . **18**·2187
Plum-Glazed Chicken . . . **14**·1707
Plum-Glazed Turkey
Roasts . . . . **14**·1768
Pork . . . . **14**·1738
Pork Chops . . . . **10**·1200
Pork Chop Treat . . . . **8**·918
Powwow Sundae . . . . **2**·153
Ribs, Best . . . . **14**·1734
Ribs Dee-Lish . . . . **2**·158
Rice-Mushroom . . . . **3**·363
Roast Canadian Bacon . . . . . **3**·365
Roasted Corn . . . . **2**·159
Roast Pork Chops . . . . **15**·1874
Rolls on a Spit . . . . **2**·159
Rotisseried Rolled Rib
Roast . . . . **2**·158
Rotisserie Duck . . . . **7**·812
Rotisserie Rib Roast . . . . . . **15**·1844
Rotisserie Round . . . . **2**·157
Rub . . . . **12**·1531
Sausage-Apple Wrap . . . . . . **3**·363
Sausage Kabobs . . . . **16**·1984
Sausage-Krauters . . . . **10**·1236
Scallion-Buttered Hard
Rolls . . . . **2**·159
Seafood Sword . . . . **10**·1228
Sesame Rainbow Trout . . . **18**·2298
Short Ribs . . . . **17**·2051
Shrimp-Out . . . . **2**·155
Shrimp with Lemon . . . . . . **16**·2033
Smoked Fish with Lemon . . . . **2**·151
Smoked Linkburgers . . . . **2**·154
Spicy Cinnamon Apples in
Foil . . . . **8**·919
Spinning Chicken . . . . **15**·1894
Spinning Ham . . . . **15**·1894
Spitted Vegetables . . . . **2**·159
Square Burgers . . . . **9**·1124
Sukiyaki Skewers . . . . **9**·1146
Sweet-Sour Sauced
Shrimp . . . . **17**·2057
Teriyaki . . . . **18**·2265

Barbecue *continued*

Turkey-Pineapple Grill . . . **14**·1772
Veal with Rice . . . . **19**·2364
Vegetables . . . . **2**·153
Zesty Luncheon Barbecue . . .**2**·155
Barquette of Tiny Shrimp . . . **16**·2022

Basic

Apple Dumplings . . . .**7**·819
Boiled Lobster . . . . **11**·1310
Broiled Chicken . . . . **4**·481
Broiled Lobster . . . . **11**·1311
Fruit Dough . . . . **3**·369
Ground Beef . . . . **9**·1090
Hamburgers . . . . **9**·1122
Mustard Sauce . . . . **12**·1453
Roll Dough . . . . **15**·1879
Scrambled Eggs . . . . **7**·833
Vanilla Ice Cream . . . . **6**·672
Waldorf Salad . . . . **19**·2413

Basil

Butter . . . . **8**·925
-Carrot Coins . . . . **11**·1321
Carrots . . . . **2**·163
Jelly, Mint or . . . . **10**·1212
Batter Rolls . . . . **2**·164
Bavarian Potato Dumplings . . **8**·1022
Bavarian-Style Stew . . . . **4**·424
Bayou Bean-Burgers . . . . **2**·175

BEAN . . . . **2**·169-179
(See also *Green Bean, Kidney
Bean, Lima Bean, Navy Bean,
Wax Bean.*)
Avocado Boats, and . . . . . **15**·1914
Bake, Apple . . . . **2**·172
Bake, Barbecued . . . . **2**·174
Bake, Canadian Bacon- . . . . . **3**·365
Bake, Deviled Ham- . . . . **7**·772
Bake, Potluck . . . . **2**·172
Bake, Wiener- . . . . **2**·175
Beef and Beans in Foil . . . . . **9**·1085
Bonanza Salad . . . . **19**·2430
Boston Beanwich . . . . **2**·175
Burgers, Big Western . . . . . **16**·1958
Burgers, Saucy . . . . **18**·2282
Calico Bean Bake . . . . **2**·174
Casserole, Rancho . . . . **2**·172
Cheese Patties, and . . . . . . **15**·1841
Dip, Hot Mexican . . . . **2**·175
Dip, Hot Sausage- . . . . **1**·71
Easy Baked . . . . **2**·172
Frank Bake, Three- . . . . **2**·175
Hearty Baked . . . . **2**·172
Maple Baked . . . . **2**·173
Orange Baked . . . . **2**·173
Oriental . . . . **2**·181
Pie, Baked . . . . **19**·2388
Pot Limas . . . . **11**·1289

Bean *continued*

Pot, Steak and . . . . **12**·1423
Pot, Wiener . . . .**8**·936
Relish . . . . **15**·1856
Roaster Baked . . . . **15**·1814

Roll-Ups, Beef and . . . . . . **12**·1424
Salad, Egg and . . . . **2**·174
Salad, Four . . . . **2**·178
Salad, Hot Five . . . . **2**·178
Salad, Marinated . . . . **19**·2430
Salad, Marinated Three- . . **11**·1354
Skillet, Smoky . . . . **11**·1301
Soup . . . . **12**·1456
Soup, Barbecue . . . . **18**·2282
Soup, Black . . . . **2**·232
-Stuffed Tomatoes . . . . **18**·2277
Succotash . . . . **18**·2193
Swedish Brown . . . . **16**·2006
Texas-Style . . . . **14**·1693
Toss, Italian . . . . **15**·1914
Toss, Red . . . . **15**·1841
Béarnaise, Blender . . . . **2**·183
Béarnaise Sauce . . . . **2**·182
Beaten Biscuits . . . . **2**·183
Béchamel Sauce . . . . **2**·183

BEEF . . . . **2**·185-199
(Listed at the end of this entry
Ground, Roast, Steak. See also
Corned Beef, Dried Beef.)
Angus Kabobs . . . . **10**·1225
Barbecued Short Ribs . . . . **17**·2051
Bavarian-Style Stew . . . . **4**·424
Bones, Deviled . . . . **10**·1272
Braised Short Ribs . . . . **17**·2052
Brisket in Beer . . . . **3**·288
Brisket with Vegetables . . . . . **3**·288
Cartwheel, Dilly . . . . **2**·197
Châteaubriand . . . . **4**·452
-Corn Chowder . . . . **5**·625
Cubes, Curried . . . . **6**·718
Della Casa, Tournedos of . **18**·2293
Fillets, Pampered . . . . **11**·1320
Fondue . . . . **8**·925
Goulash and Noodles . . . . **18**·2284

Beef *continued*

Gourmet Tenderloin on a
Spit .... 2·158
Grilled Beefwiches .... 9·1076
Hickory Brisket Slices ...... 3·287
Hungarian Short Ribs .... 19·2398
Kabobs, Fiesta .... 10·1225
Kidney Pie, and .... 7·856
Macaroni, and .... 13·1579
Mexican-Style Hash .... 5·623
Mushroom Salad, and ...... 2·199
Noodle Bake, and .... 7·800
Old-Time Oxtail Stew .... 13·1541
-Olive Spread, Zippy ..... 12·1497
Patties, Roast .... 11·1388
Pie, Pork or .... 14·1668
Potpie .... 11·1390
Pot Roast .... 14·1761
Salad Sandwiches .... 11·1364
Salad, San Marino .... 15·1918
Shanks, Simmered .... 2·163
Short Rib Stew .... 2·166
Short Rib-Vegetable
Stew .... 17·2052
Skillet, Chinese .... 4·500
Soup, Vegetable- .... 17·2084
Spaghetti, and .... 17·2101
Sprouts, and .... 11·1355
Stew Bake .... 17·2145
Stew, Burgundy .... 4·411
Stew, German .... 11·1380
Stew, Old-Time .... 1·32
Stew, Oven .... 2·196
Stew, Pioneer .... 4·424
Stew, Snappy .... 10·1271
Stew with Biscuit
Topper .... 17·2145
Stroganoff .... 17·2174
Stroganoff, Beer- .... 17·2174
Stuffed Tenderloin .... 2·197
Sweet-Sour Stew .... 4·430
Tenderloin, Roast .... 2·197
Toss, Deviled .... 11·1286

Ground

American Pizza .... 7·869
Applesauce Meat Loaf ...... 1·96
Ball Oven Stew .... 17·2147
Banana Burgers .... 2·142
Basic .... 9·1090
Basic Hamburgers .... 9·1122
Bean and Cheese Patties .. 15·1841
Beans in Foil, and .... 9·1085
Beer-Sauced Burgers .... 2·203
Biscuit Skillet, and .... 3·270
Blue Cheese Burgers .... 2·248
Boat, Saucy .... 8·950
Broiled Patties .... 9·1084
Bull's-Eye Meatballs .... 1·77
Burger Mountains .... 9·1124

Beef, Ground *continued*

Burgers, Cheese and ...... 9·1084
Burger Skillet Stew .... 4·425
Burgundy Beefburgers .... 9·1125
Campsite Stew .... 3·363
Caper Burgers .... 4·401
Cheeseburger
Chowder .... 17·2084
Cheeseburger Pie .... 20·2469
Cheeseburger Towers ..... 9·1123
Cheeseburger-Vegetable
Casserole .... 12·1411
Cheese-Filled Meat
Loaf .... 12·1439
Cheesy Stuffed Burgers .... 9·1090
Chicken-Fried Burgers ..... 8·997
Chili-Burger Rarebit .... 8·950
Chili-Burger Stack-Ups .... 9·1092
Chili-Burger Supper ..... 13·1580
Chili Con Carne .... 4·494
Chili Con Carne
(quantity) .... 15·1814
Chili Mostaccioli .... 12·1434
Corn Pancakes with Chili .... 5·624
Cranberry Meat Loaves ... 10·1234
Cucumber Burgers .... 6·708
Cumin Burgers .... 6·710
Deviled Hamburgers .... 7·771
Dilly Hamburgers .... 7·779
Dinner in Foil .... 8·916
Dip, Spicy .... 1·77
Dumplings, and .... 7·816
Egg Foo Young, and ...... 2·180
Eggplant Skillet .... 7·848
Empanadas .... 7·851
German Burgers .... 9·1124
Grilled Patties .... 9·1084
Hamburger-Bean Skillet .... 2·179
Hamburger-Cheese
Bake .... 12·1466
Hamburger-Corn Bake ... 14·1683
Hamburger-Noodle
Bake .... 15·1813
Hamburger Pie .... 9·1090
Hamburger Steak
Diane .... 20·2467
Hamburger Stroganoff ... 17·2173
Hot Dog Burgers .... 16·1951
Inside-Out Ravioli ...... 15·1840
Iowa Corn Burgers .... 9·1124
Italian Meatballs .... 10·1197
Italian Meat Loaf .... 9·1088
Italian Meat Sauce .... 18·2281
Italian Meat Sauce
(quantity) .... 15·1814
Lima-Burger Soup .... 2·179
Lima Skillet, and .... 4·446
Loaf, Favorite .... 11·1387
Loaf, Wild Rice and ...... 9·1045
Meal-In-A-Bowl Stew ..... 9·1092

Beef, Ground *continued*

Meat and Potato Pie ...... 9·1082
Meatball Barbecue .... 2·152
Meatball Dinner .... 9·1084
Meatball Heroes .... 11·1384
Meatballs à la
Burgundy .... 15·1844
Meatballs in Barbecue
Sauce .... 9·1089
Meatballs in Sauerbraten
Sauce .... 9·1089
Meatball Stroganoff .... 9·1089
Meat Loaf Supreme .... 6·656
Mexican-Style Casserole .... 5·629
Mexican Surprises .... 5·599
Midas Meat Loaf .... 11·1386
Mushroom-Bacon
Burgers .... 9·1070
Mushroom Burgers .... 9·1085
-Mushroom Loaf .... 9·1084
Noodles, and .... 14·1683
Olive Burgers .... 12·1496
Open-Face
Beefburgers .... 12·1438
Open-Face Burgers ...... 12·1512
Orange-Topped Burgers ... 9·1123
Oriental .... 13·1597
Oriental Crunch Burgers ..... 2·180
Outdoor Burgers .... 2·155
Oven Meatballs .... 9·1089
Panbroiled Patties .... 9·1084
Patties, Apple- .... 2·188
Patties Parmesan .... 11·1388
Pinwheel Burgers .... 9·1124
Pizza .... 14·1697
Planked Meat Loaf .... 9·1088
Porcupine Meatballs ..... 14·1721
Quick Chili on Buns ...... 9·1090
Rancho Bean Casserole .... 2·172
Rarebit .... 2·203
Reuben .... 9·1087
Rice Skillet, and .... 9·1090
Roll, Filled .... 18·2187
Salisbury Steak .... 16·1934
Saucy Italian Meatballs ... 11·1382
Savory Cabbage Rolls ..... 9·1087
Skilletburgers .... 9·1084
Skillet, Speedy .... 9·1090
Soup, Kohlrabi and ...... 10·1239
Sour Cream Burgers ..... 17·2094
Spaghetti and Meatballs .. 10·1197
Spaghetti and Oven
Meatballs .... 9·1089
Square Burgers .... 9·1124
Stack-A-Dinner .... 13·1597
Stroganoff, Jiffy .... 17·2173
Stuffed Hamburger Roll .... 2·199
Stuffed Manicotti .... 11·1344
Stuffed Peppers .... 12·1439
Stuffing .... 18·2185

Beef, Ground *continued*
Swedish Cabbage Rolls . . . . . . 3·327
Sweet-Sour Burgers . . . . . . 18·2218
Sweet-Sour Glazed
Loaf . . . . 9·1088
Tacos . . . . 18·2241
Taco Salad . . . . 5·629
Tangy Kraut Burger . . . . . . 16·1951
Teriyaki Burgers . . . . 17·2097
Teriyaki Miniatures . . . . 9·1087
Tostadas, Mexican . . . . . . 18·2292
Turkish Zucchini
Dolmas . . . . 7·788
Twin Meat Loaves . . . . 11·1386
Vegetable-Meatball
Soup . . . . 9·1084
Vegetable-Meatball
Stew . . . . 17·2147
Vegetable-Meat Cups . . . . . 11·1375
Vegetable Skillet, and . . . . 5·624
Wine Sauce, with . . . . 20·2460
Zwieback Meatballs . . . . . 20·2480

Roast
à la Wellington . . . . 20·2459
Barbecued Chuck . . . . 11·1354
Braised Sirloin . . . . 17·2061
Campfire Pot Roast . . . . 1·43
Cranberry Pot Roast . . . . 6·668
Dumplings, with . . . . 2·196
Fruited Pot Roast . . . . 7·803
Grilled Rib Eye . . . . 15·1894
Horseradish-Stuffed
Rib . . . . 15·1874
Individual Pot Roasts . . . . 2·194
Orange-Glazed Grilled
Chuck . . . . 11·1354
Orange Pot Roast . . . . 5·546
Pennsylvania Dutch Pot
Roast . . . . 19·2332
-Peppered Rib Eye . . . . 13·1637
Polynesian . . . . 5·534
Polynesian Pot Roast . . . . 2·194
Pot Roast . . . . 14·1761
Pot Roast in Beer . . . . 2·202
Pot Roast Variations . . . . . . 14·1761
Rib Supreme . . . . 2·196
Rolled Rump . . . . 11·1377
Rotisseried Rolled Rib . . . . 2·158
Rotisserie Rib,
Barbecue . . . . 15·1844
Rotisserie Round . . . . 2·157
Sauerbraten . . . . 16·1974
Savory Blade Pot
Roast . . . . 14·1762
Savory-Stuffed Rolled
Rib . . . . 15·1875
Sirloin Tip . . . . 17·2061
Spicy Rump . . . . 15·1843
Standing Rib . . . . 2·186

Beef, Roast *continued*
Stuffed Rolled Rib . . . . 18·2187
Tenderloin Deluxe . . . . . . 16·2042
Tenderloin, Teriyaki . . . . . 12·1536
Yankee Pot Roast . . . . 14·1761

Steak
Bean Pot, and . . . . 12·1423
Bean Roll-Ups, and . . . . . . 12·1424
Braised Flank . . . . 8·902
Broil, Herbed . . . . 16·1932
Burgundy . . . . 3·310
Canapés, Hot . . . . 3·366
Chicken-Fried . . . . 4·487
Claret Barbecue . . . . 5·555
Deviled . . . . 11·1327
Deviled Flank Rolls . . . . 2·188
Deviled Swiss . . . . 7·772
Diane . . . . 17·2143
Filet Mignon Princess . . . . . . 7·874
Filets, Broiled . . . . 18·2264
Fruit Kabobs, and . . . . 9·1145
Herb-Stuffed Flank . . . . 8·902
Island Teriyaki . . . . 2·153
Italian . . . . 17·2143
Lemon-Barbecued Chuck . . . . 2·197
London Broil . . . . 11·1315
Marchand De Vin . . . . 15·1895
Marinated Beef Cubes . . . . 16·2045
Marinated Hickory . . . . 9·1146
Mexican-Style . . . . 17·2141
Minute Steak and Capers . . 12·1424
Minute Steaks . . . . 12·1424
Minute Steak Sukiyaki . . . . . 2·186
Onion-Buttered Sirloin . . . 17·2141
Onions, and . . . . 2·196
Onions, with
(Zwiebelfleisch) . . . . 19·2395
Oriental Skillet Supper . . . . . 2·199
Oven Swiss . . . . 18·2225
Pan-Broiled . . . . 13·1550
Pan-Fried Round . . . . 13·1559
Pizza Swiss . . . . 18·2225
Planked . . . . 14·1701
Ranch House Round . . . . . 15·1854
Ranch Round . . . . 17·2143
Roll-Ups . . . . 18·2283
Round, Stuffed . . . . 18·2188
Salad, Rare Roast . . . . 16·1932
Sandwich, Saucy . . . . 11·1391
Sandwich, Stroganoff . . . . . 17·2141
Sauerbraten, Round . . . . . . 12·1467
Savory Pepper . . . . 13·1647
Skillet, Oriental . . . . 12·1530
Skillet Pizza . . . . 12·1523
Strips, Marinated . . . . 1·72
Stuffed Cube . . . . 11·1326
Stuffed Flank . . . . 8·902
Swank Porterhouse . . . . . . 14·1740
Swiss . . . . 18·2225

Beef, Steak *continued*
Teriyaki . . . . 12·1530
Teriyaki, Flank . . . . 8·902
Vegetable-Stuffed Minute
Steaks . . . . 12·1424
Zucchini Supper, and . . . . 17·2134

Beer
Beef Brisket in . . . . 3·288
Beef Pot Roast in . . . . 2·202
-Beef Stroganoff . . . . 17·2174
-Sauced Burgers . . . . 2·203
Shrimp in . . . . 2·202

Beet
Apple Skillet, and . . . . 2·208
Cabbage Slaw, and . . . . 5·591
Can-Can Borsch . . . . 2·204
Candied . . . . 3·371
Cranberry-Orange . . . . 2·204
Cream, in . . . . 2·206
Dressing, Zippy . . . . 11·1364
Harvard . . . . 9·1129
Hawaiian . . . . 2·207
-Herring Salad . . . . 9·1145
-Jellied Gefilte Fish . . . . 8·1015
-Onion Medley . . . . 2·206
Orange-Glazed . . . . 2·204
Pickled . . . . 2·207; 13·1661
-Pineapple Mold . . . . 14·1689
Raisin-Sauced . . . . 2·208
Ruby-Sauced . . . . 11·1321
Russian Borsch . . . . 2·250
Salad, Potato- . . . . 2·207
Salad, Zippy . . . . 2·207
Speedy Borsch . . . . 17·2080
Belgian Endive-Ham Rolls . . . . 2·209
Belgian Waffles . . . . 19·2409
Berks County Potato-Custard
Pie . . . . 13·1636
Berried Melon Rings . . . . . . 11·1396
Berries and Nectarines au
Rhum . . . . 17·2167

Berry
-Cereal Parfaits . . . . 4·443
-Cheesecake Pie 14·1670; 14·1679
Coupe, Cinnamon- . . . . 6·647
Jam, Double . . . . 10·1202
Meringue Cake . . . . 3·345
-Orange Coffee Cake . . . . 17·2163
-Patch Salad . . . . 6·644
-Peach Marble . . . . 13·1603
-Sour Cream Dressing . . . . 16·1925
Syrup . . . . 18·2227

Best
Barbecued Ribs . . . . 14·1734
-Ever Muffins . . . . 12·1441
Hamdogs . . . . 8·935

Best *continued*
Nut Loaf . . . . 3·275
Oven Hash . . . . 9·1130
Tomato Catsup . . . . 4·430
Two-Egg Cake . . . . 3·343
Betty, Apple Butter . . . . 2·213
Betty, Honey Rhubarb . . . . 2·213

BEVERAGE . . . . 2·215-223
Alcoholic
American-Style Glögg . . . . . 9·1036
Bacardi Cocktail . . . . 1·126
Bloody Mary . . . . 19·2403
Brandy Alexander . . . . 3·259
Bullshot . . . . 19·2403
Burgundy Punch . . . . 15·1809
Cold Duck . . . . 4·448
Daiquiri . . . . 6·732
Daiquiri Blazer . . . . 17·2149
Dry Martini . . . . 11·1360
Extra Dry Martini . . . . 11·1360
Firetong Glögg . . . . 9·1036
Fish House Punch . . . . 8·899
Grasshopper . . . . 9·1058
Highball . . . . 9·1148
Holiday Punch . . . . 19·2402
Hot Brandied Chocolate . . . . 3·260
Hot Buttered Rum . . . . 15·1897
Hot Lemon Punch . . . . 15·1809
Lime Fizz . . . . 20·2468
Margarita . . . . 11·1352
Old-Fashioned . . . . 12·1493
Orange Champagne
Cocktail . . . . 4·448
Planter's Punch . . . . 14·1701
Rosé Frappé . . . . 20·2458
Ruby Wine Punch . . . . 20·2458
Screwdriver . . . . 19·2403
Sherried Chocolate
Frappé . . . . 20·2458
Singapore Sling . . . . 17·2063
Spiced Cranberry Drink . . . . 1·64
Spiced Wassail . . . . 19·2423
Stinger . . . . 17·2149
Summer Sangria . . . . 16·1960
Syllabub . . . . 18·2226
Tomato-Vermouth
Cocktail . . . . 20·2457
Tonic . . . . 20·2465
Traditional Martini . . . . . . 11·1360
Warren's Glugg . . . . 20·2464
Watermelon-Wine Punch 19·2428
Whiskey Sour . . . . 20·2444

Beverage *continued*
Nonalcoholic
After Dinner Mocha . . . . 4·506
Amber Tea Delight . . . . . . 18·2257
American Hot Mulled
Apple Cider . . . . 5·536
Appetizer Juices . . . . 2·218
Apple Blush . . . . 1·92
Apple Cider Snap . . . . 5·536
Apple-Cot Cooler . . . . 12·1459
Apple Eggnog . . . . 19·2347
Apple Frost . . . . 2·222
Apple-Honey Tea . . . . 2·222
Apple-Lime Cooler . . . . 1·92
Apricot Shake . . . . 12·1417
Apricot Swizzle . . . . 2·232
Banana Milk Shake . . . . . . 17·2063
Blueberry Shake . . . . 12·1417
Brazilian Chocolate . . . . 5·516
Brazilian Float . . . . 5·577
Breakfast Cocoa . . . . 5·565
Breakfast Nog . . . . 12·1415
Café Aruba . . . . 5·576
Café au Lait . . . . 3·331
Café De Belgique . . . . 3·331
Cappuccino . . . . 4·403
Cherry Sparkle . . . . 2·222
Chocolate Coffee . . . . 5·576
Chocolate Soda . . . . 10·1182
Citrus Cooler . . . . 5·544
Coffee Aloha . . . . 2·220
Coffee Royal Eggnog . . . . . . 7·844
Cool Coffee Eggnog . . . . . . 5·576
Cranberry-Cherry Punch . . . . 5·524
Cranberry Cooler . . . . 2·223
Cranberry Punch . . . . 15·1808
Cranberry Sparkle . . . . 2·223
Cranberry-Tea Punch . . . . . 6·665
Demitasse . . . . 6·750
Eggnog . . . . 7·845
Eggnog Royale . . . . 2·222
Favorite Patio Refresher . . . . 8·996
Frosted Cocktail . . . . 5·544
Frosted Fruit Punch . . . . . 10·1223
Frosty Golden Punch . . . . . 8·995
Frosty Party Punch . . . . . . 15·1808
Frosty Spiced Tea . . . . . . 17·2148
Fruited Iced Tea . . . . 2·219
Fruit Flip . . . . 8·908
Golden Glow Punch . . . . . 4·406
Herbed Cocktail . . . . 2·217
Holiday Maple Punch . . . . 11·1348
Hot Apple Toddy . . . . 8·995
Hot Buttered Cranberry
Swizzle . . . . 6·666
Hot Buttered Lemonade . . 10·1275
Hot Chocolate . . . . 4·507
Hot Tomato Cocktail . . . . 18·2282
Iced Fruit Tea . . . . 18·2257
Instant Nog . . . . 7·844

Beverage, Nonalcoholic *continued*
Instant Russian Tea . . . . 2·220
Lemonade or Limeade . . . . . 1·22
Lemon Punch . . . . 15·1808
Lime Frosted Punch . . . . . 15·1808
Malted Milk . . . . 11·1341
Maple Skimmer . . . . 11·1347
Mexican Chocolate . . . . . . 4·507
Milk Shakes . . . . 12·1417
Minted Sundae Soda . . . . . 11·1293
Mint Lemonade . . . . 2·219
Mock Champagne
Punch . . . . 15·1808
Mulled Cranberry Drink . . 12·1481
1-2-3 Easy Party Punch . . . 15·1807
Orange Eggnog . . . . 10·1179
Orange-Pineapple Fizz . . . 10·1182
Passion Fruit Punch . . . . . . 9·1136
Patio Punch Soda . . . . . . 10·1182
Peach and Pineapple
Shake . . . . 14·1690
Peaches and Cream Milk
Shake . . . . 13·1606
Peachy Milk Shake . . . . . . 12·1417
Pineapple Citrus Punch . . . . 8·984
Pineapple Frostea . . . . . . 18·2257
Pineapple-Lemon Fizz . . . 10·1179
Pineapple-Lime Float . . . . 14·1690
Popfreeze Punch . . . . 15·1807
Punch for the Crowd . . . . . 15·1814
Punchmelon . . . . 19·2427
Quantity Fruit Punch . . . . . 15·1809
Raspberry Cooler . . . . 2·219
Raspberry Crush . . . . 2·223
Raspberry Mint Cooler . . . . 5·616
Rhubarb-Lemonade Punch . . 1·22
Rosy Raspberry Fizz . . . . . 8·899
Rosy Wassail . . . . 5·524
Ruby Fruit Punch . . . . 6·665
Sea Foam Punch . . . . 10·1179
Slim-Jim Frappé . . . . 8·937
Sparkle Punch . . . . 15·1808
Sparkling Mint Cooler . . . . . 5·616
Spiced Chocolate Coffee . . . 5·515
Spiced Fruit Sparkle . . . . . 17·2148
Spiced Grape Punch . . . . . 9·1049
Spiced Iced Coffee . . . . . . 5·577
Spiced Mocha . . . . 12·1425
Spiced Percolator
Punch . . . . 15·1807
Spiced Pineapple Sparkle . . 2·223
Spiced Tea . . . . 18·2257
Spicy Orange Tea . . . . 2·222
Strawberry-Banana
Shake . . . . 12·1417
Strawberry Frosted Soda . . . 2·237
Strawberry-
Lemonade Slush . . . . . 15·1820
Strawberry Shake . . . . . . 17·2159
Strawberry Sparkle Punch . 9·1029

Beverage, Nonalcoholic *continued*
Swedish Egg Coffee . . . . **5**·576
Tangy Citrus Fizz . . . . **5**·544
Tomato Refresher . . . . **11**·1319
Trader's Punch . . . . **9**·1074
Tropical Chocolate . . . . **2**·220
Tropical Punch . . . . **15**·1807
Tropic Isle Appetizer . . . . **2**·232
Tropic Isle Soda . . . . . . **10**·1182
Two-Tone Cocktail . . . . **2**·217
Viennese Coffee Float . . . . . . **8**·908
Warm Cranberry Punch . . **15**·1807
Big Apple Parfaits . . . . **1**·96
Big Western
Bean Burgers . . . . **16**·1958
Bischofsbrot
(Bishop's Bread) . . . . **19**·2396

Biscuit
Baking Powder . . . . **2**·229
Beaten . . . . **2**·183
Buttermilk . . . . **2**·229
Cheese Breakfast . . . . **2**·228
Cheese-Topped . . . . **3**·268
Drop . . . . **7**·804
Onion . . . . **2**·136
Parmesan . . . . **15**·1845
Pecan Tea . . . . **2**·229
Pie, Chicken and . . . . **15**·1819
Pizza Crust . . . . **14**·1695
Ring, Herbed . . . . **9**·1141
Sesame . . . . **16**·2018
Skillet, Beef and . . . . **3**·270
Supreme . . . . **2**·228
Topper, Beef Stew with . . . **17**·2145
Tortoni . . . . **2**·230
Whole Wheat . . . . **2**·228
Bishop's Bread
(Bischofsbrot) . . . . **19**·2396
Bismarcks, Quick . . . . **2**·230
Bite-sized
Chicken Puffs . . . . **18**·2261

Black
Bean Soup . . . . **2**·232
Bottom Pie . . . . **2**·234
Currant Pudding . . . . **6**·716
Forest Cake . . . . **3**·339
Magic Ham Towers . . . . **9**·1118
Magic Luncheon . . . . **13**·1589
Walnut Balls . . . . **19**·2416
Blackberry Sauce . . . . **2**·233
Blancmange . . . . **2**·236

Blender
Bean Soup . . . . **17**·2084
Béarnaise . . . . **2**·183
Broccoli Soup . . . . **17**·2091
Cheese Fondue . . . . **9**·1093
Cucumber Salad . . . . **6**·708

Blender *continued*
Frosting, Choco- . . . . **4**·510
Gazpacho . . . . **17**·2080
Hollandaise . . . . **9**·1148
Mayonnaise . . . . **11**·1363
Potato Pancakes . . . . **2**·240
Pots de crème . . . . **2**·238
Tartar Sauce . . . . **16**·1966
Vichyssoise . . . . **17**·2080
White Sauce . . . . **16**·1965
Blintzes, Israeli Cheese . . . . **2**·241
Blonde Lasagne . . . . **15**·1872
Bloody Mary . . . . **19**·2403

Blueberry
Berry-Cheesecake Pie . . . . **14**·1679
Buckle . . . . **2**·244
Cream Salad . . . . **2**·244
Dumplings . . . . **7**·818
Fluff, Lemon- . . . . **11**·1324
Frosty Fruit Molds . . . . **15**·1920
-Honeydew Cup . . . . **8**·987
Latkes . . . . **10**·1264
-Lemon Muffins . . . . **2**·241
Marmalade . . . . **11**·1357
Muffins . . . . **12**·1442
Pancakes . . . . **13**·1554
Peach-A-Berry
Cobbler . . . . **5**·561
Pie . . . . **2**·244
Pie, Lemon-Crusted . . . . . . **14**·1674
-Rice Bavarian . . . . **15**·1870
Sauce . . . . **2**·244; **6**·755;
13·1553; **20**·2443
Shake . . . . **12**·1417
Shortcake . . . . **2**·244
Steamed Pudding . . . . **6**·755
Strata Pie . . . . **2**·244
Tea Muffins . . . . **3**·275

Blue Cheese
-Bacon Potatoes . . . . **14**·1748
Bites . . . . **2**·247
Broilers, Salmon- . . . . **16**·1954
Burgers . . . . **2**·248
Dip, Bacon- . . . . **13**·1640
Dogs . . . . **2**·248
Dressing . . . . **11**·1363; **20**·2475
Dressing,
Pear Salad with . . . . **13**·1622
Dressing, Western . . . . **16**·1925
Fluff Dressing . . . . **19**·2428
Fruit Cups . . . . **2**·248
-Marinated Onions . . . . **1**·16
Mayonnaise . . . . **16**·1930
Salad Bowl . . . . **2**·247
Salad, Pear- . . . . **13**·1622
Sauce . . . . **16**·1971; **9**·1124
-Sauced Beans . . . . **19**·2385
Sauce, Zippy . . . . **2**·248

Blue Cheese *continued*
Slaw . . . . **5**·592
Sprouts . . . . **3**·302
-Spud Salad . . . . **2**·247
Blue Ribbon Fudge . . . . **8**·999

Boiled
Frosting . . . . **8**·968
Lobster Tails . . . . **11**·1311
Prawns . . . . **14**·1779

Bologna
Baskets . . . . **16**·1985
-Bean Chowder, Thrifty . . . **11**·1289
Burgers, Barbecued . . . . **2**·155
-Noodle Bake . . . . **12**·1468
Bombay Chicken . . . . **12**·1478
Bombe, Brandied . . . . **2**·249
Bombe, Raspberry . . . . **2**·249
Bookbinder's Snapper Soup . **19**·2335
Bordelaise Sauce . . . . **2**·250

Boston
Beanwich . . . . **2**·175
Brown Bread . . . . **2**·250
Cream Pie . . . . **2**·252
Bouillabaisse Soup . . . . **2**·253
Bouillon, Court . . . . **18**·2299
Bouillon Mushrooms . . . . . . **12**·1451
Bouquet Garni . . . . **2**·254
Bourbon Balls . . . . **20**·2467
Braided Coffee Cake . . . . **6**·745
Brains, Deep-Fried . . . . **2**·254
Brains, Scrambled . . . . **19**·2351

Braised
Celery Hearts . . . . **8**·958
Flank Steak . . . . **8**·902
Liver . . . . **11**·1306
Pork Chops . . . . **14**·1736
Short Ribs . . . . **17**·2052
Sirloin Roast . . . . **17**·2061
Veal Chops . . . . **19**·2361
Veal Shoulder Roast . . . . . . **19**·2358
Bran Apricot Squares . . . . **3**·300

Brandied
Bombe . . . . **2**·249
Chocolate, Hot . . . . **3**·260
Pâté Ring . . . . **13**·1588
Peaches . . . . **3**·259

Brandy
Alexander . . . . **3**·259
Balls . . . . **5**·531
Black Currant Pudding . . . . . . **6**·716
Black Walnut Balls . . . . . . **19**·2416
Cherries Jubilee . . . . **4**·468
Cherry-Chocolate Balls . . . . . **3**·260
Chicken Fantasia . . . . **20**·2467

Brandy *continued*
Crepes Suzette ....6·693
Escalopes de Veau
  Flambées .... **19**·2354
Golden Raisin Flambé ......**6**·766
Gourmet Salad ....**5**·588
Hamburger Steak
  Diane .... **20**·2467
Rings ....**3**·260
Singapore Sling ...... **17**·2063
Snaps ....**10**·1244
Snow-Capped Pâté ...... **20**·2466
Warren's Glugg .... **20**·2464
Braunschweiger Glacé ....**1**·70
Braunschweiger Pâté ...... **13**·1588

Brazilian
Chocolate ....**5**·516
Creams ....**3**·261
Float ....**5**·577
Pie ....**6**·760

Brazil Nut
Petals ....**3**·261
Stuffing ....**3**·261

BREAD ....**3**·263-281
(Listed at the end of this entry
*Convenience, Quick, Yeast. See
also Coffee Cake, Pancake,
Popover, Waffle.*)
Bacon Spoon .... **15**·1852
Barbecued ....**2**·159
Caraway Fingers ....**4**·406
Chapati ....**4**·448
Chive and Corn Spoon ......**4**·501
Crumb Pancakes .... **13**·1553
Crumbs ....**6**·702
Crumbs, Buttery ....**6**·702
Easy Onion ....**2**·159
French Toast ....**8**·962
French-Toasted Fondue ......**8**·963
Garlic Croutons ....**6**·699
Grilled Garlic Slices ......**2**·159
Honey Crunch Loaf .... **9**·1152
Melba Toast .... **11**·1391
Milk Toast .... **12**·1417
Onion-Butter Rolls ...... **12**·1508
Onion-Cheese Loaf ....**3**·267
Orange French Toast ....**8**·950
Parmesan Melba Toast ... **11**·1391
Pudding ....**3**·283
Pudding, Cherry ....**6**·725

Bread *continued*
Puris ....**15**·1809
Rolls on a Spit ....**2**·159
Sauce ....**16**·1966
Scallion-Buttered Hard
  Rolls ....**2**·159
Slices, Parslied ....**13**·1572
Spoon ....**17**·2120
Stuffing ....**18**·2183
Toast Cups ....**6**·698
Toasted Croutons ....**6**·699
Toasty Garlic ....**8**·1009

Convenience
Almond Crescent Rolls ......**3**·271
Apple-Raisin Loaves ....**3**·267
Apricot Ladder Loaf ....**1**·101
Bacon-Chive Corn Muffins ...**5**·637
Butterscotch-Pecan Rolls . **10**·1160
Cheese Breakfast Biscuits ...**2**·228
Cheese Crescents ....**4**·464
Cheese-Topped Biscuits .....**3**·268
Cinnamon Crescents ..... **15**·1833
Cinnamon Toast .... **18**·2270
Corn and Corn Muffins ... **12**·1441
Crescent Roll-Ups .... **16**·1942
Croissants Elegante ...... **15**·1883
Crunch Sticks ....**4**·444
Easy-Do Bacon Roll-Ups ....**3**·271
Hawaiian Muffins .... **12**·1415
Herbed Biscuit Ring ...... **9**·1141
Herb Twists .... **15**·1907
Jam Brown-and-Serves ......**3**·266
Old-Time Herb Loaf ....**3**·270
Onion Supper Muffins ... **12**·1442
Orange-Date Nut ....**3**·267
Orange-Nut Ring .... **15**·1820
Orange-Pecan Muffins ... **12**·1520
Parmesan Biscuits .... **15**·1845
Parsley Fantans ....**7**·864
Polka-Dot Muffins .... **12**·1442
Poppy Seed Rolls .... **14**·1721
Pumpkin Nut ....**3**·267
Pumpkin-Raisin Loaves .. **15**·1806
Quick Brioches ....**3**·286
Quick Christmas Braid ... **18**·2200
Quick Raisin Loaf .... **10**·1160
Quick Swedish Rye ...... **15**·1902
Spanish Corn ....**5**·627
Sticks, Easy ....**3**·270
Sticky Buns ....**3**·270
Thyme-Buttered
  Crescents .... **15**·1883
Toasty Rye Curls .... **15**·1902
Waikiki Muffins .... **12**·1441

Quick
Applesauce Puffs .... **15**·1800
Apricot Bran ....**2**·256
Baking Powder Biscuits .....**2**·229

Bread, Quick *continued*
Banana Bran Muffins ...... **9**·1045
Beaten Biscuits ....**2**·183
Best-Ever Muffins .... **12**·1441
Best Nut Loaf ....**3**·275
Biscuits Supreme ....**2**·228
Bishop's, (Bischofsbrot) .. **19**·2396
Blueberry-Lemon Muffins ....**2**·243
Blueberry Muffins .... **12**·1442
Blueberry Tea Muffins ......**3**·275
Boston Brown ....**2**·250
Buttermilk Biscuits ....**2**·229
Cheddar Bran Muffins ......**2**·256
Cheese-Caraway
  Muffins .... **12**·1441
Chocolate-Date Nut ...... **12**·1479
Coffee Cake Muffins ..... **12**·1444
Cranberry-Banana ....**6**·663
Cranberry-Cube Muffins .....**6**·669
Cranberry Nut Loaf ....**6**·663
Cranberry-Orange .... **19**·2419
Cranberry-Orange
  Muffins .... **12**·1443
Date Muffins .... **12**·1441
Double Corn Sticks ....**5**·639
Drop Biscuits ....**7**·804
Egg Muffins, Corn, and ... **12**·1445
English Muffins ....**7**·857
Fruit ....**5**·539
Fruit Rolls ....**3**·369
Ginger Muffins .... **9**·1029
Ginger-Sugar Puffs ...... **15**·1800
Glazed Lemon-Nut ....**3**·275
Golden Pumpkin
  Muffins .... **15**·1806
Graham Gems .... **12**·1444
Harvest .... **12**·1480
Hush Puppies .... **10**·1165
Jelly Muffins .... **12**·1441
Jeweled Banana ....**7**·879
Marble Muffins .... **12**·1442
Marmalade Pan .... **11**·1356
Midget Date Loaves ....**3**·276
Molasses Corn .... **12**·1430
Molasses Corn Muffins ......**5**·637
Nut Muffins .... **12**·1441
Oatmeal-Raisin Muffins .. **12**·1444
Onion Biscuits ....**2**·136
Orange Crunch Muffins .. **11**·1340
Orange-Mince Muffins ... **12**·1445
Orange-Nut .... **12**·1480
Peanut Butter Muffins .... **12**·1443
Pecan Tea Biscuits ....**2**·229
Perfect Corn ....**5**·629
Potato-Corn Triangles ..... **9**·1044
Prune-Nut .... **14**·1792
Pumpernickel .... **15**·1803
Quick Pecan Rolls .... **13**·1631
Raisin Muffins .... **12**·1441
Raisin-Nut .... **15**·1816

Bread, Quick *continued*
Sesame Biscuits .... 16·2018
Sour Milk Muffins .... 12·1442
Spiced Applesauce ...... 16·1933
Strawberry-Rhubarb Rolls 15·1862
Sugar-Crusted Muffins ... 12·1443
Whole Wheat Biscuits ......2·228
Whole Wheat Nut .... 20·2440

Yeast
Airy Cheese Rolls ....4·464
Almond Horns ....1·41
Anadama ....1·46
Basic Fruit Dough ....3·369
Basic Roll Dough .... 15·1879
Batter Rolls ....2·164
Brioche ....3·287
Bunny Rolls ....7·824
Butterhorns ....3·278
Butterscotch Dainties ....2·165
Butterscotch Swirls ....5·640
Caramel-Pecan
  Rolls .... 13·1631; 18·2216
Caramel Rolls .... 15·1882
Cardamom Braid .... 16·2002
Cheese Braid .... 20·2473
Cheese Loaves .... 17·2051
Cherry Puff Rolls ....8·988
Chocolate-Orange
  Rolls .... 16·2017
Cinnamon Crisps .... 18·2216
Cinnamon Nut Whirls ....2·165
Cinnamon Swirl ....3·281
Clothespin Rolls .... 15·1880
Coffeetime Twists .... 15·1881
Cranberry Wagon Wheel
  Rolls ....7·882
Cream of Potato Soup .... 20·2473
Croissants ....6·696
Crusty Water Rolls ....3·281
Dilly Batter .... 10·1267
Dinner Rolls ....2·165
Double Butterscotch
  Crescents .... 15·1881
Dried Fruit .... 8·1023
Fantans ....7·864
Finnish Viipuri Twist ..... 16·2005
French ....8·951
German Stollen .... 17·2152
Glazed Anise Loaf ....1·56
Glazed Orange Rolls ..... 18·2215
Hard Rolls .... 15·1882
Herb ....9·1141
Honey-Nut
  (Christopsoma) .... 9·1066
Hot Cross Buns .... 10·1158
Kolacky .... 10·1240
Lemon Puff Pillow Buns . 18·2217
Light Rye Mixer .... 15·1902
Lucia Braid .... 5·526

Bread, Yeast *continued*
Manna Rolls .... 15·1879
Mexican Holiday .... 19·2420
New Year's
  (Vasilopita) .... 9·1064
No-Knead Oatmeal ...... 12·1491
Orange Crescents ....6·695
Orange Rosettes .... 15·1880
Parker House Rolls ...... 13·1570
Peanut Butter-Jelly
  Twists .... 18·2217
Perfect White ....3·280
Poppy Seed Swirled ..... 14·1721
Potato Rolls .... 14·1749
Raisin Brioche Ring ....8·958
Raisin-Cinnamon
  Rolls .... 15·1882
Raisin Loaves .... 15·1833
Refrigerated Herb
  Rolls .... 20·2473
Refrigerator Rolls .... 15·1879
Saffron .... 15·1906
Shaker Daily Loaf .... 16·2021
Sourdough .... 17·2095
Spring Flower Rolls ....7·822
Sticks ....3·283
Swedish Lucia Buns ....3·306
Swedish Rye .... 11·1298
Sweet Banana .... 20·2473
Syrian .... 12·1458
Three-Flour .... 20·2439
Two-Tone .... 20·2472
Verona, Golden, of ...... 10·1194
Wheat .... 20·2439
Wheaten ....3·281
Whole Wheat Rolls .... 9·1045
Breaded Veal Cutlet Bake .. 19·2361

Breakfast
Cocktail Deluxe .... 13·1561
Cocoa ....5·565
Corn Bread Stacks .... 16·1951
Nog .... 12·1415
Breast of Capon Isabelle ....4·403
Brioche ....3·287

Broccoli
Casserole ....3·293
Casseroles, Tuna- .... 18·2302
-Corn Bake ....3·293
Cream-Sauced .... 19·2384
Foil, in ....3·293
Italienne ....3·291
Mold, Creamy ....3·291
Parmesan ....3·293
Puff ....3·291
Shrimp, with ....3·293
Soufflé ....3·290
Soup, Blender .... 17·2091
Specials ....3·291

Broiled
Bass Steaks .... 16·2013
Beef Filets .... 18·2264
Cornish Game Hens ....5·636
Grapefruit .... 9·1054
Ham Dinner .... 9·1113
Lake Trout ....7·894
Liver .... 11·1306
Lobster Tails .... 11·1311
Luncheon Meat
  Sandwiches .... 11·1331
Party Cake .... 11·1359
Quail .... 15·1810
Salmon Epicurean ...... 15·1891
Scallops .... 16·1989
Tomatoes .... 18·2279
Tuna Burgers .... 18·2304
Venison Steaks .... 8·1004
Broiler Banana Splits ....2·140
Brookside Fried Trout ...... 18·2298

Brown
-Butter Icing ....3·261
-Eyed Susan Cookies ....7·804
Sauce ....3·299
Stock .... 17·2152
Sugar Nut Roll ....3·299
Browned Butter Nuggets ....5·613
Browned Rice .... 15·1867

Brownie
Alaska .... 11·1403
Meringues .... 11·1404
Pudding Cake .... 15·1799
Torte .... 18·2290
Treats ....3·298

Brownies
Apple-Orange ....5·605
Butterscotch ....3·297
Cake ....3·296
Diamond Applesauce ....1·96
Fudge ....3·297
Midnight .... 9·1151
Mint-Frosted ....5·531
Tri-Level ....3·297

Brûlée
Crème ....6·686
Fast Crème ....6·762
Pumpkin Crème ....6·755
Brunch Eggs Ranchero ....7·840
Brunswick Stew .... 12·1493

Brussels Sprouts
Aspic, in ....3·302
Blue Cheesed ....3·302
Dilly ....3·301
Fix-Ups ....3·303
Marinated .... 11·1318

Brussels Sprouts *continued*
Mushrooms, and ....3·302
Polonaise ....3·302
Soufflé ....3·303
Buche de Noel ....8·959
Buckwheat Griddle Cakes ...3·303
Buffet Fruit Bowl ....9·1054
Buffet Fruit Medley ....19·2427
Bulgur Wheat Pilaf ....12·1458
Bull's-Eye Meatballs ....1·77
Bullshot ....19·2403
Bunny Rolls ....7·824
Burger Mountains ....9·1124
Burger Skillet Stew ....4·425

Burgundy
Beef ....3·310
Beefburgers ....9·1125
Beef Stew ....4·411
Chicken Livers and Rice ....4·488
Cornish Hens ....5·636
Glaze ....5·636
Glazed Ham, Cranberry ....3·310
Ham with Green Grapes ...9·1050
Jazzy Hash ....5·631
Meatballs à la ....15·1844
Olive-Spaghetti Sauce ...12·1496
Pie, Cherry- ....10·1178
Punch ....15·1809
Sauce ....16·1968

Burnt-Sugar
Cake ....3·312
Frosting ....3·312
Syrup ....3·312
Busy Bee Chippers ....10·1267
Busy-Day Cake ....15·1826

Butter
Anise-Flavored ....1·58
Apple ....1·91
-Baked Rice ....15·1868
Balls ....3·316
Banana ....3·315
Basil ....8·925
Caper ....3·315
Chive ....4·501
Clarified ....16·1971
Cookies (Kourabiedes) ....9·1066
Cranberry-Orange ....13·1553
Curls ....3·317
Frosting ....8·970
Frosting, Fluffy ....6·711
Garlic ....3·315
Herb ....3·314
Honey ....9·1152
Lemon ....3·315
Orange ....13·1553
Orange-Honey ....3·314
Pecan Cookies ....7·805

Butter *continued*
Roses ....3·315
Sauce ....6·668
Tarragon ....7·894
Whipped ....13·1553
Zippy ....3·315
Butterfly Leg of Lamb ....2·154
Butterfly Pork Chops ....3·319
Butterhorns ....3·278

Buttermilk
Biscuits ....2·229
-Chocolate Cake ....12·1416
Fondue ....18·2223
Pancakes ....3·319
Pie, Apricot- ....3·320
Soup, Cuke- ....3·320
Waffles ....19·2409
White Cake ....3·319
Buttermint Chiffon Pie .....14·1670
Butternut Chocolate Cake ...3·344
Butternut Squash Bake ......3·320

Butterscotch
Bars ....3·322
Brownies ....3·297
Cereal Bars ....15·1800
Cookies ....2·137
Crunch ....12·1416
Dainties ....2·165
Dessert ....10·1190
Dream, Frozen ....15·1797
Drops ....3·322
Filling ....7·878; 15·1881
-Nut Sauce ....10·1180
Oatmeal ....15·1822
-Pecan Rolls ....10·1160
Pie ....14·1673
Pie, Spiced ....6·680
Pudding ....15·1796
Puffs ....3·322
Sauce ....3·322
Sauce, Creamy ....6·768
Spice Cake ....15·1798
Swirls ....5·640
Topping ....5·640
Torte, Jiffy ....3·321
Torte Supreme ......15·1827
Buttery Bread Crumbs ......6·702
Buttery Peanut Brittle ....12·1480

C

Cabbage
Aspic ....11·1321
Bowls ....3·328
Bundles, Corned Beef and ...2·158
Cheese-Sauced ....3·328
Country-Style ....3·327

Cabbage *continued*
Cucumber Slaw ....6·709
Emerald ....3·327
Franks and ....8·936
Leaves, Lamb-Stuffed ....12·1457
Medley, Herbed ....13·1560
Noodles, Hungarian, and .10·1165
Pan-Fried ....3·327
Pennsylvania Red ....3·325
Peppy ....3·328
Roast Duckling with Red ....5·524
Rolls, Frank and ....8·931
Rolls, Saucy ....18·2190
Rolls, Savory ....9·1087
Rolls, Swedish ....3·327
Salad, Austrian ....4·405
Skillet, Crab- ....12·1534
Slaw ....15·1814
Slaw, Panned ....13·1560
Spicy Chops and ......17·2109
Sweet-Sour Red ....8·1022
Caesar Croutons ....3·331

Café
Aruba ....5·576
au Lait ....3·331
au Lait Cheesecake ....1·119
de Belgique ....3·331

CAKE ....3·333-350
(See also *Angel Food Cake, Chiffon
Cake, Cupcake, Fruitcake, Pound
Cake, Sponge Cake*.)
Almond Chocolate ....1·38
Almond Coffee Roll ....3·337
Almond Flip-Top ....1·38
Apple Butter ....1·91
Apple-Raisin ....13·1630
Applesauce ....1·95
Applesauce-Fig Loaf .....7·871
Apricot-Coconut Ring .....5·568
Baba au Orange ....1·125
Baba au Rhum ....1·124
Banana ....8·914
Berry Meringue ....3·345
Best Two-Egg ....3·343
Black Forest ....3·339
Boston Cream Pie ....2·252
Broiled Party ....11·1359
Brownie Pudding ......15·1799
Brownies ....3·296
Buche de Noel ....8·959

Cake *continued*
Burnt-Sugar . . . . 3·312
Busy-Day . . . . 15·1826
Buttermilk-Chocolate . . . . 12·1416
Buttermilk White . . . . 3·319
Butternut Chocolate . . . . 3·344
Butterscotch Spice . . . . . . 15·1798
Cake Mix Pronto Cookies . 16·2016
Calico Crumb . . . . 3·347
Carrot-Pineapple . . . . 4·411
Cherry-Chocolate . . . . 11·1349
Cherry Meringue . . . . 4·473
Choco-Cherry . . . . 3·347
Chocolate Chip . . . . 16·2017
Chocolate Date . . . . 3·350
Chocolate Éclair . . . . 18·2208
Chocolate Fudge . . . . 3·347
Chocolate Layer . . . . 4·509
Chocolate Marble . . . . 11·1307
Citrus Yellow . . . . 3·343
Cocoa Fudge . . . . 5·565
Cocoa Ripple Ring . . . . 5·565
Coconut-Apricot . . . . 1·100
Coconut-Lime . . . . 11·1297
Coconut-Orange . . . . 10·1265
Cranberry Kuchen . . . . 10·1267
Creamy White . . . . 3·342
Crunchy Apricot . . . . 3·350
Date . . . . 6·745
Date-Nut Ring . . . . 10·1222
Date Pudding . . . . 15·1799
Devilicious Cherry . . . . 7·774
Devil's Food . . . . 7·774
Double Mocha . . . . 8·969
Doughnuts . . . . 7·793
Feathery Crumb . . . . 12·1483
Filbert Ice Cream . . . . 7·874
Fudge Pudding . . . . 19·2341
Gingerbread . . . . 9·1030
Gingerbread Layer . . . . 3·344
Ginger-Fruit
    Upside-Down . . . . 19·2342
Ginger-Pear . . . . 9·1030
Gingerscotch . . . . 3·345
Gumdrop-Coffee Squares . . 9·1097
Honey-Pecan . . . . 7·826
Hot Fudge Sundae . . . . . . 18·2208
Jelly Roll . . . . 10·1217
Kabobs . . . . 2·152
Kaffee Kuchen . . . . 10·1241
Kris Kringle . . . . 1·31
Lady Baltimore . . . . 10·1245
Lemon Pudding . . . . 12·1415
Lincoln Log . . . . 10·1217
Linzer . . . . 11·1301
Maraschino Cherry . . . . . . 11·1349
Marble Squares à la Mode . . . 1·28
Midget Jelly Rolls . . . . 10·1218
Mincemeat . . . . 5·532
Mocha Mystery Delight . . 10·1188

Cake *continued*
Mocha-Nut Roll . . . . 12·1427
Mocha Refrigerator . . . . . . 12·1425
Molasses, Bars . . . . 12·1429
Molasses Bundt . . . . 12·1429
Mother's Best Fudge . . . . . . 3·346
Nectarine Quick . . . . 12·1459
Nutmeg . . . . 12·1483
Orange Babas . . . . 1·126
Orange Blossom . . . . 12·1519
Orange Celebration . . . . 2·136
Orange Cream . . . . 7·824
Orange-Rum . . . . 20·2467
Pain d'Épice . . . . 8·955
Peach Kuchen . . . . 10·1241
Peach Preserve . . . . 13·1607
Peachy-Almond Chiffon
    Roll . . . . 10·1218
Peanut Butter and Jelly . . . 13·1614
Peanut Butter Crunch . . . . 13·1615
Peanut Butter-Peach . . . . . 18·2201
Pears Helene . . . . 13·1625
Petits Fours . . . . 13·1653
Pineapple Crunch . . . . 5·571
Pineapple Parfait . . . . 10·1178
Pineapple Pudding . . . . . . 10·1190
Pineapple Upside-Down . . 14·1691
Pink and White Marble . . . 15·1824
Pink Cloud . . . . 17·2168
Pink Lemonade . . . . 3·345
Plymouth Cranberry . . . . . . 6·668
Prize Chocolate . . . . 2·137
Prune Spice . . . . 14·1792
Pumpkin Spice . . . . 3·350
Pumpkin, with Honey
    Cream . . . . 19·2421
Quick Upside-Down . . . . 19·2342
Raspberry Bavarian . . . . . . 17·2063
Red Devil's Food . . . . 7·774
Regal Almond . . . . 1·37
Rhubaba . . . . 18·2198
Rhubarb . . . . 15·1863
Rhubarb Upside-Down . . . 19·2341
Ribbon . . . . 15·1863
Rose Geranium . . . . 15·1889
Sacher Torte . . . . 15·1905
Scripture . . . . 16·2012
Sesame . . . . 16·2019
Snow-Capped Lemon
    Roll . . . . 10·1219
Sour Cream-Choco . . . . . . 17·2094
Spiced Chocolate . . . . 2·137
Spice-Nut . . . . 17·2111
Spicy Prune . . . . 17·2111
Starlight . . . . 18·2261
Strawberry Crunch . . . . . . 17·2163
Strawberry-Meringue . . . . . . 6·756
Strawberry, Roll . . . . 17·2169
Sweet Chocolate . . . . 4·510
Tiny Pineapple-Orange . . . 19·2342

Cake *continued*
Tiny Pineapple
    Upside-Down . . . . 14·1691
Toasted Butter Pecan . . . . 12·1476
Upside-Down Apple . . . . 3·345
Vanilla-Sour Cream . . . . . . 19·2346
Vanilla Wafer Coconut . . . . . 3·350
Velvety Fudge . . . . 4·509
Walnut Cream Roll . . . . 7·878
Walnut (Karidopita) . . . . . . 9·1064
Washington Pie . . . . 19·2423
White, Supreme . . . . 3·342
Yellow . . . . 3·342
Yellow, Deluxe . . . . 3·342

Calico
Bean Bake . . . . 2·174
Chicken . . . . 14·1683
Crumb Cake . . . . 3·347
Potato Salad . . . . 14·1753
Rice Salad . . . . 15·1869
Vegetable Bowl . . . . 14·1682
Vegetable Molds . . . . 19·2382

California
Curry Platter . . . . 12·1503
Marinade . . . . 10·1225
Potato Bake . . . . 18·2212
Camembert-Apple Sandwich . . 3·360
Camembert, French-Fried . . . 8·954
Cameo Cutouts . . . . 15·1885
Campfire Pot Roast . . . . 1·43
Campfire Spaghetti . . . . 3·363
Campsite Stew . . . . 3·363

Canadian
Bacon-Bean Bake . . . . 3·365
Bacon Stack-Ups . . . . 1·127
Pork Pie (Tourtière) . . . . 3·364

Canapé
Asparagus Fold-Overs . . . . . . 1·64
Bull's-Eye Meatballs . . . . 1·77
Cheese and Sausage Rolls . . . 1·75
Chicken Liver Boats . . . . 1·77
Crab Meat-Bacon Rounds . . . 3·366
Dried Beef . . . . 3·367
Ham and Rye Rounds . . . . . . 3·366
Ham Chippers . . . . 3·367
Hot Steak . . . . 3·366
Kabob . . . . 3·366
Lobster . . . . 3·367
Smoked Eel . . . . 17·2067
Swiss Sandwich Puffs . . . . . 3·367
Can-Can Borsch . . . . 2·204

Candied
Beets . . . . 3·371
Carrots . . . . 3·371
Ginger Sauce . . . . 6·767

Candied *continued*
Grapefruit Peel ....3·370
Orange Peel ....3·371
Popcorn ....14·1716
Sweet Potatoes ....18·2212
Tangerine Peel ....18·2245
Walnuts ....19·2416
Candlestick Bars ....5·605

CANDY ....3·372-384
(See also *Divinity, Fondant, Fudge.*)
Almond Butter Crunch ....1·38
Almond Caramels ....18·2199
Angel Sweets ....3·382
Brown Sugar Nut Roll ......3·299
Buttery Peanut Brittle ....12·1480
Candied Walnuts ....19·2416
Caramel Chocolate Clusters ..3·382
Caramel Crunch ....3·380
Caramels ....4·404
Caramel Snappers ....3·383
Chocolate Cherries ....4·512
Chocolate Peanut Pillows ....3·382
Chocolate Truffles ....8·956
Coconut Penuche ....3·379
Coffee Caramels ....3·381
Coffee Walnuts ....19·2416
Confection Bars ....3·383
Creamy Pralines ....14·1779
Crystal-Cut ....3·381
Dewdrops ....3·383
Easy Caramels ....3·381
Fondant Stuffed Dates ....19·2344
Glazed Almonds ....9·1035
Holiday Mints ....12·1420
Jewel ....1·58
Lollipop Clowns ....3·380
Mint Swirls ....3·383
Mint Wafers ....6·678
Molasses Taffy ....5·529
Nougat ....12·1469
Orange Coconut Brittle ......3·380
Peanut Brittle ....5·529
Peanut-Cereal ....13·1613
Peanut Clusters ....3·382
Pecan Log ....13·1631
Pecan Pralines ....15·1852
Penuche ....13·1636
Pralines ....14·1779
Quick Almond Brittle ....3·380
RaisinPraline Caramels ......3·381
Saltwater Taffy ....18·2241

Candy *continued*
Sea Foam ....16·2013
Sesame-Honey ....9·1127
Small Mints ....3·376
Stuffed Dates ....6·742
Tiny Red Mints ....8·907
Vanilla Taffy ....15·1802
Walnut-Covered
Chocolates ....19·2416
Caneton à l'Orange
(Duckling with Orange
Sauce) ....8·956
Canned Blackberry Pie ....2·233
Cannelloni ....10·1194
Cannelloni Filling ....10·1195
Cannelloni Noodles ....10·1195

CANNING ....4·387-398

Cantaloupe
à la Mode ....1·29
Chicken-Melon Mousse ..12·1437
Conserve, Peach- ....13·1602
Crown ....11·1397
Especiale ....8·987
Mist ....4·400
Pie, Seafoam ....4·401
Stars ....4·401
Supreme ....8·987
Tuna-Melon Dinner Salad ...4·400
Zigzag Bowl ....8·1013
Cantonese Duck ....7·813
Cantonese Turkey Casserole 19·2320

Caper
Burgers ....4·401
Butter ....3·315
Mayonnaise ....4·402
Sandwich, Shrimp-.........6·735
Sauce, Salmon Balls in ..16·1940
Cappuccino ....4·403

Caramel
Apples ....1·85
-Apple Whirls ....15·1844
Cakewiches ....4·404
Candy Frosting ....8·971
Caramels ....4·404
Chews ....5·613
Chocolate Clusters ....3·382
Coffee Ring ....3·268
Cookies, Unbaked ....15·1798
-Cream Cheese Frosting .....5·596

Caramel *continued*
Crunch ....3·380
Custard Cups ....6·724
Custard Pie ....6·723
Fudge ....3·378
Nuts ....12·1477
-Pecan Ice Cream ....10·1171
-Pecan Rolls ....13·1631; 18·2216
Popcorn Balls ....14·1716
-Raisin Sauce ....5·579
Rolls ....15·1882
Snappers ....3·383

Caraway
Chicken Halves ....4·406
Cookies ....4·405
Fingers ....4·406
Green Beans ....2·179
Skillet Slaw ....5·591
Cardamom Braid ....16·2002
Cardamom Cookies ....4·407
Carousel Salad ....13·1580

Carrot
-Apple-Ham Bake ....1·86
Bake, Golden ....4·412
Basil ....2·163
Candied ....3·371
-Cheese Pudding ....15·1795
Coins, Basil- ....11·1321
Corkscrews ....8·1012
Glazed ....4·413
Herbed ....2·178
Honey-Glazed ....9·1151
Lyonnaise ....4·413
Minted ....4·411
-Olive Slaw ....15·1857
Parslied ....4·412
Pickled ....1·14
-Pineapple Cake ....4·411
Skillet ....4·412
Sticks, Spicy ....4·412
Summertime ....4·413
Sunshine ....12·1521
Supreme ....4·412
Sweet Pickled ....13·1661
Veal and ....13·1636
Cashew Drops, Frosted ......4·419
Cashews, Snapper with .....15·1843

CASSEROLE ....4·421-429
Main Dish
à la King ....3·290
Bacon and Liver Bake ....11·1307
Baked Turkey Fondue ....19·2317
Barbecued Bean Bake ....2·174
Barbecued Veal with Rice 19·2364
Beef and Macaroni ......13·1579
Beef and Noodle Bake ......7·800
Beef and Noodles ....14·1683

Casserole, Main Dish *continued*
Beef Potpie . . . . **11**·1390
Beef Stew Bake . . . . **17**·2145
Best Oven Hash . . . . **9**·1130
Blonde Lasagne . . . . **15**·1872
Bologna-Noodle Bake . . . **12**·1468
California Curry Platter . . . **12**·1503
Canadian Bacon-Bean
    Bake . . . . **3**·365
Cannelloni . . . . **10**·1194
Cantonese Turkey . . . . **19**·2320
Carrot-Apple-Ham Bake . . . . . **1**·86
Cassola de Peix . . . . **16**·2034
Cauliflower-Ham Bake . . . . **9**·1116
Cheddar-Macaroni
    Bake . . . . **11**·1336

Cheeseburger-Vegetable . . **12**·1411
Cheese-Filled Manicotti . . **15**·1872
Cheese-Fondue Bake . . . . **8**·923
Cheese-Noodle . . . . **14**·1736
Cheese Ramekins . . . . **4**·462
Cheese-Rice Squares . . . . . **14**·1787
Chicken and Spinach-
    Filled Ravioli . . . . **15**·1840
Chicken Chip Bake . . . . **4**·486
Chicken Chow Bake . . . . **4**·427
Chicken-Dressing Bake . . **18**·2180
Chicken in . . . . **8**·1021
Chicken Livers and Rice . . . . **4**·488
Chicken-Noodle Bake . . . **13**·1581
Chicken Parisienne . . . . **4**·482
Chicken Pilaf . . . . **14**·1682
Chicken Potpie . . . . **14**·1758
Chicken Strata . . . . **17**·2155
Chicken-Vegetable Bake . . **9**·1143
Chipped Beef Puff . . . . **7**·799
Chopstick Tuna . . . . **12**·1478
Chopstick Veal Bake . . . . **4**·424
Clam Chowder . . . . **14**·1759
Clam-Mushroom Bake . . . . . **5**·554
Classic Cheese Strata . . . . **12**·1415
Classic Chicken Divan . . . . . . **7**·782
Club Chicken . . . . **4**·486
Company Strata . . . . **17**·2154
Company Tuna Bake . . . . . **18**·2304
Corn and Chicken
    Scallop . . . . **16**·1992
Corned Beef and Noodles . . **5**·631
Corned Beef Bake . . . . **5**·633
Corned Beef Pie . . . . **5**·633
Corned Beef Squares with
    Dill Sauce . . . . **7**·778

Casserole, Main Dish *continued*
Corn-Oyster Scallop . . . . . **13**·1545
Cottage Enchiladas . . . . . . **11**·1407
Crab-Mushroom
    Mornay . . . . **12**·1450
Crab-Shrimp Bake . . . . **16**·2036
Crab Supper Pie . . . . **6**·650
Creamy Chicken . . . . **13**·1581
Creamy Chicken and Rice . . . . **1**·37
Creamy Macaroni and
    Cheese Bake . . . . **4**·462
Creole Sausage-Bean
    Bake . . . . **10**·1233
Deviled Corn and Crab . . . . . **5**·622
Deviled Crab Meat
    Imperial . . . . **6**·652
Deviled Ham-Bean Bake . . . . **7**·772
Dilled Cheese . . . . **6**·643
Double Shrimp . . . . **12**·1468
Easy Chicken Divan . . . . **7**·782
Easy Lasagne . . . . **10**·1263
Easy Turkey Paella . . . . **19**·2318
Eggs au Gratin . . . . **9**·1059
Eggs in Spanish Sauce . . . . . . **2**·167
Enchilada . . . . **15**·1825
Frank and Corn Crown . . . . . **8**·933
Frank and Potato Bake . . . . . **8**·932
Franks and Cabbage . . . . **8**·936
Franks Florentine . . . . **8**·910
Frank-Vegetable Medley . . . **8**·935
Ginger-Peachy . . . . **13**·1605
Haddock-Shrimp Bake . . . . **9**·1099
Ham and Mac Bake . . . . . . **13**·1581
Ham and Potatoes
    au Gratin . . . . **1**·117
Ham and Potato
    Scallop . . . . **9**·1114
Ham and Rice . . . . **9**·1044
Ham and Turkey Divan . . **19**·2316
Ham and Vegetable
    Strata . . . . **17**·2155
Hamburger-Cheese
    Bake . . . . **12**·1466
Hamburger-Corn Bake . . . **14**·1683
Hamburger-Noodle Bake . **15**·1813
Ham in Cheese Crust . . . . **6**·657
Ham Medley . . . . **4**·427
Ham Succotash . . . . **5**·624
Hearty Baked Beans . . . . **2**·172
Hot Egg Salad Deluxe . . . . . . **7**·840
Inside-Out Ravioli . . . . **15**·1840
Jazzy Hash . . . . **5**·631
Jiffy Chili-Hominy Bake . . . **9**·1149
Lamb-Eggplant . . . . **9**·1143
Lasagne . . . . **10**·1263
Lazy-Day Lasagne . . . . **10**·1263
Lobster en Coquille . . . . . . **11**·1312
Lobster Tails Maison . . . . . **11**·1313
Lobster Thermidor Bake . . **11**·1312
Luncheon Meat Dinner . . . **15**·1826

Casserole, Main Dish *continued*
Macaroni and Cheese . . . . **11**·1335
Macaroni and Cheese
    (quantity) . . . . **15**·1813
Marmalade Ham
    Squares . . . . **11**·1356
Meat and Macaroni
    Supper . . . . **18**·2269
Meatball . . . . **15**·1871
Mexicali . . . . **11**·1408
Mexican Enchiladas . . . . . **11**·1408
Mexican-Style . . . . **5**·629
Mexican-Style Hash . . . . **5**·623
Minestrone Bake . . . . **14**·1738
Mock Lasagne . . . . **6**·643
Moussaka . . . . **12**·1436
Oven-Style Turkey Hash . . . . **6**·658
Oyster Pudding . . . . **13**·1545
Peachy Corned Beef . . . . . **13**·1605
Peppy Lasagne . . . . **15**·1872
Pork Chop Oven Dinner . . . . **2**·166
Pork Chop Risotto Bake . . . **9**·1143
Quick Frank-Kraut
    Dinner . . . . **16**·1975
Rancho Bean . . . . **2**·172
Salmagundi Bake . . . . **16**·1934
Salmon . . . . **16**·1941
Salmon and Potato
    Chip . . . . **16**·1940
Salmon Florentine . . . . **8**·910
Salmon or Tuna Pie . . . . **7**·892
Salmon Scallop . . . . **6**·656
Salmon Tetrazzini . . . . **16**·1941
San Francisco Eggs and
    Spinach . . . . **9**·1074
Sausage and
    Mostaccioli . . . . **12**·1434
Sausage and Muffin
    Bake . . . . **14**·1738
Sausage au Gratin . . . . **14**·1751
Sausage Macaroni and
    Cheese . . . . **11**·1336
Sausage-Muffin Bake . . . . **5**·637
Sausage-Squash
    Special . . . . **12**·1523
Sausage Strata . . . . **17**·2154
Savory Frank-Noodle
    Bake . . . . **8**·934
Scalloped Corn and
    Oysters . . . . **16**·1992
Scallops Elegant . . . . **16**·1991
Scallops Mornay . . . . **16**·1990
Scallops Tetrazzini . . . . **16**·1991
Seafood Bake . . . . **16**·2034
Seafood Divan . . . . **11**·1324
Shortcut Lasagne . . . . **10**·1263
Shrimp à la King . . . . **17**·2057
Shrimp à la Rockefeller . . . **17**·2116
Shrimp de Jonghe . . . . **17**·2056
Six-Layer Dinner . . . . **15**·1853

Casserole, Main Dish *continued*

Smoked Salmon and
Macaroni .... **17**·2066
Smoked Salmon Bake .... **8**·905
Spanish Rice .... **15**·1813
Speedy Corn Bread Pie ...... **5**·627
Spinach-Fish Bake .... **7**·889
Steak and Bean Pot ...... **12**·1423
Swiss and Crab Pie .... **6**·727
Swiss Cheese-Egg
Bake .... **18**·2222
Swiss Pie .... **18**·2222
Swiss Turkey-Ham
Bake .... **14**·1776
Tangiers Hash .... **9**·1130
Three-Bean Frank Bake ...... **2**·175
Tostada .... **11**·1407
Triple Seafood Bake .... **4**·427
Tufoli Stuffed with Veal ..... **2**·167
Tuna and Croutons ...... **18**·2302
Tuna-Broccoli .... **18**·2302
Tuna-Cheese Strata ...... **17**·2155
Tuna Italian .... **7**·890
Tuna Jackstraw Bake ..... **16**·2045
Tuna-Noodle .... **17**·2064
Tuna Supper Dish .... **18**·2303
Tuna-Vegetable Pie .... **4**·426
Turkey-Cheese Puff ...... **19**·2317
Turkey Crepe .... **19**·2316
Turkey-Ham .... **16**·2043
Turkey-Noodle Bake ..... **14**·1767
Turkey Parisian .... **3**·290
Turkey-Rice Bake .... **19**·2323
Turkey-Rice Squares ..... **19**·2318
Turkey-Roni .... **19**·2316
Turkey-Spaghetti Bake ... **19**·2316
Turkey-Taco Bake .... **19**·2317
Turkey Tetrazzini .... **18**·2265
Turkey Timbales .... **15**·1890
Vegetable-Meat Medley ... **9**·1069
Wiener-Bean Bake .... **2**·175
Wiener Bean Pot .... **8**·936
Wienie-Lottas .... **10**·1189
Wild Rice-Turkey Dish ... **19**·2318
Yankee Bacon Bake .... **5**·637

Vegetable
Ambrosia Potato Bake .... **5**·547
Apple and Onion
Bake .... **12**·1509
Apple Bean Bake .... **2**·172
Apricot-Sweet
Potatoes .... **18**·2213
Asparagus .... **1**·113
Bean Pot Limas .... **11**·1289
Broccoli .... **3**·293
Broccoli-Corn Bake .... **3**·293
Broccoli Puff .... **3**·291
Butternut Squash
Bake .... **3**·320

Casserole, Vegetable *continued*

Calico Bean Bake .... **2**·174
California Potato Bake ... **18**·2212
Candied Sweet
Potatoes .... **18**·2212
Carrot-Cheese
Pudding .... **15**·1795
Cauliflower Scallop .... **4**·434
Cheese-Corn Strata ...... **17**·2155
Cheesy Lima .... **11**·1289
Company Cauliflower ...... **4**·434
Company Squash
Bake .... **18**·2204
Corn and Potato Scallop ..... **4**·428
Corn-Custard .... **6**·727
Corn Pudding .... **5**·638
Creamy Celery Bake .... **4**·438
Creamy Hashed Brown
Bake .... **14**·1757
Creamy Potato Bake ..... **14**·1756
Creole Onions .... **12**·1508
Deluxe Limas .... **11**·1289
Double Potato Bake ..... **14**·1757
Easy Baked Beans .... **2**·172
Eggplant Crunch .... **7**·849
Épinards à la Crème
(Creamed Spinach) .... **17**·2116
Extra-Special Parsnips .... **13**·1573
Festive Celery .... **4**·428
Fruit-Candied Sweet
Potatoes .... **18**·2214
Golden Carrot Bake .... **4**·412
Golden Potato Bake ..... **14**·1757
Herbed Spinach Bake ...... **6**·727
Indian Corn .... **5**·623
Lima-Cheese Bake .... **4**·428
Maple Baked Beans .... **2**·173
Maple-Flavored Sweets ... **18**·2213
Mushroom .... **6**·659
New England Baked
Beans .... **2**·171
Onion Pie .... **6**·727
Oven Peas .... **13**·1595
Parslied Carrots .... **4**·412
Polynesian Yam .... **14**·1689
Potato-Cheese Custard ...... **6**·726
Potato Puff .... **15**·1799
Potluck Bean Bake .... **2**·172
Quick Corn Pudding ...... **5**·638
Saucy Zucchini .... **17**·2132
Savory Succotash .... **18**·2193
Scalloped Corn
Supreme .... **16**·1992
Scalloped Potato Bake ... **14**·1748
Scalloped Potatoes ...... **16**·1992
Scalloped Vegetables .... **19**·2382
Shaker Baked Beans ..... **16**·2021
Spiced Turban
Squash .... **18**·2304
Spinach-Carrot Custard .. **17**·2116

Casserole, Vegetable *continued*

Spinach Delight .... **17**·2116
Spinach Elegante .... **17**·2116
Spinach-Potato
Bake .... **17**·2115
Spinach Supreme .... **17**·2115
Sweet Potato-Date
Bake .... **18**·2214
Sweet Potato
Fantasia .... **18**·2213
Swiss Corn Bake .... **5**·626
Swiss Onion Bake .... **12**·1511
Tomato .... **18**·2279
Tomato Zucchini
Scallop .... **4**·428
Turnips with Cheese ..... **19**·2332
Vegetables au Gratin .... **19**·2382
Whipped Turnip Puff .... **19**·2331
Zucchini Florentine ...... **17**·2132
Zucchini Supreme .... **17**·2133
Cassola de Peix .... **16**·2034
Catsup, Best Tomato .... **4**·430

Cauliflower
Cheese Frosted .... **4**·434
Company .... **4**·434
Dilly Shrimp, and .... **4**·434
-Ham Bake .... **9**·1116
-Ham Salad .... **4**·432
Italiano .... **19**·2387
Salad, Tangy .... **4**·432
Scallop .... **4**·434
Shrimp Sauce, with .... **4**·434
Soup, Creamy .... **4**·432
Vinaigrette .... **4**·432
Caviar Appetizers .... **4**·435
Caviar-Stuffed Eggs .... **4**·436
Céleri au Jus (Braised Celery
Hearts) .... **8**·958

Celery
Aspic, Tomato- .... **1**·116
Bake, Creamy .... **4**·438
Casserole, Festive .... **4**·428
Cran-Relish .... **6**·662
Fans .... **4**·438
Hearts, Braised .... **8**·958
Luxe Peas and .... **13**·1595
Oriental .... **4**·438
Root, Marinated .... **4**·436
Root Sauté .... **4**·437
Seed Dressing .... **16**·1928
Slaw .... **4**·438
Soup, Cream of .... **4**·439
Stuffing, Speedy .... **4**·439

Cereal
Bars, Butterscotch .... **15**·1800
Candy, Peanut- .... **13**·1613
Cerealsnaps .... **4**·432

Cereal *continued*

Hot Whole Wheat and
Honey Butter . . . . **4·**442
Parfaits, Berry- . . . . **4·**443
-Peanut Bars . . . . **5·**605
Scramble . . . . **4·**443
Spicy Raisin Oatmeal . . . . . . **4·**442
Champagne Cocktail,
Orange . . . . **4·**448
Champignons Sautés (Fresh
Mushroom Sauté) . . . . **8·**956
Chapati . . . . **4·**448
Charcoaled Salmon Steaks . . . . . **7·**895

Charlotte Russe
Chocolate . . . . **4·**450
Classic Chocolate . . . . . . **10·**1246
Strawberry . . . . **8·**1019
Châteaubriand . . . . **4·**452
Chaud-Froid of Turkey . . . . **4·**452
Checkerboards . . . . **16·**1957

Cheddar
Bran Muffins . . . . **2·**256
Cheese Sauce . . . . **13·**1571;
17·2075; **19·**2318
-Macaroni Bake . . . . **11·**1336
-Squash Bake . . . . **19·**2385

CHEESE . . . . **4·**455-464
Appetizers, Snappy . . . . **1·**73
Apples . . . . **8·**1013
Asparagus with . . . . **19·**2387
Bake, Creamy Apple- . . . . **1·**93
Bake, Creamy Macaroni
and . . . . **4·**462
Bake, Hamburger- . . . . **12·**1466
Bake, Lima- . . . . **4·**428
Ball, Olive- . . . . **17·**2121
Beef Burgers, and . . . . **9·**1084
Blintzes, Israeli . . . . **2·**241
Braid . . . . **20·**2473
Breakfast Biscuits . . . . **2·**228
-Broiled Eggplant . . . . **12·**1438
-Caraway Muffins . . . . **12·**1441
Casserole, Dilled . . . . **6·**643
Chowder . . . . **5·**520
-Coated Perch, Saucy . . . . **13·**1649
-Corn Strata . . . . **17·**2155
Crab Dip, Hot, and . . . . **7·**781
Crescents . . . . **4·**464
Crunch Sandwich, Ham- . . **9·**1114
Cups, Macaroni- . . . . **11·**1364

Cheese *continued*

Custard, Potato- . . . . **6·**726
Dessert Pizza, Cherry- . . . . . . **6·**676
Dip, Clam- . . . . **2·**247
Dip, Party . . . . **11·**1318
Dip with Fruit, Hot . . . . **1·**77
Dressing, Banana- . . . . **16·**1926
Dressing, Chef's . . . . **16·**1926
Dumplings, Peach- . . . . **7·**819
Dunk, Easy . . . . **4·**446
Enchiladas . . . . **7·**852
-Filled Chocolate
Cupcakes . . . . **6·**712
-Filled Manicotti . . . . **15·**1872
-Filled Meat Loaf . . . . **12·**1439
Filling . . . . **1·**76
Fluff . . . . **1·**66
Fluffy Cream Sauce . . . . . . **19·**2406
-Fondue Bake . . . . **8·**923
Fondue, Blender . . . . **9·**1093
Fondue, Classic . . . . **8·**925
Fondue,
Monterey (or Jack) . . . . . **12·**1432
Fondue, Rarebit-Style . . . . **12·**1484
Fondue, Rosy . . . . **4·**462
Fondue, Shrimp- . . . . **17·**2058
Franks, Chili- . . . . **8·**933
Frosted Cauliflower . . . . **4·**434
Frosties, Cran- . . . . **6·**667
-Fruit Relish . . . . **6·**644
Golden Velvet Rarebit . . . **19·**2432
Loaf, Onion- . . . . **3·**267
Loaves . . . . **17·**2051
Log, Chili . . . . **4·**496
Macaroni and . . . . **11·**1335
Macaroni and (quantity) . . **15·**1813
-Marinated Onions . . . . **1·**16
Mexican Rarebit . . . . **19·**2432
Mold, Chili- . . . . **4·**496
Mold, Frosted . . . . **2·**247
Mold, Three- . . . . **4·**464
Mousse, Appetizer . . . . **1·**70
-Noodle Casserole . . . . **14·**1736
-Nut Mold . . . . **14·**1694
Parfaits, Pineapple- . . . . **6·**725
Pastries, French . . . . **8·**958
Pastries (Tyropitakia) . . . . . . **9·**1064
Pastry Crisps . . . . **1·**17
Patties, Bean and . . . . **15·**1841
Paul Revere
Cheesewiches . . . . **16·**1954
Pie, Chocolate . . . . **5·**515
Pie, Citrus . . . . **14·**1674
Pie, Cranberry . . . . **6·**669
Pie, Pear-Pineapple- . . . . . **13·**1625
Pie, Spicy Pumpkin- . . . . . **14·**1672
Pie, Strawberry- . . . . **17·**2164
Pizza . . . . **14·**1698
Pizza, Mushroom- . . . . **14·**1698
Pudding, Carrot- . . . . **15·**1795

Cheese *continued*

Puff, Macaroni- . . . . **4·**427
Puff, Turkey- . . . . **19·**2317
Quiche Lorraine . . . . **15·**1816
Rarebit, Double . . . . **19·**2431
Rarebit, Quick . . . . **19·**2432
Ramekins . . . . **4·**462
-Rice Squares . . . . **14·**1787
Rolls, Airy . . . . **4·**464
Rolls, Toasted . . . . **4·**464
Salad, Pineapple- . . . . **7·**826
Salad, Rice, Ham, and . . . **14·**1787
Salad, Salami- . . . . **16·**1933
Sandwiches,
Mexican-Style . . . . **18·**2291
Sandwich, Sardine and . . . **16·**1961
Sandwich, Turkey- . . . . . . **11·**1319
Sauce . . . . **1·**113; **3·**328; **4·**461
Sauce, Asparagus with
Two- . . . . **7·**863
-Sauced Cabbage . . . . **3·**328
-Sauced Striped Bass . . . . . **17·**2172
-Sauced Zucchini
Fritters . . . . **17·**2132
Sauce, Fish in . . . . **7·**893
Sauce, Jiffy . . . . **4·**461
Sauce, Potatoes with
Chef's . . . . **8·**919
Sausage Macaroni and . . . **11·**1336
Sausage Rolls, and . . . . **1·**75
-Scalloped Onions . . . . . . **12·**1509
Scrambled Eggs . . . . **7·**834
Snacks, Olive- . . . . **12·**1496
Soufflé . . . . **4·**462
Soufflé, Easy . . . . **17·**2075
Soufflé, Fluffy . . . . **7·**843
Soufflé, Tapioca- . . . . **18·**2247
Soup, Asparagus- . . . . **10·**1160
Soup, Chilled Tomato- . . . . . **6·**645
Soup, Golden . . . . **17·**2088
Soup, Onion- . . . . **8·**914
Spread, Crab and . . . . **17·**2121
Spread, Smoky Ham and . . . . . **1·**71
Squares, Cran- . . . . **17·**2110
Squares, Grapefruit- . . . . . . **9·**1056
Stacks, Eggplant- . . . . **7·**848
Strata, Classic . . . . **12·**1415
Strata, Tuna- . . . . **17·**2155
Straws, Peanut- . . . . **4·**468
-Stuffed Apples . . . . **1·**85
-Stuffed Mushrooms . . . . **5·**558
Tart Shells . . . . **18·**2253
Tarts, Strawberry- . . . . **18·**2252
-Topped Biscuits . . . . **3·**268
-Topped Pears . . . . **20·**2476
-Topped Tomatoes . . . . **4·**464
Topper . . . . **19·**2317
Turnips with . . . . **19·**2332
Turnovers, Shrimp- . . . . **6·**675
Waffles . . . . **11·**1314

Cheese *continued*
Waffles, Lobster- .... **11**·1314
Welsh Rabbit .... **19**·2431
Western Welsh Rarebit ... **19**·2432

Cheeseburger
Chowder .... **17**·2084
Pie .... **20**·2469
Towers .... **9**·1123
-Vegetable Casserole .... **12**·1411

Cheesecake
Angel .... **4**·465
Café au Lait .... **1**·119
Chilled Banana .... **15**·1847
Chocolate Malted .... **11**·1341
Company .... **6**·765
Fruited .... **9**·1041
Lemon .... **6**·644
Marble .... **6**·675
Pie, Berry .... **14**·1670
Pie, Speedy .... **4**·465
Strawberry-Glazed .... **4**·467
Strawberry-Rhubarb ..... **17**·2123
Supreme .... **4**·467

Cheesy
-Asparagus Soup .... **17**·2088
Corned Beef
    Sandwiches .... **13**·1662
Lima Casserole .... **11**·1289
Stuffed Burgers .... **9**·1090
Tongue on Rice .... **18**·2286
Chef's Cheese Dressing .... **16**·1926
Chef's Rice Salad .... **11**·1364

Cherries
Chocolate .... **4**·512
Jubilee .... **4**·468
Portofino .... **6**·765

Cherry
-Almond Balls .... **5**·531
-Angel Dessert .... **15**·1845
Angel Roll .... **1**·53
Bake, Peach-Cot .... **8**·991
Bavarian .... **4**·472
-Berry Compote .... **5**·595
Bread Pudding .... **6**·725
-Burgundy Pie .... **10**·1178
Cake, Choco- .... **3**·347
Cake, Devilicious .... **7**·774
Cake, Maraschino .... **11**·1349
-Cheese Dessert
    Pizza .... **6**·676
-Chocolate Balls .... **3**·260
-Chocolate Cake .... **11**·1349
-Chocolate Pie .... **14**·1679
Cookie Crisp .... **6**·756
-Cream Cheese Pie ...... **10**·1190

Cherry *continued*
-Cream Dressing .... **6**·675
-Cream Parfaits, Quick ... **13**·1568
Cream Pie .... **6**·681
Cream Puffs .... **7**·837
-Creme Parfaits .... **13**·1567
Dessert Salad .... **4**·472
Divinity .... **3**·379
Filling .... **3**·339; **4**·570; **7**·882
Fluff Divinity .... **7**·785
Fruitcake, Chip- .... **16**·2017
Ice Cream .... **11**·1350
Lattice Coffee Cake .... **7**·882
Melange .... **6**·754
Meringue Cake .... **4**·473
Nibbles, Snowcap .... **2**·224
Parfaits .... **4**·473
-Peach Pie .... **8**·906
Pie, Creamy .... **4**·474
Pie, Fresh .... **4**·475
Pie, Red .... **4**·474
Puff Rolls .... **8**·988
Refrigerator Cookies .... **5**·609
-Rhubarb Pie .... **14**·1676
Ring, Molded .... **4**·473
Salad Supreme .... **11**·1364
Sauce .... **6**·767; **16**·1973
Sauce, Apricot- .... **10**·1180
-Sauced Ham Balls ...... **11**·1382
-Sauced Pancakes .... **13**·1558
-Sauced Pork Loin ...... **14**·1782
Sauce, Ham with .... **14**·1679
Sauce, Spicy .... **16**·1970
Shortcake Towers .... **4**·473
Soup .... **17**·2091
Sparkle .... **2**·222
Sparkle, Peach- .... **13**·1603
-Strawberry Jam .... **17**·2161
Sundae Sauce .... **16**·1972
Tarts .... **14**·1675
Topper .... **19**·2406
Topping .... **4**·473
Torte, Black Forest-
    Style .... **8**·1023
Torte, Chocolate- .... **18**·2288
Torte, Forgotten .... **18**·2287
Chess Pie .... **4**·475
Chestnut Stuffing .... **18**·2183

CHICKEN .... **4**·477-487
à la France .... **14**·1777
à la King, Fancy .... **1**·26
à la King, Quick .... **1**·26

Chicken *continued*
Almond .... **2**·138
Aloha .... **13**·1642
Bake, Herbed .... **16**·1987
Barbecued .... **4**·481
Basic Broiled .... **4**·481
Biscuit Pie, and .... **15**·1819
Bombay .... **12**·1478
Breast of Capon Isabelle .....**4**·403
Breasts à la Vegetables ......**4**·499
Breasts, Curried .... **11**·1320
Breasts, Fruited .... **9**·1050
Breasts, Rolled .... **4**·484
Cacciatore .... **10**·1194
Calico .... **14**·1683
Casserole, Club .... **4**·486
Casserole, Creamy ...... **13**·1581
Casserole, in .... **8**·1021
Chinese .... **4**·486
Chinese Walnut .... **19**·2424
Chip Bake .... **4**·486
Chips, in .... **13**·1539
Chow Bake .... **4**·427
Circassian .... **19**·2327
Coq au Vin .... **5**·617
Cups, Peach and .... **13**·1605
Currant-Orange .... **6**·716
Curried, with
    Grapefruit .... **9**·1057
Curry .... **6**·719
-Curry Soup .... **17**·2090
Delicious Baked .... **4**·481
Dinner, Saucy .... **14**·1785
Dipper's Drumsticks ......**4**·482
Divan, Classic .... **7**·782
Divan, Easy .... **7**·782
-Dressing Bake .... **18**·2180
Dumplings, with .... **4**·484
Easy Italian .... **4**·444; **16**·1982
Easy Onion .... **13**·1541
-Egg Foo Yong .... **8**·929
Elegante, Roast .... **4**·480
Fantasia .... **20**·2467
Fricassee and Dumplings ....**8**·963
Fricassee, Oven .... **13**·1540
-Fried Burgers .... **8**·997
-Fried Heart .... **19**·2349
-Fried Steak .... **4**·487
-Garden, -in-the .... **8**·918
Gravy .... **4**·484
Gumbo .... **1**·23
Halves, Caraway .... **4**·406
Ham Salad, and .... **4**·419
Herb Fried .... **4**·439
Honey Barbecued
    Broilers .... **4**·481
Island Broiled .... **14**·1771
Jubilee .... **8**·901
Kiev .... **15**·1899
Liver Boats .... **1**·77

Chicken *continued*
Liver-Onion Dip ....**7**·781
Liver Pâté ....**13**·1588
Livers and Rice ....**4**·488
Livers en Brochette ......**4**·488
Livers Portugal ....**4**·488
Liver Stroganoff ....**17**·2094
Loaf ....**7**·862
Madrilene ....**11**·1339
Marinated Broiled ....**16**·2042
Maryland Fried ....**11**·1360
-Melon Mousse ....**12**·1437
Mennonite, with Sour
    Cream ....**15**·1851
-Mushroom Soup ....**17**·2090
-Noodle Bake ....**13**·1581
-Noodle Soup ....**4**·487
Open-Face
    Sandwiches ....**13**·1564
Orange Rice, with ....**16**·1969
Oven Fried ....**4**·482
Oven Herb ....**4**·481
Paprika ....**13**·1564
Parisienne ....**4**·482
Parmesan ....**14**·1772
Pecan Salad in Shimmering
    Cranberry Ring ....**6**·666
-Pecan Waffles ....**19**·2410
Perfect Fried ....**4**·482
Pies, Savory ....**14**·1759
Pilaf ....**14**·1682
Plum-Glazed ....**14**·1707
Potpie ....**14**·1758
Puffs, Bite-Sized ....**18**·2261
Raisin Dumplings,
    with ....**7**·817
Rice, Creamy, and ....**1**·37
Rice, Orange, and ....**12**·1522
-Rice Soup ....**17**·2090
Roast, with Stuffing ......**15**·1875
Romaine ....**12**·1468
Salad, Fruited ....**11**·1355
Salad, Herbed ....**18**·2249
Salad, Jacques' ....**4**·402
Salad, Jellied ....**14**·1688
Salad Oriental ....**12**·1478
Salad Pie ....**1**·40
Scallop, Corn and ....**16**·1992
Scramble ....**16**·2011
Sesame ....**6**·659
-Sesame Balls ....**16**·2018
Spanish-Style ....**14**·1772
Spinach-Filled
    Ravioli, and ....**15**·1840
Spinning ....**15**·1894
Spread, Hot ....**3**·367
Spread, Zesty ....**17**·2121
Stack-Ups, Ham and .....**13**·1556
Stewed ....**4**·486
Strata ....**17**·2155

Chicken *continued*
Supreme, Ham- ....**6**·708
Tarragon ....**18**·2249
Tater-Coated ....**13**·1539
Timbales ....**18**·2270
-Vegetable Bake ....**9**·1143
-Vegetable Chowder ....**2**·174
Velvet Soup ....**6**·684
Veronique ....**19**·2392
Washington, Rolled ......**4**·484
Wine-Broiled ....**16**·1987
Chiffonade Dressing ....**4**·489

Chiffon Cake
Chocolate ....**4**·491
Golden ....**4**·491
Grasshopper ....**8**·971
Maple ....**4**·491
Marble ....**11**·1351
Mocha ....**8**·906
Pineapple ....**14**·1691
Tropical ....**3**·338

Chiffon Pie
Apricot ....**1**·102
Brazilian ....**6**·760
Buttermint ....**14**·1670
Chocolate ....**4**·493
Chocolate-Flecked ....**4**·512
Citrus ....**5**·549
Cocktail ....**14**·1675
Coffee ....**5**·578
Creamy Pumpkin-
    Whip ....**15**·1826
Daiquiri ....**4**·493
Date ....**6**·743
Dreamy-High Pumpkin ..**14**·1670
Irish Coffee ....**14**·1678
Key Lime ....**11**·1294
Lemon ....**10**·1277
Marble-Top
    Chocolate-Rum ....**15**·1897
Mince ....**12**·1419
Orange ....**12**·1520
Pear ....**14**·1670
Peppermint ....**13**·1644
Pumpkin ....**4**·493
Raspberry ....**4**·493
Spicy Coconut ....**17**·2111
Strawberry ....**8**·1019
Tangelo ....**5**·549

Chili
-Bean Salad ....**4**·496
-Burger Rarebit ....**8**·950
-Burger Stack-Ups ....**9**·1092
-Burger Supper ....**13**·1580
-Cheese Franks ....**8**·933
Cheese Log ....**4**·496
-Cheese Mold ....**4**·496

Chili *continued*
Con Carne ....**4**·494
Con Carne (quantity) .....**15**·1814
Con Wiene ....**8**·934
-Frank Soup ....**17**·2090
Limas, with ....**11**·1291
Mayonnaise ....**11**·1363
Mostaccioli ....**12**·1434
Salad Dressing ....**4**·496
Sauce ....**4**·496
Stew, Tomato ....**17**·2146
Veal ....**19**·2364
Wax Beans ....**19**·2430
Chilies Rellenos Bake ......**13**·1641
Chilies Rellenos Con Queso ....**4**·494

Chilled
Asparagus Soup ....**1**·114
Avo-Mato Soup ....**17**·2087
Banana Cheesecake .....**15**·1847
Breakfast Compote ....**5**·595
Cream of Chive Soup ......**6**·684
Prune Whip ....**20**·2440
Tomato-Cheese Soup ......**6**·645

Chinese
Almond Cookies ....**12**·1529
Beef Skillet ....**4**·500
Brown Sauce ....**8**·929
Chicken ....**4**·486
Firepot ....**4**·498
Fried Rice ....**12**·1535
Mustard ....**4**·498
Peas and Shrimp ....**12**·1533
Pork Sauté ....**19**·2425
Smoked Ribs ....**12**·1531
Spinach ....**17**·2114
Stew ....**17**·2146
-Style Liver ....**19**·2350
Walnut Chicken· ....**19**·2424
Chip-Cherry Fruitcake .....**16**·2017
Chipped Beef Puff ....**7**·799
Chitterlings ....**1**·25
Chitterlings, Deep-Fat Fried ....**1**·25
Chitterlings, Pan-Fried ....**1**·25

Chive
Butter ....**4**·501
Corn Spoonbread, and ....**4**·501
Dip for Artichokes, Parsley- ..**1**·108
Mayonnaise ....**4**·501
Soup, Chilled Cream of .....**6**·684

Choco
-Almond Velvet ....**19**·2390
-Blender Frosting ....**4**·512
Cake, Sour Cream- ......**17**·2094
-Cherry Cake ....**3**·347
-Date Dessert ....**19**·2420
-Mallow Ice Cream ......**18**·2210

Choco *continued*
  -Mint Freeze . . . . 8·976
  -Mo Ice Cream . . . . 4·507
  -Satin Frosting . . . . 8·970

CHOCOLATE . . . . 4·503-512
  -Almond Cups . . . . 5·577
  Almond Fudge Delight . . . . 8·1000
  -Almond Ice Cream . . . . . . 10·1171
  Angel Cake . . . . 1·50
  -Angel Delight . . . . 15·1846
  Balls, Cherry- . . . . 3·260
  Bars, Double . . . . 4·510
  Black Forest Cake . . . . 3·339
  Brazilian . . . . 5·516
  Cake, Almond . . . . 1·38
  Cake, Buttermilk- . . . . . . 12·1416
  Cake, Butternut . . . . 3·344
  Cake, Cherry- . . . . 11·1349
  Cake, Prize . . . . 2·137
  Cake, Spiced . . . . 2·137
  Cake, Sweet . . . . 4·510
  Charlotte Russe . . . . 4·450
  Charlotte Russe, Classic . . 10·1246
  Cheesecake Torte . . . . 18·2201
  Cheese Pie . . . . 4·511
  Cherries . . . . 4·512
  -Cherry Torte . . . . 18·2288
  Chiffon Cake . . . . 4·491
  Chiffon Pie . . . . 4·493
  Chip Cake . . . . 16·2017
  Chip Coffee Ring . . . . 5·585
  Chippers . . . . 4·510
  Cloud Soufflé . . . . 17·2077
  Clusters, Caramel . . . . 3·382
  Coffee . . . . 5·576
  Coffee Cake, French . . . . . 18·2198
  Coffee, Spiced . . . . 5·515
  Cream Cheese Frosting . . . . . 6·675
  Cream Pie . . . . 14·1673

  Crinkle Cookies . . . . 5·597
  Crinkles . . . . 6·695
  Cupcakes, Cheese-Filled . . 6·712
  Custard, Baked . . . . 19·2345
  Daisy Cupcakes . . . . 5·565
  Date Cake . . . . 3·350
  -Date Nut Bread . . . . 12·1479
  Dessert Duet . . . . 11·1358
  Diamonds . . . . 2·160
  Dot Waffles . . . . 19·2408
  Éclair Cake . . . . 18·2208
  Filling . . . . 7·878; 8·959

Chocolate *continued*
  -Flecked Chiffon Pie . . . . 4·512
  Fondue . . . . 8·925; 18·2210
  Frosting . . . . 3·296; 18·2289
  Frosting, Creamy . . . . 4·509
  Frosting, Milk . . . . 18·2199
  Frosting, Nutty . . . . 13·1615
  Fudge Brownies . . . . 3·297
  Fudge Cake . . . . 3·347
  Fudge, Easy . . . . 15·1798
  Fudge Frosting . . . . 8·968
  Fudge Pudding Cake . . . . . 19·2341
  Glaze . . . . 9·1035
  Gloss . . . . 10·1217
  Hot . . . . 4·507
  Hot Brandied . . . . 3·260
  Hot Fudge Sundae Cake . . 18·2208
  Layer Cake . . . . 4·509
  Malted Cheesecake . . . . . . 11·1341
  Marble Cake . . . . 11·1307
  Marble Squares . . . . 4·508
  -Marshmallow Parfaits . . . 11·1360
  Meringue Pudding . . . . 4·509
  Mexican . . . . 4·507
  -Mint Dessert . . . . 6·686
  Mint-Fudge Topping . . . . . 10·1176
  -Mint Parfaits . . . . 9·1042
  Mint Sails . . . . 5·605
  Mother's Best Fudge Cake . . 3·346
  Mousse . . . . 3·339
  Mousse, French . . . . 12·1436
  No-Cook Fudge Frosting . . . 3·347
  -Nut Clusters . . . . 19·2416
  -Nut Fluff . . . . 8·970
  -Nut Sundae Cups . . . . 8·977
  -Oat Cookies . . . . 12·1489
  -Orange Rolls . . . . 16·2017
  -Peanut Bars . . . . 19·2341
  Peanut Pie . . . . 4·512
  Peanut Pillows . . . . 3·382
  -Pecan Cornucopias . . . . . . 6·763
  -Pecan Cream Puffs . . . . . . 6·683
  -Pecan Torte . . . . 18·2289
  -Pecan Whip . . . . 20·2440
  Pie, Cherry- . . . . 14·1679
  Pinwheels . . . . 15·1846
  Pots de Creme . . . . 14·1765
  Pudding . . . . 15·1796
  Pudding Frosting . . . . 15·1798
  Quick Fudge Sundaes . . . . 8·1000
  Revel Bars . . . . 18·2209
  Ripple Cake . . . . 1·53
  -Rum Pie, Marble-Top . . . 15·1897
  Sauce . . . . 6·683
  Sauce, Easy . . . . 5·516
  Sauce, Fudgy . . . . 5·578
  Sauce, Regal . . . . 5·516
  Soda . . . . 10·1182
  Soufflé . . . . 4·508
  Spritz . . . . 5·530

Chocolate *continued*
  Squares, Pineapple- . . . . 3·298
  Swirl Cookies . . . . 4·512
  Syrup . . . . 5·516
  Torte . . . . 18·2289
  Torte Frosting . . . . 15·1904
  Torte, Surprise . . . . 18·2288
  Torte, Twice- . . . . 11·1303
  Tri-Level Brownies . . . . 3·297
  Tropical . . . . 2·220
  Truffle Pie . . . . 6·680
  Truffles . . . . 8·956
  Velvet Torte . . . . 19·2390
  Velvety Fudge Cake . . . . . . 4·509
  -Wafer Crust . . . . 6·703
  Waffles . . . . 19·2407
  Walnut-Covered . . . . 19·2416
  -Walnut Sauce . . . . 16·1973
  Yummies . . . . 5·608
  Chocolaty Meringue
    Pears . . . . 13·1623
  Chop Chop Salad . . . . 4·497
  Chopped Meat Suey . . . . . . 14·1738
  Chopstick Tuna . . . . 12·1478
  Chopstick Veal Bake . . . . . . 4·424

Chop Suey
  American . . . . 2·181
  Speedy . . . . 12·1535
  Turkey . . . . 5·517
  Chow Chow . . . . 5·518

Chowder
  Beef-Corn . . . . 5·625
  Cheese . . . . 5·520
  Cheeseburger . . . . 17·2084
  Chicken-Vegetable . . . . 2·174
  Clam, au Vin . . . . 5·520
  Clam-Haddock . . . . 16·2014
  Corn . . . . 5·521
  Corned Beef . . . . 5·521
  Corn-Sausage . . . . 5·626
  Devil's . . . . 17·2090
  Fish . . . . 8·899
  Hogate's Clam . . . . 5·555
  Hot Scallop . . . . 16·1990
  Manhattan Clam . . . . 5·520
  Meatball . . . . 17·2090
  New England Clam . . . . . . 5·518
  New England Corn . . . . 5·625
  Pacific . . . . 17·2089
  Quick Clam . . . . 15·1824
  Quick Corn . . . . 15·1853
  Seafood . . . . 5·520
  Shrimp . . . . 17·2089
  Supper Corn . . . . 17·2084
  Thrifty Bologna-Bean . . . . 11·1289
  Tuna . . . . 8·899
  Chow Mein, Pork . . . . 5·521
  Chow Mein, Vegetable . . . . . 3·327

CHRISTMAS .... **5**·523-533
  Black Currant Pudding ...... **6**·716
  Braid, Quick .... **18**·2200
  Brandy Balls .... **5**·531
  Cherry-Almond Balls ...... **5**·531
  Cherry Divinity .... **3**·379
  Chocolate Spritz .... **5**·530
  Christopsoma .... **9**·1066
  Coffee Royal Eggnog .... **7**·844
  Cranberry-Cherry Punch ... **5**·524
  Crystal-Cut Candies .... **3**·381
  Currant-Glazed Ham .... **5**·526
  Date-Orange Bars .... **5**·530
  Easy Plum Pudding ...... **14**·1710
  English Plum Pudding ...... **5**·532
  Eve Salad .... **11**·1408
  Family-Style Sugar
    Cookies .... **5**·530
  Fattigmann .... **7**·868
  Fruitcake Cookies .... **5**·530
  German Stollen .... **17**·2152
  Glazed Yule Ham .... **16**·1998
  Holiday Divinity .... **5**·529
  Java Fudge .... **5**·527
  Jewel-Top Star Mold ...... **5**·527
  Lucia Braid .... **5**·526
  Lutefisk Special .... **16**·1997
  Mincemeat Cake .... **5**·532
  Mint-Frosted Brownies ..... **5**·531
  Molasses Taffy .... **5**·529
  Molded Ruby Red Salad .... **5**·526
  Nut Tree .... **12**·1477
  Pastel Popcorn Tree ..... **14**·1716
  Peanut Brittle .... **5**·529
  Peanut Butter Fudge .... **5**·527

  Regal Plum Pudding ..... **14**·1709
  Roast Duckling with Red
    Cabbage .... **5**·524
  Rosy Wassail .... **5**·524
  Santa's Fudge .... **3**·378
  Savarin Chantilly .... **16**·1988
  Snowy Cinnamon Stars ..... **5**·530
  Spiced Wassail .... **19**·2423
  Springerle .... **17**·2122
  Spritz .... **17**·2124
  Stag's Antlers .... **16**·2005
  Strawberry Torte .... **5**·532
  Sugarplum Ring .... **5**·584
  Swedish Ginger Cookies .. **18**·2206
  Swedish Lucia Buns ...... **3**·306
  Whole Nut Fruitcake .... **5**·531

Christopsoma
  (Honey-Nut Bread) .... **9**·1066
Chuck Wagon Stew .... **14**·1752

Chutney
  Cheddar Spread .... **5**·535
  Chops, Orange .... **5**·535
  Cranberry .... **6**·664
  Currant .... **5**·535
  Pears, Baked .... **5**·535

Cider
  American Hot Mulled
    Apple .... **5**·536
  Ham Baked in Apple .... **8**·996
  Snap, Apple .... **5**·536

Cinnamon
  -Apple Jelly .... **10**·1211
  Apple Rings .... **1**·94
  Apples .... **8**·907
  -Apple Salad .... **15**·1842
  Apples in Foil,
    Spicy .... **8**·919
  -Berry Coupe .... **6**·647
  Cinnamonjam Squares ... **10**·1206
  -Cream Syrup .... **18**·2227
  Crescents .... **15**·1833
  Crisps .... **18**·2216
  Crumbs .... **2**·244
  Crunch, Apple .... **1**·96
  Diamonds .... **19**·2345
  Doughnuts .... **7**·795
  English Tea Ring .... **5**·585
  -Frosted Raisin
    Bars .... **9**·1044
  Icing .... **9**·1044
  Meringue Shell .... **19**·2390
  Nut Whirls .... **2**·165
  Popcorn Balls .... **15**·1842
  Pumpkin Spice Cake .... **3**·350
  -Raisin Bars .... **5**·538
  Rolls, Raisin- .... **15**·1882
  Sauce, Apple- .... **10**·1180
  Stars, Snowy .... **5**·530
  Swirl Bread .... **3**·281
  Toast .... **18**·2270
  Toast Cobbler .... **12**·1483
Cioppino .... **5**·539
Circassian Chicken .... **19**·2327

Citrus
  -Cheese Pie .... **14**·1674
  Chiffon Pie .... **5**·549
  Cobbler .... **5**·549
  Coffee Cake .... **5**·548
  Cooler .... **5**·544
  Fluff .... **9**·1030
  Perfection Salad .... **9**·1056
  Yellow Cake .... **3**·343

CITRUS FRUIT .... **5**·541-549
City Chicken .... **5**·550

Clam
  Bisque, Creole .... **6**·690
  Casino .... **15**·1877
  -Cheese Dip .... **2**·247
  Chowder au Vin .... **5**·520
  Chowder Casserole ..... **14**·1759
  Chowder, Hogate's .... **5**·555
  Chowder, Manhattan ...... **5**·520
  Chowder, New England ..... **5**·518
  Chowder, Quick .... **15**·1824
  Clambake, Individual ...... **5**·550
  Cocktail Dunk .... **5**·553
  -Guacamole Dip .... **10**·1275
  -Haddock Chowder ..... **16**·2014
  -Mushroom Bake .... **5**·554
  -Mushroom Spaghetti .... **17**·2100
  Parmesan .... **16**·2036
  Puff .... **5**·553
  Spread .... **17**·2121
  Steamed .... **5**·554
  -Stuffed Shrimp .... **16**·2035
Clambake, Individual .... **5**·550
Claret Barbecue, Beef .... **5**·555
Clarified Butter .... **16**·1971

Classic
  Cheese Fondue· .... **8**·925
  Cheese Strata .... **12**·1415
  Chicken Divan .... **7**·782
  Chocolate Charlotte
    Russe .... **10**·1246
  Deviled Eggs .... **7**·771
  Hollandaise .... **9**·1149
Clothespin Rolls .... **15**·1880
Club Chicken Casserole .... **4**·486
Club Sandwich .... **5**·558

Cobbler
  Apple Filling .... **5**·559
  Apple-Walnut .... **7**·863
  Apricot-Scotch .... **6**·756
  Cherry Filling .... **5**·560
  Cinnamon Toast .... **12**·1483
  Citrus .... **5**·549
  Crunchy Peach .... **13**·1608
  Fruit .... **5**·559
  Fruit-Cocktail .... **8**·995
  Italian Plum .... **14**·1707
  Orange Cherry .... **5**·561

Cobbler *continued*
Peach-A-Berry .... 5·561
Peach Filling .... 5·560
Rhubarb Filling .... 5·561
Spring Rhubarb .... 5·561
Cocktail Chiffon Pie .... 14·1675
Cocktail Wieners .... 8·933

Cocoa
Breakfast .... 5·565
Crust-Lime Pie .... 11·1294
Drop Cookies .... 5·607
Fluff, Minted .... 5·566
Fudge Cake .... 5·565
-Mint Wafers .... 5·566
Ripple Ring .... 5·565

Coconut
-Apricot Cake .... 1·100
Brittle, Orange .... 3·380
Cake Doughnuts .... 7·794
Cake, Vanilla Wafer .... 3·350
Chiffon Pie, Spicy .... 17·2111
Coffee .... 3·356
Coffee Cake, Toasted ...... 5·583
Cream Pie .... 5·571
Crust .... 6·704
Cups, Tangerine- .... 18·2245
Dainties .... 16·2025
Diamonds .... 5·570
Filling, Pineapple- .... 7·881
Frosting .... 8·969
Ice Cream .... 10·1174
Ice Cream Balls, Coffee- .... 5·570
Ice Cream, Toasted .... 5·568
Kisses .... 10·1234
-Lime Cake .... 11·1297
Macaroons .... 11·1337
Minted .... 5·568
-Oatmeal Cookies .... 5·570
-Orange Cake .... 10·1265
Penuche .... 3·379
Pie, Toasted .... 6·723
Ring, Apricot- .... 5·568
Toasted .... 2·224
Topped Cupcakes .... 3·338
Codfish Balls .... 5·572

Coffee
Aloha .... 2·220
Angel Pie .... 5·579
Café Aruba .... 5·576
Café au Lait .... 3·331
Café de Belgique .... 3·331
Cappuccino .... 4·403
Caramels .... 3·381
Chiffon .... 11·1323
Chiffon Pie .... 5·578
Chiffon Torte .... 5·577
Chocolate .... 5·576

Coffee *continued*
Clouds .... 11·1403
Coconut .... 3·356
-Coconut Ice Cream Balls .... 5·570
Coffeetime Twists .... 15·1881
Demitasse .... 6·750
Dot Fudge .... 3·377
Eggnog, Cool .... 5·576
Float, Viennese .... 8·908
Frosting .... 8·969
How to make .... 5·575
Ice Cream .... 10·1173
-Ice Cream Éclairs .... 7·828
Ice Cubes .... 11·1347
-Mallow Towers .... 13·1568
-Pecan Sauce .... 7·828
Pie, Irish .... 14·1678
Roll, Almond .... 3·337
Royal Eggnog .... 7·844
Spiced Chocolate .... 5·515
Spiced Iced .... 5·577
Squares, Gumdrop- ...... 9·1097
Swedish Egg .... 5·576
Toffee Squares .... 4·508
Torte, Kona .... 5·578
Tortoni, Almond- .... 5·577
Walnuts .... 19·2416

Coffee Cake .... 5·582
Apricot-Almond .... 5·583
Apricot Bubble Balls ...... 7·881
Apricot Topped Coffee
Bread .... 19·2421
Banana Ambrosia Ring ..... 2·141
Banana Coffee Bread ...... 5·584
Berry-Orange .... 17·2163
Braided .... 6·745
Caramel Coffee Ring ...... 3·268
Cherry Lattice .... 7·882
Chocolate Chip Coffee Ring .. 5·585
Citrus .... 5·548
Cowboy .... 5·584
Crown Coffee Bread ...... 3·369
Danish Coffee Ring .... 6·736
Danish Kringle .... 6·737
Date-Jam Braid .... 10·1204
Dixie Coffee Bread ..... 13·1611
Double-Decker Coffee
Strips .... 7·881
Easter Nest .... 7·822
English Tea Ring .... 5·585
French Chocolate .... 18·2198
Frosted Almond Swirl .... 10·1160
Golden Bubble Ring ...... 3·278
Golden Crown Coffee
Bread .... 5·587
Gugelhupf .... 9·1094
Gumdrop-Nut Wreath .... 9·1096
Jelly-Filled .... 10·1215
Jewel-Top Star Mold ...... 5·527

Coffee Cake *continued*
Lazy Daisy .... 3·268
Lucia Braid .... 5·526
Mandarin .... 12·1520
Mince Coffee Circle ...... 3·276
Miniature Brunch Loaf .... 5·580
Muffins .... 12·1444
Orange Butter .... 20·2474
Orange Coffee Braid ...... 5·548
Orange-Date .... 5·583
Pear .... 13·1620
Pear-Berry .... 5·580
Petal Bread .... 3·369
Pineapple Crisscross ...... 7·881
Plum Jewel .... 14·1707
Prune-Nut Braid .... 5·582
Quick Apple Pinwheels .... 5·582
Raspberry-Cream
Cheese .... 15·1838
Sally Lunn .... 16·1934
Spicy Marble .... 19·2419
Spicy Raisin .... 12·1476
Streusel .... 17·2171
Sugarplum Loaves .... 5·587
Sugarplum Ring .... 5·584
Sunburst .... 5·587
Swedish Holiday Braid .... 5·585
Toasted Coconut .... 5·583
Topknot Loaves .... 3·369
Cold Duck .... 4·448

Coleslaw .... 5·591
Beet and Cabbage .... 5·591
Blue Cheese .... 5·592
Cabbage .... 15·1814
Cabbage-Cucumber .... 6·709
Caraway Skillet .... 5·591
Cottage Cheese .... 6·644
Cranberry .... 6·663
Creamy Cabbage .... 3·329
Kidney Bean .... 5·591
Polynesian .... 3·329
Spring Garden Toss .... 5·591
Zippy Mustard .... 3·328
Colored Easter Eggs .... 7·825
Combination Relish ...... 19·2400

Company
Cauliflower .... 4·434
Cheesecake .... 6·765
Creamed Tuna .... 18·2303
Squash Bake .... 18·2204
Strata .... 17·2154
Tuna Bake .... 18·2304

Compote
Cherry-Berry .... 5·595
Chilled Breakfast .... 5·595
Grapefruit-Berry .... 11·1324
Green and Gold .... 11·1319

Compote *continued*
Harvest Fruit . . . . 7·803
Honey-Fruit . . . . 11·1303
Hot Curried Fruit . . . . 5·595
Hot Fruit . . . . 20·2460
Nectarine-Grape . . . . 9·1050
Rhubarb-Strawberry . . . . . 15·1861
Rosy Pear . . . . 13·1623
Ruby Fruit . . . . 5·595
Spicy Peach . . . . 18·2199
Triple Strawberry . . . . 17·2169
Winter Fruit . . . . 5·595
Concord Grape Pie . . . . 9·1051
Condiments, Tempura . . . . . 18·2263
Coney Islands . . . . 5·596

Confection
Bars . . . . 3·383
Bourbon Balls . . . . 20·2467
Candied Grapefruit
Peel . . . . 3·370
Candied Orange Peel . . . . . . 3·371
Candied Tangerine
Peel . . . . 18·2245
Caramel Nuts . . . . 12·1477
Crème de Menthe Balls . . . . . 6·686
Fruit . . . . 7·803
Fruit Balls . . . . 7·803
Honey-Sugared
Walnuts . . . . 19·2417
Marzipan . . . . 11·1360
No-Bake Fruit Squares . . . . . 3·371
Confectioners' Icing . . . . 5·596

Confetti
Consommé . . . . 17·2087
Relish . . . . 15·1856
Relish Mold . . . . 15·1919
Rice Ring . . . . 15·1868
Squash . . . . 6·697

Conserve
Apple-Peach . . . . 1·85
Freezer Pineapple . . . . 18·2201
Grape . . . . 9·1052
Peach . . . . 5·598
Peach-Cantaloupe . . . . 13·1602
Plum . . . . 5·597

Consommé
Confetti . . . . 17·2087
Cooler . . . . 5·599
Hot Sherried . . . . 17·2083
Jellied . . . . 5·598
Contemporary Duckling . . . . 10·1222

Cooked
Dressing . . . . 16·1925
Giblets . . . . 8·1024
Mustard Sauce . . . . 7·841

COOKIE . . . . 5·601-613
Anise-Sugar . . . . 19·2347
Apple-Oatmeal . . . . 1·89
Apple-Orange Brownies . . . . 5·605
Apricot Foldovers . . . . 8·920
Austrian Linzer . . . . 10·1206
Black Walnut Balls . . . . . . 19·2416
Bran Apricot Squares . . . . . . 3·300
Brandy Balls . . . . 5·531
Brandy Rings . . . . 3·260
Brandy Snaps . . . . 10·1244
Brazilian Creams . . . . 3·261
Browned Butter Nuggets . . . . 5·613
Brown-Eyed Susan . . . . 7·804
Brownie Meringues . . . . . . 11·1404

Brownie Treats . . . . 3·298
Busy Bee Chippers . . . . . . 10·1267
Butter (Kourabiedes) . . . . . . 9·1066
Butter Pecan . . . . 7·805
Butterscotch . . . . 2·137
Butterscotch Bars . . . . 3·322
Butterscotch Brownies . . . . . 3·297
Butterscotch Cereal Bars . . 15·1800
Butterscotch Drops . . . . 3·322
Cake Brownies . . . . 3·296
Cake Mix Pronto . . . . 16·2016
Cameo Cutouts . . . . 15·1885
Candlestick Bars . . . . 5·605
Caramel Chews . . . . 5·613
Caraway . . . . 4·405
Cardamom . . . . 4·407
Cereal-Peanut Bars . . . . 5·605
Cerealsnaps . . . . 4·442
Cherry-Almond Balls . . . . . . 5·531
Cherry Refrigerator . . . . 5·609
Chinese Almond . . . . 12·1529
Chocolate Chippers . . . . 4·510
Chocolate Crinkle . . . . 5·597
Chocolate Crinkles . . . . 6·695
Chocolate Diamonds . . . . . . 2·160
Chocolate Mint Sails . . . . . . 5·605
Chocolate-Nut Clusters . . . 19·2416
Chocolate-Oat . . . . 12·1489
Chocolate-Peanut Bars . . . 19·2341
Chocolate Pinwheels . . . . 15·1846
Chocolate Revel Bars . . . . 18·2209
Chocolate Spritz . . . . 5·530
Chocolate Swirl . . . . 4·512
Chocolate Yummies . . . . 5·608
Cinnamon Diamonds . . . . . 19·2345
Cinnamon-Frosted Raisin
Bars . . . . 9·1044

Cookie *continued*
Cinnamon-Raisin Bars . . . . . 5·538
Cocoa Drop . . . . 5·607
Cocoa-Mint Wafers . . . . 5·566
Coconut Dainties . . . . 16·2025
Coconut Diamonds . . . . 5·570
Coconut Kisses . . . . 10·1234
Coconut Macaroons . . . . . 11·1337
Coconut-Oatmeal . . . . 5·570
Coriander . . . . 5·619
Cream Cheese . . . . 6·676
Cream Cheese Dainties . . 16·2024
Creme-Filled . . . . 5·610
Crisp Ginger . . . . 10·1244
Crisp Maple . . . . 11·1347
Crisp Pecan Slices . . . . 5·609
Crunch . . . . 5·608
Crunchy Date Rounds . . . . . 4·442
Dark Herb . . . . 1·58
Date-Filled Sugar . . . . 7·875
Date-Marmalade Pastries . . . 5·610
Date-Orange Bars . . . . 5·530
Diamond
Applesauce Brownies . . . . . 1·96
Double Buttercups . . . . . . 16·2025
Double Chocolate Bars . . . . . 4·510
Double Peanut Butter . . . . 13·1614
Easy Macaroons . . . . 5·607
Easy-Peanut Chews . . . . . . 13·1613
Family-Style Sugar . . . . 5·530
Fattigmann . . . . 7·868
Fig Bars . . . . 7·871
Filbert Macaroons . . . . 7·872
Flossie the Fish . . . . 15·1846
Frosted Cashew Drops . . . . . 4·419
Frosty Date Balls . . . . 5·613
Fruitcake . . . . 5·530
Fruit Cocktail Gems . . . . 8·995
-Fruit Freeze . . . . 8·976
Fudge Brownies . . . . 3·297
Fudge Nuggets . . . . 12·1489
Funny-Face . . . . 7·806
Gingersnaps . . . . 9·1032
Glorified Grahams . . . . 9·1042
Goober . . . . 13·1611
Grandmother's Jelly . . . . . 16·2003
Gumdrop . . . . 9·1097
Gumdrop Gems . . . . 9·1097
Holiday Peppernuts . . . . . 13·1645
Jam Shortbread . . . . 10·1206
Jam Thumbprints . . . . 5·613
Joe Froggers . . . . 12·1430
Lace . . . . 10·1243
Lacy Oatmeal Crisps . . . . . 10·1243
Layer Bar . . . . 2·161
Lebkuchen . . . . 10·1268
Lemonade . . . . 3·316
Lemon Drop . . . . 10·1279
Lemon-Mace Rounds . . . . 11·1338
Lemon-Pecan Dainties . . . 10·1278

Cookie *continued*
Lemon Tea Cakes .... 5·607
Macaroon Bonbons ...... 16·2024
Macaroons .... 11·1338
Malted Oatmeal Bars .... 11·1340
Maple Nut Chews .... 5·603
Maple Scotchies .... 12·1476
Marguerites .... 11·1352
Marmalade-Fig Bars ..... 11·1357
Marshmallow Puffs ...... 11·1359
Mincemeat Marvels ..... 15·1884
Mincemeat Star .... 5·610
Mint-Frosted Brownies ......5·531
Mocha-Frosted Drops .... 16·2017
Molasses Jumbles .... 10·1223
No-Bake Almond Balls ... 19·2347
Nut-Butter Rounds ...... 15·1885
Nut-Edged Butter Slices .....3·317
Oatmeal ....7·805
Oatmeal Chip .... 5·608
Oatmeal Crunchies ...... 15·1885
Oatmeal Rounds .... 12·1491
Old-Fashioned Raisin
  Bars .... 15·1835
Orange Drop .... 12·1416
Orange-Ginger .... 15·1847
Orange Refrigerator ..... 15·1847
Paul Bunyan Sugar ....5·610
Peanut-Bran Bars .... 13·1611
Peanut Butter Bars .... 17·2051
Peanut Butter Crinkles ... 13·1615
Peanut Butter-Oatmeal Bars ..5·566
Pecan Crispies .... 13·1630
Pecan Tassies .... 13·1630
Peppermint Kisses .... 13·1644
Pfeffernuesse .... 13·1653
Pineapple-Chocolate
  Squares .... 3·298
Pineapple Drop .... 14·1781
Polka-Dot Oatmeal Crisps 12·1491
Pumpkin .... 15·1805
Quick Sandwich .... 5·609
Raisin-Oatmeal .... 12·1491
Refrigerator Crisps ....5·557
Rolled Ginger .... 9·1028
Rosewater and Caraway .. 15·1850
Rye .... 16·2005
Sandbakkels .... 16·2005
Sandies ....8·914
Saucepan Taffy Bars ....5·597
Scotch Shortbread .... 16·2046
Scotch Teas .... 5·605
Snickerdoodles .... 17·2069
Snowy Cinnamon Stars .....5·530
Speculaas .... 17·2106
Spiced Sesame Bars ...... 16·2019
Spicy Hermits .... 9·1144
Springerle .... 17·2122
Spritz .... 17·2124
Stag's Antlers .... 16·2005

Cookie *continued*
Stuffed Date Drops .... 6·742
Sugar .... 18·2197
Sugar-Pecan Crisps ...... 15·1885
Swedish Ginger .... 18·2206
Taffy Bars .... 12·1431
Tasty Pastries .... 5·613
Toffee Bars .... 18·2271
Tri-Level Brownies ....3·297
Unbaked Caramel .... 15·1798
Uppakrakakor .... 16·2003
Vanilla Crisps .... 19·2346
Cool Coffee Eggnog ....5·576
Copenhagen Limas .... 11·1291
Coq au Vin .... 5·617
Coriander Cookies .... 5·619

Corn
Bake, Broccoli- ....3·293
Bake, Hamburger- .... 14·1683
Bake, Swiss .... 5·626
Bread and Egg Muffins ... 12·1445
Bread Stuffing .... 18·2185
Burgers, Iowa .... 9·1124
Cakes, Double- .... 13·1554
Casserole, Indian .... 5·623
Chicken Scallop, and .... 16·1992
Chowder .... 5·521
Chowder, Beef- .... 5·625
Chowder, New England ....5·625
Chowder, Quick .... 15·1853
Chowder, Supper .... 17·2084
Crab, Deviled, and ....5·622
Creamy .... 5·626
Crown, Frank and ....8·933
Curry .... 5·626
-Custard Casserole ....6·727
Foil-Baked .... 5·622
Fresh, on the Cob ...... 15·1874
Fritters .... 5·625
Fritters, Speedy .... 5·625
Fry, Golden .... 5·627
Indian-Style, on the Cob .....2·159
Muffins, Corn and ...... 12·1441
O'Brien .... 5·626
-Oyster Scallop .... 13·1545
Pancakes .... 5·624
Pancakes with Chili ....5·624
Potato Scallop, and ....4·428
Pudding .... 5·638
Pudding, Quick .... 5·638
Relish .... 5·638
Relish, Fresh .... 15·1857
Relish, Shaker .... 19·2328
Relish, Summer .... 1·15
Roasted .... 2·159
-Sausage Chowder ....5·626
Spoon Bread, Chive
  and ....4·501
Squaw .... 17·2137

Corn *continued*
Stew, Lobster and .... 17·2144
Sticks, Double ....5·639
Strata, Cheese- .... 17·2155
-Stuffed Crown
  Roast of Pork ....6·701
-Stuffed Whitefish .... 18·2188
Supreme, Scalloped ..... 16·1992
Tomato Relish, and ..... 19·2330
Triangles, Potato- .... 9·1044
Waffles .... 19·2409

Corned Beef
Bake .... 5·633
Cabbage Bundles, and .....2·158
Captains .... 12·1512
Chowder .... 5·521
Dinner .... 2·190
Double-Beef Sandwiches ....2·191
Grilled Reubens .... 5·630
Hash Burgers .... 16·1952
Jazzy Hash .... 5·631
Loaf .... 5·631
New England Dinner .... 15·1850
Noodles, and .... 5·631
Noodles, with .... 10·1157
Pâté .... 13·1587
Peach-Glazed .... 5·630
Pie .... 5·633
Reuben Roll-Ups .... 5·631
Sandwiches, Cheesy ..... 13·1662
Squares with Dill Sauce .....7·778
Sweets, with .... 5·630
Corned Pig's Knuckles ..... 16·1984
Cornflake Crust ....6·704

Cornish Game Hen
Broiled .... 5·636
Burgundy .... 5·636
Grill-Broiled .... 5·634
Pineapple-Stuffed .... 18·2187
Rice-Stuffed .... 5·634
Rice Stuffing, with ....4·480
Spit, on a .... 14·1771
Stuffed .... 7·856
Supreme .... 5·634

Cornmeal
Dumplings .... 17·2148
Griddle Cakes .... 9·1075
Mush, Fried .... 12·1447
Waffles .... 19·2409
Cornucopias .... 16·1956
Coronado Salad .... 11·1398

Cottage Cheese
Bake, Potato ....6·644
Dip, Creamy ....1·71
Dressing .... 11·1322
Enchiladas .... 11·1407

Cottage Cheese *continued*
Fluff . . . . **2**·238
Pancakes, Quick . . . . **13**·1553
Ring, ''One Cup'' . . . . **11**·1294
Sandwiches, Garden . . . . . **16**·1948
-Shrimp Toss . . . . **11**·1326
Slaw . . . . **6**·644
Cottage Fries . . . . **6**·645
Cottage Pudding . . . . **6**·646
Country Potato Salad . . . . . . **16**·2015
Country-Style Cabbage . . . . **3**·327
Court Bouillon . . . . **18**·2299
Cowboy Coffee Cake . . . . **5**·584

Crab
-Artichoke Bake . . . . **1**·109
-Artichoke Luncheon Salad . . **6**·653
Bisque . . . . **2**·231
-Cabbage Skillet . . . . **12**·1534
Cheese Spread, and . . . . . . **17**·2121
Cocktail . . . . **1**·62
Cocktail, Grapefruit- . . . . **9**·1053
Cocktail Spread, Hot . . . . **6**·650
Crown, King . . . . **6**·653
Deviled Corn and . . . . **5**·622
Dip, Hot Cheese and . . . . **7**·781
-Filled Abalone Shell . . . . . **16**·2031
Jambalaya . . . . **6**·690
Louis . . . . **6**·654
Luncheon Salad . . . . **11**·1398
Meat-Bacon Rounds . . . . **3**·366
Meat Imperial, Deviled . . . . . . **6**·652
Meat Newburg . . . . **6**·652
Meat Suzette . . . . **16**·2032
-Mushroom Mornay . . . . . **12**·1450
Open-Facers, Hot . . . . **12**·1513
Pie, Swiss and . . . . **6**·727
Rémoulade,
Artichoke and . . . . **15**·1858
Rolls . . . . **8**·918
Sandwich Broil . . . . **6**·652
Sauce, Salmon with . . . . . . **16**·1937
Sauce, Turkey- . . . . **14**·1776
-Shrimp Bake . . . . **16**·2036
Soufflé Bake . . . . **17**·2076
-Stuffed Avocados . . . . **1**·122
-Stuffed Mushrooms . . . . **6**·652
Supper Pie . . . . **6**·650
-Swiss Bites . . . . **16**·2034
-Tomato Aspic . . . . **6**·653
-Wild Rice Salad . . . . **15**·1918
Crab Apple Glaze . . . . **6**·654
Crackers, Seeded . . . . **1**·17
Cracker Stuffing . . . . **6**·659

Cranberry
-Apple Filling . . . . **7**·882
-Apricot Salad . . . . **6**·666
-Avocado Mold . . . . **6**·664
-Banana Bread . . . . **6**·663

Cranberry *continued*
-Banana Shortcake . . . . **6**·664
Burger Sauce . . . . **6**·668
-Burgundy Glazed Ham . . . . **3**·310
Cake, Plymouth . . . . **6**·668
Cheese Pie . . . . **6**·669
-Cherry Punch . . . . **5**·524
Chutney . . . . **6**·664
Coleslaw . . . . **6**·663
Cooler . . . . **2**·223
-Cube Muffins . . . . **6**·669
Cupcakes . . . . **6**·711
-Date Relish . . . . **6**·662
Drink, Mulled . . . . **12**·1481
Drink, Spiced . . . . **1**·64
Duckling . . . . **7**·811
Filled Orange Cups . . . . **1**·17
-Grape Salad . . . . **9**·1049
-Honeydew Parfaits . . . . . . **10**·1156
Ice . . . . **6**·666
Jelly . . . . **6**·664
Kuchen . . . . **10**·1267
-Marshmallow
Freeze . . . . **6**·647
Meat Loaves . . . . **11**·1387
Nut Loaf . . . . **6**·663
-Orange Beets . . . . **2**·204
-Orange Bread . . . . **19**·2419
-Orange Butter . . . . **13**·1553
-Orange Muffins . . . . **12**·1443
-Orange Relish . . . . **15**·1857
Parfaits . . . . **10**·1177
-Pear Marmalade . . . . **18**·2201
-Pear Pie . . . . **14**·1676
Pork Chops . . . . **11**·1381
Pot Roast . . . . **6**·668
Punch . . . . **15**·1808
Punch, Warm . . . . **15**·1807
-Raisin Stuffing . . . . **6**·668
Relish Salad . . . . **6**·669
Ring, Chicken Pecan Salad
in Shimmering . . . . **6**·666
Sauce . . . . **6**·662
-Sauced Bites . . . . **19**·2315
Sauce,
Roast Duckling with . . . **14**·1775
Sauce, Tangy . . . . **16**·1968
Sauce, Tuna Patties with . . **18**·2303
Sparkle . . . . **2**·223
Star Mold . . . . **6**·667
Swizzle, Hot Buttered . . . . . . **6**·666
-Tea Punch . . . . **6**·665
-Topped Ham Slices . . . . . . **9**·1111
Tuna-Berry Sandwiches . . **16**·1932
Velvet Pie, Frozen . . . . . . **14**·1677
Wagon Wheel Rolls . . . . **7**·882
Waldorf . . . . **6**·662
-Waldorf Mold . . . . **6**·664
-Wine Hors d'oeuvres . . . . **20**·2459
-Wine Salad . . . . **14**·1740

Cran(berry)
-Apple Tarts . . . . **18**·2251
-Cheese Frosties . . . . **6**·667
-Cheese Squares . . . . **17**·2110
-Mandarin Toss . . . . **6**·668
-Pineapple Jelly . . . . **10**·1212

Cream
Celery Soup, of . . . . **4**·439
Filling . . . . **7**·878; **18**·2289
Goddess Dressing . . . . **16**·1930
Ham Soup, of . . . . **15**·1823
Mushroom Soup, of . . . . . . **12**·1451
Onion Soup, of . . . . **12**·1507
Potato Soup Bread, of . . . . **20**·2473
Potato Soup, of . . . . **6**·684
-Sauced Broccoli . . . . **19**·2384
Sweetbreads . . . . **19**·2351
Tomato Soup, of . . . . **6**·684
-Topped Pears . . . . **13**·1623

Cream Cheese
Cookies . . . . **6**·676
Dainties . . . . **16**·2024
Frosting . . . . **6**·675
Frosting, Caramel- . . . . **5**·596
Pie, Cherry- . . . . **10**·1190

Creamed
Dried Beef . . . . **7**·800
Ham . . . . **9**·1114
Onions . . . . **12**·1508
Peas and New Potatoes . . . . . **6**·676
Vegetables . . . . **19**·2382

Cream Pie
Banana . . . . **2**·142
Banana-Apricot . . . . **6**·679
Butterscotch . . . . **14**·1673
Cherry . . . . **6**·681
Cherry-Chocolate . . . . **14**·1679
Chocolate . . . . **14**·1673
Chocolate Peanut . . . . **4**·512
Chocolate Truffle . . . . **6**·680
Cocoa Crust-Lime . . . . **11**·1294
Coconut . . . . **5**·571
French Lemon . . . . **10**·1276
Lemonade Meringue . . . . **6**·680
Lemon Meringue . . . . **10**·1276
Lemon Raisin . . . . **15**·1797
Lemon-Sour Cream . . . . **8**·996
Mince . . . . **6**·681
Orange Meringue . . . . **6**·680
Pineapple . . . . **11**·1403
Rum-Eggnog . . . . **15**·1897
Spiced Butterscotch . . . . **6**·680
Strawberry-Pineapple . . . . . . **6**·679
Strawberry Satin . . . . **1**·38
Vanilla . . . . **14**·1673
Vanilla-Raisin . . . . **14**·1677

Cream Puff .... 6·681
  Cherry .... 7·837
  Chocolate-Pecan .... 6·683
  Custard-Filled .... 6·683
  Ham and Eggs in Caraway ... 6·682
  Tiny .... 7·837

Creamy
  Apple-Cheese Bake .... 1·93
  Aspic .... 1·116
  Broccoli Mold .... 3·291
  Butterscotch Sauce .... 6·768
  Cabbage Slaw .... 3·329
  Cauliflower Soup .... 4·432
  Celery Bake .... 4·438
  Cherry Pie .... 4·474
  Chicken and Rice .... 1·37
  Chicken Casserole .... 13·1581
  Chocolate Frosting .... 4·509
  Corn .... 5·626
  Cottage Cheese Dip .... 1·71
  Dill Sauce .... 4·482
  Dressing .... 2·226
  Egg Sauce .... 7·845
  French Dressing .... 8·962
  Fruit Combo .... 2·226
  Green Beans .... 9·1068
  Ham Rolls .... 16·1970
  Ham Towers .... 13·1592
  Hard Sauce .... 7·871
  Hashed Brown Bake .... 14·1757
  Lentil Soup .... 10·1280
  Lima Beans .... 19·2384
  Liver over Rice .... 19·2350
  Macaroni and Cheese
    Bake .... 4·462
  Mandarin Pears .... 10·1176
  Mayonnaise .... 11·1363
  Mushroom Topper .... 12·1451
  Mustard Sauce .... 12·1453
  Onion Dip .... 17·2093
  Pear-Lime Mold .... 13·1622
  Potato Bake .... 14·1756
  Pralines .... 14·1779
  Pumpkin-Whip Pie .... 15·1826
  Salad Dressing .... 6·653
  Satin Filling .... 1·39
  Waldorf Salad .... 19·2413
  White Cake .... 3·342

Crème
  Brûlée .... 6·686
  Chantilly .... 16·1988
  -Filled Cookies .... 5·610

Crème de Menthe
  Balls .... 6·686
  Chocolate-Mint Dessert .... 6·686
  Fresh Garden Mint Ice
    Cream .... 8·976

Crème de Menthe *continued*
  Lazy Grasshopper Pie ...... 6·686
  Triple Treat Sundaes ...... 11·1302

Creole
  Clam Bisque .... 6·690
  Jambalaya .... 10·1207
  Onions .... 12·1508
  Sandwiches .... 16·1954
  Sauce .... 6·691
  Sausage-Bean
    Bake .... 10·1233
  Shrimp .... 6·688

Crepes
  Ambrosia .... 17·2162
  Frangipane .... 6·692
  Grape-Syruped .... 9·1052
  Ham-Apricot .... 6·693
  Jam-Filled .... 13·1553
  Suzette .... 6·693
Crescent Roll-Ups .... 16·1942

Crisp
  Ginger Cookies .... 10·1244
  Maple Cookies .... 11·1347
  Pecan Slices .... 5·609
  Pickle Slices .... 13·1659
Crisscross Potatoes .... 14·1748
Croissants .... 6·696
Croissants Elegante .... 15·1883
Crookneck Curry .... 6·697

Croquettes
  Ham .... 6·698
  Ham and Rice .... 6·698
  Oven Turkey .... 13·1541

Croutons
  Caesar .... 3·331
  Garlic .... 6·699
  Toasted .... 6·699
Crown Coffee Bread .... 3·369
Crown Torte .... 10·1217
Crullers .... 7·796
Crullers, Quicky .... 15·1845
Crumb-Crowned Halibut
  Steaks .... 9·1100
Crumble Topping .... 13·1625
Crumb Top Plum
  Pie .... 14·1707
Crunch Cookies .... 5·608
Crunch Sticks .... 4·444

Crunchy
  Apricot Cake .... 3·350
  Cream Dressing .... 16·1926
  Date Rounds .... 4·442
  Ham Sandwiches .... 14·1754
  Peach Cobbler .... 13·1608

Crust
  Biscuit Pizza .... 14·1695
  Chocolate-Wafer .... 6·703
  Coconut .... 6·704
  Cornflake .... 6·704
  Graham Cracker .... 6·703
  Homemade Pizza .... 14·1695
  Jiffy Pizza .... 14·1695
  Vanilla Cookie .... 19·2347
  Vanilla Wafer .... 6·702
Crusty Water Rolls .... 3·281
Crystal-Cut Candies .... 3·381
Cubaica (Sicilian Torrone) .. 10·1199

Cucumber
  Basket .... 6·709
  Burgers .... 6·708
  Cuke-Buttermilk Soup ...... 3·320
  Dressing .... 8·1015
  Relish, Fresh .... 6·709
  Ring, Shrimp- .... 9·1070
  Ring Supreme .... 6·707
  Salad .... 11·1327
  Salad, Blender .... 6·708
  Sauce .... 6·709
  Sauce, Salmon with .... 16·1937
  Scored .... 8·1013
  Sour Cream .... 6·707
Cumberland Sauce .... 6·710
Cumin Burgers .... 6·710

Cupcake
  Alaskas .... 2·133
  Cheese-Filled Chocolate ... 6·712
  Chocolate Daisy .... 5·565
  Coconut Topped .... 3·338
  Cranberry .... 6·711
  Everyday .... 6·712
  Mocha .... 3·346
  Peanut Butter .... 6·712

Currant
  Chutney .... 5·535
  Glaze .... 5·525; 6·715
  -Glazed Ham .... 5·526
  -Orange Chicken .... 6·716
  Pudding, Black .... 6·716
  -Raisin Sauce .... 6·715
  Sauce .... 11·1354

Curried
  Apple Relish .... 1·93
  Beef Cubes .... 6·718
  Chicken Breasts .... 11·1320
  Chicken with Grapefruit ... 9·1057
  Ham in Popovers .... 14·1719
  Ham, Quick .... 10·1272
  Ham Rolls .... 6·718
  Lamb .... 6·719
  Lamb Chops .... 10·1255

Curried *continued*
Onions .... **19**·2384
Scrod .... **16**·2012
Wheat Snacks .... **20**·2439

Curry
Chicken .... **6**·719
Corn .... **5**·626
Crookneck .... **6**·697
Dip, Herb- .... **17**·2093
Luncheon, Shrimp- ...... **17**·2058
Orange-Pork .... **2**·157
Quick Turkey .... **19**·2318
Salad .... **6**·720
Soup, Chicken- ....**17**·2090
-Turkey Salad ....**19**·2321

Custard
Baked .... **6**·724
Baked Caramel .... **6**·724
Baked Chocolate ..... **19**·2345
Baked (low calorie) ...... **11**·1323
Butterscotch Puffs .... **3**·322
Casserole, Corn- .... **6**·727
Cups, Caramel .... **6**·724
-Filled Cream Puffs ...... **6**·683
Filling .... **6**·725
Filling, French ....**8**·960
Flan .... **8**·901
Potato-Cheese ....**6**·726
Sauce ...... **1**·34; **6**·747; **17**·2151
-Sauced Deep-Dish
Apple Pie .... **6**·747
Stirred .... **17**·2151
Strawberry Floating
Island .... **8**·909

Custard Pie .... **6**·726
Apple .... **1**·88
Apricot-Buttermilk ....**3**·320
Black Bottom .... **2**·234
Caramel .... **7**·723
Chess .... **4**·475
Holiday Walnut .... **19**·2417
Macadamia Nut .... **11**·1332
-Peach .... **14**·1674
Pumpkin .... **15**·1805
Pumpkin-Orange
Crunch ....**7**·863
Pumpkin-Pecan .... **14**·1669
Sister Lettie's
Maple- .... **11**·1348
Slipped .... **6**·726
Sour Cream-Pumpkin .... **19**·2389
Spicy Pumpkin-
Cheese .... **14**·1672
Sweet Potato .... **1**·23
Toasted Coconut .... **6**·723
Two-Tone Holiday .... **15**·1805
Custardy Rhubarb Pie .... **6**·723

D

Dad's Denvers .... **6**·751
Daffodil Lemon Sauce ..... **10**·1278
Daiquiri .... **6**·732
Daiquiri Blazer .... **17**·2149
Daiquiri Pie .... **4**·493
Dairy-Fruit Dressing ...... **16**·1926
Daisy Marble Cake .... **11**·1351

Danish
Coffee Ring .... **6**·736
Doughnuts
(Aebleskiver) .... **16**·2004
Kringle .... **6**·737
Pastry .... **16**·2002
Dark Fruitcake .... **8**·993
Dark Herb Cookies .... **1**·58

Date
Apple Torte .... **1**·93
-Apple Waldorf .... **15**·1917
Bake, Sweet Potato- ..... **18**·2214
Balls, Frosty .... **5**·613
Cake .... **6**·745
Cake, Chocolate .... **3**·350
Chiffon Pie .... **6**·743
Coffee Cake, Orange- ...... **5**·583
Filling .... **6**·745
Dessert, Choco- .... **19**·2420
Drops, Stuffed .... **6**·742
-Filled Sugar Cookies ...... **7**·875
Fondant Stuffed .... **19**·2344
-Jam Braid .... **10**·1204
Loaves, Midget .... **3**·276
-Marmalade Pastries ....**5**·610
-Marshmallow Waldorf .. **19**·2411
Medley, Orange- .... **20**·2468
Muffins .... **12**·1441
Nut Bread, Chocolate- ... **12**·1479
Nut Bread, Orange- ....**3**·267
-Nut Filling ....**7**·878
-Nut-Ice Cream Pie .... **14**·1677
-Nut Ring .... **10**·1222
-Orange Bars ....**5**·530
-Pecan Molds .... **11**·1350
Pudding Cake .... **15**·1799
Puffs, Sweet Potato- .... **6**·740
Relish, Cranberry- ....**6**·662
-Roll Sandwiches .... **16**·1957
Rounds, Crunchy ....**4**·442
Sauce, Sherried- .... **16**·2043
Soufflé Salads .... **6**·742
Torte, Pumpkin- .... **19**·2420
Torte Waffles ....**19**·2406
Triangles, Ginger- ....**6**·740
Decorated Ham .... **16**·2006
Deep-Dish Apple Pie ...... **14**·1671
Deep-Dish Orange-Peach Pie ..**6**·747

Deep-Fried
Brains .... **2**·254
Chitterlings .... **1**·25
Oysters .... **13**·1547
Scallops .... **16**·1989
Delicata Bake .... **17**·2136
Delicious Baked Chicken ....**4**·481
Della Robbia Torte ....**7**·87
Deluxe Limas .... **11**·1289
Demitasse .... **6**·750
Denver Sandwich ....**6**·751

DESSERT .... **6**·753-765
(See also Cake, Cookie, Ice Cream,
Pie, Pudding, Sherbet.)
Almendrádo .... **1**·34
Almond Brittle Torte ..... **17**·2118
Almond-Coffee Tortoni ......**5**·577
Almond Fudge Delight .... **8**·1000
Almond-Peach Torte ..... **13**·1608
Ambrosia .... **1**·45
Ambrosia Delight .... **11**·1326
Angel Cheesecake .... **4**·465
Apple Butter Betty ....**2**·213
Apple Cinnamon Crunch ....**1**·96
Apple Crisp .... **1**·89
Apple Dumplings .... **1**·89
Apple Fritters .... **8**·965
Apple Pandowdy ...... **13**·1559
Applesauce .... **1**·94
Apple Strudel .... **17**·2175
Apple-Walnut Cobbler ......**7**·863
Apricot-Grapefruit Ice ..... **9**·1057
Apricot-Scotch Cobbler .....**6**·756
Baked Alaska .... **2**·134
Baked Ambrosia .... **6**·762
Baked Caramel Custard ....**6**·724
Baked Chocolate Custard . **19**·2345
Baked Crimson Pears ... **13**·1619
Baked Custard .... **6**·724
Baked Custard
(low calorie) .... **11**·1323
Baked Orange Cups ..... **11**·1327
Baked Pears Elegante .... **13**·1622
Baked Prune Whip ...... **17**·2151
Baklava .... **12**·1458
Banana-Brittle .... **13**·1613
Banana Pecan Crunch ......**2**·142
Banana-Raspberry Flambé **20**·2466
Bananas aux Fruits ...... **16**·1973
Bananas Foster ....**2**·142
Bananas in Nectar ...... **9**·1136
Banana-Strawberry Freeze **17**·2168

Dessert *continued*

Banbury Tarts . . . . **2**·143
Basic Apple Dumplings . . . . . **7**·819
Belgian Waffles . . . . **19**·2409
Berries and Nectarines au
   Rhum . . . . **17**·2167
Berry-Cereal Parfaits . . . . **4**·443
Big Apple Parfaits . . . . **1**·96
Biscuit Tortoni . . . . **2**·230
Blueberry Buckle . . . . **2**·244
Blueberry Dumplings . . . . **7**·818
Blueberry-Rice Bavarian . . **15**·1870
Boston Cream Pie . . . . **2**·252
Brandied Bombe . . . . **2**·249
Brandied Peaches . . . . **3**·259
Broiler Banana Splits . . . . **2**·140
Brownie Alaska . . . . **11**·1403
Brownie Torte . . . . **18**·2290
Butterscotch . . . . **10**·1190
Butterscotch Crunch . . . . . **12**·1416
Butterscotch Puffs . . . . **3**·322
Butterscotch Torte Supreme **15**·1827
Cake Kabobs . . . . **2**·152
Cantaloupe à la Mode . . . . **1**·29
Caramel-Apple Whirls . . . **15**·1844
Caramel Cakewiches . . . . **4**·404
Caramel Custard Cups . . . . . . **6**·724
Cheesecake Supreme . . . . . . **4**·467
Cheese Pastries
   (Tyropitakia) . . . . **9**·1064
Cherries Jubilee . . . . **4**·468
Cherries Portofino . . . . **6**·765
Cherry-Angel . . . . **15**·1845
Cherry Bavarian . . . . **4**·472
Cherry-Berry Compote . . . . . . **5**·595
Cherry-Chocolate Balls . . . . . . **3**·260
Cherry Cookie Crisp . . . . **6**·756
Cherry Cream Puffs . . . . **7**·837
Cherry-Creme Parfaits . . . . **13**·1567
Cherry Melange . . . . **6**·754
Cherry Parfaits . . . . **4**·473
Cherry Shortcake Towers . . . . **4**·473
Cherry Tarts . . . . **14**·1675
Cherry Torte, Black
   Forest-Style . . . . **8**·1023
Chilled Breakfast Compote . . . **5**·595
Chilled Prune Whip . . . . . **20**·2440
Choco-Almond Velvet . . . **19**·2390
Choco-Date . . . . **19**·2420
Chocolate-Angel Delight . **15**·1846
Chocolate Charlotte Russe . . **4**·450
Chocolate Cheesecake
   Torte . . . . **18**·2201
Chocolate-Cherry Torte . . **18**·2288
Chocolate Cloud Soufflé . . **17**·2077
Chocolate Dot Waffles . . . **19**·2408
Chocolate Fondue . **8**·925; **18**·2210
Chocolate Marble Squares . . **4**·508
Chocolate-Marshmallow
   Parfaits . . . . **11**·1360

Dessert *continued*

Chocolate-Mint . . . . **6**·686
Chocolate-Mint Parfaits . . . **9**·1042
Chocolate Mousse . . . . **3**·339
Chocolate-Nut Sundae
   Cups . . . . **8**·977
Chocolate-Pecan
   Cornucopias . . . . **6**·763
Chocolate-Pecan Cream
   Puffs . . . . **6**·683
Chocolate-Pecan Torte . . **18**·2289
Chocolate-Pecan Whip . . **20**·2440
Chocolate Soufflé . . . . **4**·508
Chocolate Torte . . . . **18**·2289
Chocolate Velvet Torte . . . **19**·2390
Chocolate Waffles . . . . . . **19**·2407
Chocolaty Meringue Pears **13**·1623
Choco-Mint Freeze . . . . **8**·976
Cinnamon-Berry Coupe . . . . . **6**·647
Cinnamonjam Squares . . . **10**·1206
Cinnamon Toast Cobbler . **12**·1483
Citrus Cobbler . . . . **5**·549
Classic Chocolate
   Charlotte Russe . . . . . . **10**·1246
Coffee Chiffon . . . . **11**·1323
Coffee Chiffon Torte . . . . **5**·577
Coffee Clouds . . . . **11**·1403
Coffee-Ice Cream Éclairs . . . **7**·828
Coffee-Mallow Towers . . . **13**·1568
Coffee Toffee Squares . . . . . . **4**·508
Company Cheesecake . . . . . . **6**·765
Cookie-Fruit Freeze . . . . **8**·976
Cran-Apple Tarts . . . . **18**·2251
Cranberry-Banana
   Shortcake . . . . **6**·664
Cranberry-Honeydew
   Parfaits . . . . **10**·1156
Cranberry-Marshmallow
   Freeze . . . . **6**·647
Cranberry Parfaits . . . . . . **10**·1177
Cream Puffs . . . . **6**·681
Cream-Topped Pears . . . . **13**·1623
Creamy Apple-Cheese Cake . . . **1**·93
Creamy Mandarin Pears . . **10**·1176
Crème Brûlée . . . . **6**·686
Crepes Ambrosia . . . . **17**·2162
Crepes Frangipane . . . . **6**·692
Crepes Suzette . . . . **6**·693
Crown Torte . . . . **10**·1217
Crunchy Peach Cobbler . . **13**·1608
Cubaica (Sicilian Torrone) **10**·1199
Cupcake Alaskas . . . . **2**·133
Custard-Filled Cream Puffs . . **6**·683
Danish Pastry . . . . **16**·2002
Date Apple Torte . . . . **1**·93
Date-Pecan Molds . . . . . . **11**·1350
Date Torte Waffles . . . . . . **19**·2406
Della Robbia Torte . . . . **7**·877
Devonshire Green Grapes . **9**·1050
Duet, Chocolate . . . . **11**·1358

Dessert *continued*

Easy Apricot Soufflé . . . . **1**·101
Easy Date Crumble Torte . . . . **6**·745
Easy Pineapple Parfaits . . . **10**·1177
Easy Plum Pudding . . . . . . **14**·1710
Easy Zabaglione . . . . **20**·2478
Éclairs . . . . **7**·827
Edelweiss Torte . . . . **8**·1024
Eggnog Bavarian . . . . **10**·1247
Fast Crème Brûlée . . . . **6**·762
Festive Freeze . . . . **7**·844
Fig-Nut Squares . . . . **7**·871
Filbert Meringues . . . . **7**·872
Flaming Pears Melba . . . . . **11**·1391
Flan . . . . **8**·901
Flapper Pudding . . . . **19**·2421
Flowerpot Cookie Cups . . **15**·1871
Fluffy Ambrosia . . . . **1**·45
Forgotten Cherry Torte . . . **18**·2287
French Chocolate Mousse **12**·1436
French Custard Filling . . . . . . **8**·960
French Pineapple Jubilee . **14**·1691
French Strawberry Tart . . . . . **8**·959
Fresh Fruit Aloha . . . . **17**·2167
Fresh Fruit Ambrosia . . . . **1**·44
Fresh Fruit Bars . . . . **13**·1608
Fresh Fruit Tarts . . . . **18**·2252
Fried Peach Pies . . . . **8**·964
Frosty Fruit Cup . . . . **14**·1687
Frosty Pineapple . . . . **14**·1690
Frosty Strawberry Cubes . . . . **8**·976
Frozen Apricot Torte . . . . **8**·976
Frozen Butterscotch Dream **15**·1797
Frozen Mincemeat Tarts . . **18**·2251
Fruit Cobblers . . . . **5**·559
Fruit-Cocktail Cobbler . . . . . . **8**·995
Fruit Cocktail Smoothee . . . . **6**·676
Fruit Cup Tower . . . . **8**·987
Fruited Tangerine Ice . . . . **10**·1166
Fruited Watermelon . . . . . **19**·2427
Fruit Fritters . . . . **9**·1126
Fruit Medley Elegante . . . . . . **8**·990
Fruit Melange . . . . **17**·2167
Fruit Sparkle Sundaes . . . . **10**·1183
Fruit with Dumplings . . . . . . **7**·817
Gingerettes . . . . **19**·2407
Ginger-Fruit Cooler . . . . . **19**·2428
Ginger-Fruit Oriental . . . . **12**·1531
Ginger-Maple Alaska . . . . . **9**·1031
Ginger-Peach Squares . . . . **9**·1030
Ginger-Pear Crumble . . . . **13**·1623
Golden Lemon Soufflé . . . **10**·1267
Golden Raisin Flambé . . . . . . **6**·766
Golden Sundaes . . . . **18**·2204
Green and Gold Ambrosia . **9**·1051
Green and Gold Compote
   (low calorie) . . . . **11**·1319
Harvest Fruit Compote . . . . . **7**·803
Hawaiian Fruit Crumble . . . . **6**·762
Heavenly Hawaiian Cream **11**·1349

Dessert *continued*

Heavenly Torte . . . . 6·763
Hidden Treasure Sundaes . 10·1214
Honey-Baked Bananas . . . . 9·1035
Honeydew-Berry Parfaits . 11·1396
Honeydew-Lime Mold . . . 10·1156
Honey-Fruit Compote . . . . 11·1303
Honey Rhubarb Betty . . . . . . 2·213
Hong Kong Sundaes . . . . . 10·1185
Hot Curried Fruit Compote . . 5·595
Hot Fruit Compote . . . . . . 20·2460
Hot Fruit Medley . . . . . . 14·1740
Hurry-Up Éclairs . . . . 7·828
Ice Cream Sundae Mold . . . . 5·578
Individual Meringue Shells 11·1402
Island Nut Bananas . . . . . . 9·1136
Italian Plum Cobbler . . . . . 14·1707
Italian Spumoni . . . . 17·2126
Java Tapioca Parfaits . . . . . 18·2246
Jiffy Butterscotch Torte . . . . . 3·321
Kona Coffee Torte . . . . 5·578
Lazy Grasshopper Parfaits . 9·1058
Lemonade Angel . . . . 1·52
Lemon Angel Torte . . . . 6·765
Lemon-Blueberry Fluff . . . 11·1324
Lemon Crisp . . . . 6·695
Lemon Crunch Parfaits . . . . 9·1044
Lemon Curd Tarts . . . . 10·1279
Lemon-Frosted Plum
    Squares . . . . 14·1704
Lemon-Honey . . . . 9·1152
Lime-Berry Parfaits . . . . . . 13·1567
Lime-Pineapple Fluff . . . . . 11·1296
Lime Snow . . . . 11·1327
Lime Torte . . . . 11·1296
Mandarin-Fig Whip . . . . . . 11·1342
Mandarin Pears . . . . 11·1303
Mandarin Soufflé . . . . 5·549
Maple Baked Apples . . . . 1·87
Marble Cheesecake . . . . 6·675
Marinated Skewered Fruit 17·2062
Melba Sundaes . . . . 11·1391
Melon à l'Orange . . . . 11·1303
Melon Balls Melba . . . . . . 11·1399
Melon Cocktail . . . . 8·987
Melon Medley . . . . 10·1155
Meringue Shell . . . . 1·55
Middle East Pears . . . . 13·1621
Mile-High Mocha Alaska . . 2·134
Mincemeat-Apple Crisp . . 12·1419
Mincemeat Turnovers . . . . 19·2334
Minted Cocoa Fluff . . . . . . 5·566
Mint Patty Alaskas . . . . 7·841
Mocha Blitz Torte . . . . 2·241
Mocha Brownie Pudding . 19·2420
Mocha-Dot Bavarian . . . . 12·1427
Mocha-Marshmallow
    Pudding and Chocolate-
    Almond Cups . . . . 5·577
Mocha-Nut Torte . . . . 12·1427

Dessert *continued*

Mocha Torte . . . . 12·1425
Mocha-Velvet Torte . . . . 6·768
Mock Strawberries
    Devonshire . . . . 7·775
Molded Apricot Cream . . . 19·2346
Napoleons . . . . 12·1454
Nectarine-Grape
    Compote . . . . 9·1050
Nut-Crusted Bananas . . . . . . 2·141
Orange Alaskas . . . . 2·133
Orange Cherry Cobbler . . . . 5·561
Orange Chiffon Soufflé . . . 12·1519
Orange-Date Medley . . . . 20·2468
Orange-Date Torte . . . . . . 12·1520
Orange-Spiced Peaches . . . 13·1602
Orange Sunbursts . . . . 12·1519
Orange Velvet . . . . 5·548
Orange Waffles . . . . 19·2407
Peach-A-Berry Cobbler . . . . 5·561
Peach-Angel Fluff . . . . 10·1246
Peach-Cheese Dumplings . . 7·819
Peach-Cot Cherry Bake . . . . 8·991
Peach Crumble . . . . 15·1797
Peaches à la Rum . . . . 15·1897
Peaches in Flame . . . . 13·1606
Peach-Pecan Mold . . . . 6·760
Peanut Butter Swirls . . . . . 13·1614
Pears au Gratin . . . . 1·117
Peppermint Nests . . . . 12·1422
Phony Spumoni . . . . 8·974
Pineapple-Cheese Parfaits . . 6·725
Pineapple Cream Loaf . . . . 10·1247
Pineapple Fluff . . . . 17·2070
Pineapple Jewel Squares . . 19·2345
Pineapple-Mint . . . . 12·1415
Pineapple-Mint Cup . . . . . 12·1420
Pineapple Puffs . . . . 14·1692
Pink Fruit . . . . 8·991
Pink Parfaits . . . . 17·2170
Pizza, Cherry-Cheese . . . . . . 6·676
Pizza, Nectarine . . . . 12·1461
Plum Parfaits . . . . 13·1567
Plums with Custard Sauce . 14·1709
Plum Whip . . . . 20·2441
Polka-Dot Waffles . . . . . . 19·2407
Poppy Seed Torte . . . . . . 14·1720
Portuguese Christmas Log
    (Nogados) . . . . 14·1743
Pots de Crème . . . . 14·1765
Pots de Crème Chocolate . 14·1765
Powwow Sundae . . . . 2·153
Prune and Apricot Bowl . . 14·1792
Pudding-Pear Parfaits . . . . 10·1247
Pumpkin Crème Brûlée . . . . 6·755
Pumpkin-Date Torte . . . . . 19·2420
Quick Apple Dumplings . . 15·1845
Quick Applesauce Crisp . . . . 1·94
Quick Apple Strudel . . . . . 17·2176
Quick Apricot Pastries . . . 17·2095

Dessert *continued*

Quick Cherry-Cream
    Parfaits . . . . 13·1568
Quick Jubilee Sauce . . . . 1·40
Quick Pudding Parfaits . . . 13·1567
Quick Tortoni Cups . . . . . . 18·2291
Rabanados . . . . 14·1743
Raisin-Filled Apples . . . . . 12·1411
Raspberry Angel . . . . 1·50
Raspberry Bavarian Mold . . 2·165
Raspberry Bombe . . . . 2·249
Raspberry Ice . . . . 10·1166
Raspberry-Melon Boats . . 11·1399
Raspberry-Meringue
    Squares . . . . 15·1838
Red Raspberry Fluff . . . . . . 8·1017
Red Raspberry Ring . . . . . 15·1838
Regal Plum Pudding . . . . . 14·1709
Rhubarb Crunch . . . . 15·1862
Rhubarb-Strawberry
    Compote . . . . 15·1861
Rhubarb Whip . . . . 15·1862
Rosettes . . . . 15·1891
Rosy Pear Compote . . . . . 13·1623
Rosy Pear Sundaes . . . . . . 13·1624
Ruby Fruit Compote . . . . . . 5·595
Salad, Cherry . . . . 4·472
Salad, Plum . . . . 14·1706
Savarin Chantilly . . . . 16·1988
Sherbet and Spice . . . . . . 16·2039
Sherried Ice Cream Roll . . . 6·670
Sherry-Spiced Pears . . . . . 13·1621
Shortcut Dobos Torte . . . . . 7·786
Shredded Wheat . . . . 19·2327
Skillet Strawberry
    Dumplings . . . . 7·817
S'More Pie . . . . 6·658
S'Mores . . . . 9·1041
Snowy Vanilla Torte . . . . . 19·2346
Sonhos (Dreams) . . . . 14·1743
Soufflé, Orange . . . . 17·2077
Spiced Fruit Sauce . . . . 8·991
Spiced Grapes . . . . 9·1049
Spice-Prune Dumplings . . . . 7·819
Spicy Baked Apples . . . . 1·83
Spicy Peach Compote . . . . 18·2199
Spread, Roquefort . . . . . . 15·1888
Spring Pancakes . . . . 17·2162
Spring Rhubarb Cobbler . . . 5·561
Stirred Custard . . . . 17·2151
Strawberries Juliet . . . . . . 17·2167
Strawberry-Banana Ice . . . 17·2170
Strawberry Charlotte
    Russe . . . . 8·1019
Strawberry-Cheese Tarts . . 18·2252
Strawberry Cream . . . . 6·755
Strawberry Cups . . . . 17·2168
Strawberry Delight . . . . . . 17·2170
Strawberry Dumplings . . . 17·2162
Strawberry Floating Island . . 8·909

Dessert *continued*

Strawberry-Glazed
Cheesecake . . . . 4·467
Strawberry-Lemonade
Bavarian . . . . 17·2161
Strawberry Meringue Puffs 17·2168
Strawberry Parfaits . . . . 6·759
Strawberry Scrumptious . . 17·2164
Strawberry Squares . . . . 6·760
Strawberry Swirl . . . . 17·2170
Strawberry Tarts . . . . 17·2164
Strawberry Torte . . . . 5·532
Sundae Special . . . . 18·2204
Sunny Tangerine Creme . . 18·2243
Surprise Chocolate Torte . . 18·2288
Surprise Pear Bundles . . . . 13·1625
Swiss Cream Torte . . . . 15·1802
Tangerine-Coconut Cups . 18·2245
Tiny Strawberry Soufflés . . 11·1303
Top Banana Split . . . . 10·1185
Tortoni . . . . 18·2292
Trifle . . . . 18·2294
Trifle Delight . . . . 6·723
Triple Fruit . . . . 8·991
Triple Strawberry Compote 17·2169
Triple Treat Sundaes . . . . . 11·1302
Tropical Sundaes . . . . 18·2204
Tropical Trifle . . . . 18·2295
Tutti-Frutti Tortoni . . . . 19·2335
Twice-Chocolate Torte . . . 11·1303
Two-Berry Parfaits . . . . 17·2094
Waffles . . . . 19·2407
Waffles Jubilee . . . . 19·2406
Walnut Cream Roll . . . . 7·878
Winter Fruit Compote . . . . . 5·595
Winter Fruit Medley . . . . . 10·1279
Zabaglione au Madera . . . 10·1199
Zuppa Inglese . . . . 6·725
Deutsch Dinner . . . . 10·1236

Deviled

Almonds . . . . 1·74
Baked Tomatoes . . . . 18·2279
Bass Fillets . . . . 17·2172
Beef Bones . . . . 10·1272
Beef Toss . . . . 11·1286
Corn and Crab . . . . 5·622
Crab Meat Imperial . . . . 6·652
Dip . . . . 10·1159
Eggs . . . . 7·838
Eggs, Classic . . . . 7·771
Eggs, Red . . . . 7·771
Flank Rolls . . . . 2·188
Green Beans . . . . 9·1068
Guacamole . . . . 9·1093
Ham and Tuna Sandwiches . . 7·773
Ham-Bean Bake . . . . 7·772
Hamburgers . . . . 7·771
Ham Pie . . . . 11·1389
Lamb Chops . . . . 10·1258

Deviled *continued*

Lamburgers . . . . 8·1009
Oysters on the Half Shell . 13·1546
Potatoes, Hot . . . . 7·771
Steak . . . . 11·1327
-Stuffed Potatoes . . . . 18·2190
Swiss Steak . . . . 7·772
Devilicious Cherry Cake . . . . . 7·774
Devil's Chowder . . . . 17·2090
Devil's Food Cake . . . . 7·774
Devonshire Green Grapes . . . 9·1050
Dewdrops . . . . 3·383
Diamond Applesauce
Brownies . . . . 1·96
Dieter's Dip . . . . 7·781

Dill

Dip . . . . 7·778
Pâté, Shrimp- . . . . 2·240
Pickles . . . . 13·1658
Pickles, Kosher . . . . 10·1241
Potatoes . . . . 7·778
Potatoes, Quick . . . . 14·1748
-Potato Salad, Hot . . . . . . 14·1753
Sauce . . . . 7·778
Sauce, Corned Beef
Squares with . . . . 7·778
Sauce, Creamy . . . . 4·482
-Sauced Tomatoes . . . . 18·2276
Sauce, Green Beans with . . . 2·179
Sauce, Lamb Patties with . 16·1969
Sauce, Pompano with . . . . 14·1714

Dilled

Cheese Casserole . . . . 6·643
Lamb Stew . . . . 17·2147
Mushroom Sauce . . . . 17·2076
Salmon Steaks . . . . 16·1937
Veal Special . . . . 10·1235
Vegetable Sticks . . . . 19·2381

Dilly

Batter Bread . . . . 10·1267
Beef Cartwheel . . . . 2·197
-Brussels Sprouts . . . . 3·301
Green Tomatoes . . . . 18·2278
Hamburgers . . . . 7·779
Shrimp, Cauliflower and . . . . 4·434
Dinner Rolls . . . . 2·165

Dip

à la Spaghetti . . . . 7·781
Anchovy . . . . 1·47
Artichokes, Parsley-Chive,
for . . . . 1·108
Bacon-Blue . . . . 13·1640
Cheese Fluff . . . . 1·66
Chicken Liver-Onion . . . . . . 7·781
Clam-Cheese . . . . 2·247
Clam Cocktail Dunk . . . . 5·553

Dip *continued*

Clam-Guacamole . . . . 10·1275
Creamy Cottage Cheese . . . . . 1·71
Creamy Onion . . . . 17·2093
Deviled . . . . 10·1159
Deviled Guacamole . . . . . . 9·1093
Dieter's . . . . 7·781
Dill . . . . 7·778
Easy Cheese Dunk . . . . 4·446
Elegante, Lobster . . . . 7·781
Fruit, Hot Cheese,'with . . . . . 1·77
Ginger . . . . 1·71
Guacamole . . . . 9·1093
Herb-Curry . . . . 17·2093
Hot Cheese and Crab . . . . . . 7·781
Hot Mexican Bean . . . . 2·175
Hot Sausage-Bean . . . . 1·71
Jiffy Braunschweiger . . . . . . 1·66
Mustard 'n Ham . . . . 7·777
Party Cheese . . . . 11·1318
Pepper Cup Trio . . . . 13·1640
Pineapple-Orange Yogurt . 20·2476
Quick Fruit . . . . 17·2167
Spaghetti . . . . 13·1640
Spicy Beef . . . . 1·77
Zesty Zucchini . . . . 11·1318
Zippy Ham . . . . 5·629
Diploma Sandwiches . . . . . 16·1957
Dipper's Drumsticks . . . . 4·482
Divan, Classic Chicken . . . . . 7·782
Divan, Easy Chicken . . . . 7·782

Divinity . . . . 7·784

Cherry . . . . 3·379
Cherry Fluff . . . . 7·785
Holiday . . . . 5·529
Rainbow . . . . 7·785
Dixie Coffee Bread . . . . . . 13·1611

Double

-Beef Sandwiches . . . . 2·191
Berry Jam . . . . 10·1202
Buttercups . . . . 16·2025
Butterscotch Crescents . . . 15·1881
Cheese Rarebit . . . . 19·2431
Chocolate Bars . . . . 4·510
-Corn Cakes . . . . 13·1554
Corn Sticks . . . . 5·639
-Decker Coffee Strips . . . . . . 7·881
-Decker Honeydew Mold . 11·1396
Fruit-Glazed Pork Chops . . 9·1135
-Layer Fudge . . . . 8·999
Mocha Cake . . . . 8·969
Peanut Butter Cookies . . . . 13·1614
Potato Bake . . . . 10·1189
Shrimp Casserole . . . . 12·1468

Doughnut

Applesauce . . . . 1·96
Apricot Split-Ups . . . . 7·793

Doughnut *continued*
Balls .... 7·794
Cake .... 7·793
Cinnamon .... 7·795
Coconut Cake .... 7·794
Crullers .... 7·796
Danish (Aebleskiver) ... 16·2004
Filled .... 7·795
Jiffy .... 7·793
New Orleans Square .... 7·795
Orange .... 7·796
Potato .... 7·794
Raised .... 7·795
Rocky-Road Rings ..... 7·796
Shaggy Mochas .... 7·793
Spicy Cake .... 3·273
Twists .... 7·794
Dreamy-High Pumpkin Pie . 14·1670
Dressed-Up Pork Steaks .... 13·1664

Dried Beef
Beef and Noodle Bake ..... 7·800
Canapés .... 3·367
Chipped Beef Puff ...... 7·799
Creamed .... 7·800
Double-Beef Sandwiches ... 2·191
Log .... 7·799
Dried Fruit Bread .... 8·1023
Drop Biscuits .... 7·804
Dry Martini .... 11·1360
Dublin Fruitcake .... 3·348
Dublin Potato Salad ..... 7·778
Duchess Potatoes ...... 7·808

Duck, Duckling
à la Orange, Wild ...... 7·812
Cantonese .... 7·813
Contemporary .... 10·1222
Cranberry .... 7·811
Elegant, with Sauce ..... 8·1003
Kowloon .... 2·150
Navy Bean-Stuffed ...... 7·813
Orange Sauce, with ..... 8·956
Roast Domestic .... 7·813
Roast, with Cranberry
  Sauce .... 14·1775
Roast, with Oranges .... 7·813
Roast, with Red Cabbage . 5·524
Rotisserie .... 7·812
Wild, in Wine .... 8·1005

Dumpling
Apple .... 1·89
Basic Apple .... 7·819
Bavarian Potato .... 8·1022
Beef and .... 7·816
Beef with .... 2·196
Blueberry .... 7·818
Chicken Fricassee and ... 8·963
Chicken with .... 4·484

Dumpling *continued*
Chicken with Raisin ...... 7·817
Cornmeal .... 17·2148
Easy .... 7·817
Fluffy .... 7·817
Fruit with .... 7·817
Lamb Stew 'n .... 7·816
Lemon .... 8·963
Marrow .... 8·1021
Parsley .... 17·2052
Peach-Cheese .... 7·819
Potato (Kartoffel Klösse) . 10·1230
Quick Apple .... 15·1845
Skillet Strawberry ..... 7·817
Spice-Prune .... 7·819
Strawberry .... 17·2162
Dutch-Glazed Onions .... 12·1509
Dutch Green Beans ...... 9·1067

E

Easter
Bunny Rolls .... 7·824
Eggs, Colored .... 7·825
Ham 'n Egg Triple Deckers .. 7·826
Honey-Pecan Cake ..... 7·826
Nest Coffee Cake ...... 7·822
Orange Cream Cake .... 7·824
Pineapple-Cheese Salad .. 7·826
Spring Flower Rolls .... 7·822

Easy
Apricot Soufflé .... 1·101
Baked Beans .... 2·172
Bread Sticks .... 3·270
Caramels .... 3·381
Cheese Dunk .... 4·446
Cheese Soufflé .... 17·2075
Chicken Divan .... 7·782
Chicken-Noodle
  Soup .... 17·2090
Chocolate Fudge ..... 15·1798
Chocolate Sauce ..... 5·516
Daffodil Cake .... 6·731
Date Crumble Torte ... 6·745
-Do Bacon Roll-Ups ... 3·271
Dumplings .... 7·817
Eggs à la King ...... 7·840
Italian Chicken ... 4·444; 16·1982
Lasagne .... 10·1263
Macaroons .... 5·607
Mexican Skillet ..... 11·1337
Onion Bread .... 2·159
Onion Chicken ..... 13·1541
-Peanut Chews ..... 13·1613
Pineapple Parfaits ... 10·1177
Plum Pudding ...... 14·1710
Seafood Sauce ..... 16·1970
Shrimp Sauté ...... 4·446

Easy *continued*
Sourdough Flapjacks ...... 8·904
Turkey Paella .... 19·2318
Vegetable Soup .... 19·2382
Zabaglione .... 20·2478
Éclairs .... 7·827
Éclairs, Coffee-Ice Cream ... 7·828
Éclairs, Hurry-Up ...... 7·828
Edam Sage Spread ...... 1·70
Edam, Stuffed .... 7·829
Edelweiss Torte .... 8·1024

EGG .... 7·831-843
À La King .... 1·27
À La King, Easy ...... 7·840
au Gratin .... 15·1871
Bake, Swiss Cheese- .... 18·2222
Basic Scrambled ...... 7·833
Bean Salad, and ...... 2·174
Benedict .... 7·850
Caraway Puffs, Ham and, in .. 6·682
Caviar-Stuffed .... 4·436
Cheese Scrambled ..... 7·834
Classic Deviled ...... 7·771
Coffee, Swedish ...... 5·576
Colored Easter .... 7·825
Deviled .... 7·838
Filling .... 1·76
Fluffy Scrambled ..... 7·834
Foo Yong, Beef and ... 2·180
Foo Yong, Chicken- ... 8·929

Fried .... 7·836
Hard-Cooked .... 7·834
Herb Scrambled ...... 9·1143
Mornay, Wine- ...... 12·1433
Pastry .... 13·1586
Poached .... 7·834
Puffs .... 9·1116
Puffs, Ham-Turkey Sauce
  on .... 9·1116
Ranchero, Brunch .... 7·840
Red Deviled .... 7·771
Salad Bake, Olive- ... 19·2394
Salad Deluxe, Hot .... 7·840
Salad Filling .... 16·1959
Salad, Ham and ..... 15·1917
Sauce .... 7·890
Sauce, Creamy ..... 7·845
Scrambled, with Tomatoes 16·2011
Shirred (Baked) ..... 7·835
Soft-Cooked .... 7·834
Spanish .... 7·838

Egg *continued*
Spanish Sauce, in ....2·167
Spinach, San Francisco,
   and .... 9·1074
-Tomato-Sardine Sandwiches 6·735
Triple Deckers, Ham 'n ......7·826

Eggnog ....7·845
Apple .... 19·2347
Bavarian .... 10·1247
Breakfast .... 12·1415
Coffee Royal ....7·844
Cool Coffee ....5·576
Instant ....7·844
Orange .... 10·1179
Pie, Rum- .... 15·1897
Royale ....2·222
Sauce .... 15·1795

Eggplant
Baked ....7·849
-Cheese-Broiled .... 12·1438
-Cheese Stacks ....7·848
Crunch Casserole ....7·849
Elegant ....7·848
Italian ....7·848
Pan-Fried ....7·847
Ratatouille .... 15·1839
Scalloped ....7·849
Skillet ....7·848
Electric Mixer Pastry .... 13·1586

Elegant
Duckling with Sauce ...... 8·1003
Eggplant ....7·848
Grapefruit .... 9·1054
Onion Soup .... 12·1511
Emerald Cabbage ....3·327
Empanadas ....7·851

Enchilada
Casserole .... 15·1825
Cheese ....7·852
Cottage .... 11·1407
Mexican .... 11·1408
Endive-Avocado Salad ....7·852

English
Muffins ....7·857
Plum Pudding ....5·532
Tea Ring ....5·585
Toffee Ice Cream ...... 18·2209
Epicurean Peas .... 13·1595
Épinards à la Crème .... 17·2116
Escalopes De Veau Flambées 19·2354
European Apple Pie .... 14·1675
Everyday Cupcakes ....6·712
Everyday Waffles .... 19·2409
Extra Dry Martini .... 11·1360
Extra-Special Parsnips ...... 13·1573

F

Family
Green Salad .... 11·1286
Skillet Supper ....4·425
-Style Sugar Cookies ....5·530
Fancy Chicken à la King ....1·26
Fancy Franks ....1·75
Fantans ....7·864
Fast Crème Brûlée ....6·762
Fattigmann ....7·868

Favorite
Beef Loaf .... 11·1387
Pancakes .... 13·1552
Patio Refresher ....8·996
Feather Pancakes .... 13·1552
Feathery Crumb Cake ...... 12·1483

Festive
Celery Casserole ....4·428
Freeze ....7·844
Lettuce Salad .... 15·1920
Fiesta Beef Kabobs .... 10·1225
Fiesta Wax Beans ....2·179

Fig
Bars ....7·871
Bars, Marmalade- .... 11·1357
Filling ....7·871
Fruit Salad ....7·871
Loaf, Applesauce- ....7·871
-Nut Squares ....7·871
Whip, Mandarin- .... 11·1342

Filbert
Ice Cream Cake ....7·874
Macaroons ....7·872
Meringues ....7·872
Sponge Cake ....7·872
Filet Mignon Princess ....7·874

Filled
Artichoke Casings ....1·109
Beef Roll .... 18·2187
Doughnuts ....7·795
Ham Schnitzel .... 16·2008

Filling
Almond .... 1·41; 5·610; 16·2002
Almond Cream ....6·692
Apple ....5·559
Butterscotch .... 7·878; 15·1881
Cannelloni .... 10·1195
Cheese ....1·76
Cherry ...... 3·339; 5·560; 7·882
Chocolate .... 7·878; 8·959
Cranberry-Apple ....7·882
Cream .... 7·878; 18·2289

Filling *continued*
Creamy Satin ....1·39
Custard ....6·725
Date .... 6·745; 7·875
Date-Nut ....7·878
Egg ....1·76
Egg Salad .... 16·1959
Fig ....7·871
French Custard ....8·960
Grasshopper ....8·971
Ham ....1·76
Ham Salad .... 16·1959
Lemon ....7·879
Lime .... 11·1297
Mincemeat ....5·610
Orange .... 1·38; 5·578
Peach ....5·560
Pineapple-Coconut ....7·881
Poppy Seed .... 14·1721
Prune .... 10·1240
Rhubarb ....5·561
Tomato .... 18·2278
Vanilla Nut ....5·532
Finnish Viipuri Twist .... 16·2005
Firetong Glögg .... 9·1036

FISH ....7·884-896
Bake, Hickory .... 9·1146
Bake, Luau .... 18·2188
Bake, Spinach- ....7·889
Barbecued Bass Steaks ... 16·2013
Beet-Jellied Gefilte .... 8·1015
Broiled Bass Steaks ...... 16·2013
Cheese-Sauced Striped Bass 17·2172
Cheese Sauce, in ....7·893
Chips, and ....7·896
Chowder ....8·899
Cioppino ....5·539
Codfish Balls ....5·572
Corn-Stuffed Whitefish ... 18·2188
Crab-Filled Abalone Shell 16·2031
Curried Scrod .... 16·2012
Deviled Bass Fillets ...... 17·2197
Fillets, Baked ....7·889
Fillets, Zippy ....7·895
Fried ....7·895
Fried Mullet Parmesan ... 13·1559
Grilled Abalone ...... 15·1854
Herb-Baked ....7·890
Horseradish-Sauced
   Steamed .... 16·1997
Italian-Sauced .... 11·1320
Lemon-Stuffed ....7·890

Fish *continued*
Lutefisk Special . . . . **16**·1997
Mint-Stuffed Striped Bass . **17**·2171
Oriental Abalone . . . . **12**·1531
Oven-Fried . . . .**7**·895
Planked Stuffed Walleye . . . . .**7**·893
Poached . . . .**7**·896
Pompano Amandine . . . . . **14**·1714
Pompano En Papillote . . . . **13**·1563
Pompano with Dill Sauce . **14**·1714
Portions, Taco-Style . . . . . **18**·2241
Salad Club Sandwich . . . . **16**·1949
Smelts . . . . **17**·2065
Smelts in Barbecue Sauce . **17**·2065
Smoked Eel Canapés . . . . . **17**·2067
Smoked, with Lemon . . . .**2**·151
Snapper with Cashews . . . **15**·1843
Sole with Grapes . . . . **17**·2071
Steamed . . . .**7**·896
Tarragon Butter, with . . . . . .**7**·894
Fisherman's Luck . . . . **9**·1100
Fish House Punch . . . .**8**·899
Flambé, Banana-Raspberry . **20**·2466
Flambé, Golden Raisin . . . .**6**·766
Flaming Pears Melba . . . . . . **11**·1391
Flan . . . .**8**·901
Flank Steak Teriyaki . . . .**8**·902
Flapper Pudding . . . . **19**·2421
Flossie the Fish . . . . **15**·1846

Flounder
Provençale . . . .**8**·911
Stuffed . . . .**8**·911
Wine, in . . . .**8**·911
Flowerpot Cookie Cups . . . . **15**·1871

Fluffy
Ambrosia . . . .**1**·45
Butter Frosting . . . .**6**·711
Cheese Soufflé . . . .**7**·843
Citrus Dressing . . . .**5**·546
Cream Sauce . . . . **19**·2406
Dumplings . . . .**7**·817
Frosting . . . . **11**·1297
Hard Sauce . . . .**9**·1128
Maple Sauce . . . .**8**·963
Rice . . . . **15**·1867
Scrambled Eggs . . . .**7**·834
Tapioca Pudding . . . . **18**·2246
White Frosting . . . . **12**·1416
Fluted Mushrooms . . . . **12**·1450
Foamy Sauce . . . .**8**·915
Foil-Baked Halibut . . . .**8**·918
Foiled Potatoes . . . .**8**·919
Foiled Vegetables . . . .**8**·919

Fondant . . . .**8**·921
Peppermint . . . .**8**·921
Stuffed Dates . . . . **19**·2344
Vanilla . . . .**8**·921

Fondue
Bake, Cheese- . . . .**8**·923
Baked Turkey . . . . **19**·2317
Beef . . . .**8**·925
Blender Cheese . . . .**9**·1093
Buttermilk . . . . **18**·2223
Chocolate . . . . **8**·925; **18**·2210
Classic Cheese . . . .**8**·925
Dippers . . . . **12**·1432
French-Toasted . . . .**8**·963
Monterey (or Jack) Cheese **12**·1432
Rarebit-Style . . . . **12**·1484
Rosy Cheese . . . .**4**·462
Shrimp-Cheese . . . . **17**·2058
Teriyaki Meatballs . . . .**1**·64
Teriyaki Miniatures . . . .**9**·1087
Veal Strips . . . .**6**·729

Foo Yong
Beef and Egg . . . .**2**·180
Sauce . . . .**8**·929
Toss . . . . **19**·2424

Foreign Cookery
Austrian
Bischofsbrot . . . . **19**·2396
Sacher Torte . . . . **15**·1905
Wiener Schnitzel . . . . **20**·2446
Wiener Schnitzel à la
  Holstein . . . . **20**·2446
Zwiebelfleisch . . . . **19**·2395

Canadian
Maple Syrup Pie . . . .**3**·365
Tourtière (Canadian Pork
  Pie) . . . .**3**·364

Czechoslovakian
Kolacky . . . . **10**·1240

Dutch
Crullers . . . .**7**·796
Speculaas . . . . **17**·2106

English
Banbury Tarts . . . .**2**·143
Beef and Kidney Pie . . . .**7**·856
Cumberland Sauce . . . .**6**·710
Fish and Chips . . . .**7**·896
Hot Cross Buns . . . . **10**·1158
Individual Yorkshire
  Puddings . . . . **20**·2476
Lemon Curd Tarts . . . . **10**·1279
Mixed Grill . . . . **10**·1232
Plum Pudding . . . .**5**·532
Sally Lunn . . . . **16**·1934
Simnel Cake . . . . **17**·2060
Stuffed Cornish Game Hens . .**7**·856
Trifle . . . . **18**·2294
Welsh Rabbit . . . . **19**·2431

Foreign Cookery *continued*
French
Allemande Sauce . . . .**1**·32
Baked Liver Pâté . . . .**8**·956
Béarnaise Sauce . . . .**2**·182
Béchamel Sauce . . . .**2**·183
Biscuit Tortoni . . . .**2**·230
Blancmange . . . .**2**·236
Bouillabaisse . . . .**2**·253
Bread . . . .**8**·951
Brioche . . . .**3**·287
Buche de Noel . . . .**8**·959
Caneton à l'Orange
  (Duckling with Orange
  Sauce) . . . .**8**·956
Cassola de Peix . . . . **16**·2034
Céleri au Jus (Braised
  Celery Hearts) . . . .**8**·958
Champignons Sautés (Fresh
  Mushroom Sauté) . . . .**8**·956
Châteaubriand . . . .**4**·452
Chaud-Froid of Turkey . . . . . .**4**·452
Chocolate Mousse . . . . **12**·1436
Chocolate Truffles . . . .**8**·956
Coq au Vin . . . .**5**·617
Croissants . . . .**6**·696
Eggplant Ratatouille . . . . . **15**·1839
Épinards à la Créme
  (Creamed Spinach) . . . . **17**·2116
Escalopes De Veau
  Flambées . . . . **19**·2354
-Fried Camembert . . . .**8**·954
Napoleons . . . . **12**·1454
Omelet . . . . **12**·1501
Onion Soup . . . .**8**·958
Pain d'Épice . . . .**8**·955
Pâté Feuilleté au Fromage
  (French Cheese Pastries) . .**8**·958
Petits Fours . . . . **13**·1653
Pots de Crème . . . . **14**·1765
Quiche Lorraine . . . . **15**·1816
Quick Brioche . . . .**3**·286
Ragout . . . . **15**·1829
Raisin Brioche Ring . . . .**8**·958
Sauce Provençale . . . . **14**·1789
Savarin Chantilly . . . . **16**·1988
Savory Chestnut Stuffing . . . .**8**·955
Shrimp Étouffé . . . .**7**·861
Strawberry Tart . . . .**8**·959
Veal Cordon Bleu . . . . **19**·2354
Veal Stew . . . .**8**·959
Vichyssoise . . . . **19**·2393

German
Apple Strudel . . . . **17**·2175
Bavarian Potato
  Dumplings . . . . **8**·1022
Cherry Torte, Black Forest-
  Style . . . . **8**·1023
Chicken in Casserole . . . . . **8**·1021

Foreign Cookery, German *continued*
Cranberry Kuchen .... **10**·1267
Dried Fruit Bread .... **8**·1023
Edelweiss Torte .... **8**·1024
Gugelhupf .... **9**·1094
Hasenpfeffer .... **9**·1129
Kaffee Kuchen .... **10**·1241
Kartoffel Klösse (Potato
    Dumplings) .... **10**·1230
Kartoffel Pfannkuchen
    (Potato Pancakes) ..... **10**·1230
Königsberger
    Klops .... **10**·1240
Lebkuchen .... **10**·1268
Linzer Cake .... **11**·1301
Marrow
    Dumplings .... **8**·1021
Peach Kuchen .... **10**·1241
Peasant Platter .... **8**·1022
Pfeffernuesse .... **13**·1653
Sauerbraten .... **16**·1974
Springerle .... **17**·2122
Stollen .... **17**·2152
Sweet-Sour Red
    Cabbage .... **8**·1022

Greek
Christopsoma (Honey-Nut
    Bread) .... **9**·1066
Karidopita (Walnut
    Cake) .... **9**·1064
Kourabiedes (Butter
    Cookies) .... **9**·1066
Moussaka .... **12**·1436
Tyropitakia (Cheese
    Pastries) .... **9**·1064
Vasilopita (New Year's
    Bread) .... **9**·1064

Hungarian
Cabbage and
    Noodles .... **10**·1165
Goulash .... **10**·1164
Noodle Bake .... **10**·1164
Spaetzels .... **10**·1165

Indian
Chapati .... **4**·448
Curried Lamb .... **6**·719
Kima .... **10**·1187
Mulligatawny .... **12**·1446
Puris .... **15**·1809
Yellow Rice .... **10**·1187

Indonesian
Peanut Sauce .... **15**·1873
Pisang Goreng .... **14**·1694
Pork Sate (Pork
    Kabobs) .... **15**·1873
Rijsttafel Rice .... **15**·1873

Foreign Cookery *continued*
Italian
Antipasto .... **1**·60
Antipasto Sandwich .... **1**·59
Cannelloni .... **10**·1194
Cannelloni Filling ...... **10**·1195
Cannelloni Noodles ..... **10**·1195
Cappuccino .... **4**·403
Chicken and Spinach-
    Filled Ravioli .... **15**·1840
Chicken Cacciatore ..... **10**·1194
Cubaica (Sicilian
    Torrone) .... **10**·1199
Gnocchi .... **9**·1038
Golden Bread of
    Verona .... **10**·1194
Individual Antipasto .... **1**·59
Lasagne .... **10**·1263
Meatballs .... **10**·1197
Pastafazool .... **10**·1195
Polenta .... **14**·1711
Prosciutto and
    Artichokes .... **14**·1788
Roasted Sweet Peppers ... **10**·1195
Spaghetti and
    Meatballs .... **10**·1197
Spumoni .... **17**·2126
Stuffed Manicotti .... **11**·1344
Tomato Polenta .... **14**·1711
Veal Parmesan with
    Spaghetti .... **17**·2101
Veal Scallopine .... **13**·1579
Vitello Tonnato .... **19**·2355
Zabaglione au Madera ... **10**·1199
Zuppa Inglese .... **6**·725

Jewish
Beet-Jellied Gefilte Fish ... **8**·1015
Blueberry Latkes .... **10**·1264
Contemporary Duckling .. **10**·1222
Date-Nut Ring .... **10**·1222
Fruit Fritters .... **9**·1126
Israeli Cheese Blintzes ..... **2**·241
Potato Kugels .... **10**·1242
Sesame-Honey Candy .... **9**·1127

Lithuanian
Strawberry Torte .... **5**·532

Mexican
Almendrado .... **1**·34
Beef Tostadas .... **18**·2292
Cheese Enchiladas .... **7**·852
Chilies Rellenos Con
    Queso .... **4**·494
Christmas Eve Salad .... **11**·1408
Cottage Enchiladas ..... **11**·1407
Deviled Guacamole ..... **9**·1093
Empanadas .... **7**·851
Enchiladas .... **11**·1408

Foreign Cookery, Mexican *continued*
Fried Beans .... **18**·2292
Frijoles Refritos .... **8**·965
Guacamole .... **9**·1093
Hot Sauce for
    Tostadas .... **18**·2293
Mexicali Casserole ...... **11**·1408
Salsa .... **15**·1857
Tostada Casserole .... **11**·1407

Near Eastern
Baklava .... **12**·1458
Bulgar Wheat Pilaf ...... **12**·1458
Lamb Shish Kabobs ...... **16**·2044
Lamb-Stuffed Cabbage
    Leaves .... **12**·1457
Lebanese Cacic .... **12**·1456
Shish Kabob .... **12**·1457
Syrian Bread .... **12**·1458
Turkish Zucchini Dolmas ....**7**·788

Oriental
Abalone .... **12**·1531
Beef Skillet .... **12**·1530
Beef Teriyaki .... **12**·1530
Chi Chow .... **12**·1530
Chicken-Egg Foo Yong ...... **8**·929
Chinese Almond
    Cookies .... **12**·1529
Chinese Firepot .... **4**·498
Chinese Fried Rice ...... **12**·1535
Chinese Peas and
    Shrimp .... **12**·1533
Chinese Smoked Ribs .... **12**·1531
Crab-Cabbage Skillet .... **12**·1534
Ginger-Fruit Oriental .... **12**·1531
Japanese Custard
    Soup .... **12**·1530
Japanese Tempura .... **18**·2263
Lobster Salad .... **12**·1534
Pineapple-Pork Skillet .... **12**·1535
Pork and Shrimp .... **12**·1534
Rice .... **12**·1536
Scallop Skillet .... **12**·1533
Shrimp Foo Yong .... **8**·929
Speedy Chop Suey ...... **12**·1535
Sukiyaki .... **18**·2202
Sweet and Sour Pork ..... **12**·1535
Sweet and Sour Tuna .... **12**·1534
Sweet-Sour Shrimp ...... **12**·1533
Teriyaki Roast
    Tenderloin .... **12**·1536
Veal Chops .... **12**·1532
Yakamish .... **12**·1531

Portuguese
Nogados (Portuguese
    Christmas Log) .... **14**·1743
Rabanados .... **14**·1743
Sonhos (Dreams) .... **14**·1743

Foreign Cookery *continued*
Russian
Borsch . . . .**2**·250
Chicken Kiev . . . . **15**·1899
Kulebiaka . . . . **15**·1900
Lamb Shashlik . . . . **16**·2025

Scandinavian
Aebleskiver (Danish
   Doughnuts) . . . . **16**·2004
Baked Liver and Rice . . . . **16**·1998
Cardamom Braid . . . . **16**·2002
Cardamom Cookies . . . .**4**·407
Chocolate Spritz . . . .**5**·530
Danish Coffee Ring . . . .**6**·736
Danish Kringle . . . .**6**·737
Danish Pastry . . . . **16**·2002
Decorated Ham . . . . **16**·2006
Egg-Tomato-Sardine
   Sandwiches . . . .**6**·735
Fattigmann . . . .**7**·868
Finnish Viipuri Twist . . . . . **16**·2005
Firetong Glögg . . . .**9**·1036
Glazed Yule Ham . . . . **16**·1998
Grandmother's Jelly
   Cookies . . . . **16**·2003
Ham Pinwheel
   Sandwiches . . . .**6**·735
Horseradish-Sauced
   Steamed Fish . . . . **16**·1997
Jellied Veal Loaf
   (Kalvsylta) . . . . **19**·2355
Lingonberry Sauce . . . . . . **11**·1298
Lucia Braid . . . . **16**·2004
Lutefisk Special . . . . **16**·1997
Quick Swedish Meatballs . **16**·2007
Roast Duckling with Red
   Cabbage . . . .**5**·524
Rum Pudding . . . . **16**·2003
Rye Cookies . . . . **16**·2005
Sandbakkels . . . . **16**·2005
Shrimp-Capers Sandwich . . . .**6**·735
Spritz . . . . **17**·2124
Stag's Antlers . . . . **16**·2005
Stuffed Celery . . . . **16**·2006
Swedish Brown Beans . . . . **16**·2006
Swedish Egg Coffee . . . .**5**·576
Swedish Fruit Soup . . . . . . **17**·2091
Swedish Ginger Cookies . . **18**·2206
Swedish Holiday Braid . . . . . .**5**·585
Swedish Lucia Buns . . . .**3**·306
Swedish Meatballs . . . . . . **16**·1999
Swedish Pancakes . . . . **13**·1557
Swedish Rye Bread . . . . . **11**·1298
Swedish Veal Roast . . . . . . **19**·2359
Uppakrakakor . . . . **16**·2003

Scottish
Scotch Broth . . . . **16**·2009
Tea Scones . . . . **16**·2008

Foreign Cookery *continued*
Spanish
Flan . . . .**8**·901
Gazpacho . . . . **8**·1014
Paella . . . . **13**·1549
Potato Omelet . . . . **17**·2103

Swiss
Cream Torte . . . . **15**·1802

Turkish
Circassian Chicken . . . . . . **19**·2327
   Shredded Wheat Dessert . **19**·2327
Forgotten Cherry Torte . . . **18**·2287
Four Bean Salad . . . .**2**·178
Four-Star Sandwich . . . . . . **12**·1513

Frankfurter
Best Hamdogs . . . .**8**·935
Blue Cheese Dogs . . . .**2**·248
Cocktail Wieners . . . .**8**·933
Coney Islands . . . .**5**·596
Doubles . . . .**8**·935
Hot Dogs Delicious . . . .**8**·936
Kettle-Cooked . . . .**8**·931
Nutty Pups . . . .**8**·934
Skewer Dogs . . . . **12**·1430
Wiener-Bean Bake . . . .**2**·175
Wiener Bean Pot . . . .**8**·936
Wienie-Lottas . . . . **10**·1189

Frank(furter)
Barbecue, Tangy . . . .**8**·935
Cabbage, and . . . .**8**·936
Cabbage Rolls, and . . . .**8**·931
Chili-Cheese . . . .**8**·933
Corn Crown, and . . . .**8**·933
Fancy . . . .**1**·75
Florentine . . . .**8**·910
Foil, in . . . . **14**·1780
Frankrauts . . . . **16**·1975
Fries . . . .**8**·931
Glazed Apples and . . . .**8**·936
Hilo . . . . **15**·1854
-Kraut Dinner, Quick . . . . . **16**·1975
Kraut Stew, and . . . . **16**·1975
-Noodle Bake, Savory . . . . . .**8**·934
Plum-Glazed . . . .**1**·75
Potato Bake, and . . . .**8**·932
-Reuben Sandwich . . . .**8**·935
Sassy . . . . **10**·1214
Saucy . . . .**8**·934
Skillet, Sweet Potato- . . . . **18**·2213
Snapperoni . . . . **16**·1982
Spirals, Swiss and . . . .**8**·937
Sweet and Sour . . . . **14**·1690
Triangles . . . . **16**·1982
-Vegetable Medley . . . .**8**·935
Freezer Pineapple Conserve . **18**·2201

FREEZING . . . .**8**·938-949

French
Bread . . . .**8**·951
Bread Stuffing . . . . **18**·2185
Cheese Pastries . . . .**8**·958
Chocolate Coffee
   Cake . . . . **18**·2198
Chocolate Mousse . . . . **12**·1436
Custard Filling . . . .**8**·960
Dressing . . . .**8**·962
-Fried Butterfly Shrimp . . . . .**6**·748
-Fried Camembert . . . .**8**·954
-Fried Liver . . . . **11**·1306
-Fried Onion Rings . . . .**8**·961
-Fried Potato Puffs . . . .**8**·960
-Fried Shrimp . . . . **16**·2036
-Fried Sweet Potatoes . . . . **18**·2212
-Fried Vegetable Bites . . . . . .**8**·960
Fries . . . .**8**·960
Lemon Pie . . . . **10**·1276
Omelet . . . . **12**·1501
Onion Pie . . . . **14**·1669
Onion Soup . . . .**1**·16
Ragout . . . . **15**·1829
Shrimp in Shells . . . . **17**·2056
Strawberry Tart . . . .**8**·959
Toast . . . .**8**·962
-Toasted Fondue . . . .**8**·963
Veal Stew . . . .**8**·959
Vichyssoise . . . . **19**·2393

Fresh
Apple Waffles . . . .**3**·273
Apricot Pie . . . .**1**·100
Cherry Pie . . . .**4**·475
Cooked Shrimp . . . . **17**·2055
Corn on the Cob . . . . **15**·1874
Corn Relish . . . . **15**·1857
Cucumber Relish . . . .**6**·709
Fruit Aloha . . . . **17**·2167
Fruit Ambrosia . . . .**1**·44
Fruit Bars . . . . **13**·1608
Fruit Tarts . . . . **18**·2252
Garden Mint Ice Cream . . . . .**8**·976
Gooseberry Pie . . . .**9**·1040
Herb Salad . . . .**9**·1141
Mint Sauce . . . . **16**·1970
Mushroom Sauté . . . .**8**·956
Peach Ice Cream . . . . **15**·1853
Pineapple Jubilee . . . . **14**·1691
Pineapple Pie . . . . **14**·1692

Fried
Cornmeal Mush .... **12·**1447
Eggs .... **7·**836
Fish .... **7·**895
Haddock .... **9·**1099
Mullet Parmesan .... **13·**1559
Peach Pies .... **8·**964
Plantains .... **14·**1701
Rabbit .... **15·**1828
Salmon Sandwich .... **18·**2249
Shad Roe .... **15·**1877
Squid .... **17·**2137
Squirrel .... **17·**2138
Tomatoes .... **18·**2279
Frijoles Refritos .... **8·**965

Fritter
Apple .... **8·**965
Banana .... **2·**141
Cheese-Sauced
   Zucchini .... **17·**2132
Corn .... **5·**625
Fruit .... **9·**1126
Speedy Corn .... **5·**625
Vegetable .... **8·**965
Frog Legs, Oven-Fried ...... **13·**1540
Frog Legs with Sauce .... **8·**965

Frosted
Almond Swirl .... **10·**1160
Cashew Drops .... **4·**419
Cheese Mold .... **2·**247
Cocktail .... **5·**544
Fruit Punch .... **10·**1223
Luncheon Meat .... **11·**1330
Ribbon Loaf .... **16·**1959
Rose Geranium Leaves ... **15·**1890

FROSTING .... **8·**966-973
Almond Paste .... **3·**348
Apple .... **3·**348
Boiled .... **8·**968
Brown-Butter Icing .... **3·**261
Burnt-Sugar .... **3·**312
Butter .... **8·**970
Caramel Candy .... **8·**971
Caramel-Cream Cheese ..... **5·**596
Choco-Blender .... **4·**510
Chocolate .... **3·**296; **18·**2289
Chocolate-Cream Cheese ... **6·**675
Chocolate-Nut Fluff ...... **8·**970
Chocolate Pudding ...... **15·**1798
Chocolate Torte .... **15·**1904

Frosting *continued*
Choco-Satin .... **8·**970
Cinnamon Icing .... **9·**1044
Coconut .... **8·**969
Coffee .... **8·**969
Confectioners' Icing .... **5·**596
Cream Cheese .... **6·**675
Creamy Chocolate .... **4·**509
Fluffy .... **11·**1297
Fluffy Butter .... **6·**711
Fluffy White .... **12·**1416
Fudge .... **8·**968
Golden Butter .... **3·**350
Golden Butter Icing .... **4·**419
Jelly .... **10·**1214
Lemon Butter ..... **5·**597; **18·**2199
Maple Fluff .... **17·**2111
Milk Chocolate .... **18·**2199
Mint .... **5·**531
Mocha .... **16·**2017
No-Cook Fudge .... **3·**347
Nutty Chocolate .... **13·**1615
Orange-Butter .... **13·**1630
Orange Cream .... **7·**824
Orange Icing .... **15·**1880
Ornamental .... **3·**353
Peanut Butter Quick
   Cake .... **8·**969
Petits Fours Icing .... **13·**1653
Pink .... **8·**968
Prune Butter .... **14·**1792
Rocky-Road .... **8·**970
Rose Geranium .... **15·**1890
Royal .... **3·**353
Sea Foam .... **16·**2013
Seven-Minute .... **8·**968
Shadow Icing .... **1·**31
Sour Cream .... **17·**2095
Speedy .... **13·**1615
Uncooked .... **8·**970

Frosty
Date Balls .... **5·**613
Fruit Cup .... **14·**1687
Fruit Molds .... **15·**1920
Golden Punch .... **8·**995
Party Punch .... **15·**1808
Pineapple Dessert ...... **14·**1690
Salad Loaf .... **15·**1920
Spiced Tea .... **17·**2148
Strawberry Cubes .... **8·**976

Frozen
Apricot Torte .... **8·**976
Butterscotch Dream .... **15·**1797
Cranberry Velvet Pie ..... **14·**1677
Fruit Slices .... **15·**1920
Limeade Pudding .... **8·**977
Mincemeat Tarts ...... **18·**2251
Strawberry Jam .... **10·**1204

FRUIT .... **8·**979-991
(See also Apple, Apricot, Avocado,
Banana, Blueberry, Cantaloupe,
Cranberry, Currant, Date, Fig,
Grape, Grapefruit, Honeydew,
Lemon, Lime, Mandarin Orange,
Nectarine, Orange, Papaya, Peach,
Pear, Pineapple, Plum, Prune,
Raisin, Raspberry, Rhubarb,
Strawberry, Tangerine,
Watermelon.)

Aloha, Fresh .... **17·**2167
Ambrosia, Fresh .... **1·**44
Balls .... **7·**803
Banana-Berry Cup .... **8·**987
Bars, Fresh .... **13·**1608
Baskets .... **8·**1013
Boats, Ham Salad- .... **14·**1689
Bowl, Buffet .... **9·**1054
Bowl, Fresh .... **19·**2428
Bowl, Low-Cal .... **5·**545
Bread .... **5·**539
-Candied Sweet Potatoes . **18·**2214
Canned Blackberry Pie ..... **2·**233
Chilled Breakfast Compote ... **5·**595
Cobblers .... **5·**559
-Cocktail Cobbler .... **8·**995
Cocktail Gems .... **8·**995
Cocktail Mold .... **8·**994
Cocktail Pie .... **8·**994
Cocktail Smoothee .... **6·**676
Cocktail, Summer .... **5·**562
Combo, Creamy .... **2·**226
Compote, Harvest .... **7·**803
Compote, Honey- .... **11·**1303
Compote, Hot .... **20·**2460
Compote, Hot Curried ..... **5·**595
Compote Pie .... **7·**803
Compote, Ruby .... **5·**595
Compote, Winter .... **5·**595
Confections .... **7·**803
Cooler, Ginger- .... **19·**2428
Cream, Fresh, and ..... **19·**2428
Crumble, Hawaiian .... **6·**762
Cup Combinations .... **8·**984
Cup, Frosty .... **14·**1687
Cup, 1-2-3 .... **5·**563
Cups, Blue Cheese .... **2·**248
Cup Tower .... **8·**987
Dessert, Pink .... **8·**991
Dessert, Triple .... **8·**991
Dip Fluff .... **16·**1924

Fruit *continued*
Dip, Quick .... **17**·2167
Dough, Basic ....**3**·369
Dumplings, with ....**7**·817
-Filled Squash ....**1**·19
Flip ....**8**·908
Freeze, Cookie- ....**8**·976
Freeze, Oriental ....**3**·371
French Dressing ....**16**·1928
Fresh Gooseberry Pie .....**9**·1040
Fried Plantains ....**14**·1701
Fritters ....**9**·1126
Galaxy Salad ....**20**·2475
-Glazed Pork Chops,
   Double ....**9**·1135
Kabobs, Beef and ....**9**·1145
Kabobs, Ham and ....**9**·1111
Lingonberry Sauce ......**11**·1298
Mangoes on the
   Half Shell ....**11**·1343
Mango Sherbet ....**11**·1344
Marinated Skewered .....**17**·2062
Medley, Buffet ....**19**·2427
Medley Elegante ....**8**·990
Medley, Hot ....**14**·1740
Medley, Midwinter .....**13**·1624
Medley, Winter ....**10**·1279
Melange ....**17**·2167
Melon Medley ....**10**·1155
Orange Fluff, and ....**8**·987
Oriental, Ginger- ....**12**·1531
Plate, Hawaiian ....**8**·988
Punch, Quantity ......**15**·1809
Punch, Ruby ....**6**·665
Platter, Summer ....**5**·546
Refresher ....**16**·2043
Relish, Cheese- ....**6**·644
Rolls ....**3**·369
Salad, Fig ....**7**·871
Salad, Refrigerated ....**9**·1049
Salad, Salmon- ....**14**·1688
Salad, Tuna- ....**18**·2303
Sauce, Spiced ....**8**·991
Sauce, Spring ....**10**·1180
Sauce, Wine ....**5**·634
Sherbet, Three- ....**8**·996
Soufflé, Winter- ....**9**·1056
Soup, Swedish ....**17**·2091
Sparkle Cup ....**9**·1047
Sparkle, Spiced ....**17**·2148
Sparkle Sundaes ......**10**·1183
Squares, No-Bake ....**3**·371
Steamed Blackberry
   Pudding ....**2**·233
Strawberry Dressing,
   with ....**10**·1215
-Stuffed Goose ....**14**·1775
-Stuffed Pork Chops ......**8**·990
Stuffing, Three ....**18**·2184
Tarts, Fresh ....**18**·2252

Fruit *continued*
Tea, Iced ....**18**·2257
Tea Sandwiches ....**16**·1958
Topper, Tropical ......**18**·2286
Toss, Slim-Trim ......**19**·2428
-Turkey Kabobs ....**8**·990
Upside-Down Cake,
   Ginger ....**19**·2342
-Vegetable Toss ....**12**·1521
Wheels ....**16**·1948

Fruitcake
Chip-Cherry ....**16**·2017
Cookies ....**5**·530
Dark ....**8**·993
Dublin ....**3**·348
Golden ....**8**·992
Groom's Cake ....**9**·1077
Harvest Apple Cake ....**3**·348
Light ....**8**·993
No-Bake ....**8**·993
Simnel Cake ....**17**·2060
Whole Nut ....**5**·531

Fruited
Cheesecake ....**9**·1041
Chicken Breasts ....**9**·1050
Chicken Salad ....**11**·1355
Iced Tea ....**2**·219
Luncheon Loaf ....**11**·1330
Nectar Salad ....**8**·1018
Parfait Salad ....**11**·1398
Pot Roast ....**7**·803
Tangerine Ice ....**10**·1166
Watermelon ....**19**·2427

Fruit Pie
Apple-Apricot ....**14**·1671
Apple Crumb ....**1**·87
Apple-Raisin ....**1**·88
Blueberry ....**2**·244
Canned Blackberry ....**2**·233
Cherry-Peach ....**8**·906
Cherry-Rhubarb ....**14**·1676
Concord Grape ....**9**·1051
Cranberry-Pear ....**14**·1676
Creamy Cherry ....**4**·474
Crumb Top Plum ....**14**·1707
Custard-Peach ....**14**·1674
Custard-Sauced Deep-Dish
   Apple ....**6**·747
Deep-Dish Apple ....**14**·1671
Deep-Dish Orange-Peach ...**6**·747
European Apple ....**14**·1675
Fresh Apricot ....**1**·100
Fresh Cherry ....**4**·475
Fresh Gooseberry ....**9**·1040
Fresh Pineapple ....**14**·1692
Fried Peach ....**8**·964
Fruit Cocktail ....**8**·994

Fruit Pie *continued*
Ginger-Fruit ....**9**·1032
Homemade Mincemeat ..**12**·1419
King Kamehameha ......**14**·1679
Lemon-Crusted Blueberry **14**·1674
Lemony Mince-Meringue .**12**·1418
Marmalade-Plum ....**11**·1357
Mock Mince ....**1**·88
1-2-3 Apple ....**15**·1797
Peach ....**13**·1608
Peach-Marshmallow ....**11**·1359
Peach-Mince ....**12**·1418
Pear Crumble ....**13**·1625
Pear-Pineapple-Cheese ..**13**·1625
Perfect Apple ....**1**·87
Petite Peach ....**13**·1608
Pizza-Peach ....**13**·1607
Raisin ....**15**·1835
Red Cherry ....**4**·474
Rhubarb ....**15**·1860
Rosy Raspberry ....**18**·2247
Sliced Pear ....**14**·1675
Strawberry Glamour .....**17**·2163
Strawberry Glaze ....**17**·2164
Strawberry-Rhubarb .....**15**·1860
Tart and Saucy Apple ....**12**·1484
Topsy-Turvy Apple ....**1**·87
Fruity Ginger Ale Mold ......**9**·1049

Fudge
Blue Ribbon ....**8**·999
Brownies ....**3**·297
Caramel ....**3**·378
Coffee Dot ....**3**·377
Double-Layer ....**8**·999
Easy Chocolate ....**15**·1798
Frosting ....**8**·968
Java ....**5**·527
Nuggets ....**12**·1489
Old-Time ....**8**·999
Opera ....**8**·999
Peanut Butter ....**5**·527
Pudding Cake ....**19**·2341
Remarkable ....**8**·1000
Ribbon Pie ....**13**·1644
Rocky Road ....**8**·1000
Santa's ....**3**·378
Sauce ....**1**·28
Sauce, Quick ....**6**·768
Two-Tone ....**3**·378
Fudgy Chocolate Sauce ....**5**·578
Funny-Face Cookies ....**7**·806

G

Game
Broiled Quail ....**15**·1810
Broiled Venison Steaks ....**8**·1004
Fried Rabbit ....**15**·1828

Game *continued*

Fried Squirrel .... **17**·2138
Opossum .... **12**·1513
Partridge in Red Wine .... **13**·1574
Pheasant in Wine Sauce .. **13**·1655
Pheasant with Wild Rice .. **13**·1655
Roast Sherried Pheasant .. **13**·1655
Roast Wild Goose .... **9**·1039
Savory Squab .... **17**·2127
Smothered Quail .... **8**·1005
Smothered Pheasant ..... **13**·1654
Squab on a Spit .... **17**·2127
Squab with Apricot Sauce . **8**·1004
Sweet-Sour Squab .... **17**·2127
Wine-Sauced Birds .... **8**·1005

Garden

Cottage Cheese
  Sandwiches .... **16**·1948
Pepper Boats .... **9**·1073
Vegetable Bowl .... **17**·2133

Garlic

Bread, Toasty .... **8**·1009
Butter .... **3**·315
Croutons .... **6**·699
Dressing, Snappy .... **16**·1929
French Dressing .... **8**·1009
Lamb Kabobs .... **16**·2045
Olive Oil .... **3**·331
Olives .... **12**·1497
Slices, Grilled .... **2**·159

Garnish

Apple Rings .... **8**·1010
Brazil-Nut Petals ....**3**·261
Carrot Corkscrews .... **8**·1012
Carrot Curls or Zigzags .... **8**·1012
Cheese Apples .... **8**·1013
Chocolate Curls .... **8**·1008
Coffee Coconut .... **3**·356
Cucumber Basket .... **6**·709
Fluted Mushrooms ...... **12**·1450
Frosted Rose Geranium
  Leaves .... **15**·1890
Fruit Baskets .... **8**·1013
Grapes, Frosted .... **9**·1052
Kumquat Flowers ...... **10**·1242
Melon Balls .... **8**·1013
Minted Coconut ....**5**·568
Orange Chrysanthemum . **8**·1013
Orange Garnishes ...... **12**·1517
Ornamental Frosting ....**3**·353
Panned Apple Rings ....**3**·360
Pickle Fans .... **8**·1012
Pickle Garnishes .... **8**·1012
Radish Accordions .... **8**·1011
Radish Daisies .... **8**·1012
Radish Roses .... **8**·1012
Scalloped Bowl .... **8**·1013

Garnish *continued*

Scored Cucumbers .... **8**·1013
Stuffed Pickle Slices ...... **8**·1012
Sugar Bells ....**3**·285
Tomato Roses .... **8**·1012
Turnip Lilies .... **8**·1013
Vegetable Flowers .... **8**·1013
Zigzag Bowl .... **8**·1013
Gazpacho, Blender .... **17**·2080
Gazpacho, Spanish .... **8**·1014

German

Beef Stew .... **11**·1380
Burgers .... **9**·1124
Peasant Platter .... **8**·1022
Potato Salad .... **14**·1754
Stollen .... **17**·2152
Giant Pecan Popovers ....**2**·238

Giblet

Cooked .... **8**·1024
Gravy .... **9**·1062
Stuffing .... **19**·2309

Gin

Lime Fizz .... **20**·2468

Ginger

Cookies, Crisp .... **10**·1244
Cookies, Orange- .... **15**·1847
Cookies, Rolled .... **9**·1028
Cookies, Swedish ...... **18**·2206
-Date Triangles .... **6**·740
Dip .... **1**·71
-Fruit Cooler .... **19**·2428
-Fruit Oriental .... **12**·1531
-Fruit Pie .... **9**·1032
-Fruit Upside-Down
  Cake .... **19**·2342
-Glazed Crown Roast of
  Pork .... **6**·701
-Honey Dressing .... **9**·1152
-Maple Alaska .... **9**·1031
Muffins .... **9**·1029
-Peach Squares .... **9**·1030
-Peachy Casserole ...... **13**·1605
-Pear Cake .... **9**·1030
-Pear Crumble .... **13**·1623
Rice .... **12**·1530
Sauce .... **12**·1531
Sauce, Candied ....**6**·767
-Sauced Tongue .... **18**·2285
Soy ....**4**·498
-Sugar Puffs .... **15**·1800
Gingerbread .... **9**·1030
Gingerbread Layer Cake .....**3**·344
Gingered Ham Slice ..... **17**·2109
Gingered-Rhubarb
  Jam .... **15**·1861
Gingerettes .... **19**·2407

Gingerscotch Cake ....**3**·345
Gingersnaps .... **9**·1032
Gingery Macaroni Salad .... **15**·1835

Glaze

Apple .... **3**·267
Apricot .... **16**·1988
Burgundy ....**5**·636
Chocolate .... **9**·1035
Chocolate Gloss ' .... **10**·1217
Crab Apple ....**6**·654
Currant .... **5**·526; **6**·715
Golden .... **3**·267
Jewel .... **11**·1384
Lemon .... **5**·607; **10**·1268
Mustard, for Ham .... **9**·1111
Orange ....**6**·695
Peking .... **10**·1159
Vanilla ....**1**·58
Wine ....**7**·856

Glazed

Almonds .... **9**·1035
Anise Loaf ....**1**·56
Apples and Franks ....**8**·936
Carrots .... **4**·413
Ham-Raisin Balls .... **9**·1117
Ham Ring .... **11**·1387
Ham Slice .... **14**·1733
Lemon-Nut Bread ....**3**·275
Orange Rolls .... **18**·2215
Pork Shoulder .... **14**·1782
Sausage Bites ....**1**·75
Sausage Loaf .... **14**·1732
Smoked Shoulder .... **14**·1734
Squash Rings .... **1**·21
Squash with Onions ....**1**·20
Yule Ham .... **16**·1998
Glorified Grahams .... **9**·1042
Glorified Rice .... **15**·1870
Glossy Fruit Dressing ...... **16**·1928

Golden

Apricot Sauce ....**6**·767
Bread of Verona .... **10**·1194
Bubble Ring ....**3**·278
Butter Frosting ....**3**·350
Butter Icing ....**4**·419
Carrot Bake ....**4**·412
Cheese Soup .... **17**·2088
Chiffon Cake ....**4**·491
Corn Fry ....**5**·627
Crown Coffee Bread ....**5**·587
Fruitcake ....**8**·992
Gate Salad Loaf .... **16**·1950
Glaze ....**3**·267
Glow Punch ....**4**·406
Lemon Soufflé .... **10**·1267
Potato Bake .... **14**·1757
Pumpkin Muffins .... **15**·1806

Golden *continued*
Raisin Flambé .... **6·**766
Squash Soup .... **17·**2136
Sundaes .... **18·**2204
Velvet Rarebit .... **19·**2432
Goober Cookies .... **13·**1611
Good Neighbor Stew ...... **17·**2148

Goose
Fruit-Stuffed .... **14·**1775
Roast Domestic .... **9·**1040
Roast Wild .... **9·**1039
Gooseberry Cups .... **9·**1040
Goulash and Noodles, Beef . **18·**2284
Goulash, Hungarian .... **10·**1164

Gourmet
Dagwoods .... **19·**2312
Onions .... **12·**1509
Pork Chops .... **6·**672
Potato Soup .... **14·**1749
Salad .... **5·**588
Sauce .... **3·**299
Shrimp .... **17·**2058
Tenderloin on a Spit .... **2·**158

Graham Cracker
Crust .... **6·**703
Pudding .... **9·**1041
Tart Shells .... **18·**2252
Graham Gems .... **12·**1444
Grandmother's Jelly Cookies **16·**2003

Grape
Burgundy Ham with Green **9·**1050
Compote, Nectarine- ..... **9·**1050
Conserve .... **9·**1052
Devonshire Green .... **9·**1050
Jam, Spiced .... **10·**1204
Jelly .... **10·**1212
Parfait Pie .... **9·**1052
Pie, Concord .... **9·**1051
Punch, Spiced .... **9·**1049
Salad, Cranberry- .... **9·**1049
Sole with .... **17·**2071
Spiced .... **9·**1049
-Syruped Crepes .... **9·**1052

Grapefruit
-Berry Compote .... **11·**1324
Broiled .... **9·**1054
-Cheese Squares .... **9·**1056
-Crab Cocktail .... **9·**1053
Curried Chicken with ..... **9·**1057
Elegant .... **9·**1054
Ice, Apricot- .... **9·**1057
Molds, Apple- .... **9·**1054
Peel, Candied .... **3·**370
Salad, Artichoke- .... **9·**1057
-Sherbet Ring .... **9·**1054

Grasshopper .... **9·**1058
Cake .... **8·**971
Filling .... **8·**971
Parfaits, Lazy .... **9·**1058
Pie .... **9·**1059
Pie, Lazy .... **6·**686

Gravy
Chicken .... **4·**484
Giblet .... **9·**1062
Herb .... **11·**1377
Hurry-Up .... **9·**1061
Onion .... **17·**2052
Pan .... **3·**296
Perfect Pan .... **9·**1061
Pot Roast .... **9·**1060
Sour Cream ..... **9·**1061; **13·**1564
Yankee Pot Roast .... **14·**1761
Greek Salad .... **9·**1066
Green and Gold
Ambrosia .... **9·**1051
Green and Gold Compote
(low calorie) .... **11·**1319

Green Bean
Amandine .... **1·**44
Bacon Flavored .... **19·**2385
Blue Cheese-Sauced ..... **19·**2385
Caesar .... **9·**1068
Caraway .... **2·**179
Combo, Tomato- .... **9·**1068
Creamy .... **9·**1068
Deviled .... **9·**1068
Dill Sauce, with .... **2·**179
Dutch .... **9·**1067
Far East .... **19·**2387
Pickled Dilled .... **13·**1660
Plus .... **15·**1825
Salad, Chili- .... **4·**496
Saucy Vegetable Trio ...... **2·**179
Savory .... **16·**1988
Skillet, Hamburger- .... **2·**179
Snappy .... **9·**1067
Succotash .... **18·**2193
Greengage Plum
Squares .... **9·**1069
Green Goddess Salad .... **9·**1069
Green Goddess Sauce .... **8·**925

Green Pepper
Boats, Garden .... **9·**1073
Cups, Stuffed .... **13·**1641
Cups, Tuna in .... **14·**1683
Cup Trio .... **13·**1640
Indian-Stuffed .... **9·**1073
Roasted Sweet .... **10·**1195
Steak, Savory .... **13·**1647
Stuffed .... **12·**1439
Tongue-Stuffed .... **19·**2351
Turkey-Stuffed .... **9·**1073

Green Rice Bake .... **15·**1868
Green Salad Quintet .... **9·**1074
Green Tomato Dill Pickles .. **13·**1661
Grill-Broiled Cornish Game
Hens .... **5·**634

Grilled
Abalone .... **15·**1854
Beefwiches .... **9·**1076
Garlic Slices .... **2·**159
Halibut .... **9·**1101
Ham Slice .... **10·**1214
Perch with Parsley Sauce . **13·**1648
Reubens .... **5·**630
Rib Eye Roast .... **15·**1894
Salmon Steaks .... **16·**1939
Salmonwiches .... **9·**1076
Sausage Treats .... **9·**1075
Tomatoes .... **9·**1075
Turkey Pieces .... **2·**155
Vegetables in Foil .... **2·**159
Grits Ring, Parmesan ...... **9·**1077
Groom's Cake .... **9·**1077

GROUND BEEF ...... **9·**1079-1092
Pizza .... **14·**1697
Reuben .... **9·**1087
Stuffing .... **18·**2185
Ground Lamb Pie .... **10·**1261
Guacamole .... **9·**1093
Guacamole, Deviled .... **9·**1093
Guacamole Dip, Clam- .... **10·**1275
Gugelhupf .... **9·**1094
Guinea Hens and Kraut ..... **9·**1096

Gumbo
Chicken .... **1·**23
Soup, Tomato- .... **9·**1096
Z'Herbs .... **6·**690

Gumdrop
-Coffee Squares .... **9·**1097
Cookies .... **9·**1097
Gems .... **9·**1097
-Nut Wreath .... **9·**1096

H

Haddock
Chowder, Clam- .... **16·**2014
Fried .... **9·**1099
Herbed Fish Bake ...... **9·**1099

Haddock *continued*
Polynesian .... **9**·1070
-Shrimp Bake .... **9**·1099
Stuffed Fillet Roll-Ups .... **7**·890

Halibut
Fisherman's Luck .... **9**·1100
Foil-Baked ....**8**·918
Grilled .... **9**·1101
Herb-Crumb Topped Fish ....**7**·894
Royale .... **9**·1101
Steaks, Crumb-Crowned ... **9**·1100

HAM .... **9**·1103-1119
-Apricot Crepes .... **6**·693
-Asparagus Broil ...... **18**·2223
Bake, Carrot-Apple- ....**1**·86
Bake, Cauliflower- ...... **9**·1116
Baked in Apple Cider ...... **8**·996
Bake, Swiss Turkey- ..... **14**·1776
Ball ....**1**·70
Balls, Cherry-Sauced ..... **11**·1382
Barbecue .... **11**·1320
-Bean Bake, Deviled ....**7**·772
Best Hamdogs ....**8**·935
Birds, Veal and .... **19**·2362
Bites, Artichoke- .... **9**·1113
Black Magic Luncheon ... **13**·1589
Blanket, in a .... **1**·17
Burgandy, with Green
    Grapes .... **9**·1050
California Curry Platter ... **12**·1503
Casserole, Turkey- ..... **16**·2043
-Cheese Crunch Sandwich . **9**·1114
Cheese Crust, in .... **6**·657
Cheese Salad, Rice, and .. **14**·1787
Cheese Spread, Smoky, and ...**1**·71
Cherry Sauce, with ...... **14**·1679
Chicken Stack-Ups, and .. **13**·1556
-Chicken Supreme .... **6**·708
Chippers ....**3**·367
Crab Apple Glaze, with .. **13**·1662
Cranberry-Burgundy Glazed **3**·310
Creamed .... **9**·1114
Croquettes .... **6**·698
Currant-Glazed .... **5**·526
Curried, in Popovers ..... **14**·1719
Decorated .... **16**·2006
Dinner, Broiled .... **9**·1113
Dip, Mustard 'n ....**7**·777
Dip, Zippy ....**5**·629
Egg Salad, and .... **15**·1917
Eggs in Caraway Puffs, and ...**6**·682

Ham *continued*
Egg Triple Deckers, 'n ....**7**·826
Filling .... **1**·76
Fruit Kabobs, and .... **9**·1111
Glazed Yule .... **16**·1998
Kabobs, Lamb 'n .... **10**·1227
Loaf .... **9**·1117
Loaf, Spicy .... **11**·1387
Loaf, Upside-Down .... **9**·1117
Mac Bake, and .... **13**·1581
Medley ....**4**·427
Mustard Glaze for .... **9**·1111
Newburg Tarts .... **18**·2253
Omelet, Sour Cream- ..... **9**·1114
Pâté .... **13**·1587
Patties .... **11**·1388
Patties, Apricot- .... **14**·1782
Peachy Glazed .... **9**·1035
Pea Soup, and .... **17**·2090
Pie, Deviled .... **11**·1389
Pie, Hawaiian .... **9**·1071
Pinwheel Sandwiches ....**6**·735
Potatoes au Gratin, and .....**1**·117
Potato Salad, and .... **14**·1754
Potato Scallop, and .... **9**·1114
-Pretzel Teasers .... **14**·1785
Prosciutto and Artichokes . **14**·1788
Puffs .... **9**·1117
Quick Curried .... **10**·1272
-Raisin Balls, Glazed ..... **9**·1117
Rice Casserole, and .... **9**·1044
Rice Croquettes, and ....**6**·698
-Rice Loaves .... **11**·1387
Ring, Glazed .... **11**·1387
Rolls, Belgian Endive- ....**2**·209
Rolls, Creamy .... **16**·1970
Rolls, Curried .... **6**·718
Rye Rounds, and ....**3**·366
Rye Stuffing, with .... **15**·1903
Salad, Apple and .... **9**·1113
Salad, Cauliflower- ....**4**·432
Salad, Chicken and ....**4**·419
Salad Filling .... **16**·1959
Salad-Fruit Boats .... **14**·1689
Salad, Rice and .... **19**·2389
Salad Sandwich Spread .. **17**·2121
Salad Supreme .... **14**·1780
Sandwiches, Crunchy ... **14**·1754
Schnitzel, Filled ...... **16**·2008
Slice, Gingered .... **17**·2109
Slice, Glazed .... **14**·1733
Slice, Grilled .... **10**·1214
Slices, Cranberry-Topped .. **9**·1111
Slices, Hawaiian ..... **9**·1113
Soup, Cream of .... **15**·1823
Spinning .... **15**·1894
Squares, Marmalade- .....**11**·1356
-Squash Skillet .... **1**·21
Steak Barbecue .... **9**·1111
-Stuffed Potatoes ....**14**·1751

Ham *continued*
-Stuffed Tomatoes .... **9**·1114
Succotash ....**5**·624
Sweet-Sour, over Rice ..... **9**·1116
Swisser, Peach- .... **13**·1605
Towers, Black Magic ..... **9**·1118
Towers, Creamy .... **13**·1592
Tropicale .... **9**·1111
Turkey Divan, and .... **19**·2316
Turkey Pie, Top Hat, and .. **9**·1118
-Turkey Sauce on Egg Puffs . **9**·1116
Vegetable Stew, and ..... **9**·1116
Vegetable Strata, and .... **17**·2155
Waffles .... **19**·2409
Wafflewiches .... **19**·2408

Hamburger
-Bean Skillet ....**2**·179
-Cheese Bake .... **12**·1466
-Corn Bake .... **14**·1683
-Noodle Bake .... **15**·1813
Pie .... **9**·1090
Steak Diane .... **20**·2467
Stroganoff .... **17**·2173
Hard Rolls .... **15**·1882
Hard Sauce .... **5**·532; **9**·1128
Harvard Beets .... **9**·1129

Harvest
Apple Cake ....**3**·348
Bread .... **12**·1480
Fruit Compote ....**7**·803
Fruit Mold .... **15**·1919
Hasenpfeffer .... **9**·1129

Hash
Best Oven .... **9**·1130
Jazzy ....**5**·631
Mexican-Style ....**5**·623
Oriental .... **10**·1272
Oven-Style Turkey ....**6**·658
Skillet .... **9**·1130
Tangiers .... **9**·1130
Yankee Red-Flannel ..... **9**·1129
Hashed Brown Omelet ..... **12**·1501
Hashed Browns .... **14**·1747
Hausplatte .... **16**·1984

Hawaiian
Beets ....**2**·207
Fruit Crumble ....**6**·762
Fruit Plate ....**8**·988
Ham Pie .... **9**·1071
Ham Slices .... **9**·1113
Muffins .... **12**·1415
Pancakes .... **13**·1554
Shrimp Platter .... **9**·1135
Heart, Chicken-Fried ...... **19**·2349
Hearts of Palm Salad ..... **9**·1138
Heart, Stuffed Beef .... **9**·1138

Hearty
Baked Beans . . . .**2**·172
Hodgepodge . . . . **14**·1737
Oyster Stew . . . . **13**·1546
Vegetable Soup . . . . **19**·2332

Heavenly
Hawaiian Cream . . . . **11**·1349
Orange Fluff . . . .**5**·545
Torte . . . .**6**·763

Herb
-Baked Fish . . . .**7**·890
Bouquet Garni . . . .**2**·254
Bread . . . . **9**·1141
Butter . . . .**3**·314
-Crumb Topped Fish . . . .**7**·894
-Curry Dip . . . . **17**·2093
Dressing . . . . **11**·1363
Fried Chicken . . . .**4**·439
Gravy . . . . **11**·1377
Honey Basting Sauce, 'n . . . **9**·1151
Scrambled Eggs . . . . **9**·1143
-Stuffed Flank Steak . . . .**8**·902
Stuffing . . . . **18**·2184
Twists . . . . **15**·1907

Herbed
Biscuit Ring . . . . **9**·1141
Cabbage Medley . . . . **13**·1560
Carrots . . . .**2**·178
Chicken Bake . . . . **16**·1987
Chicken Salad . . . . **18**·2249
Cocktail . . . .**2**·217
Fish Bake . . . . **9**·1099
Onion Slices . . . . **12**·1509
Pea Salad . . . . **13**·1597
Riblets and Limas . . . . **11**·1291
Spinach Bake . . . .**6**·727
Steak Broil . . . . **16**·1932
Tomato Broth . . . . **17**·2082
Tomatoes . . . . **18**·2276
Tomato Halves . . . . **9**·1141
Turkey on Spit . . . . **19**·2311
Hibachi Totem Poles . . . . **9**·1145

Hickory
Brisket Slices . . . .**3**·287
Fish Bake . . . . **9**·1146
Lamb Kabobs . . . . **10**·1261
Smoked Turkey . . . .**2**·151
Hidden Treasure Sundaes . . **10**·1214
Highball . . . . **9**·1148
Hilo Franks . . . . **15**·1854
Hobo Rice . . . .**2**·159
Hogate's Clam Chowder . . . . . .**5**·555

Holiday
Bread, Mexican . . . . **19**·2420
Cocktail Deluxe . . . . **14**·1713

Holiday *continued*
Divinity . . . .**5**·529
Maple Punch . . . . **11**·1348
Mints . . . . **12**·1420
Peppernuts . . . . **13**·1645
Punch . . . . **19**·2402
Rice Stuffing . . . . **18**·2187
Turkey Salad . . . . **14**·1713
Walnut Pie . . . . **19**·2417

Hollandaise
Blender . . . . **9**·1148
Classic . . . . **9**·1149
Jiffy . . . . **9**·1149

Homemade
Mincemeat Pie . . . . **12**·1419
Noodles . . . . **12**·1467
Pizza Crust . . . . **14**·1695
Strawberry Ice Cream . . . . **16**·1943
Hominy in Sour Cream . . . . . . **9**·1149

Honey
-Baked Bananas . . . . **9**·1035
-Banana Mold . . . .**7**·863
-Banana Syrup . . . . **9**·1152
Barbecued Broilers . . . .**4**·481
Basting Sauce, Herb 'n . . . . **9**·1151
Butter . . . . **9**·1152
Butter,
    Hot Whole Wheat and . . . .**4**·442
Butter, Orange- . . . .**3**·314
-Citrus Syrup . . . . **18**·2227
Cream, Pumpkin Cake with **19**·2421
Crunch Loaf . . . . **9**·1152
Dessert, Lemon- . . . . **9**·1152
Dressing . . . . **11**·1395
Dressing, Ginger- . . . . **9**·1152
-Fruit Compote . . . . **11**·1303
-Glazed Carrots . . . . **9**·1151
Honeyberry Dressing . . . . **12**·1521
Lime . . . .**5**·546
-Lime Dressing . . . . **11**·1296
-Lime Lamb Roast . . . . **10**·1256
Mayonnaise . . . . **16**·1930
-Nut Bread (Christopsoma) . **9**·1066
Pecan Cake . . . .**7**·826
Rhubarb Betty . . . .**2**·213
-Sugared Walnuts . . . . **19**·2417

Honeydew
-Berry Parfaits . . . . **11**·1396
Cup, Blueberry- . . . .**8**·987
-Lime Mold . . . . **10**·1156
Mold, Double-Decker . . . **11**·1396
Parfaits, Cranberry- . . . . . . **10**·1156
Red-Jeweled . . . . **10**·1156
Stack-Up . . . . **20**·2475
Hong Kong Sundaes . . . . . . **10**·1185
Hopping John . . . .**2**·235

Horseradish
Dressing . . . . **2**·207; **16**·1926
Dressing, Mustard- . . . . . . **11**·1286
-Sauced Steamed Fish . . . . **16**·1997
Sauces . . . . **10**·1157
-Stuffed Rib Roast . . . . **15**·1874

Hot
Apple Toddy . . . .**8**·995
Brandied Chocolate . . . .**3**·260
Buttered Cranberry Swizzle . .**6**·666
Buttered Lemonade . . . . . . **10**·1275
Buttered Rum . . . . **15**·1897
Cheese and Crab Dip . . . . . .**7**·781
Cheese Dip with Fruit . . . .**1**·77
Chicken Spread . . . .**3**·367
Chocolate . . . .**4**·507
Cider Sauce . . . . . . **3**·273; **13**·1556
Crab Cocktail Spread . . . .**6**·650
Crab Open-Facers . . . . **12**·1513
Cross Buns . . . . **10**·1158
Curried Fruit Compote . . . . . .**5**·595
Curried Turkey
    Sandwiches . . . . **19**·2313
Deviled Potatoes . . . .**7**·771
Dill-Potato Salad . . . . **14**·1753
Dog Burgers . . . . **16**·1951
Dogs Delicious . . . .**8**·936
Egg Salad Deluxe . . . .**7**·840
Five Bean Salad . . . .**2**·178
Fruit Compote . . . . **20**·2460
Fruit Medley . . . . **14**·1740
Fudge-
    Peanut Butter Sauce . . . **16**·1972
Fudge Sundae Cake . . . . . . **18**·2208
Lemon Punch . . . . **15**·1809
Mexican Bean Dip . . . .**2**·175
Milk Sponge Cake . . . . **17**·2120
Mustard Sauce . . . . **16**·1970
Potato Salad Fix-Up . . . . . **14**·1756
Sauce for Tostadas . . . . **18**·2293
Sausage-Bean Dip . . . .**1**·71
Scallop Chowder . . . . **16**·1990
Sherried Consommé . . . . **17**·2083
Steak Canapés . . . .**3**·366
Tomato Bouillon . . . . **18**·2281
Tomato Cocktail . . . . **18**·2282
Turkey Sandwiches . . . . . . **19**·2313
Vegetable Platter . . . . **19**·2383
Whole Wheat and Honey
    Butter . . . .**4**·442
Hubbard Squash in Sour
    Cream . . . . **10**·1161

Hungarian
Cabbage and Noodles . . . **10**·1165
Goulash . . . . **10**·1164
Noodle Bake . . . . **10**·1164
Short Ribs . . . . **19**·2398
Spaetzels . . . . **10**·1165

Hurry-Up Éclairs ....7·828
Hurry-Up Gravy .... 9·1061
Hurry-Up Ham Puffs .... 1·76
Hush Puppies .... 10·1165

I

Ice
Cranberry .... 6·666
Fruited Tangerine .... 10·1166
Raspberry .... 10·1166
Ring .... 2·223
Strawberry-Banana ...... 17·2170

ICE CREAM .... 10·1169-1179
Balls, Coffee-Coconut .... 5·570
Banana .... 2·140
Basic Vanilla .... 6·672
Caramel-Pecan .... 10·1171
Cherry .... 11·1350
Chocolate-Almond ...... 10·1171
Choco-Mallow .... 18·2210
Choco-Mo .... 4·507
Coconut .... 10·1174
Coffee .... 10·1173
Cups ....10·1176
Éclairs, Coffee- .... 7·828
English Toffee ....18·2209
Fresh Garden Mint ....8·976
Fresh Peach .... 15·1853
Homemade Strawberry ... 16·1943
Kona Sunset .... 9·1136
Lotus ....8·974
Maple-Almond .... 10·1174
Mauna Loa Parfaits .... 9·1136
Party Spumoni .... 10·1177
Peach .... 6·672
Peach-Almond .... 1·40
Peach Melba .... 10·1173
Peppermint .... 10·1174; 18·2209
Pie, Lemon .... 10·1277
Pie, Mile High ....6·761
Pie, Peanut- .... 14·1678
Refrigerator Vanilla ...... 15·1858
Rhubarb .... 15·1863
Roll, Sherried ....6·670
Strawberry .... 10·1174
Sundae Mold ....5·578
Toasted Coconut ....5·568
Tropical .... 10·1173
Vanilla .... 10·1171
Vanilla Custard .... 10·1173
Waikiki Sundae ....8·906

Iced Fruit Tea .... 18·2257

Indian
Corn Casserole ....5·623
-Stuffed Peppers .... 9·1073
-Style Corn on the Cob ......2·159

Individual
Antipasto .... 1·59
Clambake .... 5·550
Meringue Shells .... 11·1402
Pot Roasts .... 2·194
Yorkshire Puddings ...... 20·2476
Inside-Out Ravioli .... 15·1840
Instant Nog .... 7·844
Instant Russian Tea .... 2·220
Iowa Corn Burgers .... 9·1124
Irish Coffee Pie .... 14·1678
Irish Lamb Stew .... 17·2145

Island
Broiled Chicken .... 14·1771
Nut Bananas .... 9·1136
Sweet-Sour Pork .... 18·2247
Teriyaki .... 2·153
Israeli Cheese Blintzes ....2·241

Italian
Anchovy Salad .... 9·1072
Bean Toss .... 15·1914
Dressing .... 16·1928
Eggplant ....7·848
Gnocchi .... 9·1038
Green Salad .... 1·47
Meatballs .... 10·1197
Meat Loaf .... 9·1088
Meat Sauce .... 18·2281
Meat Sauce (quantity) .... 15·1814
Picnic Shoulder .... 13·1663
Plum Cobbler .... 14·1707
Polenta .... 14·1711
Salad Bowl .... 11·1285
Salad Dressing .... 10·1200
-Sauced Fish .... 11·1320
Spaghetti Toss .... 13·1645
Spumoni .... 17·2126
Steak .... 17·2143
Stuffing .... 18·2185
Veal Chops .... 19·2363
Veal Cutlets .... 19·2361

J

Jacques' Chicken Salad ....4·402

Jam
Apricot-Pineapple .... 10·1202
Braid, Date- .... 10·1204
Brown-and-Serves .... 10·1206

Jam *continued*
Cherry-Strawberry .... 17·2161
Double Berry .... 10·1202
-Filled Crepes .... 13·1553
Frozen Strawberry .... 10·1204
Gingered-Rhubarb ...... 15·1861
Peach-Plum .... 10·1203
Peach-Rum .... 10·1203
Plum .... 10·1204
Raspberry-Rhubarb ...... 10·1203
Shortbread Cookies ...... 10·1206
Spiced Grape .... 10·1204
Strawberry .... 10·1204
Strawberry-Rhubarb ..... 10·1203
Thumbprints ....5·613

Jambalaya
Crab ....6·690
Creole .... 10·1207
Turkey .... 19·2324
Japanese Custard Soup ... 12·1530
Japanese Tempura .... 18·2263
Java Fudge ....5·527
Java Tapioca Parfaits .... 18·2246
Jazzy Hash ....5·631

Jellied
Chicken Salad .... 14·1688
Consommé ....5·598
Potato Salad .... 15·1842
Veal Loaf (Kalvsylta) ..... 19·2355

JELLY .... 10·1209-1215
Apple-Mint .... 10·1213
Cinnamon-Apple .... 10·1211
Cranberry ....6·664
Cran-Pineapple .... 10·1212
-Filled Coffee Cake .... 10·1215
Frosting .... 10·1214
Grape .... 10·1212
Mint-Apple .... 12·1423
Mint or Basil .... 10·1212
Muffins .... 12·1441
Orange-Sauterne .... 10·1212
Uncooked
Strawberry .... 10·1213

Jelly Roll .... 10·1217
Almond Coffee ....3·337
Crown Torte .... 10·1217
Lincoln Log .... 10·1217
Midget .... 10·1218
Mocha-Nut .... 12·1427

Jelly Roll *continued*
Peachy-Almond Chiffon .. **10**·1218
Snow-Capped Lemon .... **10**·1219
Strawberry Cake .... **17**·2169
Jewel Candies .... **1**·58
Jeweled Banana Bread .... **7**·879
Jewel Glaze .... **11**·1384
Jewel-Top Star Mold .... **5**·527

Jiffy
Braunschweiger Dip .... **1**·66
Butterscotch Torte .... **3**·321
Cheese Sauce .... **4**·461
Chili-Hominy Bake .... **9**·1149
Doughnuts .... **7**·793
Hollandaise .... **9**·1149
Mexican Dinner .... **18**·2242
Mustard Sauce .... **12**·1452
Orange Pancakes .... **13**·1557
Pizza Crust .... **14**·1695
Shrimp Skillet .... **17**·2055
Spaghetti Sauce .... **14**·1784
Stroganoff .... **17**·2173
Joe Froggers .... **12**·1430
Johnnycakes .... **10**·1222
Jubilee Salad Mold .... **10**·1215
Jubilee Sauce .... **14**·1781

K

Kabob
Appetizer Skewer Dogs .....**2**·153
Armenian Shish .... **10**·1227
Beef and Fruit .... **9**·1145
Beef Angus .... **10**·1225
Cake .... **2**·152
Canapés .... **3**·366
Fiesta Beef .... **10**·1225
Fruit-Turkey .... **8**·990
Garlic Lamb .... **16**·2045
Ham and Fruit .... **9**·1111
Hibachi Totem Poles ...... **9**·1145
Hickory Lamb .... **10**·1261
Italiano, Shish .... **16**·2045
Kau Kau .... **16**·2044
Kidney .... **19**·2350
Lamb .... **2**·152
Lamb 'n Ham .... **10**·1227
Lamb Shashlik .... **16**·2025
Lamb Shish .... **16**·2044
Liver .... **11**·1306
Mandarin Dinner .... **10**·1227
Marinated Beef Cubes .... **16**·2045
Marinated Skewered Fruit **17**·2062
Meatball Barbecue .... **2**·152
Mile-Long Sandwiches ... **10**·1227
Plum-Sauced Lamb ...... **10**·1225
Pork (Pork Sate) .... **15**·1873
Red Hots on .... **18**·2269

Kabob *continued*
Sausage .... **16**·1984
Seafood .... **10**·1228
Seafood Sword .... **10**·1228
Shish .... **12**·1457
Skewer Dogs .... **12**·1430
Smoked Linkburgers ....**2**·154
Speedy .... **11**·1331
Sukiyaki Skewers .... **9**·1146
Kaffee Kuchen .... **10**·1241
Karidopita (Walnut Cake) .... **9**·1064
Kartoffel Klösse (Potato
Dumplings) .... **10**·1230
Kartoffel Pfannkuchen
(Potato Pancakes) .... **10**·1230
Kau Kau Kabobs .... **16**·2044
Kettle-Cooked Frankfurters .....**8**·931
Kettle-of-Bean Stew .... **2**·174
Key Lime Pie .... **11**·1294

Kidney
Kabobs .... **19**·2350
Mixed Grill .... **10**·1232
Pie, Beef and ....**7**·856
-Vegetable Pie .... **14**·1759
Wine Sauce, in .... **10**·1231

Kidney Bean
Bake, Creole Sausage- ... **10**·1233
-Burgers, Bayou ....**2**·175
Chicken-Vegetable
Chowder .... **2**·174
Coleslaw ....**5**·591
Mexican Fried .... **18**·2292
Speedy Brown .... **10**·1233
Kima .... **10**·1187
King Crab Crown ....**6**·653
King Kamehameha Pie .... **14**·1679
Kohlrabi and Ground Beef
Soup .... **10**·1239
Kolacky .... **10**·1240
Kona Coffee Torte ....**5**·578
Kona Sunset .... **9**·1136
Königsberger Klops .... **10**·1240
Kosher Dill Pickles .... **10**·1241
Kourabiedes (Butter
Cookies) .... **9**·1066
Kowloon Duckling ....**2**·150
Kraut-Pork Pinwheel .... **14**·1732
Kris Kringle Cake ....**1**·31
Kulebiaka .... **15**·1900
Kumquat Flowers .... **10**·1242
Kumquat Marmalade ...... **10**·1242

L

Lace Cookies .... **10**·1243
Lacy Oatmeal Crisps .... **10**·1243
Lady Baltimore Cake .... **10**·1245

LAMB .... **10**·1249-1261
(Listed at the end of this entry
Chop, Ground, Roast.)
Armenian Shish Kabobs .. **10**·1227
Curried ....**6**·719
-Eggplant Casserole .... **9**·1143
Ham Kabobs, 'n .... **10**·1227
Kabobs ....**2**·152
Kabobs, Garlic .... **16**·2045
Kabobs, Hickory .... **10**·1261
Kabobs, Plum-Sauced .... **10**·1225
Paprikash .... **10**·1259

Racks with Herb Jackets .....**2**·157
Roll-Ups ....**5**·599
Shanks, Armenian-Italian . **16**·2024
Shanks, Barbecued ...... **10**·1258
Shanks, Mandarin- ...... **12**·1522
Shashlik .... **16**·2025
Shepherd's Pie .... **16**·2038
Shish Kabobs .... **16**·2044
Shish Kabobs Italiano .... **16**·2045
Spanish, with Spaghetti ... **10**·1258
Stew, Dilled .... **17**·2147
Stew 'n Dumplings ....**7**·816
Stew, Scottish .... **17**·2145
Stew, Spring .... **10**·1261
-Stuffed Artichokes ....**1**·107
-Stuffed Cabbage Leaves .. **12**·1457
-Vegetable Supper .... **14**·1751

Chop
Broil .... **12**·1422
Curried .... **10**·1255
Deviled .... **10**·1258
Mixed Grill .... **10**·1232
Orange-Thyme .... **10**·1256
Oriental .... **17**·2097
Shoulder, Tangy .... **13**·1642
Stew, Irish .... **17**·2145
Supreme .... **17**·2123
Sweet-Sour ....**2**·255
Tangy .... **10**·1255

Ground
Broiler Dinner .... **10**·1261
Deviled Lamburgers ...... **8**·1009
-Eggplant Balls .... **18**·2283
Frank Burgers, and ...... **11**·1379
Patties with Dill Sauce ... **16**·1969
Patties with Mint Sauce ... **10**·1256
Pie .... **10**·1261
Roll-Ups ....**5**·599

Lamb *continued*
Roast
Butterfly Leg of . . . .**2**·154
Honey-Lime . . . . **10**·1256
Leg of, with Pineapple . . **10**·1259
Leg of, with Plum Sauce . . **10**·1259
Minted Leg of, on a Spit . . **12**·1423
Rack of, with
   Vegetables . . . .**10**·1256
Roast Leg of . . . .**10**·1254
Shoulder Roll . . . .**10**·1255
Shoulder, Stuffed . . . . **10**·1259
Stuffed . . . . **18**·2188

Lasagne . . . . **10**·1263
Blonde . . . . **15**·1872
Casserole, Mock . . . .**6**·643
Easy . . . . **10**·1263
Lazy-Day . . . . **10**·1263
Peppy . . . . **15**·1872
Shortcut . . . . **10**·1263
Layer Bar Cookies . . . .**2**·161

Lazy
Daisy Coffee Cake . . . .**3**·268
-Day Lasagne . . . . **10**·1263
Grasshopper Parfaits . . . . . . **9**·1058
Grasshopper Pie . . . . **6**·686
Lebanese Cacic . . . . **12**·1556
Lebkuchen . . . . **10**·1268
Leek Lorraine . . . . **10**·1269
Leeks with Lemon . . . . **10**·1269
Leg of Lamb with Pineapple . **10**·1259
Leg of Lamb with Plum
   Sauce . . . . **10**·1259

Lemon
Angel Torte . . . .**6**·765
Apple Salad . . . .**1**·85
-Barbecued Chuck Steak . . . .**2**·197
Barbecued Shrimp with . . **16**·2033
-Blueberry Fluff . . . . **11**·1324
Butter . . . .**3**·315
Butter Frosting . . . . **5**·597; **18**·2199
Cheesecake . . . .**6**·644
Chiffon Pie . . . . **10**·1277
Chiffon Sherbet . . . . **16**·2040
Crisp . . . .**6**·695
Crunch Parfaits . . . . **9**·1044
-Crusted Blueberry Pie . . . **14**·1674
Curd Tarts . . . . **10**·1279
Drop Cookies . . . . **10**·1279
Dumplings . . . .**8**·963
Filling . . . .**7**·879
Fizz, Pineapple- . . . . **10**·1179
-Frosted Plum Squares . . . **14**·1704
Frost Pie . . . . **20**·2443
Glaze . . . . **5**·607; **10**·1268
Glow Angel Cake . . . .**3**·338
-Honey Dessert . . . .**9**·1152

Lemon *continued*
Ice Cream Pie . . . . **10**·1277
Leeks with . . . . **10**·1269
Lemondown Fancy . . . . . . **10**·1278
Loaf, Tuna- . . . . **18**·2304
Mace Rounds . . . . **11**·1338
Meringue Pie . . . . **10**·1276
Muffins, Blueberry- . . . .**2**·243
-Nut Bread, Glazed . . . .**3**·275
-Parslied Turnips . . . . **19**·2332
Pastry . . . . **14**·1674
-Pecan Dainties . . . . **10**·1278
Pie, French . . . . **10**·1276
Pound Cake . . . . **10**·1278
Pudding Cake . . . . **12**·1415
Puff Pillow Buns . . . . **18**·2217
Punch . . . . **15**·1808
Punch, Hot . . . . **15**·1809
Raisin Pie . . . . **15**·1797
Roll, Snow-Capped . . . . **10**·1219
Sauce . . . . . **2**·213; **7**·819; **14**·1706
Sauce, Daffodil . . . . **10**·1278
Sauce, Orange- . . . .**2**·141
Sauce, Potatoes in . . . . **14**·1748
Sherbet . . . . **10**·1278
Soufflé, Golden . . . . **10**·1267
-Sour Cream Pie . . . .**8**·996
-Stuffed Fish . . . .**7**·890
Tea Cakes . . . .**5**·607

Lemonade . . . .**1**·22
Angel Dessert . . . .**1**·52
Bavarian, Strawberry- . . . . **17**·2161
Cake, Pink . . . .**3**·345
Cookies . . . .**3**·316
Dressing . . . . **16**·1925
Hot Buttered . . . . **10**·1275
Meringue Pie . . . .**6**·680
Mint . . . .**2**·219
Pudding . . . . **15**·1797
Punch, Rhubarb- . . . .**1**·22
Slush, Strawberry- . . . . **15**·1820
Lemony
Mince-Meringue Pie . . . . . **12**·1418
Lentil-Vegetable Soup . . . . . . **10**·1280

Lettuce
Pennsylvania Dutch . . . . . **11**·1286
Tomato Salad, Bacon,
   and . . . . **18**·2277
Toss, Spinach- . . . . **17**·2113
Toss, Wilted . . . . **10**·1266
Light Fruitcake . . . .**8**·993
Light Rye Mixer Bread . . . . . . **15**·1902

Lima Bean
-Burger Soup . . . .**2**·179
Casserole, Cheesy . . . . . . **11**·1289
-Cheese Bake . . . .**4**·428
Chili with . . . . **11**·1291

Lima Bean *continued*
Chowder, Thrifty
   Bologna- . . . . **11**·1289
Copenhagen . . . . **11**·1291
Creamy . . . . **19**·2384
Deluxe . . . . **11**·1289
Herbed Riblets and . . . . . . **11**·1291
Mushrooms, and . . . . **11**·1291
One Bean Toss . . . .**2**·178
Pot . . . .·. . . . **11**·1289
Saucy Vegetable Trio . . . .**2**·179
Skillet, Beef and . . . .**4**·446
Skillet, Pork and . . . . **11**·1291
Skillet, Tongue and . . . . . . **18**·2285

Lime
-Berry Parfaits . . . . **13**·1567
Cake, Coconut- . . . . **11**·1297
Cooler, Apple- . . . .**1**·92
Dressing, Honey- . . . . **11**·1296
Dressing, Poppy Seed- . . . **14**·1720
Filling . . . . **11**·1297
Fizz . . . .**20**·2468
Float, Pineapple- . . . .**14**·1690
Frosted Punch . . . .**15**·1808
Honey . . . .**5**·546
Lamb Roast, Honey- . . . . . **10**·1256
Limeade . . . .**1**·22
Mold, Creamy Pear- . . . . . **13**·1622
Mold, Honeydew- . . . . **10**·1156
Mold, Turkey- . . . . **19**·2320
Parfait Pie . . . . **11**·1294
Pie, Cocoa Crust- . . . . **11**·1294
Pie, Key . . . . **11**·1294
-Pineapple Fluff . . . . **11**·1296
Snow . . . . **11**·1327
Torte . . . . **11**·1296
Lincoln Log . . . . **10**·1217
Lingonberry Sauce . . . . **11**·1298
Linzer Cake . . . . **11**·1301

Liqueur
Banana-Raspberry
   Flambé . . . . **20**·2466
Honey-Fruit Compote . . . **11**·1303
Mandarin Pears . . . . **11**·1303
Melon à l'Orange . . . . **11**·1303
Orange-Date Medley . . . . **20**·2468
Tiny Strawberry Soufflés . . **11**·1303
Twice-Chocolate Torte . . . **11**·1303

Liver . . . . **11**·1306
Apples and Onions, with . **19**·2350
Bake, Bacon and . . . . **11**·1307
Boats, Chicken . . . .**1**·77
Braised . . . . **11**·1306
Broiled . . . . **11**·1306
Chinese-Style . . . . **19**·2350
Creamy, over Rice . . . . **19**·2350
en Brochette, Chicken . . . . .**4**·488

Liver *continued*
French-Fried .... **11**·1306
Gourmet Salad .... **5**·588
Kabobs .... **11**·1306
Loaf .... **11**·1306
Mushrooms, with .... **16**·1931
-Onion Dip, Chicken .... **7**·781
Panfried .... **11**·1306
Pâté, Chicken .... **1**·65
Portugal, Chicken .... **4**·488
Rice, Chicken, and .... **4**·488
Rolls, Sausage- .... **11**·1306
Snow-Capped Pâté ...... **20**·2466
Stroganoff, Chicken ...... **17**·2094
Tomato Skillet, and ...... **11**·1307
Loaf Pound Cake .... **14**·1778

Lobster
Basic Boiled .... **11**·1310
Basic Broiled .... **11**·1311
Canapés .... **3**·367
-Cheese Waffles .... **11**·1314
Corn Stew, and .... **17**·2144
Dip Elegante .... **7**·781
en Coquille .... **11**·1312
Newburg .... **12**·1463
-Orange Cups .... **11**·1314
Ring Mold .... **11**·1314
Salad .... **11**·1314
Salad, Oriental .... **12**·1534
Savannah, Baked .... **11**·1311
Stew .... **11**·1313
Supreme .... **11**·1313
Tails .... **11**·1311
Tails, Boiled .... **11**·1311
Tails, Broiled .... **11**·1311
Tails Maison .... **11**·1313
Tails, Over-the-Coals .... **16**·2033
Thermidor Bake .... **11**·1312
Lollipop Clowns .... **3**·380
London Broil .... **11**·1315
Lotus Ice Cream .... **8**·974
Louis Dressing .... **6**·654
Low-Cal Fruit Bowl .... **5**·545
Low-Cal Snow Dressing ...... **5**·545

LOW-CALORIE
    COOKERY .... **11**·1317-1327

Luau Fish Bake .... **18**·2188
Luau Ribs .... **17**·2104
Lucia Braid .... **16**·2004
Luncheon Cooler .... **11**·1398

Luncheon Meat
Best Hamdogs .... **8**·935
Dinner .... **15**·1826
Frosted .... **11**·1330
Fruited Luncheon Loaf ... **11**·1330
Mandarin Roasts .... **11**·1331
Sandwiches, Broiled ..... **11**·1331
Skillet Barbecue .... **11**·1330
Skillet, Macaroni .... **11**·1331
Speedy Kabobs .... **11**·1331
Yam Skillet, and .... **11**·1330
Zesty Luncheon Barbecue ... **2**·155
Luncheon Salad .... **2**·226
Lush Strawberry Meringue
    Pie .... **17**·2166
Lutefisk Special .... **16**·1997
Luxe Peas and Celery ...... **13**·1595

M

Macadamia Nut Pie .... **11**·1332

Macaroni
Bake, Cheddar- .... **11**·1336
Bake, Ham and .... **13**·1581
Beef and .... **13**·1579
Casserole, Turkey- .... **19**·2316
Cheese, and .... **11**·1335
Cheese, and (quantity) ... **15**·1813
Cheese Bake, Creamy, and ...**4**·462
-Cheese Cups .... **11**·1364
-Cheese Puff .... **4**·427
Cheese, Sausage, and .... **11**·1336
-Meat Skillet .... **11**·1331
Omelet .... **11**·1336
Puff Soufflé .... **17**·2076
Salad, Gingery .... **15**·1835
-Salmon Salad .... **11**·1304
Shells Florentine .... **11**·1337
Smoked Salmon and ..... **17**·2066
Supper, Meat and ...... **18**·2269

Macaroon .... **11**·1338
Bonbons .... **16**·2024
Easy .... **5**·607
Filbert .... **7**·872
Mallow-Mint Sauce .... **6**·767
Malted Milk .... **11**·1341
Malted Oatmeal Bars ...... **11**·1340

Mandarin Orange
Angel Pie .... **1**·55
Coffee Cake .... **12**·1520
Delight Salad .... **10**·1179
Dinner .... **10**·1227
-Fig Whip .... **11**·1342
Fluff, Heavenly .... **5**·545
-Lamb Shanks .... **12**·1522
Mold, Spiced .... **5**·545

Mandarin Orange *continued*
Pears .... **11**·1303
-Pear Salad .... **11**·1342
Pears, Creamy .... **10**·1176
Pork .... **11**·1342
Pot Roast .... **5**·546
Roasts .... **11**·1331
Soufflé .... **5**·549
Spicy, 'n Prunes .... **14**·1792
Toss, Cran- .... **6**·668
Mangoes on the Half
    Shell .... **11**·1343
Mango Sherbet .... **11**·1344
Manhattan Clam Chowder .....**5**·520
Manicotti, Cheese-Filled ... **15**·1872
Manna Rolls .... **15**·1879

Maple
Alaska, Ginger- .... **9**·1031
-Almond Ice Cream ...... **10**·1174
-Apricot Syrup .... **11**·1348
Baked Apples .... **1**·87
Baked Beans .... **2**·173
Chiffon Cake .... **4**·491
Cookies, Crisp .... **11**·1347
-Custard Pie, Sister
    Lettie's .... **11**·1348
-Flavored Sweets .... **18**·2213
Fluff Frosting .... **17**·2111
Nut Chews .... **5**·603
Punch, Holiday .... **11**·1348
Scotchies .... **12**·1476
Skimmer .... **11**·1347
Syrup .... **11**·1348
Syrup Pie .... **3**·365
Whip .... **11**·1348
Mapled Appetizers .... **9**·1072
Maraschino Cherry Cake ... **11**·1349

Marble
Cheesecake .... **6**·675
Chiffon Cake .... **11**·1351
Muffins .... **12**·1442
Pound Cake .... **14**·1778
Squares à la Mode .... **1**·28
-Top Chocolate-Rum
    Pie .... **15**·1897
Margarita .... **11**·1352
Marguerites .... **11**·1352
Marinade, Armenian .... **11**·1352
Marinade, California .... **10**·1225

Marinated
Artichoke Hearts .... **1**·59
Artichokes .... **1**·108
Barbecued Chuck
    Roast .... **11**·1354
Bean Salad .... **19**·2430
Beef Cubes .... **16**·2045
Beef Strips .... **1**·72

Marinated *continued*
Broiled Chicken .... **16**·2042
Celery Root .... **4**·436
Hickory Steaks .... **9**·1146
Orange-Glazed Grilled
Chuck .... **11**·1354
Pork Roast .... **11**·1354
Skewered Fruit .... **17**·2062
Sprouts .... **11**·1318
Three-Bean Salad .... **11**·1354

Marmalade
Blueberry .... **11**·1357
Cranberry-Pear .... **18**·2201
-Fig Bars .... **11**·1357
-Ham Squares .... **11**·1356
Kumquat .... **10**·1242
Orange .... **11**·1356
Pan Bread .... **11**·1356
Pastries, Date- .... **5**·610
-Plum Pie .... **11**·1357
Marrow Dumplings .... **8**·1021

Marshmallow .... **11**·1359
Blizzard .... **5**·546
Cream .... **17**·2162
Dressing .... **11**·1363
Freeze, Cranberry- .... **6**·647
Pie, Peach- .... **11**·1359
Pie, Strawberry- .... **14**·1671
Puffs .... **11**·1359
Sauce .... **6**·683; **6**·766
Sauce, Peanut Butter- ...... **6**·768
S'Mores .... **9**·1041
Sparkles .... **14**·1716
Towers, Coffee- .... **13**·1568
Waldorf, Date- .... **19**·2411

Martini
Dry .... **11**·1360
Extra Dry .... **11**·1360
Traditional .... **11**·1360
Maryland Fried
Chicken .... **11**·1360
Marzipan .... **11**·1360
Mashed Potatoes .... **14**·1747
Mashed Sweet
Potatoes .... **18**·2212
Mauna Loa Parfaits .... **9**·1136

Mayonnaise .... **11**·1362
Blender .... **11**·1363
Blue Cheese .... **16**·1930
Caper .... **4**·402
Chili .... **11**·1363
Chive .... **4**·501
Creamy .... **11**·1363
Honey .... **16**·1930
Pink Fruit .... **11**·1362
Meal-in-a-Bowl Stew .... **9**·1092

MEAT .... **11**·1371-1381
(See also *Barbecue, Beef,
Frankfurter, Ham, Lamb,
Luncheon Meat, Pork,
Sausage, Variety Meat.*)

Macaroni Supper, and ... **18**·2269
Pie, Monday .... **14**·1752
Potato Balls, and .... **14**·1752
Potato Pie, and .... **9**·1082
Vegetable Soup, and ..... **17**·2088
Yam Skillet, and .... **11**·1330

Meatball
à la Burgundy .... **15**·1844
Barbecue .... **2**·152
Barbecue Sauce, in .... **9**·1089
Bull's-Eye .... **1**·77
Casserole .... **15**·1871
Chowder .... **17**·2090
Dinner .... **9**·1084
Glazed Ham-Raisin .... **9**·1117
Heroes .... **11**·1384
Italian .... **10**·1197
Königsberger Klops ...... **10**·1240
Lamb-Eggplant .... **18**·2283
Meat and Potato .... **14**·1752
Mexican Surprises .... **5**·599
Oven .... **9**·1089
Oven Stew, Beef .... **17**·2147
Pie .... **12**·1503
Porcupine .... **14**·1721
Quick Swedish .... **16**·2007
Salmon, in Caper
Sauce .... **16**·1940
Sauerbraten Sauce, in ..... **9**·1089
-Sauerkraut Skillet .... **16**·1976
Soup, Vegetable- .... **9**·1084
Spaghetti and .... **10**·1197
Spaghetti and Oven .... **9**·1089
Stew, Vegetable- .... **17**·2147
Stroganoff .... **9**·1089
Swedish .... **16**·1999
Sweet-Sour .... **15**·1827
Teriyaki .... **1**·64
Zwieback .... **20**·2480

Meat Loaf
Applesauce ....**1**·96
Apricot-Topped Veal .... **19**·2365
Beef-Mushroom .... **9**·1084
Cheese-Filled .... **12**·1439
Chicken .... **7**·862

Meat Loaf *continued*
Cranberry .... **10**·1234
Favorite Beef .... **11**·1387
Glazed Ham Ring .... **11**·1387
Glazed Sausage .... **14**·1732
Ham .... **9**·1117
Ham-Rice .... **11**·1387
Italian .... **9**·1088
Kraut-Pork Pinwheel ..... **14**·1732
Liver .... **11**·1306
Midas .... **11**·1386
Planked .... **9**·1088
Pork-Apricot .... **11**·1307
Salmon .... **16**·1940
Spicy Ham .... **11**·1387
Splits .... **16**·1952
Stuffed Hamburger Roll ....**2**·199
Supreme ....**6**·656
Sweet-Sour Glazed .... **9**·1088
Top-Notch Turkey ....**19**·2315
Tuna-Lemon ....**18**·2304
Twin .... **11**·1386
Upside-Down Ham ...... **9**·1117
Veal .... **19**·2365
Wild Rice and Beef ...... **9**·1045

Meat Pie
Beef and Kidney ....**7**·856
Beef Potpie .... **11**·1390
Canadian Pork (Tourtière) ...**3**·364
Cheeseburger .... **20**·2469
Chicken and Biscuit ..... **15**·1819
Chicken Potpie .... **14**·1758
Corned Beef ....**5**·633
Crab Supper ....**6**·650
Deviled Ham .... **11**·1389
Empanadas ....**7**·851
Ground Lamb .... **10**·1261
Hamburger .... **9**·1090
Ham in Cheese Crust ......**6**·657
Hawaiian Ham .... **9**·1071
Kidney-Vegetable .... **14**·1759
Kulebiaka .... **15**·1900
Meat and Potato .... **9**·1082
Monday .... **14**·1752
Pork or Beef .... **14**·1668
Quick Turkey .... **12**·1414
Rice and Tuna .... **15**·1869
Salmon or Tuna ....**7**·892
Savory Chicken .... **14**·1759
Seafood Soufflé .... **16**·2032
Shepherd's .... **16**·2038
Short-Cut Shepherd's ..... **16**·2038
Sweet Potato-Turkey ..... **19**·2320
Swiss and Crab ....**6**·727
Top Hat Ham and Turkey .. **9**·1118
Tuna-Vegetable ....**4**·426
Vegetable- .... **19**·2389
Mediterranean Salad .... **10**·1200
Mediterranean Sauce ....**5**·547

Melba Sundaes .... **11**·1391
Melba Toast .... **11**·1391

MELON .... **11**·1393-1399
à l'Orange .... **11**·1303
Balls Melba .... **11**·1399
Basket .... **10**·1156
Bowls .... **8**·1013
Cocktail .... **8**·987
Julep, Rainbow .... **1**·73
Medley .... **10**·1155
Polka-Dot Mold .... **11**·1398
Rings, Berried .... **11**·1396
Salad .... **11**·1396
Supreme .... **11**·1396
Toss, Apple- .... **11**·1395
Tower .... **11**·1399
Wedges .... **11**·1395
Mennonite Chicken with
Sour Cream .... **15**·1851
Men's Favorite Salad .... **15**·1826

Menus
Breakfast
Lazy Saturday .... **16**·1951
Make-Ahead .... **15**·1823

Brunch
Easter Morning .... **7**·822
Sunday .... **8**·988
Sunday Morning .... **3**·273

Dinner
Boss, for the .... **2**·217
Christmas .... **5**·526
Company .... **6**·765
Company for .... **17**·2091
Easter .... **7**·824
Good Home Cooking ...... **8**·991
Ham .... **6**·762
He-Man .... **8**·990
Holiday .... **6**·765
Holiday Feast .... **5**·524
Italian Fiesta .... **3**·281
Jiffy Company .... **15**·1826
Meal Planning Chart ... **11**·1366
Midsummer Cookout ...... **3**·367
Oven-Going .... **2**·220
Oven Meal .... **15**·1826
Sunday Chicken .... **4**·427
Thanksgiving .... **3**·278
2, for .... **17**·2087

Menus *continued*
Low Calorie
Luncheon .... **16**·1949
1000 Calories .... **11**·1324
1200 Calories .... **11**·1326
1500 Calories .... **11**·1327

Lunch
After the Hunt .... **7**·826
Box Menus .... **11**·1329
Bridge .... **3**·270
Cookout Feast .... **2**·219
Mexican .... **15**·1825
Oriental .... **4**·424
Quick-Fixing .... **17**·2088
Quick Weekend .... **15**·1824
Saturday .... **6**·762
School Day .... **3**·270
Summertime .... **2**·219
Summertime Special ..... **19**·2389

Other Occasions
Afternoon Snack .... **2**·222
Afternoon Tea .... **3**·275
After the Game .... **16**·1954
Cocktails at Six .... **19**·2382
Fireside Get-Together .....**2**·223
Get Acquainted Coffee .....**3**·268
Holiday Open House ......**2**·223
New Neighbor, for the ... **16**·1958
Snow Shoveling Break .....**2**·222
Spring Wedding
Reception .... **8**·984
Stag Party .... **16**·1958

Supper
In-A-Jiffy .... **8**·991
Man-Pleasing .... **17**·2088
Patio, on the .... **19**·2387
Post-Holiday .... **8**·990

Meringue
Filbert .... **7**·872
Shell .... **11**·1402
Shell, Cinnamon .... **19**·2390
Shells, Individual .... **11**·1402
Soft .... **11**·1402
Topknot .... **19**·2390
Mexicali Casserole .... **11**·1408

Mexican
Beef Tostadas .... **18**·2292
Chocolate .... **4**·507
Enchiladas .... **11**·1408
Fried Beans .... **18**·2292
Holiday Bread .... **19**·2420
Hot Sauce .... **18**·2284
Mex-ocado Sauce .... **1**·15
Mix-Ups .... **18**·2281
Rarebit .... **19**·2432

Mexican *continued*
-Style Casserole .... **5**·629
-Style Cheese
Sandwiches .... **18**·2291
-Style Hash .... **5**·623
-Style Steak .... **17**·2141
Surprises .... **5**·599
-Taco Sandwiches .... **16**·1954
Tostadas .... **1**·77
Midas Meat Loaf .... **11**·1386
Middle East Pears .... **13**·1621
Midget Date Loaves .... **3**·276
Midget Jelly Rolls .... **10**·1218
Midwinter Fruit Medley .... **13**·1624
Mile High Ice Cream Pie ...... **6**·761
Mile-High Mocha Alaska ..... **2**·134
Mile-Long Sandwiches ..... **10**·1227

Milk (See also *Shake.*)
Chocolate Frosting ...... **18**·2199
Shakes .... **12**·1417
Toast .... **12**·1417

Mincemeat
-Apple Crisp .... **12**·1419
Cake .... **5**·532
Filling .... **5**·610
Marvels .... **15**·1884
Pancakes .... **13**·1557
Pie, Homemade .... **12**·1419
Spareribs .... **17**·2104
Star Cookies .... **5**·610
Stuffing .... **18**·2185
Sundae Sauce .... **12**·1419
Tarts, Frozen .... **18**·2251
Turnovers .... **19**·2334

Mince(meat)
Chiffon Pie .... **12**·1419
Coffee Circle .... **3**·276
Cottage Pudding .... **6**·646
Cream Pie .... **6**·681
-Meringue Pie, Lemony .. **12**·1418
Pie, Peach- .... **12**·1418
Minestrone Bake .... **14**·1738
Miniature Brunch Loaf .... **5**·580

Mint
-Apple Jelly .... **12**·1423
Basil Jelly, or .... **10**·1212
Cooler, Raspberry .... **5**·616
Cooler, Sparkling .... **5**·616
Cup, Pineapple- .... **12**·1420
Dessert, Chocolate- .... **6**·686
Dessert, Pineapple- ...... **12**·1414
Freeze, Choco- .... **8**·976
Freeze, Pineapple- .... **8**·927
-Frosted Brownies .... **5**·531
Frosting .... **5**·531
-Fudge Topping .... **10**·1176

Mint *continued*
Holiday .... 12·1420
Ice Cream, Fresh
    Garden .... 8·976
Jelly, Apple- .... 10·1213
Limeade .... 2·219
Parfaits, Chocolate- .... 9·1042
Patty Alaskas .... 7·841
Sails, Chocolate .... 5·605
Sauce .... 12·1423
Sauce, Fresh .... 16·1970
Sauce, In-a-Hurry ...... 16·1970
Sauce, Lamb Patties
    with .... 10·1256
Sauce, Mallow- .... 6·767
Sauce, Tangy .... 10·1215
Small .... 3·376
-Stuffed Striped Bass ..... 17·2171
Swirls .... 3·383
Tiny Red .... 8·907
Wafers .... 6·678
Wafers, Cocoa- .... 5·566

Minted
Carrots .... 4·411
Cocoa Fluff .... 5·566
Coconut .... 5·568
Leg of Lamb on a Spit ... 12·1423
Peas .... 12·1422
Sundae Soda .... 11·1293
Minute Steaks and Capers .. 12·1424
Minute Steak Sukiyaki .... 2·186
Mixed Grill .... 10·1232
Mixed Pickles .... 13·1659

Mocha
Blitz Torte .... 2·241
Brownie Pudding .... 19·2420
Chiffon Cake .... 8·906
Cupcakes .... 3·346
-Dot Bavarian .... 12·1427
-Frosted Drops .... 16·2017
Frosting .... 16·2017
-Marshmallow Pudding and
    Chocolate-Almond Cups ..5·577
Mystery Delight .... 10·1188
-Nut Roll .... 12·1427
-Nut Torte .... 12·1427
Refrigerator Cake .... 12·1425
Sauce .... 6·767
Torte .... 12·1425
-Velvet Torte .... 6·768

Mock
Champagne Punch ...... 15·1808
Indian Pudding .... 4·444
Lasagne Casserole .... 6·643
Mince Pie .... 1·88
Strawberries Devonshire ...7·775
Modern Caesar Salad ..... 15·1886

Molasses
Bundt Cake .... 12·1429
Cake Bars .... 12·1429
Corn Bread .... 12·1430
Corn Muffins .... 5·637
Jumbles .... 10·1223
Taffy .... 5·529

Molded
Apricot Cream .... 19·2346
Asparagus Salad .... 1·114
Cherry Ring .... 4·473
Ruby Red Salad .... 5·526
Mondae Sauce .... 10·1185
Monterey (or Jack)
    Cheese Fondue .... 12·1432
Mornay Sauce .... 12·1433

Mostaccioli
Chili .... 12·1434
Sauced .... 12·1434
Sausage and .... 12·1434
Mother's Best Fudge
    Cake .... 3·346
Moussaka .... 12·1436

Mousse
Appetizer Cheese .... 1·70
Chicken-Melon .... 12·1437
Chocolate .... 3·339
French Chocolate .... 12·1436
Salmon .... 10·1275
Tuna .... 12·1437

Muffin
Applesauce Puffs .... 15·1800
Bacon-Chive Corn .... 5·637
Bake, Sausage and .... 14·1738
Banana-Bran .... 9·1045
Best-Ever .... 12·1441
Blueberry .... 12·1442
Blueberry-Lemon .... 2·243
Blueberry Tea .... 3·275
Cheddar Bran .... 2·256
Cheese-Caraway .... 12·1441
Coffee Cake .... 12·1444
Corn and Corn .... 12·1441
Corn Bread and Egg ..... 12·1445
Cranberry-Cube .... 6·669
Cranberry-Orange .... 12·1443
Date .... 12·1441
English .... 7·857
Ginger .... 9·1029
Ginger-Sugar Puffs ...... 15·1800
Golden Pumpkin .... 15·1806
Graham Gems .... 12·1444
Hawaiian .... 12·1415
Jelly .... 12·1441
Marble .... 12·1442
Molasses Corn .... 5·637

Muffin *continued*
Nut .... 12·1441
Oatmeal-Raisin .... 12·1444
Onion Supper .... 12·1442
Orange Crunch .... 11·1340
Orange-Mince .... 12·1445
Orange-Pecan .... 12·1520
Peanut Butter .... 12·1443
Polka-Dot .... 12·1442
Raisin .... 12·1441
Sour Milk .... 12·1442
Spicy Fruit Puffs .... 1·83
Sugar-Crusted .... 12·1443
Waikiki .... 12·1441
Mulled Cranberry
    Drink .... 12·1481
Mulligatawny .... 12·1446
Mush, Fried
    Cornmeal .... 12·1447

Mushroom
-Bacon Burgers .... 9·1070
Bake, Clam- .... 5·554
Barbecue, Rice- .... 3·363
Bouillon .... 12·1451
Brussels Sprouts
    and .... 3·302
Burgers .... 9·1085
Casserole .... 6·659
-Cheese Pizza .... 14·1698
Cheese-Stuffed .... 5·558
Cocktail .... 12·1450
Crab-Stuffed .... 6·652
Dressing .... 16·1925
Fluted .... 12·1450
Limas and .... 11·1291
Liver with .... 16·1931
Loaf, Beef- .... 9·1084
Mornay, Crab- .... 12·1450
Pasta Sauce .... 2·163
Pickled .... 12·1451
Pickled, and
    Onions .... 13·1660
Salad, Beef and .... 2·199
Salad, Turkey- .... 15·1918
Sauce ...... 3·290; 6·656; 7·862;
        9·1117; 11·1388; 19·2317
Sauce, Dilled .... 17·2076
Sauce, Quick .... 12·1451
Sauce, Wine- .... 16·1970
Sauté, Fresh .... 8·956
Soufflé, Shrimp- .... 12·1416
Soup, Chicken .... 17·2090
Soup, Cream of .... 12·1451
Spaghetti, Clam- .... 17·2100
Stuffed .... 12·1450
Stuffing .... 18·2183
Topper, Creamy .... 12·1451
Wild Rice and .... 20·2447
Zippy .... 1·14

Mustard
Barbecued Ribs .... **17**·2104
Beans .... **1**·14
Chinese .... **4**·498
Glaze for Ham .... **9**·1111
Ham Dip, 'n ....**7**·777
-Horseradish
  Dressing .... **11**·1286
Pickles .... **13**·1658
Sauce .... **6**·729; **9**·1117
Sauce, Basic .... **12**·1453
Sauce, Cooked ....**7**·841
Sauce, Creamy .... **12**·1453
Sauce, Hot .... **16**·1970
Sauce, Jiffy .... **12**·1452
Sauce, Zippy .... **12**·1453
Slaw, Zippy ....**3**·328

N

Napoleons .... **12**·1454

Navy Bean
New England
  Baked ....**2**·171
Salad, Tuna- .... **18**·2302
Soup .... **12**·1456
Soup, Blender .... **17**·2084
-Stuffed Duck .... **7**·813
Stuffing Supreme,
  Sausage- .... **18**·2182
Neapolitan Cake .... **3**·340

Nectarine
Berries and,
  au Rhum .... **17**·2167
Dessert Pizza .... **12**·1461
Fruit-Vegetable Toss ..... **12**·1521
-Grape Compote .... **9**·1050
Quick Cake .... **12**·1459
Sauté .... **12**·1459
Sherbet .... **16**·2040
Nesselrode Pie .... **12**·1461

Newburg
Crab Meat .... **12**·1463
Lobster .... **12**·1463
Shrimp .... **13**·1591

New England
Baked Beans ....**2**·171
Clam Chowder ....**5**·518
Corn Chowder ....**5**·625
Dinner .... **15**·1850
New Orleans
Square Doughnuts ....**7**·795
New Year's Bread
  (Vasilopita) .... **9**·1064
Nippy Nectar Dressing ..... **16**·1925

No-Bake
Almond Balls .... **19**·2347
Fruitcake ....**8**·993
Fruit Squares ....**3**·371
Strawberry Shortcake .... **17**·2161
No-Cook Fudge Frosting ......**3**·347
No-Flip Oven Pancakes .... **13**·1552
Nogados (Portuguese
  Christmas Log) .... **14**·1743
No-Knead Oatmeal Bread .. **12**·1491

Noodle
Bake, Beef and ....**7**·800
Bake, Bologna- .... **12**·1468
Bake, Chicken- .... **13**·1581
Bake, Hamburger- .... **15**·1813
Bake, Hungarian .... **10**·1164
Bake, Savory Frank- ....**8**·934
Bake, Turkey- .... **14**·1767
Beef and .... **14**·1683
Beef Goulash and .... **18**·2284
Cannelloni .... **10**·1195
Casserole, Cheese- .... **14**·1736
Casserole, Tuna- .... **17**·2064
Corned Beef with .... **10**·1157
Homemade .... **12**·1467
Hungarian Cabbage and .. **10**·1165
Nibbles ....**5**·521
Parsley-Buttered ....**7**·845
Poppy Seed .... **10**·1271
Romano .... **15**·1887
Soup, Chicken- ....**4**·487
Soup, Easy Chicken- ..... **17**·2090
Spaetzle .... **17**·2097
Stroganoff with Poppy
  Seed .... **14**·1720
Notches .... **11**·1407
Nougat .... **12**·1469

NUT .... **12**·1471-1478
Bananas, Island .... **9**·1136
Braid, Prune- ....**5**·582
Bread, Chocolate-Date ... **12**·1479
Bread, Glazed Lemon ....**3**·275
Bread, Honey- .... **9**·1066
Bread, Orange- .... **12**·1480
Bread, Orange-Date ....**3**·267
Bread, Prune- .... **14**·1792
Bread, Raisin- .... **15**·1816
Bread, Whole Wheat .... **20**·2440
-Butter Rounds .... **15**·1885
Cake, Spice- .... **17**·2111
Caramel .... **12**·1477

Nut *continued*
Chestnut Stuffing .... **18**·2183
-Crusted Bananas ....**2**·141
-Edged Butter Slices ....**3**·317
Filling, Date- ....**7**·878
Fluff, Chocolate- ....**8**·970
Fruitcake, Whole .... **5**·531
-Ice Cream Pie, Date- .... **14**·1677
Loaf, Best .... **3**·275
Loaf, Cranberry ....**6**·663
Mold, Cheese- .... **14**·1694
Muffins .... **12**·1441
Pudding,
  Steamed Pumpkin- .....**12**·1475
Ring, date- ....**10**·1222
Ring, Orange- .... **15**·1820
Roll, Brown Sugar ....**3**·299
Sauce, Butterscotch- ..... **10**·1180
Sauce, Peach- .... **10**·1180
Savory Chestnut Stuffing .....**8**·955
Squares, Fig- ....**7**·871
Sundae Cups, Chocolate- ....**8**·977
Swedish ....**12**·1476
Torte, Mocha- .... **12**·1427
Tree .... **12**·1477
Whirls, Cinnamon ....**2**·165
Wreath, Gumdrop- .... **9**·1096

Nutmeg
Cake .... **12**·1483
-Pineapple Sauce ....**6**·767
Whipped Squash ....**1**·21
Nutty Chocolate Frosting ... **13**·1615
Nutty Pups ....**8**·934

O

Oatmeal
Bars, Malted .... **11**·1340
Bars, Peanut Butter- ....**5**·566
Bread, No-Knead .... **12**·1491
Butterscotch .... **15**·1822
Chip Cookies ....**5**·608
Cookies ....**7**·805
Cookies, Apple-Filled .... **12**·1489
Cookies, Chocolate- ..... **12**·1489
Cookies, Coconut- ....**5**·570
Cookies, Raisin- .... **12**·1491
Crisps, Lacy .... **10**·1243
Crisps, Polka-Dot .... **12**·1491
Crunchies .... **15**·1885
-Raisin Muffins .... **12**·1444
Rounds .... **12**·1491
Spicy Raisin ....**4**·442
"Oh Boy" Waffles .... **10**·1267
Oil Pastry .... **13**·1586
Okra, Tomatoes and .... **12**·1493
Old-Fashioned .... **12**·1493
Old-Fashioned Raisin Bars .. **15**·1835

Old-Time
Beef Stew .... 1·32
Fudge .... 8·999
Herb Loaf .... 3·270
Oxtail Stew .... 13·1541

Olive
Burgers .... 12·1496
-Cheese Ball .... 17·2121
-Cheese Snacks .... 12·1496
-Egg Salad Bake .... 19·2394
Sauce .... 8·925
Sauté, Veal- .... 19·2363
Slaw, Carrot- .... 15·1857
-Spaghetti Sauce .... 12·1496
Spread, Zippy Beef- ...... 12·1497

Omelet
French .... 12·1501
Hashed Brown .... 12·1501
Macaroni .... 11·1336
Parmesan .... 13·1571
Puffy .... 12·1501
Sour Cream .... 7·843
Sour Cream-Ham .... 9·1114
Spanish Potato .... 17·2103
Tuna .... 18·2303
One Bean Toss .... 2·178
"One Cup" Cottage Ring .... 11·1294
One-Step Creamed Peas .... 13·1594
1-2-3 Apple Pie .... 15·1797
1-2-3 Easy Party Punch .... 15·1807
1-2-3 Fruit Cup .... 5·563
1-2-3 Sauce .... 16·1970

Onion
Bake, Apple and .... 12·1509
Bake, Swiss .... 12·1511
Beef with (Zwiebelfleisch) 19·2395
Biscuits .... 2·136
Bread, Easy .... 2·159
-Buttered Sirloin .... 17·2141
-Butter Rolls .... 12·1508
-Cheese Loaf .... 3·267
Cheese-Marinated .... 1·16
Cheese-Scalloped .... 12·1509
-Cheese Soup .... 8·914
Chicken, Easy .... 13·1541
Creamed .... 12·1508
Creole .... 12·1508
Curried .... 19·2384
Dip, Chicken Liver- .... 7·781
Dutch-Glazed .... 12·1509
Fries .... 13·1539
Glazed Squash with .... 1·20
Gourmet .... 12·1509
Gravy .... 17·2052
Liver with Apples and .... 19·2350
Medley, Beet- .... 2·206
Pickled .... 12·1507; 13·1660

Onion *continued*
Pickled Mushrooms and .. 13·1660
Pie .... 6·727
Pie, French .... 14·1669
Potatoes .... 13·1662
Relish, Pimiento- .... 7·883
Rings, French-Fried .... 8·961
Rings, Pickled .... 5·557
Sauce, Ribs with .... 14·1734
Slices, Herbed .... 12·1509
Slices, Skillet .... 11·1321
Soup .... 8·958
Soup, Cream of .... 12·1507
Soup, Elegant .... 12·1511
Soup, French .... 1·16
Sour Cream-Pimiento .... 12·1511
Steak and .... 2·196
Stuffed .... 12·1509
Supper Muffins .... 12·1442
Tripe and .... 2·190
-Wine Soup .... 20·2459

Open-Face
Beefburgers .... 12·1438
Burgers .... 12·1512
Sandwich Supreme ...... 16·1949
Opera Fudge .... 8·999
Opossum .... 12·1513

Orange
Alaskas .... 2·133
-Apricot Freeze .... 1·101
-Apricot Ring ...... 2·240; 5·546
-Avocado Toss .... 1·122
Baba au .... 1·125
Babas .... 1·126
Baked Beans .... 2·173
Bars, Date- .... 5·530
Beets, Cranberry- .... 2·204
Blossom Cake .... 12·1519
Bowl, Winter .... 12·1521
Bread, Cranberry- ...... 19·2419
Brownies, Apple- .... 5·605
Butter .... 13·1553
Butter Coffee Cake ..... 20·2474
Butter, Cranberry- ..... 13·1553
-Butter Frosting .... 13·1630
Cake, Coconut- .... 10·1265
Celebration Cake .... 2·136
Champagne Cocktail ...... 4·448
Cherry Cobbler .... 5·561
Chicken and Rice ...... 12·1522
Chicken, Currant- .... 6·716
Chiffon Pie .... 12·1520
Chiffon Soufflé .... 12·1519
Chrysanthemum .... 8·1013
Chutney Chops .... 5·535
Coconut Brittle .... 3·380
Coffee Braid .... 5·548
Coffee Cake, Berry- .... 17·2163

Orange *continued*
Cream Cake .... 7·824
Cream Frosting .... 7·824
Crescents .... 6·695
Crunch Muffins .... 11·1340
Crunch Pie, Pumpkin- ..... 7·863
Cups, Baked .... 11·1327
Cups, Lobster- .... 11·1314
-Date Coffee Cake .... 5·583
-Date Fold-Ups .... 16·1956
-Date Medley .... 20·2468
-Date Nut Bread .... 3·267
-Date Torte .... 12·1520
Delight Salad .... 10·1179
Dessert Soufflé .... 17·2077
Doughnuts .... 7·796
Drop Cookies .... 12·1416
Eggnog .... 10·1179
Filling .... 1·38; 5·578
Fluff, Fruit and .... 8·987
French Toast .... 8·950
Fruit Mold, Papaya .... 12·1521
-Ginger Cookies .... 15·1847
Glaze .... 5·605
-Glazed Beets .... 2·204
-Glazed Grilled Chuck .. 11·1354
-Glazed Pork Chops .... 14·1736
-Honey Butter .... 3·314
Icing .... 15·1880
-Lemon Sauce .... 2·141
Marmalade .... 11·1356
Melon à l' .... 11·1303
Meringue Pie .... 6·680
-Mince Muffins .... 12·1445
Muffins, Cranberry- .... 12·1443
Nut Bread .... 12·1480
-Nut Ring .... 15·1820
Pancakes, Jiffy .... 13·1557
-Peach Pie, Deep-Dish .... 6·747
-Pear Salad .... 9·1152
-Pecan Muffins .... 12·1520
Peel, Candied .... 3·371
-Pineapple Fizz .... 10·1182
-Pork Curry .... 2·157
Pork Steaks .... 13·1664
-Port Mold .... 20·2460
Pot Roast .... 5·546
-Pumpkin Pudding .... 6·724
Refrigerator Cookies ... 15·1847
Relish, Cranberry- ..... 15·1857
Rice .... 6·716
Rice, Chicken with .... 16·1969
-Rice Stuffed Perch .... 13·1649
Ring Mold, Papaya- .... 12·1521
Roast Duckling with ..... 7·813
Rolls, Chocolate- ..... 16·2017
Rolls, Glazed .... 18·2215
Rosettes .... 15·1880
-Rum Cake .... 20·2467
Salads, Fruit-Filled ... 12·1521

Orange *continued*
Sauce .... **8**·956
Sauce, Duckling with .... **8**·956
-Sauced Waffles .... **19**·2406
Sauce, Tenderloin with ... **18**·2263
-Sauterne Jelly .... **10**·1212
Shortcake, Peach- .... **13**·1606
-Sour Cream Topper .... **8**·987
-Spiced Peaches .... **13**·1602
-Spinach Toss .... **17**·2113
Sponge Cake .... **17**·2118
Stuffing .... **18**·2184
Sunbursts .... **12**·1519
Sunshine Cake .... **3**·339
Syrup .... **13**·1553
Tapioca Fluff .... **15**·1796
Tea, Spicy .... **2**·222
-Thyme Lamb Chops ..... **10**·1256
-Topped Burgers .... **9**·1123
Toss, Apple- .... **1**·85
Velvet .... **5**·548
Waffles .... **19**·2407
Waldorf .... **19**·2413
Wild Duck Á La .... **7**·812
Yogurt Dip, Pineapple- ... **20**·2476

Oriental
Abalone .... **12**·1531
Beef Skillet .... **12**·1530
Chi Chow .... **12**·1530
Crunch Burgers .... **2**·180
Fruit Freeze .... **3**·371
Hash .... **10**·1272
Lobster Salad .... **12**·1534
Pork and Shrimp .... **12**·1534
Rice .... **12**·1536
Scallop Skillet .... **12**·1533
Skillet Supper .... **2**·199
Veal Chops .... **12**·1532

ORIENTAL COOKERY 12·1525-1536

Original Caesar Salad .... **3**·331
Ornamental Frosting .... **3**·353
Outdoor Burgers .... **2**·155

Oven
Beef Stew .... **2**·196
-Browned Potatoes ...... **14**·1747
Chicken Fricassee .... **13**·1540
-Cooked Frozen Vegetables **19**·2379
Fried Chicken .... **4**·482
-Fried Fish .... **7**·895
-Fried Frog Legs .... **13**·1540
Fried Turkey .... **19**·2322

Oven *continued*
Herb Chicken .... **4**·481
Meatballs .... **9**·1089
Peas .... **13**·1595
-Style Turkey Hash .... **6**·658
Swiss Steak .... **18**·2225
Tomato Sandwich .... **13**·1540
Turkey Croquettes ...... **13**·1541
Over-the-Coals
Lobster Tails .... **16**·2033

Oyster
Angels on Horseback .... **1**·56
Bienville .... **15**·1852
Cocktail .... **13**·1544
Corn-, Scallop .... **13**·1545
Deep-Fried .... **13**·1547
Deviled, on the Half Shell **13**·1546
Half Shell, on the .... **13**·1544
Pudding .... **13**·1545
Rockefeller .... **13**·1547
Scalloped .... **13**·1545
Scalloped Corn and ..... **16**·1992
Stew .... **13**·1546
Stew, Hearty .... **13**·1546
Stuffing .... **13**·1546

P

Pacific Chowder .... **17**·2089
Paella, Easy Turkey .... **19**·2318
Paella, Spanish .... **13**·1549
Pain d'Épice .... **8**·955
Pampered Beef Fillets ...... **11**·1320
Panama Radish Salad ...... **15**·1829
Pan-Broiled Steak .... **13**·1550

Pancake (See also *Crepes*.)
à la Mode .... **13**·1557
Apple .... **13**·1554
Apple-Sauced Potato Cakes **13**·1556
Blender Potato .... **2**·240
Blueberry .... **13**·1554
Blueberry Latkes .... **10**·1264
Bread Crumb .... **13**·1553
Buckwheat Griddle Cakes ...**3**·303
Buttermilk .... **13**·1552
Cherry-Sauced .... **13**·1558
Corn .... **5**·624
Cornmeal Griddle Cakes .. **9**·1075
Corn, with Chili .... **5**·624
Double-Corn Cakes ..... **13**·1554
Easy Sourdough Flapjacks ...**8**·904
Favorite .... **13**·1552
Feather .... **13**·1552
Hawaiian .... **13**·1554
Israeli Cheese Blintzes ...... **2**·241
Jiffy Orange .... **13**·1557
Johnnycakes .... **10**·1222

Pancake *continued*
Mincemeat .... **13**·1557
No-Flip Oven .... **13**·1552
Potato (Kartoffel
Pfannkuchen) .... **10**·1230
Pumpkin Puff .... **13**·1556
Quick Cottage
Cheese .... **13**·1553
Spring .... **17**·2162
Super Strawberry .... **13**·1557
Swedish .... **13**·1557
Toppers .... **13**·1553
Turkey-Potato .... **14**·1751
Western Flapjacks .... **8**·904

Pan-Fried
Cabbage ....**3**·327
Chitterlings ....**1**·25
Eggplant ....**7**·847
Liver .... **11**·1306
Papaya Rings .... **13**·1559
Parsnips .... **13**·1573
Round Steak .... **13**·1559
Tomatoes .... **13**·1559
Pan Gravy ....**3**·296
Panned Apple Rings ....**3**·360
Panned Cabbage
Slaw .... **13**·1560

Papaya
-Orange Ring Mold ...... **12**·1521
-Raspberry Marble .... **13**·1563
Rings, Pan-Fried .... **13**·1559
Paprika Chicken .... **13**·1564

Parfait
Berry-Cereal ....**4**·443
Big Apple ....**1**·96
Cherry ....**4**·473
Cherry-Creme .... **13**·1567
Chocolate-Marshmallow ..**11**·1360
Chocolate-Mint .... **9**·1042
Coffee-Mallow Towers ... **13**·1568
Cranberry .... **10**·1177
Cranberry-Honeydew .... **10**·1156
Easy Pineapple .... **10**·1177
Honeydew-Berry .... **11**·1396
Java Tapioca .... **18**·2246
Lazy Grasshopper .... **9**·1058
Lemon Crunch .... **9**·1044
Lime-Berry .... **13**·1567
Mauna Loa .... **9**·1136
Peanut Butter Swirls ..... **13**·1614
Pineapple-Cheese ....**6**·725
Plum .... **13**·1567
Pudding-Pear .... **10**·1247
Quick Cherry-Cream .... **13**·1568
Quick Pudding .... **13**·1567
Strawberry ....**6**·759
Two-Berry .... **17**·2094

Parfait Pie
Cherry-Burgundy .... **10**·1178
Grape .... **9**·1052
Lime .... **11**·1294
Peach .... **13**·1569
Pineapple .... **14**·1677
Pink ....**2**·238
Pumpkin .... **13**·1569
Sea Foam Cantaloupe ....**4**·401
Strawberry .... **13**·1570
Strawberry-Cheese ...... **17**·2164
Strawberry Ribbon ...... **17**·2166
Parker House Rolls .... **13**·1570

Parmesan
Beef Patties .... **11**·1388
Biscuits .... **15**·1845
Broccoli ....**3**·293
Cheese Sauce .... **16**·1972
Chicken .... **14**·1772
Clams .... **16**·2036
Dressing .... **16**·1929
Fried Mullet .... **13**·1559
Grits Ring .... **9**·1077
Melba Toast .... **11**·1391
Nibble Mix .... **14**·1785
Omelet .... **13**·1571
Popcorn .... **14**·1715
-Rice Squares .... **13**·1571
Shoestrings .... **16**·2045
Supper, Veal .... **11**·1381
Zucchini .... **20**·2479

Parsley
-Buttered Noodles ....**7**·845
-Chive Dip for
    Artichokes ....**1**·108
Dumplings .... **17**·2052
Fantans ....**7**·864
Rice Ring ....**6**·688

Parslied
Bread Slices .... **13**·1572
Carrots ....**4**·412
New Potatoes .... **13**·1572
Potato Salad .... **13**·1573
Parsnips, Extra-
Special .... **13**·1573
Parsnips, Pan-Fried .... **13**·1573
Partridge in Red Wine ...... **13**·1574

Party
Cheese Dip .... **11**·1318
Potato Chips ....**1**·75
Pumpkin Pie ....**6**·672
Sandwiches .... **16**·1958
Spumoni .... **10**·1177
Passion Fruit Punch .... **9**·1136
Pastafazool .... **10**·1195
Pastel Popcorn Tree .... **14**·1716

Pastry
Egg .... **13**·1586
Electric Mixer .... **13**·1586
Lemon .... **14**·1674
Oil .... **13**·1586
Petal Cups ....**6**·652
Plain .... **13**·1585
Puff .... **9**·1118
Rich Tart Shell .... **13**·1586
Shell, Rich ....**4**·475
Tart Shells, for .... **18**·2250
Topper ....**4**·424

Pâté
Baked Liver ....**8**·956
Braunschweiger .... **13**·1588
Chicken Liver ....**1**·65
Corned Beef .... **13**·1587
Feuilleté au Fromage ....**8**·958
Ham .... **13**·1587
Ring, Brandied .... **13**·1588
Shrimp-Dill ....**2**·240
Snow-Capped .... **20**·2466
Tuna .... **13**·1586
Patio Potato Salad ....**4**·439
Patio Punch Soda .... **10**·1182
Paul Bunyan Sugar Cookies ....**5**·610
Paul Revere Cheesewiches .. **16**·1954

Pea
Almonds, and ....**4**·499
Celery, Luxe, and .... **13**·1595
Cream, in .... **13**·1594
Epicurean .... **13**·1595
Minted .... **12**·1422
One-Step Creamed ...... **13**·1594
Oven .... **13**·1595
Potage, Potato- .... **17**·2086
Potatoes, Smoky, and .... **13**·1595
Potato Soup, and .... **13**·1592
Quick Creole .... **13**·1597
Salad, Herbed .... **13**·1597
Shrimp, Chinese, and .... **12**·1533
Snow, with Water
    Chestnuts .... **19**·2384
Soup, Ham and .... **17**·2090
Soup, Split .... **17**·2117
Springtime .... **13**·1594

PEACH .... **13**·1599-1608
-A-Berry Cobbler ....**5**·561
à la Rum .... **15**·1897

Peach *continued*
-Almond Ice Cream ....**1**·40
-Angel Fluff .... **10**·1246
Brandied ....**3**·259
Cake, Peanut Butter- ..... **18**·2201
-Cantaloupe Conserve ... **13**·1602
-Cheese Dumplings ....**7**·819
-Cherry Sparkle .... **13**·1603
Chicken Cups, and ...... **13**·1605
Cobbler, Crunchy .... **13**·1608
Compote, Spicy .... **18**·2199
Conserve ....**5**·598
Conserve, Apple- ....**1**·85
-Cot Cherry Bake ....**8**·991
Cream Milk
    Shake, and .... **13**·1606
Crumble .... **15**·1797
-Easy Shortcake .... **13**·1606
Filling ....**5**·560
Flame, in .... **13**·1606
Freeze, Spicy .... **15**·1920
Frosty Fruit Molds .... **15**·1920
-Ham Swisser .... **13**·1605
Ice Cream ....**6**·672
Ice Cream, Fresh .... **15**·1853
Kuchen .... **10**·1241
Marble, Berry- .... **13**·1603
-Marshmallow Pie .... **11**·1359
Melba Ice Cream .... **10**·1173
-Mince Pie .... **12**·1418
Mold, Spiced .... **13**·1603
-Nut Sauce .... **10**·1180
-Orange Shortcake ...... **13**·1606
Orange-Spiced .... **13**·1602
Parfait Pie .... **13**·1569
-Pecan Mold ....**6**·760
Pie .... **13**·1608
Pie, Cherry- ....**8**·906
Pie, Custard- .... **14**·1674
Pie, Deep-Dish Orange- .....**6**·747
Pie, Pizza- .... **13**·1607
Pies, Fried ....**8**·964
Pies, Petite .... **13**·1608
-Pineapple Ring .... **11**·1350
Pineapple Shake, and .... **14**·1690
-Plum Jam .... **10**·1203
Preserve Cake .... **13**·1607
-Rum Jam .... **10**·1203
Salad, Applesauce- ...... **13**·1603
Sauce .... **6**·760; **10**·1182
Sauce, Spicy .... **9**·1035
Shortcakes .... **16**·2048
Spiced **13**·1602; **17**·2068; **17**·2110
Squares, Ginger- .... **9**·1030
Torte, Almond- .... **13**·1608

Peachy
-Almond Chiffon Roll .... **10**·1218
Casserole, Ginger- .... **13**·1605
Corned Beef .... **13**·1605

Peachy *continued*
Glazed Ham .... **9**·1035
Milk Shake .... **12**·1417
Rice Pudding .... **4**·444
Peaked Pineapple Salad .... **11**·1332

Peanut
Bars, Cereal- .... **5**·605
Bars, Chocolate- .... **19**·2341
-Bran Bars .... **13**·1611
Brittle .... **5**·529
Brittle, Buttery .... **12**·1480
Brittle Pie .... **13**·1611
-Cereal Candy .... **13**·1613
-Cheese Straws .... **4**·468
Chews, Easy- .... **13**·1612
Clusters .... **3**·382
Coco Roons .... **18**·2210
Crunch Pie .... **13**·1613
-Ice Cream Pie .... **14**·1678
-Mallow Dressing .... **16**·1930
Pie, Chocolate .... **4**·512
Pillows, Chocolate .... **3**·382
Sauce .... **4**·498; **15**·1873
Soup .... **1**·24
Topper .... **13**·1611

Peanut Butter
-Bacon Sandwich .... **15**·1803
Bars .... **17**·2051
Cookies, Double .... **13**·1614
Crinkles .... **13**·1615
Crunch Cake .... **13**·1615
Cupcakes .... **6**·712
Fudge .... **5**·527
Jelly Cake, and .... **13**·1614
Jelly Twists .... **18**·2217
-Marshmallow Sauce ...... **6**·768
Muffins .... **12**·1443
-Oatmeal Bars .... **5**·566
-Peach Cake .... **18**·2201
Pork .... **13**·1615
Quick Cake Frosting ...... **8**·969
Sauce, Hot Fudge- .... **16**·1972
Swirls .... **13**·1614
Waffles .... **19**·2409

PEAR .... **13**·1617-1625
au Gratin .... **1**·117
Baked Chutney .... **5**·535
Baked Crimson .... **13**·1619
-Berry Coffee Cake .... **5**·580
-Blue Cheese Salad ...... **13**·1622

Pear *continued*
Bundles, Surprise .... **13**·1625
Cake, Ginger- .... **9**·1030
Cheese-Topped .... **20**·2476
Chiffon Pie .... **14**·1670
Chocolaty Meringue ..... **13**·1623
Coffee Cake .... **13**·1620
Compote, Rosy .... **13**·1623
Cream-Topped .... **13**·1623
Creamy Mandarin .... **10**·1176
Crumble, Ginger- ...... **13**·1623
Crumble Pie .... **13**·1625
Elegante, Baked .... **13**·1622
Helene Cake .... **13**·1625
-Lime Mold, Creamy ..... **13**·1622
Marmalade, Cranberry- .. **18**·2201
Melba, Flaming .... **11**·1391
Middle East .... **13**·1621
Parfaits, Pudding- ...... **10**·1247
Pie, Cranberry- .... **14**·1676
Pie, Sliced .... **14**·1675
-Pineapple-Cheese Pie ... **13**·1625
-Pineapple Ring .... **13**·1621
Salad, Mandarin- ...... **11**·1342
Salad, Pink .... **13**·1621
Salad, Orange- .... **9**·1152
Salad with Cheese
Dressing .... **13**·1622
Sherry-Spiced .... **13**·1621
Sundaes, Rosy .... **13**·1624
Waldorf Salad .... **13**·1619

Pecan
Cake, Honey- .... **7**·826
Cake, Toasted Butter ..... **12**·1476
Cookies, Butter .... **7**·805
Cornucopias, Chocolate- ... **6**·763
Cream Puffs, Chocolate- ... **6**·683
Crispies .... **13**·1630
Crisps, Sugar- .... **15**·1885
Dainties, Lemon- ...... **10**·1278
Ice Cream, Caramel- ..... **10**·1171
Log .... **13**·1631
Pie, Pumpkin- .... **14**·1669
Pie, Southern .... **13**·1628
Popovers .... **14**·1719
Popovers, Giant .... **2**·238
Pralines .... **15**·1852
-Raisin Pie .... **13**·1628
Rolls, Butterscotch- ...... **10**·1160
Rolls, Caramel- . **13**·1631; **18**·2216
Rolls, Quick .... **13**·1631
Sauce, Coffee- .... **7**·828
Slices, Crisp .... **5**·609
Tassies .... **13**·1630
Tea Biscuits .... **2**·229
Torte, Chocolate- ...... **18**·2289
Waffles .... **19**·2409
Waffles, Chicken- ...... **19**·2410
Whip, Chocolate- ...... **20**·2440

Peking Glaze .... **10**·1159
Pennsylvania Dutch Lettuce . **11**·1286
Pennsylvania Dutch Pot Roast **19**·2332
Pennsylvania Red Cabbage ....**3**·325
Penuche .... **13**·1636
Pepper Cup Trio .... **13**·1640

Peppermint
Chiffon Pie .... **13**·1644
Fondant .... **8**·921
Ice Cream ...... **10**·1174; **18**·2209
Kisses .... **13**·1644
Nests .... **12**·1422
Pepperoni Pizza .... **14**·1700
Pepperoni Salad .... **8**·1006
Pepper Pot Soup .... **13**·1647
Peppers, Pickled Sweet Red . **13**·1660

Peppy
Cabbage .... **3**·328
Lasagne .... **15**·1872
Potato Salad .... **14**·1753

Perch
Grilled, with Parsley Sauce **13**·1648
Orange-Rice Stuffed ..... **13**·1649
Saucy Cheese-Coated .... **13**·1649

Perfect
Apple Pie .... **1**·87
Corn Bread .... **5**·629
Fried Chicken .... **4**·482
Pan Gravy .... **9**·1061
Waffles .... **19**·2410
White Bread .... **3**·280
Perfection Salad .... **13**·1650
Petal Bread .... **3**·369
Petite Peach Pies .... **13**·1608
Petits Fours .... **13**·1653
Petits Four Icing .... **13**·1653
Pfeffernuesse .... **13**·1653

Pheasant
Apples, with .... **8**·1005
Roast Sherried .... **13**·1655
Smothered .... **13**·1654
Wild Rice, with .... **13**·1655
Wine Sauce, in .... **13**·1655
Phony Spumoni .... **8**·974

Pickle
Dill .... **13**·1658
Fans .... **8**·1012
Garnishes .... **8**·1012
Green Tomato Dill ...... **13**·1661
Kosher Dill .... **10**·1241
Mixed .... **13**·1659
Mustard .... **13**·1658
Relish, Apple- .... **15**·1856
Sauce .... **7**·894

Pickle *continued*
Shaker Cut . . . . **19**·2330
Slices, Crisp . . . . **13**·1659
Slices, Stuffed . . . . **8**·1012
Sweet . . . . **13**·1659
Sweet-Sour . . . . **13**·1658
Watermelon . . . . **13**·1658

Pickled
Apricots . . . . **15**·1856
Artichoke Hearts . . . . **13**·1661
Beets . . . . **2**·207; **13**·1661
Carrots . . . . **1**·14
Carrots, Sweet . . . . **13**·1661
Dilled Beans . . . . **13**·1660
Mushrooms . . . . **12**·1451
Mushrooms and Onions . . **13**·1660
Onion Rings . . . . **5**·557
Onions . . . . **12**·1507; **13**·1660
Shrimp . . . . **16**·1931
Sweet Red Peppers . . . . . . **13**·1660

PIE . . . . **14**·1667-1678
(See also *Chiffon Pie, Cream Pie,*
Custard Pie, Fruit Pie, Parfait Pie.)
Banana Split . . . . **6**·768
Berry-
Cheesecake . . **14**·1670; **14**·1679
Blueberry Strata . . . . **2**·244
Cherry-Cream Cheese . . . . **10**·1190
Chocolate Cheese . . . . **5**·515
Citrus-Cheese . . . . **14**·1674
Coffee Angel . . . . **5**·579
Cranberry Cheese . . . . **6**·669
Date-Nut-Ice Cream . . . . . **14**·1677
Frozen Cranberry Velvet . . **14**·1677
Fruit Compote . . . . **7**·803
Fudge Ribbon . . . . **13**·1644
Grasshopper . . . . **9**·1059
Lazy Grasshopper . . . . **6**·686
Lemondown Fancy . . . . . . **10**·1278
Lemon Frost . . . . **20**·2443
Lemon Ice Cream . . . . **10**·1277
Lush Strawberry Meringue **17**·2166
Mandarin Angel . . . . **1**·55
Maple Syrup . . . . **3**·365
Mile High Ice Cream . . . . . . **6**·761
Party Pumpkin . . . . **6**·672
Peanut Brittle . . . . **13**·1611
Peanut Crunch . . . . **13**·1613
Peanut-Ice Cream . . . . . . **14**·1678
Pecan-Raisin . . . . **13**·1628
Pineapple-Sour Cream . . . **14**·1692

Pie *continued*
Shoofly . . . . **16**·2046
S'More . . . . **6**·658
Southern Pecan . . . . **13**·1628
Speedy Cheesecake . . . . **4**·465
Strawberry Alaska . . . . . . **14**·1674
Strawberry Angel . . . . **1**·55
Strawberry Frozen . . . . . . **17**·2166
Strawberry-Mallow . . . . . **14**·1671
Strawberry Sunshine . . . . **2**·133
Pilaf, Bulgar Wheat . . . . **12**·1458
Pilaf, Chicken . . . . **14**·1682

Pimiento
-Onion Relish . . . . **7**·883
Onions, Sour Cream- . . . . . **12**·1511
Sauce . . . . **19**·2315

Pineapple
Acorn Squash . . . . **1**·20
Cake, Carrot- . . . . **4**·411
-Carrot Toss . . . . **4**·409
-Cheese Parfaits . . . . **6**·725
-Cheese Pie, Pear- . . . . **13**·1625
-Cheese Salad . . . . **7**·826
Chiffon Cake . . . . **14**·1691
-Chocolate Squares . . . . **3**·298
Citrus Punch . . . . **8**·984
Cocktail . . . . **5**·563
-Coconut Filling . . . . **7**·881
Conserve, Freezer . . . . **18**·2201
Cream Loaf . . . . **10**·1247
Cream Pie . . . . **11**·1403
Cream Pie, Strawberry- . . . . . **6**·679
Crisscross Coffee Cake . . . . . **7**·881
Crunch Cake . . . . **5**·571
Dessert, Frosty . . . . **14**·1690
Dressing . . . . **14**·1689
Drop Cookies . . . . **14**·1781
Fizz, Orange- . . . . **10**·1182
Fluff . . . . **17**·2070
Fluff Cake . . . . **17**·2120
Freeze . . . . **18**·2210
-French Dressing . . . . **8**·988
Frostea . . . . **18**·2257
Grill, Turkey- . . . . **14**·1772
Jam, Apricot- . . . . **10**·1202
Jelly, Cran- . . . . **10**·1212
Jewel Squares . . . . **19**·2345
Jubilee, Fresh . . . . **14**·1691
Leg of Lamb with . . . . **10**·1259
-Lemon Fizz . . . . **10**·1179
-Lime Float . . . . **14**·1690
-Mint Cup . . . . **12**·1420
-Mint Dessert . . . . **12**·1415
-Mint Freeze . . . . **8**·927
Mold, Beet- . . . . **14**·1689
Mold, Upside-Down . . . . . **14**·1688
-Orange Cakes, Tiny . . . . . **19**·2342
-Orange Yogurt Dip . . . . . **20**·2476

Pineapple *continued*
Parfait Cake . . . . **10**·1178
Parfait Pie . . . . **14**·1677
Parfaits, Easy . . . . **10**·1177
Pie, Fresh . . . . **14**·1692
-Pork Skillet . . . . **12**·1535
Pudding Cake . . . . **10**·1190
Puffs . . . . **14**·1692
Ring, Peach- . . . . **11**·1350
Ring, Pear- . . . . **13**·1621
Salad, Peaked . . . . **11**·1332
Sauce, Nutmeg- . . . . **6**·767
Shake, Peach and . . . . **14**·1690
Sherbet . . . . **16**·2040
-Sour Cream Pie . . . . **14**·1692
Spareribs . . . . **10**·1234
-Stuffed Cornish Hens . . . . **18**·2187
-Turkey Salad . . . . **19**·2321
Upside-Down Cake . . . . . . **14**·1691
Upside-Down Cakes,
Tiny . . . . **14**·1691
-Veal Patties . . . . **19**·2365
-Whipped Topping . . . . . . **14**·1691

Pink
Cloud Cake . . . . **17**·2168
Frosting . . . . **8**·968
Fruit Dessert . . . . **8**·991
Fruit Mayonnaise . . . . **11**·1362
Lemonade Cake . . . . **3**·345
Parfait Pie . . . . **2**·238
Parfaits . . . . **17**·2170
Pear Salad . . . . **13**·1621
Popcorn Balls . . . . **14**·1716
Velvet Sherbet . . . . **16**·2040
White Marble Cake, and . . **15**·1824
Pinwheel Burgers . . . . **9**·1124
Pioneer Beef Stew . . . . **4**·424
Piquant Salad . . . . **10**·1167
Piquant Sauce . . . . **16**·1940
Pisang Goreng . . . . **14**·1694

Pizza
American . . . . **7**·869
Cheese . . . . **14**·1698
Crust, Biscuit . . . . **14**·1695
Crust, Homemade . . . . **14**·1695
Crust, Jiffy . . . . **14**·1695
Ground Beef . . . . **14**·1697
Mushroom-Cheese . . . . . . **14**·1698
-Peach Pie . . . . **13**·1607
Pepperoni . . . . **14**·1700
Pronto . . . . **15**·1845
Sausage . . . . **14**·1697
Sausage-Salami . . . . **14**·1697
Short-Cut . . . . **14**·1698
Swiss Steak . . . . **18**·2225
Wheels . . . . **18**·2283
Yard, by the . . . . **16**·1952
Plain Pastry . . . . **13**·1585

Planked
Meat Loaf .... **9**·1088
Steak .... **14**·1701
Stuffed Walleye .... **7**·893
Planter's Punch .... **14**·1701

Plum
Cobbler, Italian .... **14**·1707
Conserve .... **5**·597
Custard Sauce, with ..... **14**·1709
Dessert Salad .... **14**·1706
-Glazed Chicken .... **14**·1707
-Glazed Franks .... **1**·75
-Glazed Ribs .... **14**·1781
-Glazed Turkey Roasts ... **14**·1768
Jam .... **10**·1204
Jam, Peach- .... **10**·1203
Jewel Coffee Cake ...... **14**·1707
Parfaits .... **13**·1567
Pie, Crumb Top .... **14**·1707
Pie, Marmalade- .... **11**·1357
Pudding, Easy .... **14**·1710
Sauce .... **10**·1180
-Sauced Lamb Kabobs ... **10**·1225
Squares, Greengage ..... **9**·1069
Squares, Lemon-Frosted .. **14**·1704
Whip .... **20**·2441
Plump Prunes .... **1**·66
Plymouth Cranberry Cake ..... **6**·668
Poached Eggs .... **7**·834
Poached Fish .... **7**·896
Poached Salmon .... **7**·896
Polish Cutlets .... **6**·730

Polka-Dot
Muffins .... **12**·1442
Oatmeal Crisps .... **12**·1491
Pinwheels .... **14**·1693
Waffles .... **19**·2407

Polynesian
Beef Roast .... **5**·534
Coleslaw .... **3**·329
Haddock .... **9**·1070
Pork Steaks .... **17**·2110
Pot Roast .... **2**·194
Yam Casserole .... **14**·1689

Pompano
Amandine .... **14**·1714
Dill Sauce, with .... **14**·1714
En Papillote .... **13**·1563

Popcorn .... **14**·1715
Balls, Caramel .... **14**·1716
Balls, Cinnamon .... **15**·1842
Candied .... **14**·1716
Parmesan .... **14**·1715
Pops .... **14**·1715
Tree, Pastel .... **14**·1716

Popfreeze Punch .... **15**·1807
Po Po .... **9**·1135

Popovers .... **14**·1719
Curried Ham in .... **14**·1719
Giant Pecan .... **2**·238
Pecan .... **14**·1719

Poppy Seed
Dressing .... **11**·1363
Filling .... **14**·1721
-Lime Dressing .... **14**·1720
Rolls .... **14**·1721
Swirled Bread .... **14**·1721
Torte .... **14**·1720
Porcupine Meatballs ...... **14**·1721

PORK .... **14**·1723-1738
(Listed at the end of this entry *Chop, Ground, Roast, Spareribs*. See also *Bacon, Ham, Sausage*.)
Barbecued .... **14**·1738
Beef Pie, or .... **14**·1668
Chow Mein .... **5**·521
Corned Pig's Knuckles ... **16**·1984
Island Sweet-Sour ...... **18**·2247
Kabobs (Pork Sate) ...... **15**·1873
Mandarin .... **11**·1342
Peanut Buttered .... **13**·1615
Potato Supper, and ..... **13**·1664
Salad Jamboree .... **14**·1736
Sate (Pork Kabobs) ...... **15**·1873
Sauté, Chinese .... **19**·2425
Skillet, Pineapple- ...... **12**·1535
Steaks, Dressed-Up ..... **13**·1664
Steaks, Orange .... **13**·1664
Steaks, Polynesian ...... **17**·2110
Sweet and Sour .... **12**·1535

Chop
Amber Rice, on .... **15**·1869
Apricot Stuffed .... **1**·99
Barbecue .... **10**·1200
Braised .... **14**·1736
Butterfly .... **3**·319
Cabbage, Spicy, and .... **17**·2109
Cranberry .... **11**·1381
Dinner, Seasoned ...... **13**·1581
Double Fruit-Glazed ..... **9**·1135
Fruit-Stuffed .... **8**·990
Gourmet .... **6**·672
Lima Skillet, Smoked .... **14**·1731
Orange Chutney .... **5**·535

Pork, Chop *continued*
Orange-Glazed .... **14**·1736
Oven Dinner .... **2**·166
Risotto Bake .... **9**·1143
Roast .... **15**·1874
Saffron Rice, with ...... **15**·1906
Sour Cream, in .... **14**·1736
Spanish Rice, in .... **4**·426
Stuffed .... **18**·2180
Supper .... **14**·1784
Sweet and Sour .... **18**·2218
Treat .... **8**·918

Ground
American Chop Suey ..... **2**·181
-Apricot Loaf .... **11**·1307
Chopped Meat Suey .... **14**·1738
Meat Loaf Supreme ..... **6**·656
Pie, Canadian (Tourtière) .. **3**·364
Pinwheel, Kraut- .... **14**·1732
Savory Cabbage Rolls ... **9**·1087
Swedish Cabbage Rolls .. **3**·327
Twin Meat Loaves ...... **11**·1386

Roast
Corn-Stuffed Crown ..... **6**·701
Curry, Orange- .... **2**·157
Dinner, Smoked .. **2**·252; **13**·1664
Ginger-Glazed Crown ... **6**·701
Glazed Smoked Shoulder . **14**·1734
Italian Picnic Shoulder ... **13**·1663
Loin .... **14**·1723
Loin, Apple-Buttered .... **14**·1734
Loin, Cherry-Sauced .... **14**·1782
Marinated .... **11**·1354
Rio Grande .... **14**·1733
Rolled Veal and .... **19**·2361
Shoulder, Glazed ...... **14**·1782
Tangerine .... **18**·2243
Tenderloin .... **18**·2264
Tenderloin, Stuffed ..... **14**·1733
Tenderloin with Orange
   Sauce .... **18**·2263

Spareribs
Abacus .... **10**·1227
Best Barbecued .... **14**·1734
Cantonese .... **17**·2104
Chinese Smoked .... **12**·1531
Dee-Lish .... **2**·158
Far East .... **5**·618
Kraut, Quick, and ...... **14**·1784
Kraut, with .... **16**·1976
Luau .... **17**·2104
Mincemeat .... **17**·2104
Mustard Barbecued ..... **17**·2104
Onion Sauce, with ..... **14**·1734
Pineapple .... **10**·1234
Plum-Glazed .... **14**·1781
Sweet-Sour .... **18**·2218

Port
Cherries Portofino ....**6**·765
Mold, Orange- .... **20**·2460
Quick Jubilee Sauce ....**1**·40
Portuguese Christmas Log .. **14**·1743

Potato
au Gratin, Ham and ....**1**·117
Bake, Creamy ....**14**·1756
Baked ....**14**·1747
Bake, Double ....**10**·1189
Baked-Stuffed ....**11**·1326
Bake, Golden ....**14**·1757
Bake, Scalloped ....**14**·1748
Bake, Spinach ....**17**·2115
Balls, Meat and ....**14**·1752
-Beet Salad ....**2**·207
Blue Cheese-Bacon ....**14**·1748
Blue Cheese-Spud Salad .....**2**·247
Cakes, Apple-Sauced ....**13**·1556
-Cheese Custard ....**6**·726
Chef's Cheese Sauce, with ...**8**·919
Chips, Party ....**1**·75
Clouds ....**14**·1757
-Corn Triangles ....**9**·1044
-Cottage Bake ....**6**·644
Cottage Fries ....**6**·645
Creamed Peas and New .....**6**·676
Creamy
    Hashed Brown Bake ... **14**·1757
Crisscross ....**14**·1748
-Custard Pie,
    Berks County ....**13**·1636
Deviled-Stuffed ....**18**·2190
Dill ....**7**·778
Doughnuts ....**7**·794
Duchess ....**7**·808
Dumplings, Bavarian .... **8**·1022
Dumplings ....**10**·1230
Fish and Chips ....**7**·896
Foiled ....**8**·919
French Fries ....**8**·960
Ham-Stuffed ....**14**·1751
Hashed Brown Omelet ... **12**·1501
Hashed Browns ....**14**·1747
Hot Deviled ....**7**·771
Kugels ....**10**·1242
Lemon Sauce, in ....**14**·1748
Mashed ....**14**·1747
Omelet, Spanish ....**17**·2103
Onion ....**13**·1662
Oven-Browned ....**14**·1747
Pancakes, Blender ....**2**·240
Pancakes (Kartoffel
    Pfannkuchen) ....**10**·1230
Pancakes, Turkey ....**14**·1751
Parmesan Shoestrings ...**16**·2045
Parslied New ....**13**·1572
-Pea Potage ....**17**·2086
Pie, Meat and ....**9**·1082

Potato *continued*
Puff ....**15**·1799
Puffs, French-Fried ....**8**·960
Puff Soufflé ....**17**·2075
Quick Dill ....**14**·1748
Rolls ....**14**·1749
Salad, Calico ....**14**·1753
Salad, Country ....**16**·2015
Salad, Dublin ....**7**·778
Salad Fix-Up, Hot ....**14**·1756
Salad, German ....**14**·1754
Salad, Ham and ....**14**·1754
Salad, Hot Dill- ....**14**·1753
Salad, Jellied ....**15**·1842
Salad Mold ....**15**·1919
Salad, Parslied ....**13**·1573
Salad, Patio ....**4**·439
Salad, Peppy ....**14**·1753
Salad, Potluck ....**14**·1753
Salad, Skillet ....**15**·1820
Salad, Sour Cream ....**17**·2093
Salad Special ....**15**·1914
Salad, Swiss ....**4**·501
Salad, Turkey- ....**10**·1157
Scallop, Corn and ....**4**·428
Scalloped ....**16**·1992
Scallop, Ham and ....**9**·1114
Shredded au Gratin ....**1**·117
Skillet, Sausage- ....**16**·1975
Smoky Peas and ....**13**·1595
Soup ....**14**·1749
Soup, Cream of ....**6**·684
Soup, Gourmet ....**14**·1749
Soup, Peas and ....**13**·1592
Sour Cream Baked ....**6**·710
Stuffed Baked ....**19**·2335
Supper, Pork and ....**13**·1664
Tater-Coated Chicken ....**13**·1539
Toppers, Baked ....**14**·1747
Volcano ....**20**·2442
Potluck Bean Bake ....**2**·172
Potluck Potato Salad ....**14**·1752
Pot Roast Gravy ....**9**·1060
Pot Roast Variations ....**14**·1761
Pots de Crème ....**14**·1765
Pots de crème, Blender ......**2**·238
Pots de Crème, Chocolate .. **14**·1765

POULTRY ....**14**·1767-1776
(See also *Chicken, Cornish Game
Hen, Duck and Duckling, Goose,
Turkey.*)
Guinea Hens and Kraut ... **9**·1096

Pound Cake
Lemon ....**10**·1278
Loaf ....**14**·1778
Marble ....**14**·1778
Powwow Sundae ....**2**·153
Pralines ....**14**·1779
Preserves, Winter ....**14**·1781
Prize Chocolate Cake ....**2**·137
Prosciutto and Artichokes ... **14**·1788

Prune
Apricot Bowl, and ....**14**·1792
Butter Frosting ....**14**·1792
Cake, Spicy ....**17**·2111
Dumplings, Spice- ....**7**·819
Filling ....**10**·1240
-Nut Braid ....**5**·582
-Nut Bread ....**14**·1792
Plump ....**1**·66
Salad, Stuffed ....**14**·1792
Spice Cake ....**14**·1792
Spicy Oranges 'n ....**14**·1792
Stewed ....**14**·1791
Whip, Baked ....**17**·2151
Whip, Chilled ....**20**·2440

Pudding
Applesauce ....**15**·1796
Baked Indian ....**10**·1188
Baked Rice ....**15**·1869
Black Currant ....**6**·716
Blancmange ....**2**·236
Blender Pots de Crème ......**2**·238
Blueberry Steamed ....**6**·755
Bread ....**3**·283
Butterscotch ....**15**·1796
Cherry Bread ....**6**·725
Chocolate ....**15**·1796
Chocolate Meringue ....**4**·509
Cottage ....**6**·646
English Plum ....**5**·532
Fluffy Tapioca ....**18**·2246
Frozen Limeade ....**8**·977
Graham Cracker ....**9**·1041
Lemonade ....**15**·1797
Mince Cottage ....**6**·646
Mocha Marshmallow ....**5**·577
Mock Indian ....**4**·444
Orange-Pumpkin ....**6**·724
Orange Tapioca Fluff .... **15**·1796
Peachy Rice ....**4**·444
-Pear Parfaits ....**10**·1247
Potato Kugels ....**10**·1242
Raspberry Cream ....**6**·672
Rice ....**15**·1870
Royale, Rice ....**15**·1870
Rum ....**16**·2003
Saucepan Rice ....**15**·1869
Snow ....**6**·728
Snowflake ....**6**·759

Pudding *continued*
Snow, with Berries ...... **17**·2151
Steamed Blackberry ....**2**·233
Steamed Pumpkin-Nut ... **12**·1475
Strawberry-Vanilla ...... **10**·1190
Vanilla .... **15**·1796
Walnut Crunch .... **19**·2417
Puff Pastry .... **15**·1800
Puffy Omelet .... **12**·1501
Pumpernickel Bread ...... **15**·1803

Pumpkin
Cake with Honey Cream . **19**·2421
-Cheese Pie, Spicy .... **14**·1672
Chiffon Pie .... **4**·493
Cookies .... **15**·1805
Crème Brûlée .... **6**·755
-Date Torte .... **19**·2420
Muffins, Golden .... **15**·1806
Nut Bread .... **3**·267
-Nut Pudding, Steamed ... **12**·1475
-Orange Crunch Pie ....**7**·863
Parfait Pie .... **13**·1569
-Pecan Pie .... **14**·1669
Pie .... **15**·1805
Pie, Dreamy-High .... **14**·1670
Pie, Party .... **6**·672
Pie, Sour Cream .... **19**·2389
Pudding, Orange- .... **6**·724
Puff Pancakes .... **13**·1556
-Raisin Loaves .... **15**·1806
Spice Cake .... **3**·350
-Whip Pie, Creamy ...... **15**·1826

Punch
Burgundy .... **15**·1809
Cranberry .... **15**·1808
Cranberry-Cherry .... **5**·524
Cranberry-Tea .... **6**·665
Crowd, for the .... **15**·1814
Eggnog Royale .... **2**·222
Fish House .... **8**·899
Frosted Fruit .... **10**·1223
Frosty Golden ....**8**·995
Frosty Party .... **15**·1808
Golden Glow .... **4**·406
Holiday .... **19**·2402
Holiday Maple .... **11**·1348
Hot Lemon .... **15**·1809
Lemon .... **15**·1808
Lime Frosted .... **15**·1808
Mock Champagne .... **15**·1808
1-2-3 Easy Party .... **15**·1807
Passion Fruit .... **9**·1136
Pineapple Citrus .... **8**·984
Planter's .... **14**·1701
Popfreeze .... **15**·1807
Punchmelon .... **19**·2427
Quantity Fruit .... **15**·1809
Raspberry Crush ....**2**·223

Punch *continued*
Rhubarb-Lemonade ....**1**·22
Rosy Wassail ....**5**·524
Ruby Fruit ....**6**·665
Ruby Wine .... **20**·2458
Sea Foam .... **10**·1179
Sparkle .... **15**·1808
Spiced Grape .... **9**·1049
Spiced Percolator .... **15**·1807
Strawberry Sparkle .... **9**·1029
Trader's .... **9**·1074
Tropical .... **15**·1807
Warm Cranberry .... **15**·1807
Warren's Glugg .... **20**·2464
Watermelon-Wine ...... **19**·2428
Puris .... **15**·1809

Q

Quail
Broiled .... **15**·1810
Smothered .... **8**·1005
Wine-Sauced Birds .... **8**·1005

Quantity
Amber Tea Delight ...... **18**·2257
Burgundy Punch .... **15**·1809
Cabbage Slaw .... **15**·1814
Chili Con Carne .... **15**·1814
Cranberry-Cherry Punch ....**5**·524
Cranberry Cooler ....**2**·223
Frosty Party Punch .... **15**·1808
Fruit Punch .... **15**·1809
Hamburger-Noodle Bake . **15**·1813
Holiday Punch .... **19**·2402
Italian Meat Sauce .... **15**·1814
Lemon Punch .... **15**·1808
Lime Frosted Punch ...... **15**·1808
Macaroni and Cheese .... **15**·1813
Mock Champagne Punch . **15**·1808
Punch for the Crowd .... **15**·1814
Roaster Baked Beans ..... **15**·1814
Scramble .... **4**·443
Spanish Rice .... **15**·1813
Spiced Percolator Punch . **15**·1807
Tossed Green Salad ...... **15**·1814
Tropical Punch .... **15**·1807
Warm Cranberry Punch .. **15**·1807
Warren's Glugg .... **20**·2464
Quiche Lorraine .... **15**·1816
Quiche, Shrimp .... **15**·1816

Quick
Almond Brittle ....**3**·380
Apple Dumplings .... **15**·1845
Apple Pinwheels ....**5**·582
Applesauce Crisp ....**1**·94
Apple Strudel .... **17**·2175
Apricot Pastries .... **17**·2095

Quick *continued*
Bismarcks .... **2**·230
Brioches .... **3**·286
Cheese Rarebit .... **19**·2432
Cherry-Cream Parfaits .... **13**·1568
Chicken à la King ....**1**·26
Chili on Buns .... **9**·1090
Christmas Braid .... **18**·2200
Clam Chowder .... **15**·1824
Corn Chowder .... **15**·1853
Corn Pudding ....**5**·638
Cottage Cheese
Pancakes .... **13**·1553
Creole Peas .... **13**·1597
Crullers .... **15**·1845
Curried Ham .... **10**·1272
Dill Potatoes .... **14**·1748
Frank-Kraut Dinner ...... **16**·1975
Fruit Dip .... **17**·2167
Fudge Sauce .... **6**·768
Fudge Sundaes .... **8**·1000
Jubilee Sauce .... **1**·40
Mushroom Sauce .... **12**·1451
Pecan Rolls .... **13**·1631
Pudding Parfaits .... **13**·1567
Raisin Loaf .... **10**·1160
Ribs and Kraut .... **14**·1784
Sandwich Cookies ....**5**·609
Swedish Meatballs ...... **16**·2007
Swedish Rye Bread ...... **15**·1902
Tortoni Cups .... **18**·2291
Tuna Salad .... **18**·2278
Turkey Curry .... **19**·2318
Turkey Pie .... **12**·1414
Turnovers .... **19**·2333
Upside-Down Cake ...... **19**·2342
Vegetable Soup .... **13**·1579
Vichyssoise .... **19**·2393

QUICK COOKERY ... **15**·1819-1827
(See *Jiffy, Speedy.*)

R

Rabanados .... **14**·1743

Rabbit (Cheese)
Welsh .... **19**·2431

Rabbit (Hare)
Fried .... **15**·1828
Hasenpfeffer .... **9**·1129

Rack of Lamb
  with Vegetables .... **10**·1256

Radish
  Daisies .... **8**·1012
  Roses .... **8**·1012
  Salad, Panama .... **15**·1829
Rainbow Divinity ....**7**·785
Rainbow Melon Julep ....**1**·73
Raised Doughnuts ....**7**·795

Raisin
  Balls, Glazed Ham- .... **9**·1117
  Bars, Cinnamon- ....**5**·538
  Bars, Cinnamon-Frosted ... **9**·1044
  Bars, Old-Fashioned ..... **15**·1835
  Brioche Ring .... **8**·958
  Cake, Apple- .... **13**·1630
  -Cinnamon Rolls .... **15**·1882
  Coffee Cake, Spicy .... **12**·1476
  Dumplings, Chicken with ...**7**·817
  -Filled Apples .... **12**·1411
  -Filled Sweet Potatoes .... **12**·1522
  Flambé, Golden ....**6**·766
  Loaves .... **15**·1833
  Loaves, Apple- ....**3**·267
  Loaves, Pumpkin- ...... **15**·1806
  Muffins .... **12**·1441
  Muffins, Oatmeal .... **12**·1444
  -Nut Bread .... **15**·1816
  -Oatmeal Cookies .... **12**·1491
  Oatmeal, Spicy ....**4**·442
  Pie .... **15**·1835
  Pie, Apple- ....**1**·88
  Pie, Lemon .... **15**·1797
  Pie, Pecan- .... **13**·1628
  Pie, Vanilla- .... **14**·1677
  Praline Caramels ....**3**·381
  Rice .... **12**·1522
  Sauce .... **15**·1835
  Sauce, Caramel- ....**5**·579
  Sauce, Currant- ....**6**·715
  -Sauced Beets ....**2**·208
  Stuffing, Cranberry- ......**6**·668
Ranch House Round
  Steak .... **15**·1854
Rancho Bean Casserole ....**2**·171
Ranch Round Steak .... **17**·2143

Rarebit
  Beef ....**2**·203
  Chili-Burger ....**8**·950
  Double Cheese .... **19**·2431
  Fondue, -Style .... **12**·1484
  Golden Velvet .... **19**·2432
  Mexican .... **19**·2432
  Quick Cheese .... **19**·2432
  Welsh Rabbit .... **19**·2431
  Western Welsh .... **19**·2432
Rare Roast Beef Salad ...... **16**·1932

Raspberry
  Angel Berry Cake ....**3**·339
  Angel Dessert ....**1**·50
  Bavarian Cake .... **17**·2063
  Bavarian Mold ....**2**·155
  Bombe ....**2**·249
  Cherry-Berry Compote ......**5**·595
  Chiffon Pie ....**4**·493
  Cooler ....**2**·219
  -Cream Cheese Coffee
    Cake .... **15**·1838
  Cream Pudding ....**6**·672
  Crush ....**2**·223
  Fizz, Rosy ....**8**·899
  Flambé, Banana- .... **20**·2466
  Fluff, Red .... **8**·1017
  Grapefruit-Berry Compote **11**·1324
  Ice .... **10**·1166
  Lime-Berry Parfaits ..... **13**·1567
  Marble, Papaya- .... **13**·1563
  Melba Sauce .... **10**·1180
  -Melon Boats .... **11**·1399
  -Meringue Squares ..... **15**·1838
  Mint Cooler ....**5**·616
  -Nectarine Cocktail ....**8**·987
  Pie, Rosy .... **18**·2247
  -Rhubarb Jam .... **10**·1203
  Ring, Red .... **15**·1838
  Salad, Red .... **15**·1839
  Sauce ....**6**·759
Ravigote Sauce .... **15**·1839

Ravioli
  Chicken and Spinach-Filled **15**·1840
  Inside-Out .... **15**·1840
  Veal Stew with .... **17**·2147

Red
  Bean Toss .... **15**·1841
  Cherry Pie ....**4**·474
  Currant Dressing .... **16**·1929
  Deviled Eggs ....**7**·771
  Devil's Food Cake ....**7**·774
  Dot Turnips .... **19**·2331
  Grape Waldorf .... **19**·2413
  Hots on Kabob .... **18**·2269
  -Jeweled Honeydew ..... **10**·1156
  Sauce ....**4**·498

Red Raspberry
  Fluff .... **8**·1017
  Ring .... **15**·1838
  Salad .... **15**·1839
Refrigerated Fruit Salad ...... **9**·1049
Refrigerated Herb Rolls ..... **20**·2473

Refrigerator
  Crisps ....**5**·557
  Rolls .... **15**·1879
  Vanilla Ice Cream .... **15**·1858

Regal
  Almond Cake ....**1**·37
  Chocolate Sauce ....**5**·516
  Plum Pudding .... **14**·1709

**REGIONAL
COOKERY** .... **15**·1849-1854
Afro-American
  Chicken Gumbo ....**1**·23
  Chitterlings ....**1**·25
  Deep-Fat Fried
    Chitterlings ....**1**·25
  Pan-fried Chitterlings ......**1**·25
  Peanut Soup ....**1**·24
  Salt Pork and Greens ....**1**·24
  Sweet Potato Pie ....**1**·23

Creole
  Clam Bisque ....**6**·690
  Crab Jambalaya ....**6**·690
  Gumbo Z'Herbs ....**6**·690
  Jambalaya .... **10**·1207
  Sauce ....**6**·691
  Shrimp ....**6**·688

Hawaiian
  Bananas in Nectar .... **9**·1136
  Double Fruit-Glazed Pork
    Chops .... **9**·1135
  Island Nut Bananas .... **9**·1136
  Kona Sunset .... **9**·1136
  Macadamia Nut Pie ..... **11**·1332
  Mauna Loa Parfaits ..... **9**·1136
  Passion Fruit Punch .... **9**·1136
  Po Po .... **9**·1135
  Shrimp Platter .... **9**·1135

Midwest
  Apple-Buttered Pork
    Loin .... **14**·1734
  Beef with Dumplings ....**2**·196
  Broiled Lake Trout ....**7**·894
  Denver Sandwich ....**6**·751
  Fresh Corn Relish .... **15**·1857
  Fresh Peach Ice
    Cream .... **15**·1853
  Indian Corn Casserole ......**5**·623
  Quick Corn Chowder ... **15**·1853
  Scramble ....**4**·443
  Six-Layer Dinner .... **15**·1853
  Wild Rice Stuffing .... **20**·2447
  Wild Rice-Turkey
    Dish .... **19**·2318

Regional Cookery *continued*

New England
Anadama Bread . . . . 1·46
Baked Beans . . . . 2·171
Baked Indian Pudding . . . . 10·1188
Boston Brown Bread . . . . 2·250
Boston Cream Pie . . . . 2·252
Clam Chowder . . . . 5·518
Dinner . . . . 15·1850
Manhattan Clam
　Chowder . . . . 5·520
Snickerdoodles . . . . 17·2069

Northeast
Apple Butter Betty . . . . 2·213
Apple Pandowdy . . . . 13·1559
Buckwheat Griddle
　Cakes . . . . 3·303
Classic Chicken Divan . . . . . . 7·782
Codfish Balls . . . . 5·572
Corn Chowder . . . . 5·625
Cranberry Sauce . . . . 6·662
Individual Clambake . . . . 5·550
Mennonite Chicken with
　Sour Cream . . . . 15·1851
Pepperpot Soup . . . . 13·1647
Rosewater and Caraway
　Cookies . . . . 15·1850
Yankee Red-Flannel
　Hash . . . . 9·1129

Pennsylvania Dutch
Berks County Potato-
　Custard Pie . . . . 13·1636
Lettuce . . . . 11·1286
Pot Roast . . . . 19·2332
Red Cabbage . . . . 3·325
Sausage Scrapple . . . . 16·2011
Shoofly Pie . . . . 16·2046
Sweet Potato Relish . . . . . . 13·1636
Veal and Carrots . . . . 13·1636

Shaker
Baked Beans . . . . 16·2021
Cut Pickles . . . . 19·2330
Daily Loaf . . . . 16·2021
Special Cabbage Salad . . . 16·2021

Southern
Bacon Spoon Bread . . . . . . 15·1852
Bananas Foster . . . . 2·142
Beaten Biscuits . . . . 2·183
Hopping John . . . . 2·235
Hush Puppies . . . . 10·1165
Johnnycakes . . . . 10·1222
Key Lime Pie . . . . 11·1294
Maryland Fried
　Chicken . . . . 11·1360
Opposum . . . . 12·1513
Oysters Bienville . . . . 15·1852

Regional Cookery, Southern *continued*
Oysters Rockefeller . . . . . . 13·1547
Pecan Pie . . . . 13·1628
Pecan Pralines . . . . 15·1852
Spoon Bread . . . . 17·2120

Southwest and West
California Potato Bake . . . 18·2212
Chili Con Carne . . . . 4·494
Cioppino . . . . 5·539
Crab Louis . . . . 6·654
Denver Sandwich . . . . 6·751
Grilled Abalone . . . . 15·1854
Ranch House Round
　Steak . . . . 15·1854
Snowcap Cherry Nibbles . . . 2·224
Sourdough Bread . . . . 17·2095
Taco Salad . . . . 5·629
Texas-Style Beans . . . . 14·1693
Western Salad . . . . 15·1854

Relish
Apple-Pickle . . . . 15·1856
Bean . . . . 15·1856
Celery Cran- . . . . 6·662
Celery Fans . . . . 4·438
Cheese-Fruit . . . . 6·644
Chili Sauce . . . . 4·496
Chow Chow . . . . 5·518
Cinnamon Apple Rings . . . . . 1·94
Combination . . . . 19·2400
Confetti . . . . 15·1856
Corn . . . . 5·638
Corn and Tomato . . . . 19·2330
Cranberry-Date . . . . 6·662
Cranberry-Orange . . . . . . 15·1857
Curried Apple . . . . 1·93
Deviled Guacamole . . . . . . 9·1093
Fresh Corn . . . . 15·1857
Fresh Cucumber . . . . 6·709
Garlic Olives . . . . 12·1497
Pickled Apricots . . . . 15·1856
Pickled Mushrooms . . . . . 12·1451
Pickled Onion Rings . . . . . . 5·557
Pickled Onions . . . . 12·1507
Pimiento-Onion . . . . 7·883
Salsa . . . . 15·1857
Shaker Corn . . . . 19·2328
Speedy Salsa . . . . 2·240
Summer Corn . . . . 1·15
Sweet Potato . . . . 13·1636
Vegetable Medley . . . . . . 19·2328
Remarkable Fudge . . . . 8·1000
Reuben Roll-Ups . . . . 5·631
Reubens, Grilled . . . . 5·630

Rhubarb
Betty, Honey . . . . 2·213
Cake . . . . 15·1863
Cheesecake, Strawberry- . 17·2123

Rhubarb *continued*
Cobbler, Spring . . . . 5·561
Crunch . . . . 15·1862
Filling . . . . 5·561
Ice Cream . . . . 15·1863
Jam, Gingered- . . . . 15·1861
Jam, Raspberry- . . . . 10·1203
Jam, Strawberry- . . . . 10·1203
-Lemonade Punch . . . . 1·22
Pie . . . . 15·1860
Pie, Cherry- . . . . 14·1676
Pie, Custardy . . . . 6·723
Pie, Strawberry- . . . . 15·1860
Rhubaba . . . . 18·2198
Rolls, Strawberry- . . . . . . 15·1862
Salad, Ruby . . . . 15·1861
Sauce . . . . 15·1860
-Strawberry Compote . . . . 15·1861
Upside-Down Cake . . . . . 19·2341
Whip . . . . 15·1862
Ribbon Cake . . . . 15·1863
Ribbon Sandwiches . . . . . . 16·1957
Ribs Dee-Lish . . . . 2·158
Ribs with Onion Sauce . . . . 14·1734

Rice
Baked . . . . 4·428
Bake, Green . . . . 15·1868
Bake, Turkey- . . . . 19·2323
Barbecued Veal with . . . . . 19·2364
Bavarian, Blueberry- . . . . . 15·1870
Beef Loaf, Wild, and . . . . . . 9·1045
Browned . . . . 15·1867
Butter-Baked . . . . 15·1868
Casserole, Ham and . . . . . . 9·1044
Cheesy Tongue on . . . . . . 18·2286
Chicken Livers and . . . . 4·488
Chicken with Orange . . . . 16·1969
Chinese Fried . . . . 12·1535
Creamy Chicken and . . . . . . 1·37
Creamy Liver over . . . . . . 19·2350
Croquettes, Ham and . . . . . 6·698
Deluxe, Shrimp and . . . . . 17·2057
Fluffy . . . . 15·1867
Ginger . . . . 12·1530
Glorified . . . . 15·1870
Ham, and Cheese
　Salad . . . . 14·1787
Ham Salad, and . . . . 19·2389
Hobo . . . . 2·159
Loaves, Ham- . . . . 11·1387
-Mushroom Barbecue . . . . . 3·363
Mushrooms, Wild, and . . . 20·2447
Orange . . . . 6·716
Orange Chicken and . . . . . 12·1522
Oriental . . . . 12·1536
Pheasant with Wild . . . . . 13·1655
Pork Chops in Spanish . . . . 4·426
Pork Chops on Amber . . . . 15·1869
Pork Chops with Saffron . . 15·1906

Rice *continued*

Pudding . . . . **15**·1870
Pudding, Baked . . . . **15**·1869
Pudding, Peachy . . . . **4**·444
Pudding Royale . . . . **15**·1870
Pudding, Saucepan . . . . . . **15**·1869
Raisin . . . . **12**·1522
Rijsttafel . . . . **15**·1873
Ring, Confetti . . . . **15**·1868
Ring, Parsley . . . . **6**·688
Salad, Calico . . . . **15**·1869
Salad, Chef's . . . . **11**·1364
Salad, Crab-Wild . . . . **15**·1918
Salad, Tuna- . . . . **18**·2268
Shrimp Elegante with . . . . **15**·1868
Skillet, Beef and . . . . **9**·1090
Soufflé, Tuna 'n . . . .**7**·892
Soup, Chicken- . . . . **17**·2090
Soup, Tomato- . . . . **18**·2281
Spanish . . . . **15**·1813
Squares, Cheese- . . . . **14**·1787
Squares, Turkey- . . . . **19**·2318
-Stuffed Cornish Game
      Hens . . . .**5**·634
Stuffed Perch,
      Orange- . . . . **13**·1649
Stuffing, Cornish
      Hens with . . . . **4**·480
Stuffing, Holiday . . . . **18**·2187
Stuffing, Sesame- . . . . **18**·2185
Stuffing, Wild . . . . **20**·2447
Sweet-Sour Ham over . . . . . **9**·1116
Sweet-Sour Veal with . . . . **19**·2364
Tuna Pie, and . . . . **15**·1869
-Turkey Dish, Wild . . . . . . **19**·2318
Yellow . . . . **10**·1187
Rich Pastry Shell . . . . **4**·475
Rich Tart Shell . . . . **13**·1586
Rijsttafel Rice . . . . **15**·1873
Rio Grande Pork Roast . . . . . **14**·1733

Roast

Beef Patties . . . . **11**·1388
Beef Tenderloin . . . . **2**·197
Canadian Bacon . . . . **3**·365
Chicken Elegante . . . . **4**·480
Chicken with Stuffing . . . . **15**·1875
Domestic Duck . . . . **7**·813
Domestic Goose . . . . **9**·1040
Duckling with Cranberry
      Sauce . . . . **14**·1775
Duckling with Oranges . . . . . .**7**·813
Duckling with Red
      Cabbage . . . .**5**·524
Leg of Lamb . . . . **10**·1254
-Peppered Rib Eye . . . . **13**·1637
Pork Chops . . . . **15**·1874
Pork Loin . . . . **14**·1723
Pork Tangerine . . . . **18**·2243
Pork Tenderloin . . . . **18**·2264

Roast *continued*

Sherried Pheasant . . . . **13**·1655
Stuffed Lamb . . . . **18**·2188
Turkey (Covered Pan) . . . . **19**·2311
Turkey Halves or
      Quarters . . . . **19**·2322
Turkey (Open Pan) . . . . . . **19**·2310
Wild Goose . . . . **9**·1039
Roasted Corn . . . .**2**·159
Roasted Sweet Peppers . . . . . **10**·1195
Roaster Baked Beans . . . . . . **15**·1814
Rocky Road . . . . **8**·1000
Rocky-Road Frosting . . . . **8**·970
Rocky-Road Rings . . . .**7**·796
Roe, Fried Shad . . . . **15**·1877

Roll

Airy Cheese . . . .**4**·464
Almond Crescent . . . . **3**·271
Almond Horns . . . .**1**·41
Batter . . . .**2**·164
Brioche . . . .**3**·287
Bunny . . . .**7**·824
Butterhorns . . . .**3**·278
Butterscotch Dainties . . . .**2**·165
Butterscotch-Pecan . . . . . . **10**·1160
Butterscotch Swirls . . . .**5**·640
Caramel . . . . **15**·1882
Caramel-Pecan . **13**·1631; **18**·2216
Cheese Crescents . . . .**4**·464
Cherry Puff . . . .**8**·988
Chocolate-Orange . . . . **18**·2217
Clothespin . . . . **15**·1880
Coffeetime Twists . . . . **15**·1881
Cranberry Wagon Wheel . . . .**7**·882
Croissants . . . .**6**·696
Croissants Elegante . . . . . . **15**·1883
Crusty Water . . . .**3**·281
Dinner . . . .**2**·165
Double Butterscotch
      Crescents . . . . **15**·1881
Dough, Basic . . . . **15**·1879
Easy-Do Bacon Roll-Ups . . . .**3**·271
Fantans . . . .**7**·864
Fruit . . . .**3**·369
Glazed Orange . . . . **18**·2215
Hard . . . . **15**·1882
Jam Brown-and-Serves . . . **10**·1206
Kolacky . . . . **10**·1240
Manna . . . . **15**·1879
Onion-Butter . . . . **12**·1508
Orange Crescents . . . .**6**·695
Orange Rosettes . . . . **15**·1880
Parker House . . . . **13**·1570
Parsley Fantans . . . .**7**·864
Poppy Seed . . . . **14**·1721
Potato . . . . **14**·1749
Quick Brioches . . . .**3**·286
Quick Pecan . . . . **13**·1631
Raisin-Cinnamon . . . . **15**·1882

Roll *continued*

Refrigerated Herb . . . . **20**·2473
Refrigerator . . . . **15**·1879
Scallion-Buttered Hard . . . . . .**2**·159
Spit, on a . . . .**2**·159
Spring Flower . . . .**7**·822
Sticky Buns . . . .**3**·270
Strawberry-Rhubarb . . . . . **15**·1862
Swedish Lucia Buns . . . .**3**·306
Thyme-Buttered Crescents **15**·1883
Toasted Cheese . . . .**4**·464
Whole Wheat . . . . **9**·1045

Rolled

Chicken Breasts . . . .**4**·484
Chicken Washington . . . .**4**·484
Ginger Cookies . . . . **9**·1028
Rump Roast . . . . **11**·1377
Veal and Pork Roast . . . . . **19**·2361
Roquefort Dessert Spread . . . **15**·1888
Roquefort Dressing . . . . **15**·1888
Rosé Frappé . . . . **20**·2458
Rose Geranium Cake . . . . . . **15**·1889
Rose Geranium Frosting . . . . **15**·1890
Rosettes . . . . **15**·1891
Rosewater and Caraway
      Cookies . . . . **15**·1850

Rosy

Cheese Fondue . . . .**4**·462
Pear Compote . . . . **13**·1623
Pear Sundaes . . . . **13**·1624
Raspberry Fizz . . . .**8**·899
Raspberry Pie . . . . **18**·2247
Salad Dressing . . . . **16**·1926
Strawberry Ring . . . . **17**·2169
Wassail . . . .**5**·524

Rotisserie

Duck . . . .**7**·812
Rib Roast Barbecue . . . . . . **15**·1844
Round . . . .**2**·157
Rotisseried Rolled Rib Roast . . . .**2**·158
Round Steak Sauerbraten . . . **12**·1467
Royal Frosting . . . .**3**·353
Royal Red Sauce . . . .**4**·482

Ruby

Fruit Compote . . . .**5**·595
Fruit Punch . . . .**6**·665
Rhubarb Salad . . . . **15**·1861
-Sauced Beets . . . . **11**·1321
Wine Punch . . . . **20**·2458

Rum

Baba au Rhum . . . .**1**·124
Berries and Nectarines au . **17**·2167
Daiquiri . . . .**6**·732
Daiquiri Blazer . . . . **17**·2149
Daiquiri Pie . . . .**4**·493

Rum *continued*

-Eggnog Pie .... **15**·1897
Hot Buttered .... **15**·1897
Peaches à la .... **15**·1897
Pie, Marble-Top Chocolate- **15**·1897
Pudding .... **16**·2003
Russian Borsch .... **2**·250
Russian Dressing .... **15**·1901
Rutabaga Whip .... **15**·1901

Rye

Bread, Quick Swedish ... **15**·1902
Bread, Swedish .... **11**·1298
Cookies .... **16**·2005
Curls, Toasty .... **15**·1902
Mixer Bread, Light .... **15**·1902
Stuffing, Ham with ...... **15**·1903

S

Sacher Torte .... **15**·1905
Saffron Bread .... **15**·1906

Salad .... **15**·1909-1920
(See also *Coleslaw*.)
Artichoke-Grapefruit ...... **9**·1057
Bean and Avocado Boats . **15**·1914
Beet-Pineapple Mold ... **14**·1689
Berried Melon Rings ..... **11**·1396
Calico Rice .... **15**·1869
Carousel .... **13**·1580
Cheese-Nut Mold .... **14**·1694
Christmas Eve .... **11**·1408
Citrus Perfection .... **9**·1056
Deluxe, Hot Egg ....**7**·840
Egg and Bean .... **2**·174
Endive-Avocado ....**7**·852
Frosted Cheese Mold ......**2**·247
Fruit-Vegetable Toss ..... **12**·1521
Gingery Macaroni ...... **15**·1835
Guacamole .... **9**·1093
Molded Ruby Red ....**5**·526
"One Cup" Cottage Ring . **11**·1294
Orange-Avocado Toss ....**1**·122
Orange-Spinach Toss ... **17**·2113
Pear-Blue Cheese .... **13**·1622
Pineapple-Carrot Toss ....**4**·409
Ring, Spring ....**8**·1017
Sandwich Tower .... **16**·1958
Sea Lime .... **19**·2421
Spinach-Avocado Bowl .. **17**·2112
Tangerine-Walnut Toss ... **18**·2245

Salad *continued*

Tangy Cauliflower ....**4**·432
Walnut Croutons for ..... **19**·2419
Western .... **15**·1854

Fruit

Apple-Avocado Ring ....**1**·122
Apple-Grapefruit Molds ... **9**·1054
Apple-Melon Toss .... **11**·1395
Apple-Orange Toss ....**1**·85
Apple Ring Waldorf ....**1**·86
Applesauce-Peach ...... **13**·1603
Apple Snow ....**1**·85
Avocado-Citrus ....**1**·122
Basic Waldorf .... **19**·2413
Berry-Patch ....**6**·644
Berry-Peach Marble ..... **13**·1603
Blueberry Cream ....**2**·244
Bowl, Buffet .... **9**·1054
Bowl, Fresh .... **19**·2428
Bowl, Low-Cal ....**5**·545
Cantaloupe Crown ...... **11**·1397
Cantaloupe Stars ....**4**·401
Cheese-Topped Pears .... **20**·2476
Cherry Dessert ....**4**·472
Cinnamon-Apple .... **15**·1842
Cocktail Mold ....**8**·994
Combo, Creamy ....**2**·226
Combo, Yogurt- .... **15**·1917
Cranberry-Apricot .... **6**·666
Cranberry-Avocado Mold ...**6**·664
Cranberry-Grape .... **9**·1049
Cranberry Relish ....**6**·669
Cranberry Star Mold ......**6**·667
Cranberry Waldorf ....**6**·662
Cranberry-Waldorf Mold ....**6**·664
Cranberry-Wine .... **14**·1740
Cran-Cheese Frosties ....**6**·667
Cran-Cheese Squares .... **17**·2110
Cran-Mandarin Toss ....**6**·668
Cream, Fresh, and .... **19**·2428
Creamy Pear-Lime
Mold .... **13**·1622
Creamy Waldorf .... **19**·2413
Cups, Blue Cheese ....**2**·248
Date-Apple Waldorf ..... **15**·1917
Date-Marshmallow
Waldorf .... **19**·2411
Date Soufflé ....**6**·742
Double-Decker Honeydew
Mold .... **11**·1396
Fig ....**7**·871
-Filled Orange .... **12**·1521
Freeze, Avocado ....**1**·121
Freeze, Oriental ....**3**·371
Frosty Fruit Molds ...... **15**·1920
Fruited Nectar ....**8**·1018
Fruited Parfait .... **11**·1398
Fruity Ginger Ale Mold .... **9**·1049
Galaxy .... **20**·2475

Salad, Fruit *continued*

Gooseberry Cups .... **9**·1040
Grapefruit-Cheese
Squares .... **9**·1056
Grapefruit-Sherbet Ring ... **9**·1054
Green and Gold
Compote .... **11**·1319
Greengage Plum Squares .. **9**·1069
Heavenly Orange Fluff ......**5**·545
Honey-Banana Mold ....**7**·863
Honeydew Stack-Up ..... **20**·2475
Lemon Apple ....**1**·85
Loaf, Frosty .... **15**·1920
Luncheon ....**2**·226
Luncheon Cooler .... **11**·1398
Mandarin-Pear .... **11**·1342
Medley, Buffet .... **19**·2427
Medley, Midwinter ..... **13**·1624
Melon .... **11**·1396
Melon Basket .... **10**·1156
Melon Polka-Dot
Mold .... **11**·1398
Melon Supreme .... **11**·1396
Melon Tower .... **11**·1399
Melon Wedges .... **11**·1395
Molded Cherry Ring ....**4**·473
Mold, Harvest .... **15**·1919
Mold, Jubilee .... **10**·1215
Mold, Papaya-Orange ... **12**·1521
Orange-Apricot Freeze ......**1**·101
Orange-Apricot Ring ..**2**·240; **5**·546
Orange Delight .... **10**·1179
Orange Fluff, and ....**8**·987
Orange-Pear .... **9**·1152
Orange-Port Mold ...... **20**·2460
Orange Waldorf .... **19**·2413
Papaya-Orange Ring Mold **12**·1521
Papaya-Raspberry
Marble .... **13**·1563
Peach-Cherry Sparkle .... **13**·1603
Peach-Pineapple Ring .... **11**·1350
Peaked Pineapple .... **11**·1332
Pear-Pineapple Ring ..... **13**·1621
Pear Waldorf .... **13**·1619
Pear, with Cheese
Dressing .... **13**·1622
Pineapple-Cheese .... **7**·826
Pineapple-Mint Freeze ..... **8**·927
Pink Pear .... **13**·1621
Platter, Summer ....**5**·546
Plum Dessert .... **14**·1706
Red Grape Waldorf ..... **19**·2413
Red-Jeweled Honeydew .. **10**·1156
Red Raspberry .... **15**·1839
Refresher .... **16**·2043
Refrigerated .... **9**·1049
Rosy Strawberry Ring .... **17**·2169
Ruby Rhubarb .... **15**·1861
Salmon- .... **14**·1688
Slices, Frozen .... **15**·1920

Salad, Fruit *continued*

Soufflé, Winter .... **9**·1056
Sparkling Melon Loaf .... **10**·1275
Spiced Mandarin Mold ......**5**·545
Spiced Peach Mold ...... **13**·1603
Spiced Waldorf .... **19**·2411
Spicy Apricot Mold ....**5**·557
Spicy Peach Freeze ...... **15**·1920
Strawberry-Banana
  Mold ....**2**·141
Strawberry Cups .... **17**·2168
Strawberry Soufflé ...... **17**·2170
Strawberry Yogurt .... **17**·2167
Strawberry Yogurt
  Medley .... **20**·2476
Stuffed Prune .... **14**·1792
Sunshine Citrus
  Cups .... **9**·1056
Supreme, Cherry .... **11**·1364
Sweet Apple Ring ....**1**·83
Swiss Apple .... **17**·2093
Tangerine-Apricot
  Mold .... **18**·2245
Toss, Slim-Trim .... **19**·2428
Tropical Apple .... **19**·2419
24-Hour .... **15**·1917
Upside-Down Pineapple
  Mold .... **14**·1688
Winter Orange Bowl ..... **12**·1521

Main Dish

Apple and Ham .... **9**·1113
Apple Tuna Toss ....**1**·86
Artichoke and Crab
  Rémoulade .... **15**·1858
Bacon, Lettuce, and
  Tomato .... **18**·2277
Bake, Tuna .... **18**·2302
Beef and Mushroom ....**2**·199
Beet-Herring .... **9**·1145
Beet-Jellied Gefilte
  Fish .... **8**·1015
Bowl, Aladdin's .... **16**·1933
Cauliflower-Ham ....**4**·432
Coronado .... **11**·1398
Cottage-Shrimp Toss ..... **11**·1326
Chef's Rice .... **11**·1364
Chicken and Ham ....**4**·419
Chicken Pecan, in
  Shimmering Cranberry
  Ring ....**6**·666
Chop Chop ....**4**·497
Corned Beef Loaf ....**5**·631
Crab-Artichoke
  Luncheon ....**6**·653
Crab Louis ....**6**·654
Crab Luncheon .... **11**·1398
Crab-Tomato Aspic ....**6**·653
Crab-Wild Rice .... **15**·1918
Curry-Turkey .... **19**·2321

Salad, Main Dish *continued*

Deviled Beef Toss .... **11**·1286
-Fruit Boats, Ham .... **14**·1689
Fruited Chicken .... **11**·1355
Gourmet ....**5**·588
Ham and Egg .... **15**·1917
Ham-Chicken
  Supreme ....**6**·708
Ham-Stuffed Tomatoes .... **9**·1114
Herbed Chicken .... **18**·2249
Holiday Turkey .... **14**·1713
Jacques' Chicken ....**4**·402
Jamboree, Pork .... **14**·1736
Jellied Chicken .... **14**·1688
King Crab Crown ....**6**·653
Lobster .... **11**·1314
Lobster-Orange Cups .... **11**·1314
Lobster Ring Mold ...... **11**·1314
Macaroni-Cheese Cups .. **11**·1364
Macaroni-Salmon .... **11**·1304
Oriental, Chicken .... **12**·1478
Oriental Lobster .... **12**·1534
Peach and Chicken
  Cups .... **13**·1605
Pepperoni .... **8**·1006
Pie, Chicken ....**1**·40
Pineapple-Turkey .... **19**·2321
Quick Tuna .... **18**·2278
Rare Roast Beef .... **16**·1932
Rice and Ham .... **19**·2389
Rice, Ham, and
  Cheese .... **14**·1787
Salami-Cheese .... **16**·1933
Salmon-Avocado Mold ... **16**·1939
Salmon-Filled
  Tomatoes .... **16**·1939
Salmon Mousse .... **10**·1275
San Marino Beef .... **15**·1918
Scallop .... **16**·1991
Scallop Toss .... **12**·1439
Seafood .... **16**·2031
Shrimp-Cucumber
  Ring .... **9**·1070
Shrimp in Avocado
  Ring .... **15**·1919
Skillet Chef's .... **19**·2399
Skillet Potato .... **15**·1820
Spinach-Shrimp .... **16**·2030
Supreme, Ham .... **14**·1780
Taco ....**5**·629
Tangy Seafood Toss ..... **9**·1057
Tokyo Turkey Toss ....**2**·181
Tuna .... **11**·1321
Tuna-Bean .... **18**·2302
Tuna-Fruit .... **18**·2303
Tuna, in Iceberg Ring .. **11**·1321
Tuna-Melon Dinner ....**4**·400
Tuna-Rice .... **18**·2268
Tuna-Spinach Toss ...... **17**·2114
Tuna-Waldorf .... **19**·2411

Salad, Main Dish *continued*

Turkey-Apple Toss ...... **19**·2321
Turkey Aspic .... **19**·2320
Turkey-Chip .... **19**·2321
Turkey-Lime Mold .... **19**·2320
Turkey-Mushroom ...... **15**·1918
Turkey-Potato .... **10**·1157
Turkey Waldorf .... **12**·1478

Vegetable

Anchovy ....**1**·47
Artichoke Heart ....**1**·108
Asparagus-Tomato ....**1**·114
Asparagus Toss ....**1**·114
Austrian Cabbage ....**4**·405
Bean Bonanza .... **19**·2430
Bean-Stuffed
  Tomatoes .... **18**·2277
Blender Cucumber ....**6**·708
Blue Cheese-Spud ....**2**·247
Bowl, Blue Cheese ....**2**·247
Bowl, Calico .... **14**·1682
Bowl, Italian .... **11**·1285
Bowl, Spring .... **19**·2425
Bowl, Summer .... **11**·1286
Brussels Sprouts in
  Aspic ....**3**·302
Cabbage Aspic .... **11**·1321
Calico Potato .... **14**·1753
Carrot-Olive Slaw .... **15**·1857
Cauliflower
  Vinaigrette ....**4**·432
Celery Slaw ....**4**·438
Chili-Bean ....**4**·496
Confetti Relish Mold .... **15**·1919
Country Potato .... **16**·2015
Creamy Aspic ....**1**·116
Creamy Broccoli Mold ......**3**·291
Cucumber .... **11**·1327
Cucumber Ring
  Supreme ....**6**·707
Curry ....**6**·720
Dublin Potato ....**7**·778
Family Green .... **11**·1286
Fix-Up, Hot Potato ...... **14**·1756
Foo Yung Toss .... **19**·2424
Four Bean ....**2**·178
Fresh Herb .... **9**·1141
German Potato .... **14**·1754
Greek .... **9**·1066
Green Beans
  Caesar .... **9**·1068
Green Goddess .... **9**·1069
Ham and Potato .... **14**·1754
Hearts of Palm .... **9**·1138
Herbed Pea .... **13**·1597
Hot Dill-Potato .... **14**·1753
Hot Five Bean ....**2**·178
Italian Anchovy .... **9**·1072
Italian Bean Toss .... **15**·1914

Salad, Vegetable *continued*
Italian Green . . . . **1**·47
Jellied Potato . . . . **15**·1842
Lebanese Cacic . . . . **12**·1456
Marinated Bean . . . . **19**·2430
Marinated Three-Bean . . . **11**·1354
Mediterranean . . . . **10**·1200
Medley . . . . **6**·707
Men's Favorite . . . . **15**·1826
Modern Caesar . . . . **15**·1886
Molded Asparagus . . . . **1**·114
Mold, Potato . . . . **15**·1919
Molds, Calico . . . . **19**·2382
One Bean Toss . . . . **2**·178
Original Caesar . . . . **3**·331
Panama Radish . . . . **15**·1829
Parslied Potato . . . . **13**·1573
Patio Potato . . . . **4**·439
Pennsylvania Dutch
   Lettuce . . . . **11**·1286
Peppy Potato . . . . **14**·1753
Perfection . . . . **13**·1650
Piquant . . . . **10**·1167
Potato-Beet . . . . **2**·207
Potluck Potato . . . . **14**·1753
Quintet, Green . . . . **9**·1074
Red Bean Toss . . . . **15**·1841
Salata . . . . **9**·1070
Sour Cream Cucumbers . . . . . **6**·707
Sour Cream Potato . . . . . . **17**·2093
Special Cabbage . . . . **16**·2021
Special, Potato . . . . **15**·1914
Spinach-Lettuce Toss . . . . . **17**·2113
Sunshine Aspic . . . . **1**·116
Superb . . . . **11**·1286
Swiss Potato . . . . **4**·501
Tangy Spinach Toss . . . . . . **17**·2114
Tomato Aspic Soufflé . . . . **7**·862
Tomato-Bean Combo . . . . . **9**·1068
Tomato-Celery Aspic . . . . **1**·116
Tossed Green . . . . **15**·1814
Tossed Western . . . . **15**·1914
Wilted Lettuce Toss . . . . . . **10**·1266
Wilted Spinach . . . . **17**·2114
Zippy Beet . . . . **2**·207
Zucchini Vinaigrette . . . . . **18**·2204

SALAD DRESSING . . . **16**·1923-1932
Apricot . . . . **16**·1929
Avocado . . . . **1**·122
Avocado-Cream **17**·2093; **19**·2427
Banana-Cheese . . . . **16**·1926
Berry-Sour Cream . . . . **16**·1925

Salad Dressing *continued*
Blender Mayonnaise . . . . . **11**·1363
Blue Cheese . . . . **11**·1363; **20**·2475
Blue Cheese Fluff . . . . **19**·2428
Blue Cheese Mayonnaise . **16**·1930
Caper Mayonnaise . . . . **4**·402
Celery Seed . . . . **16**·1928
Chef's Cheese . . . . **16**·1926
Cherry-Cream . . . . **6**·675
Chiffonade . . . . **4**·489
Chili . . . . **4**·496
Chili Mayonnaise . . . . **11**·1363
Cooked . . . . **16**·1925
Cottage Cheese . . . . **11**·1322
Cottage Cheese Fluff . . . . **2**·238
Cream Goddess . . . . **16**·1930
Creamy . . . . **2**·226; **6**·653
Creamy French . . . . **8**·962
Creamy Mayonnaise . . . . . **11**·1363
Crunchy Cream . . . . **16**·1926
Cucumber . . . . **8**·1015
Dairy-Fruit . . . . **16**·1926
Fluffy Citrus . . . . **5**·546
French . . . . **8**·962
Fruit Dip Fluff . . . . **16**·1924
Fruit French . . . . **16**·1928
Garlic French . . . . **8**·1009
Garlic Olive Oil . . . . **3**·331
Ginger-Honey . . . . **9**·1152
Glossy Fruit . . . . **16**·1928
Herb . . . . **11**·1363
Honey . . . . **11**·1395
Honeyberry . . . . **12**·1521
Honey-Lime . . . . **11**·1296
Honey Mayonnaise . . . . . . **16**·1930
Horseradish . . . . . . **2**·207; **16**·1926
Italian . . . . **10**·1200; **16**·1928
Lemonade . . . . **16**·1925
Lime Honey . . . . **5**·546
Louis . . . . **6**·654
Low-Cal Snow . . . . **5**·545
Marshmallow . . . . **11**·1363
Marshmallow Blizzard . . . . . . **5**·546
Mayonnaise . . . . **11**·1362
Mushroom . . . . **16**·1925
Mustard-Horseradish . . . . . **11**·1286
Nippy Nectar . . . . **16**·1925
Parmesan . . . . **16**·1929
Peanut-Mallow . . . . **16**·1930
Pineapple . . . . **14**·1689
Pineapple-French . . . . **8**·988
Pink Fruit Mayonnaise . . . **11**·1362
Poppy Seed . . . . **11**·1363
Poppy Seed-Lime . . . . **14**·1720
Red Currant . . . . **16**·1929
Roquefort . . . . **15**·1888
Rosy . . . . **16**·1926
Russian . . . . **15**·1901
Sesame . . . . **16**·1929
Shawano . . . . **16**·1928

Salad Dressing *continued*
Slim-Trim . . . . **11**·1322
Snappy Garlic . . . . **16**·1929
Spicy Fruit . . . . **17**·2110
Sweet-Sour . . . . **16**·1925
Tarragon . . . . **16**·1926
Thousand Island . . . . **18**·2268
Tomato . . . . **18**·2283
Tomato Soup . . . . **16**·1928
Two-Way . . . . **13**·1637
Vinaigrette . . . . **19**·2397
Walnut . . . . **12**·1478
Western Blue Cheese . . . . . **16**·1925
Whipped Cream . . . . **19**·2428
Yogurt **11**·1327; **11**·1363; **20**·2475
Zippy Beet . . . . **11**·1364
Zippy Cooked . . . . **14**·1753
Zippy Emerald . . . . **16**·1927
Salami-Cheese Salad . . . . **16**·1933
Salami Topping, Trout with . . **18**·2298
Salata . . . . **9**·1070
Salisbury Steak . . . . **16**·1934
Sally Lunn . . . . **16**·1934
Salmagundi Bake . . . . **16**·1934

Salmon
-Avocado Mold . . . . **16**·1939
Bake, Smoked . . . . **8**·905
Balls in Caper Sauce . . . . . **16**·1940
-Blue Cheese Broilers . . . . **16**·1954
Casserole . . . . **16**·1941
Crab Sauce, with . . . . **16**·1937
Cucumber Sauce, with . . . **16**·1937
Epicurean, Broiled . . . . **15**·1891
-Filled Tomatoes . . . . **16**·1939
Florentine . . . . **8**·910
-Fruit Mold . . . . **14**·1688
Grilled Salmonwiches . . . . . **9**·1076
Loaf . . . . **16**·1940
Macaroni, Smoked, and . . **17**·2066
Mousse . . . . **10**·1275
Party Log . . . . **1**·70
Poached . . . . **7**·896
Potato Chip Casserole, and **16**·1940
Roll-Ups . . . . **16**·1941
Salad, Macaroni- . . . . **11**·1304
Sandwich, Fried . . . . **18**·2249
Scallop . . . . **6**·656
Steaks . . . . **16**·1939
Steaks, Charcoaled . . . . **7**·895
Steaks, Dilled . . . . **16**·1937
Steaks, Grilled . . . . **16**·1939
Tetrazzini . . . . **16**·1941
Tuna Pie, or . . . . **7**·892
Salsa . . . . **15**·1857
Salsa (Sauce) . . . . **17**·2141
Salt Pork and Greens . . . . **1**·24
Saltwater Taffy . . . . **18**·2241
Sandbakkels . . . . **16**·2005
Sandies . . . . **8**·914

SANDWICH .... 16·1945-1959
Antipasto ....1·59
Apple Turkey ....1·87
Avocado Open-Facers ... 15·1824
Bacon Big Boys ....1·128
Barbecued Bologna Burgers ..2·155
Bayou Bean-Burgers ....2·175
Beef Rarebit ....2·203
Beef Salad .... 11·1364
Beer-Sauced Burgers ....2·203
Best Hamdogs ....8·935
Big Western Bean
   Burgers .... 16·1958
Blue Cheese Burgers ....2·248
Blue Cheese Dogs ....2·248
Boston Beanwich ....2·175
Broil, Crab ....6·652
Broiled Luncheon Meat .. 11·1331
Broiled Tuna Burgers ..... 18·2304
Burger Mountains .... 9·1124
Burgundy Beefburgers .... 9·1125
Camembert-Apple ....3·360
Checkerboards .... 16·1957
Cheese and Beef Burgers .. 9·1084
Cheeseburger Towers .... 9·1123
Cheesy Corned Beef .. 13·1662
Chicken Open-Face ..... 13·1564
Chili-Burger Rarebit ....8·950
Chili-Cheese Franks ....8·933
Chili Con Wiene ....8·934
Club ....5·558
Coney Islands ....5·596
Corned Beef Captains .... 12·1512
Corned Beef Hash
   Burgers .... 16·1952
Cornucopias .... 16·1956
Crab Rolls ....8·918
Creole .... 16·1954
Crunchy Ham .... 14·1754
Dad's Denvers ....6·751
Date-Roll .... 16·1957
Denver ....6·751
Deviled Ham and Tuna .....7·773
Deviled Hamburgers ....7·771
Dilly Beef Cartwheel ....2·197
Dilly Hamburgers ....7·779
Diploma .... 16·1957
Double-Beef ....2·191
Egg-Tomato-Sardine ......6·735
Fish Salad Club .... 16·1949
Four-Star .... 12·1513
Frankfurter Doubles ....8·935

Sandwich *continued*
Frank-Reuben ....8·935
Frank Triangles .... 16·1982
Fried Salmon .... 18·2249
Frosted Ribbon Loaf ..... 16·1959
Fruit Tea .... 16·1958
Fruit Wheels .... 16·1948
Garden Cottage Cheese .. 16·1948
German Burgers .... 9·1124
Ginger-Date Triangles .....6·740
Golden Gate Salad Loaf .. 16·1950
Gourmet Dagwoods ..... 19·2312
Grilled Beefwiches .... 9·1076
Grilled Reubens ....5·630
Grilled Salmonwiches .... 9·1076
Ground Beef Reuben .... 9·1087
Ham-Asparagus Broil .... 18·2223
Ham-Cheese Crunch ..... 9·1114
Ham 'n Egg Triple Deckers ...7·826
Ham Pinwheel ....6·735
Ham Wafflewiches ...... 19·2408
Hot Crab Open-Facers ... 12·1513
Hot Curried Turkey ..... 19·2313
Hot Dog Burgers ...... 16·1951
Hot Dogs Delicious ....8·936
Hot Turkey .... 19·2313
Iowa Corn Burgers .... 9·1124
Loaf, Ten-in-One ....2·188
Meatball Heroes .... 11·1384
Meat Loaf Splits .... 16·1952
Mexican-Style Cheese ... 18·2291
Mexi-Taco .... 16·1954
Mile-Long .... 10·1227
Mushroom Burgers ..... 9·1085
Nutty Pups ....8·934
Olive Burgers .... 12·1496
Olive-Egg Salad Bake .... 19·2394
Open-Face Beefburgers .. 12·1438
Open-Face Burgers ...... 12·1512
Orange-Date Fold-Ups ... 16·1956
Orange-Topped Burgers ... 9·1123
Oriental Crunch Burgers .....2·180
Oven Tomato .... 13·1540
Party .... 16·1958
Paul Revere
   Cheesewiches .... 16·1954
Peach-Ham Swisser .... 13·1605
Peanut Butter-Bacon ..... 15·1803
Pizza by the Yard ..... 16·1952
Polka-Dot Pinwheels ... 14·1693
Puffs, Spring .... 19·2388
Quick Chili on Buns .... 9·1090
Reuben Roll-Ups ....5·631
Ribbon .... 16·1957
Salmon-Blue Cheese
   Broilers .... 16·1954
Sardine .... 16·1961
Sardine and Cheese ...... 16·1961
Saucy Bean Burgers ...... 18·2282
Saucy Beef Boat ....8·950

Sandwich *continued*
Saucy Steak .... 11·1391
Seafood Diamonds .... 16·1956
Shrimp .... 17·2058
Shrimp Boat .... 16·1950
Shrimp-Capers ....6·735
Skilletburgers .... 9·1084
Snapperoni Franks .... 16·1982
Sour Cream Burgers ..... 17·2094
Square Burgers .... 9·1124
Stroganoff .... 16·1952
Stroganoff Steak .... 17·2141
Submarine .... 18·2192
Supper, Turkey .... 19·2313
Supreme, Open-Face .... 16·1949
Tamale Hero .... 9·1144
Tangy Kraut Burger .... 16·1951
Teatime .... 16·1956
Tower, Salad .... 16·1958
Triple-Layered .... 16·1949
Tuna-Berry .... 16·1932
Tuna Open-Facer .... 16·1949
Tuna Tugs .... 12·1513
Turkey-Cheese .... 11·1319
Turkey Double-Decker .... 9·1075
Turkey Joes .... 19·2313
Turkey Swisswiches .... 19·2313
Watercress Pinwheels .... 19·2425
Zesty Luncheon Barbecue ...2·155
San Francisco Eggs and
   Spinach .... 9·1074
San Marino Beef Salad ... 15·1918
Santa's Fudge ....3·378

Sardine
Appetizer Spread .... 16·1961
Cheese Sandwich, and ... 16·1961
Sandwiches .... 16·1961
Sandwiches, Egg-Tomato- ...6·735
Sassy Franks .... 10·1214

SAUCE .... 16·1963-1973
Allemande ....1·32
Anchovy Butter ....1·47
Apple-Cinnamon ..... 10·1180
Apricot ....6·693
Apricot-Cherry ...... 10·1180
Basic Mustard .... 12·1453
Béarnaise ....2·182
Béchamel ....2·183
Best Tomato Catsup ....4·430
Blackberry ....2·233
Blender Béarnaise ....2·183

Sauce *continued*

Blender Hollandaise ...... **9**·1148
Blender Tartar .... **16**·1966
Blender White .... **16**·1965
Blueberry .... **2**·244; **6**·755;
           13·1553; **20**·2443
Blue Cheese ..... **9**·1124; **16**·1971
Bordelaise .... **2**·250
Bread .... **16**·1966
Brown .... **3**·299
Burgundy .... **16**·1968
Butter .... **6**·668
Butterscotch ....**3**·322
Butterscotch-Nut .... **10**·1180
Candied Ginger .... **6**·767
Caramel-Raisin ....**5**·579
Cheddar Cheese .... **13**·1571;
      17·2075; **19**·2318
Cheese ...... **1**·113; **3**·328; **4**·461
Cherry .... **6**·767; **16**·1973
Cherry Sundae .... **16**·1972
Chili .... **4**·496
Chinese Brown .... **8**·929
Chinese Mustard .... **4**·498
Chive Mayonnaise .... **4**·501
Chocolate .... **6**·683
Chocolate-Walnut .... **16**·1973
Classic Hollandaise .... **9**·1149
Coffee-Pecan .... **7**·828
Cooked Mustard .... **7**·841
Cranberry .... **6**·662
Cranberry Burger .... **6**·668
Creamy Butterscotch ...... **6**·768
Creamy Dill .... **4**·482
Creamy Egg .... **7**·845
Creamy Hard .... **7**·871
Creamy Mustard .... **12**·1453
Creole .... **6**·691
Cucumber .... **6**·709
Cumberland .... **6**·710
Currant .... **11**·1354
Currant-Raisin .... **6**·715
Custard ..... **1**·34; **6**·747; **17**·2151
Daffodil Lemon .... **10**·1278
Deluxe, Tartar .... **16**·1966
Diable .... **7**·775
Dill .... **7**·778
Dilled Mushroom ...... **17**·2076
Easy Chocolate .... **5**·516
Easy Seafood .... **16**·1970
Egg .... **7**·890
Fluffy Cream .... **19**·2406
Fluffy Hard .... **9**·1128
Fluffy Maple .... **8**·963
Foamy .... **8**·915
Foo Yong .... **8**·929
Fresh Mint .... **16**·1970
Fruit Sparkle .... **16**·1972
Fudge .... **1**·28
Fudgy Chocolate .... **5**·578

Sauce *continued*

Ginger .... **12**·1531
Ginger Soy ....**4**·598
Golden Apricot .... **6**·767
Gourmet ....**3**·299
Green Goddess ....**8**·925
Hard ....**5**·532
Herb 'n Honey Basting .... **9**·1151
Horseradish .... **10**·1157
Hot Cider .... **3**·273; **13**·1556
Hot, for Tostadas ...... **18**·2293
Hot Fudge-Peanut Butter . **16**·1972
Hot Mustard .... **16**·1970
In-a-Hurry Mint .... **16**·1970
Italian Meat .... **18**·2281
Italian Meat (quantity) .... **15**·1814
Jiffy Cheese ....**4**·461
Jiffy Hollandaise .... **9**·1149
Jiffy Mustard .... **12**·1452
Jiffy Spaghetti .... **14**·1784
Jubilee .... **14**·1781
Lemon .... **2**·213; **7**·819; **14**·1706
Lingonberry .... **11**·1298
Mallow-Mint .... **6**·767
Maple Whip .... **11**·1348
Marshmallow ...... **6**·683; **6**·766
Mediterranean ....**5**·547
Mexican Hot .... **18**·2284
Mex-ocado ....**1**·15
Mincemeat Sundae ..... **12**·1419
Mint .... **12**·1423
Mocha ....**6**·767
Mondae .... **10**·1185
Mornay .... **12**·1433
Mousseline .... **12**·1438
Mushroom .. **3**·290; **6**·656; **7**·862;
      9·1117; **11**·1388; **19**·2317
Mushroom Pasta .... **2**·163
Mustard .... **6**·729; **9**·1117
Nutmeg-Pineapple .... **6**·767
Olive ....**8**·925
Olive-Spaghetti .... **12**·1496
1-2-3 .... **16**·1970
Orange ....**8**·956
Orange-Lemon .... **2**·141
Parmesan Cheese ...... **16**·1972
Peach .... **6**·760; **10**·1182
Peach-Nut .... **10**·1180
Peanut .... **15**·1873
Peanut Butter-Marshmallow .**6**·768
Pickle ....**7**·894
Pimiento .... **19**·2315
Piquant .... **16**·1940
Plum .... **10**·1180
Potatoes with Chef's
    Cheese ....**8**·919
Provençale .... **14**·1789
Quick Fudge ....**6**·768
Quick Jubilee .... **1**·40
Quick Mushroom ...... **12**·1451

Sauce *continued*

Raisin .... **15**·1835
Raspberry ....**6**·759
Raspberry Melba .... **10**·1180
Ravigote .... **15**·1839
Regal Chocolate ....**5**·516
Rhubarb .... **15**·1860
Royal Red ....**4**·482
Salsa .... **17**·2141
Sauterne .... **16**·1987
Sherried-Date .... **16**·2043
Sherry .... **13**·1655
Shrimp .... **17**·2059
Shrimp-Almond .... **15**·1825
Sour Cream .... **16**·1972
Spiced Fruit ....**8**·991
Spicy Cherry .... **16**·1970
Spicy Peach .... **9**·1035
Spicy Tomato .... **15**·1840
Spring Fruit .... **10**·1180
Strawberry .... **17**·2162
Sweet-Sour .... **12**·1534
Swiss-Cheddar ....**4**·461
Swiss Cheese ....**4**·461
Tangy Barbecue ....**1**·43
Tangy Cranberry ...... **16**·1968
Tangy Mint .... **10**·1215
Tartar .... **18**·2253
Tropical Sundae ...... **16**·1972
Turkey-Crab .... **14**·1776
Vanilla ....**6**·646
Vanilla Dessert ...... **19**·2346
Velouté .... **19**·2390
Whipped Cream ...... **12**·1475
White .... **20**·2445
Wine ....**8**·925
Wine Fruit ....**5**·634
Wine-Mushroom ...... **16**·1970
Zippy Blue Cheese ....**2**·248
Zippy Mustard .... **12**·1453
Zippy Pineapple ....**4**·482
Sauced Mostaccioli .... **12**·1434

Saucepan

Rice .... **15**·1868
Rice Pudding .... **15**·1869
Taffy Bars ....**5**·597

Saucy

Bean Burgers .... **18**·2282
Beef Boat ....**8**·950
Cabbage Rolls .... **18**·2190
Cheese-Coated Perch .... **13**·1649
Chicken Dinner .... **14**·1785
Dilled Butternut .... **17**·2135
Franks ....**8**·934
Italian Meatballs ...... **11**·1382
Steak Sandwich .... **11**·1391
Vegetable Trio ....**2**·179
Zucchini .... **17**·2132

Sauerbraten .... **16**·1974
Sauerbraten, Round
  Steak .... **12**·1467

Sauerkraut
  Dinner, Quick Frank- .... **16**·1975
  Frankrauts .... **16**·1975
  Guinea Hens and .... **9**·1096
  Provençale .... **16**·1976
  Quick Ribs and .... **14**·1784
  Skillet, Meatball- .... **16**·1976
  Spareribs with .... **16**·1976
  Stew, Frank and .... **16**·1975
  Tomato .... **18**·2279
  Weinkraut .... **16**·1984

Sausage
  -Apple Wrap .... **3**·363
  au Gratin .... **14**·1751
  -Bean Bake, Creole ...... **10**·1233
  -Bean Dip, Hot .... **1**·71
  -Bean Stuffing
    Supreme .... **18**·2182
  Biscuits, in .... **16**·1984
  Bites, Glazed .... **1**·75
  Chowder, Corn- .... **5**·626
  Kabobs .... **16**·1984
  -Krauters .... **10**·1236
  -Liver Rolls .... **11**·1306
  Loaf, Glazed .... **14**·1732
  Macaroni and Cheese .... **11**·1336
  Mock Lasagne
    Casserole .... **6**·643
  Mostaccioli, and .... **12**·1434
  -Muffin Bake .... **5**·637
  Muffin Bake, and .... **14**·1738
  Pizza .... **14**·1697
  -Potato Skillet .... **16**·1975
  Rolls, Cheese and .... **11**·1300
  -Salami Pizza .... **14**·1679
  Scrapple .... **16**·2011
  Skillet, Yam and .... **11**·1300
  Squash and .... **1**·19
  -Squash Special .... **12**·1523
  Stew, Savory .... **11**·1300
  Strata .... **17**·2154
  -Stuffed Apples .... **1**·86
  -Stuffed Breast of Veal .... **19**·2359
  -Stuffed Squash .... **18**·2190
  Stuffing .... **15**·1907
  Treats, Grilled .... **9**·1075
Sautéed Apples .... **8**·1005

Sauterne
  Jelly, Orange- .... **10**·1212
  Rosy Wassail .... **5**·524
  Sauce .... **16**·1987
  Sole with Grapes .... **17**·2071
Savarin Chantilly .... **16**·1988
Savarin Syrup .... **16**·1988

Savory
  Blade Pot Roast .... **14**·1762
  Cabbage Rolls .... **9**·1087
  Chestnut Stuffing .... **8**·955
  Chicken Pies .... **14**·1759
  Frank-Noodle Bake .... **8**·934
  Green Beans .... **16**·1988
  Pepper Steak .... **13**·1647
  Sausage Stew .... **11**·1300
  Squab .... **17**·2127
  -Stuffed Rolled Rib
    Roast .... **15**·1875
  Stuffing .... **10**·1259
  Succotash .... **18**·2193
  Tomato Soup .... **17**·2087
  Vegetable Trio .... **17**·2131
Scallion-Buttered
  Hard Rolls .... **2**·159

Scalloped
  Bacon and Eggs .... **16**·1993
  Corn and Oysters .... **16**·1992
  Corn Supreme .... **16**·1992
  Eggplant .... **7**·849
  Melon Bowl .... **8**·1013
  Oysters .... **13**·1545
  Potato Bake .... **14**·1748
  Potatoes .... **16**·1992
  Squash .... **16**·1993
  Vegetables .... **19**·2382
Scallopine, Veal .... **13**·1579
Scallopine with Wine,
  Veal .... **16**·1993
Scallopine Burgers .... **20**·2460

Scallops
  à la Jimmy .... **16**·2033
  Bacon, and .... **16**·1991
  Broiled .... **16**·1989
  Chowder, Hot .... **16**·1990
  Deep-Fried .... **16**·1989
  Elegant .... **16**·1991
  Mornay .... **16**·1990
  Salad .... **16**·1991
  Skillet, Oriental .... **12**·1533
  Teriyaki .... **18**·2265
  Tetrazzini .... **16**·1991
  Toss .... **12**·1439

**SCANDINAVIAN
  COOKERY** .... **16**·1995-2007
Scones, Tea .... **16**·2008
Scored Cucumbers .... **8**·1013

Scotch
  Broth .... **16**·2009
  Shortbread .... **16**·2046
  Teas .... **5**·605
Scottish Lamb Stew .... **17**·2145
Scramble .... **4**·443
Scrambled Brains .... **19**·2351
Scrambled Eggs with
  Tomatoes .... **16**·2011
Screwdriver .... **19**·2403
Scripture Cake .... **16**·2012

Sea Foam .... **16**·2013
  Cantaloupe Pie .... **4**·401
  Frosting .... **16**·2013
  Punch .... **10**·1179

Seafood (See also *Fish, Shellfish.*)
  Bake .... **16**·2034
  Bake, Triple .... **4**·427
  Bisque .... **2**·231
  Cassola de Peix .... **16**·2034
  Chowder .... **5**·520
  Diamonds .... **16**·1956
  Divan .... **11**·1324
  Fried Squid .... **17**·2137
  Kabobs .... **10**·1228
  Salad .... **16**·2031
  Sauce, Easy .... **16**·1970
  Shore Dinner .... **16**·2014
  Soufflé Pie .... **16**·2032
  Stuffing .... **18**·2184
  Sword .... **10**·1228
  Toss, Tangy .... **9**·1057
  Turnovers .... **7**·893
Sea Lime Salad .... **19**·2421
Seasoned Pork Chop Dinner . **13**·1581
Seasoned Salt .... **16**·2015
Seeded Crackers .... **1**·17

Sesame Seed
  Biscuits .... **16**·2018
  Cake .... **16**·2019
  Chicken .... **13**·1540
  Dressing .... **16**·1929
  -Honey Candy .... **9**·1127
  Rainbow Trout .... **18**·2298
  -Rice Stuffing .... **18**·2185
Seven-Minute Frosting .... **8**·968
Shadow Icing .... **1**·31
Shaggy Mochas .... **7**·793

Shake
  Apricot .... **12**·1417
  Banana Milk .... **17**·2063
  Blueberry .... **12**·1417
  Milk .... **12**·1417
  Peaches and Cream Milk . **13**·1606
  Peach-Pineapple .... **10**·1179
  Peachy Milk .... **12**·1417

Shake *continued*
Strawberry .... **17·**2159
Strawberry-Banana ...... **12·**1417

Shaker
Baked Beans .... **16·**2021
Corn Relish .... **19·**2328
Cut Pickles .... **19·**2330
Daily Loaf .... **16·**2021
Shawano Dressing .... **16·**1928

SHELLFISH .... **16·**2027-2036
(See also *Clam, Crab, Lobster,*
Oyster, Scallops, Shrimp.)
Bouillabaisse Soup .... **2·**253
Broiled Prawns .... **14·**1779
Cioppino .... **5·**539
Shepherd's Pie .... **16·**2038

Sherbet
Lemon .... **10·**1278
Lemon Chiffon .... **16·**2040
Mango .... **11·**1344
Nectarine .... **16·**2040
Pineapple .... **16·**2040
Pink Velvet .... **16·**2040
Ring, Grapefruit- .... **9·**1054
Spice, and .... **16·**2039
Strawberry .... **11·**1402
Three-Fruit .... **8·**996

Sherried
Chocolate Frappé .... **20·**2458
-Date Sauce .... **16·**2043
Ice Cream Roll .... **6·**670
Pheasant, Roast .... **13·**1655

Sherry
Chicken Breasts à la
Vegetables .... **4·**499
Cioppino .... **5·**539
Easy Zabaglione .... **20·**2478
French Shrimp in Shells .. **17·**2056
Fruit Refresher .... **16·**2043
Harvest Fruit Compote ...... **7·**803
Hot Sherried Consommé . **17·**2083
Marinated Broiled Chicken **16·**2042
Roast Duckling with
Oranges .... **7·**813
Rolled Veal and Pork Roast **19·**2361
-Spiced Pears .... **13·**1621
Tenderloin Deluxe ...... **16·**2042
Trifle .... **18·**2294

Sherry *continued*
Trifle Delight .... **6·**723
Tropical Trifle .... **18·**2295
Turkey-Ham Casserole ... **16·**2043
Turkey in Sour Cream .... **19·**2315
Turkey Sandwich Supper . **19·**2313
Shirred (Baked) Eggs .... **7·**835
Shish Kabob .... **12·**1457
Shish Kabobs Italiano ...... **16·**2045
Shoofly Pie .... **16·**2046
Shore Dinner .... **16·**2014

Shortcake
Blueberry .... **2·**244
Cranberry-Banana .... **6·**664
No-Bake Strawberry ..... **17·**2161
Peach .... **16·**2048
Peach-Easy .... **13·**1606
Peach-Orange .... **13·**1606
Strawberry .... **16·**2048
Sunshine .... **17·**2161
Towers, Cherry .... **4·**473

Shortcut
Dobos Torte .... **7·**786
Lasagne .... **10·**1263
Pizza .... **14·**1698
Shepherd's Pie .... **16·**2038
Short Rib Stew .... **2·**166
Short Rib-Vegetable Stew ... **17·**2052
Shredded au Gratin Potatoes ... **1·**117
Shredded Wheat Dessert ... **19·**2327

Shrimp
à la King .... **17·**2057
à la Rockefeller .... **17·**2116
à l'Imperatrice .... **17·**2057
-Almond Sauce .... **15·**1825
Avocado Ring, in .... **15·**1919
Bake, Crab- .... **16·**2036
Bake, Haddock- .... **9·**1099
Barbecued, with Lemon .. **16·**2033
Barquette of Tiny .... **16·**2022
Beer, in .... **2·**202
Boat .... **16·**1950
Capers Sandwich .... **6·**735
Casserole, Double ...... **12·**1468
Cauliflower and Dilly .... **4·**434
-Cheese Fondue .... **17·**2058
-Cheese Turnovers .... **6·**675
Chinese Peas and .... **12·**1533
Chowder .... **17·**2089
Clam-Stuffed .... **16·**2035
Cocktail .... **5·**563
Creole .... **6·**688
-Cucumber Ring .... **9·**1070
-Curry Luncheon ....**17·**2058
deJonghe ....**17·**2056
-Dill Pâté .... **2·**240
Elegante with Rice ....**15·**1868

Shrimp *continued*
Étouffé .... **7·**861
Foo Yong .... **8·**929
French Fried ....**16·**2036
French-Fried Butterfly .... **6·**748
French, in Shells .... **17·**2056
Fresh Cooked .... **17·**2055
Gourmet .... **17·**2058
Jackets, in .... **1·**75
Kettle, Sole- .... **17·**2071
-Mushroom Soufflé ...... **12·**1416
Newburg .... **13·**1591
Oriental Pork and .... **12·**1534
-Out .... **2·**155
Pickled .... **16·**1931
Platter, Hawaiian .... **9·**1135
Quiche .... **15·**1816
Rémoulade, Avocado with .. **1·**123
Rice Deluxe, and .... **17·**2057
-Rice Salad .... **18·**2278
Saki .... **16·**2035
Salad, Spinach- .... **16·**2030
Sandwiches .... **17·**2058
Sauce .... **17·**2059
Sauté, Easy .... **4·**446
Skillet, Jiffy .... **17·**2055
Sweet-Sour .... **12·**1533
Sweet-Sour Sauced ..... **17·**2057
Thermidor .... **13·**1589
Toss, Cottage- .... **11·**1326
Simmered Beef Shanks .... **2·**163
Simnel Cake .... **17·**2060
Simple Syrup .... **20·**2464
Singapore Sling .... **17·**2063
Sirloin Tip Roast .... **17·**2061
Sister Lettie's Maple-
Custard Pie .... **11·**1348
Six-Layer Dinner .... **15·**1853
Skewer Dogs .... **12·**1430

Skillet
Barbecue .... **11·**1330
Beef and Biscuit .... **3·**270
Beef and Lima .... **4·**446
Beef and Rice .... **9·**1090
Beef and Vegetable .... **5·**624
Beet and Apple .... **2·**208
Carrots .... **4·**412
Chef's Salad .... **19·**2399
Chinese Beef .... **4·**500
Crab-Cabbage .... **12·**1534
Easy Mexican .... **11·**1337
Eggplant .... **7·**848
Hamburger-Bean .... **2·**179
Ham-Squash .... **1·**21
Hash .... **9·**1130
Liver and Tomato .... **11·**1307
Macaroni-Meat .... **11·**1331
Meat and Yam .... **11·**1330

Skillet *continued*
Meatball-Sauerkraut ..... **16**·1976
Onion Slices .... **11**·1321
Oriental Beef .... **12**·1530
Oriental Scallop .... **12**·1533
Pineapple-Pork .... **12**·1535
Pizza Steak .... **12**·1523
Pork and Lima .... **11**·1291
Potato Salad .... **15**·1820
Sausage-Potato .... **16**·1975
Skilletburgers .... **9**·1084
Smoked Pork Chop and
   Lima .... **14**·1731
Smoky Bean .... **11**·1301
Spaghetti .... **17**·2101
Speedy Beef .... **9**·1090
Squash .... **17**·2132
Stew, Burger .... **4**·425
Strawberry Dumplings .....**7**·817
Supper, Family ....**4**·425
Supper, Oriental ....**2**·199
Sweet Potato-Frank ...... **18**·2213
Tongue and Bean .... **18**·2285
Veal .... **19**·2364
Yam and Sausage ...... **11**·1300
Sliced Pear Pie .... **14**·1675
Slim-Jim Frappé ....**8**·937
Slim-Trim Dressing ...... **11**·1322
Slim-Trim Fruit Toss ..... **19**·2428
Slipped Custard Pie ....**6**·726
Small Mints ....**3**·376
Smelts .... **17**·2065
Smelts in Barbecue Sauce ... **17**·2065

Smoked
Beef Luncheon .... **17**·2068
Eel Canapés .... **17**·2067
Fish with Lemon ....**2**·151
Linkburgers ....**2**·154
Pork Chop and Lima Skillet **14**·1731
Pork Dinner .... **2**·252; **13**·1664
Salmon and Macaroni .... **17**·2066
Salmon Bake ....**8**·905

Smoky
Bean Skillet .... **11**·1301
Ham and Cheese Spread .....**1**·71
Peas and Potatoes .... **13**·1595
S'More Pie ....**6**·658
S'Mores .... **9**·1041
Smothered Pheasant .... **13**·1654
Smothered Quail .... **8**·1005
Snapperoni Franks .... **16**·1982
Snapper with Cashews ..... **15**·1843

Snappy
Beef Stew .... **10**·1271
Cheese Appetizers ....**1**·73
Garlic Dressing .... **16**·1929
Green Beans .... **9**·1067

Snickerdoodles .... **17**·2069
Snowcap Cherry
   Nibbles ....**2**·224
Snow-Capped Lemon
   Roll .... **10**·1219
Snow-Capped
   Pâté .... **20**·2466
Snowflake Pudding ....**6**·759
Snow Peas with Water
   Chestnuts .... **19**·2384
Snow Pudding ....**6**·728
Snow Pudding with
   Berries .... **17**·2151
Snowy Cinnamon
   Stars ....**5**·530
Snowy Vanilla Torte .... **19**·2346

Soda
Chocolate .... **10**·1182
Minted Sundae .... **11**·1293
Patio Punch .... **10**·1182
Strawberry Frosted ....**2**·237
Tropic Isle .... **10**·1182
Soft Meringue .... **11**·1402
Sole-Shrimp Kettle .... **17**·2071
Sole with Grapes .... **17**·2071
Sombrero Spread ....**4**·446
Sonhos (Dreams) .... **14**·1743

Soufflé
Bake, Crab .... **17**·2076
Broccoli ....**3**·290
Brussels Sprouts .... **3**·303
Cheese ....**4**·462
Chocolate ....**4**·508
Chocolate Cloud ...... **17**·2077
Clam Puff ....**5**·553
Easy Apricot ....**1**·101
Easy Cheese .... **17**·2075
Fluffy Cheese ....**7**·843
Golden Lemon .... **10**·1267
Macaroni-Cheese
   Puff ....**4**·427
Macaroni Puff .... **17**·2076
Mandarin ....**5**·549
Orange Chiffon .... **12**·1519
Orange Dessert .... **17**·2077
Potato Puff .... **17**·2075
Shrimp-Mushroom .... **12**·1416
Spinach .... **17**·2075
Squash .... **17**·2136
Sweet Potato
   Puff .... **18**·2214
Tapioca-Cheese .... **18**·2247
Tiny Strawberry .... **11**·1303
Tomato Aspic ....**7**·862
Tuna .... **17**·2077
Tuna 'n Rice ....**7**·892
Turkey .... **17**·2076
Winter Fruit .... **9**·1056

SOUP .... **17**·2079-2091
(See also *Chowder*.)
Asparagus-Cheese .... **10**·1160
Barbecue Bean .... **18**·2282
Bean .... **12**·1456
Black Bean ....**2**·232
Blender Bean .... **17**·2084
Blender Broccoli .... **17**·2091
Blender Gazpacho ...... **17**·2080
Blender Vichyssoise ...... **17**·2080
Bookbinder's Snapper .... **19**·2335
Bouillabaisse ....**2**·253
Can-Can Borsch ....**2**·204
Cantaloupe Mist ....**4**·400
Cheesy-Asparagus .... **17**·2088
Cherry .... **17**·2091
Chicken-Curry .... **17**·2090
Chicken Gumbo ....**1**·23
Chicken Madrilene ...... **11**·1339
Chicken-Mushroom ..... **17**·2090
Chicken-Noodle ....**4**·487
Chicken-Rice .... **17**·2090
Chicken Velvet ....**6**·684
Chili-Frank .... **17**·2090
Chili with Limas .... **11**·1291
Chilled Asparagus ....**1**·114
Chilled Avo-Mato .... **17**·2087
Chilled Cream of
   Chive ....**6**·684
Chilled Tomato-Cheese .....**6**·645
Confetti Consommé ...... **17**·2087
Consommé Cooler ....**5**·599
Crab Bisque ....**2**·231
Cream of Celery ....**4**·439
Cream of Ham .... **15**·1823
Cream of Mushroom ..... **12**·1451
Cream of Onion .... **12**·1507
Cream of Potato ....**6**·684
Cream of Tomato ....**6**·684
Creamy Cauliflower ....**4**·432
Creamy Lentil .... **10**·1280
Creole Clam Bisque ....**6**·690
Cuke-Buttermilk ....**3**·320
Easy Chicken-Noodle .... **17**·2090
Easy Vegetable .... **19**·2382
Elegant Onion .... **12**·1511

French Onion ....**1**·16
French Vichyssoise ...... **19**·2393
Golden Cheese .... **17**·2088
Golden Squash .... **17**·2136
Gourmet Potato .... **14**·1749
Gumbo Z'Herbs ....**6**·690

Soup *continued*
Ham and Pea .... **17**·2090
Hearty Hodgepodge ..... **14**·1737
Hearty Vegetable .... **19**·2332
Herbed Tomato Broth .... **17**·2082
Hot Sherried
    Consommé .... **17**·2083
Hot Tomato Bouillon .... **18**·2281
Japanese Custard .... **12**·1530
Jellied Consommé .... **5**·598
Kohlrabi and Ground
    Beef .... **10**·1239
Lentil-Vegetable .... **10**·1280
Lima-Burger .... **2**·179
Meat and Vegetable ..... **17**·2088
Mexican Mix-Ups .... **18**·2281
Mulligatawny .... **12**·1446
Onion .... **8**·958
Onion-Cheese .... **8**·914
Onion-Wine .... **20**·2459
Peanut .... **1**·24
Peas and Potato .... **13**·1592
Pepper Pot .... **13**·1647
Potato .... **14**·1749
Potato-Pea Potage ...... **17**·2086
Quick Vegetable .... **13**·1579
Quick Vichyssoise ...... **19**·2393
Russian Borsch .... **2**·250
Savory Tomato .... **17**·2087
Scotch Broth .... **16**·2009
Seafood Bisque .... **2**·231
Spanish Gazpacho ...... **8**·1014
Speedy Borsch .... **17**·2080
Speedy Minestrone ..... **12**·1420
Split Pea .... **17**·2117
Swedish Fruit .... **17**·2091
Tomato-Gumbo .... **9**·1096
Tomato-Rice .... **18**·2281
Turkey-Vegetable ...... **19**·2317
Vegetable-Beef .... **17**·2084
Vegetable Cocktail ..... **18**·2282
Vegetable-Meatball .... **9**·1084

Sour Cream
Baked Potatoes .... **6**·710
Burgers .... **17**·2094
-Choco Cake .... **17**·2094
Cucumbers .... **6**·707
Frosting .... **17**·2095
Gravy .... **9**·1061; **13**·1564
-Ham Omelet .... **9**·1114
Omelet .... **7**·843
-Pimiento Onions .... **12**·1511
Potato Salad .... **17**·2093
-Pumpkin Pie .... **19**·2389
Sauce .... **16**·1972
Sourdough Bread .... **17**·2095
Sour Milk Muffins .... **12**·1442
Southern Pecan Pie ...... **13**·1628
Spaetzle .... **17**·2097

Spaghetti
Baked .... **17**·2100
Bake, Turkey- .... **19**·2316
Beef and .... **17**·2101
Campfire .... **3**·363
Clam-Mushroom .... **17**·2100
Dip .... **13**·1640
Marina .... **17**·2100
Meatballs, and .... **10**·1197
Oven Meatballs, and ...... **9**·1089
Sauce, Jiffy .... **14**·1784
Sauce, Olive- .... **12**·1496
Skillet .... **17**·2101
Spanish Lamb with ...... **10**·1258
Toss, Italian .... **13**·1645
Turnover .... **17**·2101
Veal Parmesan with ..... **17**·2101

Spanish
Corn Bread .... **5**·627
Eggs .... **7**·838
Gazpacho .... **8**·1014
Lamb with Spaghetti .... **10**·1258
Paella .... **13**·1549
Potato Omelet .... **17**·2103
Rice .... **15**·1813
-Style Chicken .... **14**·1772
Zucchini .... **20**·2480

Sparerib
Cantonese .... **17**·2104
Far East .... **5**·618
Kraut, with .... **16**·1976
Sparkle Punch .... **15**·1808
Sparkling Melon Loaf ..... **10**·1275
Sparkling Mint Cooler .... **5**·616
Special Cabbage Salad ..... **16**·2021
Speculaas .... **17**·2106

Speedy
Beef Skillet .... **9**·1090
Borsch .... **17**·2080
Brown Beans .... **10**·1233
Celery Stuffing .... **4**·439
Cheesecake Pie .... **4**·465
Chop Suey .... **12**·1535
Corn Bread Pie .... **5**·627
Corn Fritters .... **5**·625
Frosting .... **13**·1615
Kabobs .... **11**·1331
Minestrone .... **12**·1420
Salsa .... **2**·240

Spiced
Applesauce Bread .... **16**·1933
Butterscotch Pie .... **6**·680
Chocolate Cake .... **2**·137
Chocolate Coffee .... **5**·515
Citrus Appetizer Cup .... **5**·544
Cranberry Drink .... **1**·64

Spiced *continued*
Fruit Sauce .... **8**·991
Fruit Sparkle .... **17**·2148
Grape Jam .... **10**·1204
Grape Punch .... **9**·1049
Grapes .... **9**·1049
Iced Coffee .... **5**·577
Mandarin Mold .... **5**·545
Mocha .... **12**·1425
Peaches .... **13**·1602;
                17·2068; **17**·2110
Peach Mold .... **13**·1603
Percolator Punch ...... **15**·1807
Pineapple Sparkle .... **2**·223
Sesame Bars .... **16**·2019
Tea .... **18**·2257
Tongue .... **19**·2351
Turban Squash .... **18**·2304
Waldorf Salad .... **19**·2411
Wassail .... **19**·2423
Spice-Nut Cake .... **17**·2111
Spice-Prune Dumplings ...... **7**·819

Spicy
Apricot Mold .... **5**·557
Baked Apples .... **1**·83
Beef Dip .... **1**·77
Cake Doughnuts .... **3**·273
Carrot Sticks .... **4**·412
Cherry Sauce .... **16**·1970
Chops and Cabbage ..... **17**·2109
Cinnamon Apples in Foil ... **8**·919
Coconut Chiffon Pie ..... **17**·2111
Fruit Dressing .... **17**·2110
Fruit Puffs .... **1**·83
Ham Loaf .... **11**·1387
Hermits .... **9**·1144
Marble Coffee Cake ..... **19**·2419
Oranges 'n Prunes ..... **14**·1792
Orange Tea .... **2**·222
Peach Compote .... **18**·2199
Peach Freeze .... **15**·1920
Peach Sauce .... **9**·1035
Prune Cake .... **17**·2111
Pumpkin-Cheese Pie ..... **14**·1672
Raisin Coffee Cake ..... **12**·1476
Raisin Oatmeal .... **4**·442
Rump Roast .... **15**·1843
Tomato Sauce .... **15**·1840
Whole Tomatoes .... **2**·167

Spinach
-Avocado Bowl .... **17**·2112
Bake, Herbed .... **6**·727
-Carrot Custard .... **17**·2116
Chinese .... **17**·2114
Delight .... **17**·2116
Elegante .... **17**·2116
Epinards à la Crème
    (Creamed Spinach) .... **17**·2116

Spinach *continued*
-Filled Ravioli,
  Chicken and .... **15**·1840
-Fish Bake .... **7**·889
-Lettuce Toss .... **17**·2113
Macaroni Shells
  Florentine .... **11**·1337
-Potato Bake .... **17**·2115
Salad, Wilted .... **17**·2114
Salmon Florentine .... **8**·910
San Francisco Eggs and .... **9**·1074
-Shrimp Salad .... **16**·2030
Soufflé .... **17**·2075
-Stuffed Breast of Veal .... **19**·2359
-Stuffed Zucchini .... **19**·2385
Supreme .... **17**·2115
Surprise .... **17**·2114
Toss, Orange- .... **17**·2113
Toss, Tangy .... **17**·2114
Toss, Tuna- .... **17**·2114
Spinning Chicken .... **15**·1894
Spinning Ham .... **15**·1894
Spitted Vegetables .... **2**·159
Split Pea Soup .... **17**·2117

Sponge Cake
Filbert .... **7**·872
Hot Milk .... **17**·2120
Orange .... **17**·2118
Pineapple Fluff .... **17**·2120
Spoon Bread .... **17**·2120

Spread (See also *Pâté*.)
Appetizer Cheese Mousse ....**1**·70
Avocado Cocktail ....**1**·121
Braunschweiger Glacé ....**1**·70
Chili Cheese ....**4**·496
Chili Cheese Log ....**4**·496
Chutney Cheddar ....**5**·535
Clam .... **17**·2121
Crab and Cheese .... **17**·2121
Dried Beef Log ....**7**·799
Edam Sage ....**1**·70
Ham Ball ....**1**·70
Ham Salad Sandwich .... **17**·2121
Hot Chicken ....**3**·367
Hot Crab Cocktail ....**6**·650
Olive-Cheese Ball .... **17**·2121
Roquefort Dessert .... **15**·1888
Salmon Party Log ....**1**·70
Sardine Appetizer .... **16**·1961
Smoky Ham and Cheese .....**1**·71
Sombrero ....**4**·446
Three-Cheese Mold ....**4**·464
Zesty Chicken .... **17**·2121
Zippy Beef-Olive .... **12**·1497

Spring
Flower Rolls ....**7**·822
Fruit Sauce .... **10**·1180

Spring *continued*
Garden Toss ....**5**·591
Lamb Stew .... **10**·1261
Pancakes .... **17**·2162
Rhubarb Cobbler ....**5**·561
Salad Bowl .... **19**·2425
Salad Ring .... **8**·1017
Sandwich Puffs .... **19**·2388
Springerle .... **17**·2122
Springtime Peas .... **13**·1594
Spritz .... **17**·2124
Spumoni, Italian .... **17**·2126

Squab
Apricot Sauce, with .... **8**·1004
Savory .... **17**·2127
Spit, on a .... **17**·2127
Sweet-Sour .... **17**·2127
Square Burgers .... **9**·1124

SQUASH .... **17**·2129-2136
(See also *Acorn Squash,
Zucchini Squash*.)
Applesauce, and ....**1**·19
Bake, Butternut ....**3**·320
Bake, Company .... **18**·2204
Baked Banana ....**2**·143
Chips .... **17**·2136
Confetti ....**6**·697
Crookneck Curry ....**6**·697
Delight .... **17**·2136
Hubbard, in Sour Cream .. **10**·1161
Saucy Dilled Butternut .. **17**·2135
Sausage, and ....**1**·19
Scalloped .... **16**·1993
Skillet, Summer .... **17**·2131
Soufflé .... **17**·2136
Soup, Golden .... **17**·2136
Special, Sausage- .... **12**·1523
Spiced Turban .... **18**·2304
Squaw Corn .... **17**·2137
Squid, Fried .... **17**·2137
Stack-a-Dinner .... **13**·1597
Stag's Antlers .... **16**·2005
Standing Rib Roast .... **2**·186
Starlight Cakes .... **18**·2261

Steak
Bean Pot, and .... **12**·1423
Diane .... **17**·2143
Marchand De Vin .... **15**·1895
Onions, and ....**2**·196
Zucchini Supper, and .... **17**·2134

Steamed
Blackberry Pudding ....**2**·233
Clams .... **5**·554
Fish ....**7**·896
Pumpkin-Nut Pudding ... **12**·1475

Stew
Bavarian-Style ....**4**·424
Beef Ball Oven .... **17**·2147
Beef, with Biscuit
  Topper .... **17**·2145
Brunswick .... **12**·1493
Burger Skillet ....**4**·425
Burgundy Beef ....**4**·411
Campsite ....**3**·363
Chinese .... **17**·2146
Chuck Wagon .... **14**·1752
Cioppino ....**5**·539
Dilled Lamb .... **17**·2147
Dumplings, Lamb, 'n ....**7**·816
Dumplings, Veal, 'n ...... **17**·2148
Frank and Kraut ....**8**·932
French Ragout .... **15**·1829
French Veal ....**8**·959
German Beef .... **11**·1380
Good Neighbor .... **17**·2148
Ham and
  Vegetable .... **9**·1116
Hasenpfeffer ....**9**·1129
Hearty Oyster .... **13**·1546
Hungarian Goulash ...... **10**·1164
Irish Lamb .... **17**·2145
Kettle-of-Bean ....**2**·174
Lobster .... **11**·1313
Lobster and Corn .... **17**·2144
Meal-in-a-Bowl ....**9**·1092
Old-Time Beef ....**1**·32
Old-Time Oxtail .... **13**·1541
Oven Beef ....**2**·196
Oyster .... **13**·1546
Pioneer Beef ....**4**·424
Savory Sausage .... **11**·1300
Scottish Lamb .... **17**·2145
Short Rib ....**2**·166
Short Rib-
  Vegetable .... **17**·2052
Snappy Beef .... **10**·1271
Spring Lamb .... **10**·1261
Sweet-Sour ....**4**·430
Tomato Chili .... **17**·2146
Veal .... **19**·2363
Veal, with Ravioli .... **17**·2147
Vegetable-Meatball ...... **17**·2147
Stewed Chicken ....**4**·486
Stewed Prunes .... **14**·1791
Sticky Buns ....**3**·270
Stinger .... **17**·2149
Stirred Custard .... **17**·2151
Stock, Brown .... **17**·2152
Stock, White .... **17**·2152

STRAWBERRY .... 17·2157-2170
  Alaska Pie .... 14·1674
  Angel Pie .... 1·55
  Banana Ice .... 17·2170
  -Banana Mold .... 2·141
  -Banana Shake .... 12·1417
  Berries and Nectarines au
    Rhum .... 17·2167
  Berry Cheesecake Pie .... 14·1670
  Berry Meringue Cake .... 3·345
  Berry-Orange Coffee Cake 17·2163
  Berry-Patch Salad .... 6·644
  Berry-Sour Cream Dressing 16·1925
  Cake Roll .... 17·2169
  Charlotte Russe .... 8·1019
  -Cheese Pie .... 17·2164
  -Cheese Tarts .... 18·2252
  Chiffon Pie .... 8·1019
  Compote, Rhubarb- ..... 15·1861
  Compote, Triple .... 17·2169
  Cream .... 6·755
  Crunch Cake .... 17·2163
  Cubes, Frosty .... 8·976
  Cups .... 17·2168
  Delight .... 17·2170
  Devonshire, Mock .... 7·775
  Dressing, Fruit with ...... 10·1215
  Dumplings .... 17·2162
  Dumplings, Skillet .... 7·817
  Floating Island .... 8·909
  Freeze, Banana- .... 17·2168
  Frosted Soda .... 2·237
  Frozen Pie .... 17·2166
  Glamour Pie .... 17·2163
  -Glazed Cheesecake .... 4·467
  Glaze Pie .... 17·2164
  Honeydew-Berry Parfaits . 11·1396

  Ice Cream .... 10·1174
  Ice Cream, Homemade ... 16·1943
  Jam .... 10·1204
  Jam, Cherry- .... 17·2161
  Jam, Frozen .... 10·1204
  Jelly, Uncooked .... 10·1213
  Juliet .... 17·2167
  -Lemonade Bavarian ..... 17·2161
  -Lemonade Slush .... 15·1820
  -Mallow Pie .... 14·1671
  -Meringue Cake .... 6·756
  Meringue Pie, Lush ...... 17·2166
  Meringue Puffs .... 17·2168
  Pancakes, Super .... 13·1557
  Parfait Pie .... 13·1570

Strawberry *continued*
  Parfaits .... 6·759
  -Pineapple Cream Pie ...... 6·679
  Pink Parfait Pie .... 2·238
  -Rhubarb Cheesecake .... 17·2123
  -Rhubarb Jam .... 10·1203
  -Rhubarb Pie .... 15·1860
  -Rhubarb Rolls .... 15·1862
  Ribbon Pie .... 17·2166
  Ring, Rosy .... 17·2169
  Ruby Fruit Compote .... 5·595
  Satin Pie .... 1·38
  Sauce .... 17·2162
  Scrumptious .... 17·2164
  Shake .... 17·2159
  Sherbet .... 11·1402
  Shortcake .... 16·2048
  Shortcake, No-Bake ..... 17·2161
  Snow Pudding
    with Berries .... 17·2151
  Soufflé Salads .... 17·2170
  Soufflés, Tiny .... 11·1303
  Sparkle Punch .... 9·1029
  Squares .... 6·760
  Starter .... 8·987
  Sunshine Pie .... 2·133
  Swirl .... 17·2170
  Tart, French .... 8·959
  Tarts .... 17·2164
  Torte .... 5·532
  -Vanilla Pudding .... 10·1190
  Whipped Cream .... 2·141
  Yogurt Medley .... 20·2476
  Yogurt Salad .... 17·2167
Streusel Coffee Cake .... 17·2171

Stroganoff
  Beef .... 17·2174
  Beer-Beef .... 17·2174
  Chicken Liver .... 17·2094
  Hamburger .... 17·2173
  Jiffy .... 17·2173
  Meatball .... 9·1089
  Poppy Seed Noodles, with 14·1720
  Sandwich .... 16·1952
  Steak Sandwich .... 17·2141
  Strudel, Apple .... 17·2175
  Strudel, Quick Apple ...... 17·2176

Stuffed
  Acorn Squash .... 1·20
  Baked Potatoes .... 19·2335
  Beef Heart .... 9·1138
  Beef Round .... 18·2188
  Celery .... 16·2006
  Cornish Game Hens .... 7·856
  Cube Steaks .... 11·1326
  Date Drops .... 6·742
  Dates .... 6·742
  Edam .... 7·829

Stuffed *continued*
  Fillet Roll-Ups .... 7·890
  Flank Steaks .... 8·902
  Flounder .... 8·911
  Hamburger Roll .... 2·199
  Lamb Shoulder .... 10·1259
  Manicotti .... 11·1344
  Mushrooms .... 12·1450
  Onions .... 12·1509
  Pepper Cups .... 13·1641
  Peppers .... 12·1439
  Pickle Slices .... 8·1012
  Pork Chops .... 18·2180
  Pork Tenderloin .... 14·1733
  Prune Salad .... 14·1792
  Rolled Rib
    Roast .... 18·2187
  Sweet Potatoes .... 18·2213
  Tenderloin .... 2·197
  Tomato Cups .... 18·2190
  Tomatoes .... 18·2278

STUFFING .... 18·2179-2191
  Brazil Nut .... 3·261
  Bread .... 18·2183
  Chestnut .... 18·2183
  Corn Bread .... 18·2185
  Cracker .... 6·659
  Cranberry-Raisin .... 6·668
  French Bread .... 18·2185
  Giblet .... 19·2309
  Ground Beef .... 18·2185
  Herb .... 18·2184
  Holiday Rice .... 18·2187
  Italian .... 18·2185
  Mincemeat .... 18·2185
  Mushroom .... 18·2183
  Orange .... 18·2184
  Oyster .... 13·1546
  Sausage .... 15·1907
  Savory .... 10·1259
  Savory Chestnut .... 8·955
  Seafood .... 18·2184
  Sesame-Rice .... 18·2185
  Speedy Celery .... 4·439
  Supreme, Sausage-
    Bean .... 18·2182
  Three Fruit .... 18·2184
  Wild Rice .... 20·2447
Submarine
  Sandwich .... 18·2192
Succotash .... 18·2193
Succotash, Ham .... 5·624

SUGAR . . . . 18·2195-2201
  Bells .3·285
  Cookies . . . . 18·2197
  -Crusted Muffins . . . . 12·1443
  -Pecan Crisps . . . . 15·1885
Sugarplum Loaves . . . . .5·587
Sugarplum Ring . . . . .5·584
Sukiyaki . . . . 18·2202
Sukiyaki Skewers . . . . 9·1146

Summer
  Corn Relish . . . . .1·15
  Fruit Cocktail . . . . .5·562
  Fruit Platter . . . . .5·546
  Salad Bowl . . . . 11·1286
  Sangria . . . . 16·1960
  Scramble . . . . .4·433
  Squash Skillet . . . . 17·2131
Summertime Carrots . . . . 4·413
Sunburst Coffee Cake . . . . .5·587

Sundae
  Fruit Sparkle . . . . 10·1183
  Golden . . . . 18·2204
  Hidden Treasure . . . . .10·1214
  Hong Kong . . . . 10·1185
  Melba . . . . 11·1391
  Rosy Pear . . . . 13·1624
  Sauce, Cherry . . . . 16·1972
  Sauce, Tropical . . . . 16·1972
  Special . . . . 18·2204
  Triple Treat . . . . 11·1302
  Tropical . . . . 18·2204
Waikiki . . . . .8·906
Sunny Citrus-Cream
  Topping . . . . 18·2286
Sunny Tangerine Creme . . . . 18·2243

Sunshine
  Aspic . . . . .1·116
  Carrots . . . . 12·1521
  Citrus Cups . . . . 9·1056
  Shortcake . . . . 17·2161
Super Strawberry
  Pancakes . . . . 13·1557
Superb Salad . . . . 11·1286
Supper Corn Chowder . . . . . 17·2084
Surprise Chocolate Torte . . . 18·2288
Surprise Pear Bundles . . . . . 13·1625
Svengali Tomatoes . . . . 18·2276
Swank Porterhouse
  Steak . . . . 14·1740

Swedish
  Brown Beans . . . . 16·2006
  Cabbage Rolls . . . . .3·327
  Egg Coffee . . . . .5·576
  Fruit Soup . . . . 17·2091
  Ginger Cookies . . . . 18·2206
  Holiday Braid . . . . .5·585
  Lucia Buns . . . . .3·306
  Meatballs . . . . 16·1999
  Nuts . . . . 12·1476
  Pancakes . . . . 13·1557
  Rye Bread . . . . 11·1298
  Timbale Cases . . . . 18·2270
  Veal Roast . . . . 19·2359
Sweet Apple Ring . . . . .1·83
Sweet Banana Bread . . . . 20·2473
Sweetbread Bake . . . . .18·2207
Sweetbreads, Cream . . . . . . .19·2351
Sweet Chocolate Cake . . . . . . .4·510
Sweet Pickled Carrots . . . . . 13·1661
Sweet Pickles . . . . 13·1659

Sweet Potato
  Apricot- . . . . 18·2213
  Bake, Ambrosia . . . . .5·547
  Bake, California . . . . 18·2212
  Boats . . . . 18·2214
  Candied . . . . 18·2212
  -Date Bake . . . . 18·2214
  -Date Puffs . . . . .6·740
  Fantasia . . . . 18·2213
  -Frank Skillet . . . . 18·2213
  French-Fried . . . . 18·2212
  Fruit-Candied . . . . 18·2214
  Mashed . . . . 18·2212
  Pie . . . . .1·23
  Puff . . . . 18·2214
  Raisin-Filled . . . . 12·1522
  Relish . . . . 13·1636
  Stuffed . . . . 18·2213
  Toasted Croquettes . . . . . . 18·2213
  -Turkey Pie . . . . 19·2320

Sweet-Sour
  Burgers . . . . 18·2218
  Chops . . . . 18·2218
  Dressing . . . . 16·1925
  Franks . . . . 14·1690
  Glazed Loaf . . . . 9·1088
  Ham over Rice . . . . 9·1116
  Lamb Chops . . . . .2·255
  Meatballs . . . . 15·1827
  Pickles . . . . 13·1658
  Pork . . . . 12·1535
  Red Cabbage . . . . 8·1022
  Sauce . . . . 12·1534
  Sauced Shrimp . . . . 17·2057
  Shrimp . . . . 12·1533
  Spareribs . . . . 18·2218
  Squab . . . . 17·2127

Sweet-Sour *continued*
  Stew . . . . .4·430
  Surprises . . . . .4·446
  Tuna . . . . 12·1534; 18·2218
  Veal with Rice . . . . 19·2364

Swiss Cheese
  Apple Salad . . . . 17·2093
  Bites, Crab- . . . . 16·2034
  -Cheddar Sauce . . . . .4·461
  Corn Bake . . . . .5·626
  Crab Pie, and . . . . .6·727
  -Egg Bake . . . . 18·2222
  Frank Spirals, and . . . . .8·937
  Onion Bake . . . . 12·1511
  Pie . . . . 18·2222
  Potato Salad . . . . .4·501
  Sandwich Puffs . . . . .3·367
  Sauce . . . . .4·461
  Turkey-Ham Bake . . . . 14·1776
  Turkey Swisswiches . . . . . . 19·2313
Swiss Cream Torte . . . . 15·1802
Swiss Steak . . . . 18·2225
Swiss Steak, Deviled . . . . .7·772
Syllabub . . . . 18·2226
Syrian Bread . . . . 12·1458

Syrup
  Berry . . . . 18·2227
  Burnt-Sugar . . . . .3·312
  Chocolate . . . . .5·516
  Cinnamon-Cream . . . . 18·2227
  Honey-Banana . . . . 9·1152
  Honey-Citrus . . . . 18·2227
  Maple . . . . 11·1348
  Maple-Apricot . . . . 11·1348
  Orange . . . . 13·1553
  Savarin . . . . 16·1988
  Simple . . . . 20·2464

T

Taco
  Beef . . . . 18·2241
  Salad . . . . .5·629
Taffy Bars . . . . 12·1431
Tamale Hero Sandwiches . . . . 9·1144
Tamale Pie . . . . 14·1758
Tangelo Chiffon Pie . . . . .5·549

Tangerine
  -Apricot Mold . . . . 18·2245
  -Coconut Cups . . . . 18·2245
  Creme, Sunny . . . . 18·2243
  Ice, Fruited . . . . 10·1166
  Peel, Candied . . . . 18·2245
  Roast Pork . . . . 18·2243
  -Walnut Toss . . . . 18·2245
Tangiers Hash . . . . 9·1130

Tangy
Barbecue Sauce . . . . .1·43
Cauliflower Salad . . . . .4·432
Citrus Fizz . . . . .5·544
Cranberry Sauce . . . . 16·1968
Frank Barbecue . . . . .8·935
Kraut Burger . . . . 16·1951
Lamb Chops . . . . 10·1255
Lamb Shoulder Chops . . . . 13·1642
Mint Sauce . . . . 10·1215
Seafood Toss . . . . 9·1057
Spinach Toss . . . . 17·2114
Tuna . . . . 13·1589

Tapioca
-Cheese Soufflé . . . . 18·2247
Parfaits, Java . . . . 18·2246
Pudding, Fluffy . . . . 18·2246
Tarragon Butter . . . . .7·894
Tarragon Dressing . . . . 16·1926

Tart
Banbury . . . . .2·143
Cherry . . . . 14·1675
Cran-Apple . . . . 18·2251
French Strawberry . . . . .8·959
Fresh Fruit . . . . 18·2252
Frozen Mincemeat . . . . 18·2251
Ham Newburg . . . . 18·2253
Lemon Curd . . . . 10·1279
Saucy Apple Pie, and . . . . .12·1484
Shells, Cheese . . . . .18·2253
Shells, Graham Cracker . . .18·2252
Shells, Pastry for . . . . 18·2250
Strawberry . . . . 17·2164
Strawberry-Cheese . . . . . . 18·2252
Tartar Sauce . . . . 18·2253
Tartar Sauce, Blender . . . . . . 16·1966
Tartar Sauce Deluxe . . . . . . 16·1966
Tasty Bran Waffles . . . . .3·273
Tasty Pastries . . . . .5·613
Tater-Coated Chicken . . . . . . 13·1539

Tea
Apple-Honey . . . . .2·222
Delight, Amber . . . . 18·2257
Frosty Spiced . . . . 17·2148
Fruited Ice . . . . .2·219
How to Make . . . . 18·2257
Iced Fruit . . . . 18·2257
Instant Russian . . . . .2·220
Pineapple Frostea . . . . 18·2257
Punch, Cranberry- . . . . .6·665
Scones . . . . 16·2008
Spiced . . . . 18·2257
Spicy Orange . . . . .2·222
Teatime Sandwiches . . . . . . 16·1956
Tempura Condiments . . . . . . 18·2263
Tempura, Japanese . . . . 18·2263
Tenderloin Deluxe . . . . 16·2042

Tenderloin with Orange
Sauce . . . . 18·2263
Ten-in-One Sandwich Loaf . . . .2·188

Teriyaki . . . . 18·2265
Beef . . . . 12·1530
Burgers . . . . 17·2097
Meatballs . . . . .1·64
Miniatures . . . . 9·1087
Roast Tenderloin . . . . 12·1536
Scallops . . . . 18·2265
Tetrazzini, Turkey . . . . 18·2265
Texas-Style Beans . . . . 14·1693

Thanksgiving . . . . 18·2265-2266
Candied Sweet Potatoes . . 18·2212
Celery Cran-Relish . . . . .6·662
Cranberry Sauce . . . . .6·662
Creamed Onions . . . . 12·1508
Indian Corn Casserole . . . . . . .5·623
Pumpkin Pie . . . . 15·1805
Roast Turkey
(Covered Pan) . . . . 19·2311
Roast Turkey (Open Pan) . 19·2310
Two-Tone Holiday Pie . . . 15·1805
Thermidor Bake, Lobster . . . 11·1312
Thermidor, Shrimp . . . . 13·1589
Thousand Island· . . . . 18·2268

Three
-Bean Frank Bake . . . . .2·175
-Cheese Mold . . . . .4·464
-Flour Bread . . . . 20·2439
-Fruit Sherbet . . . . .8·996
Fruit Stuffing . . . . 18·2184
Thrifty Bologna-Bean
Chowder . . . . 11·1289
Thyme-Buttered Crescents . . 15·1883

Timbales
Cases, Swedish . . . . 18·2270
Chicken . . . . 18·2270
Turkey . . . . 15·1890

Tiny
Cream Puffs . . . . .7·837
Pineapple-Orange Cakes . 19·2342
Pineapple Upside-Down
Cakes . . . . 14·1691
Red Mints . . . . .8·907
Strawberry Soufflés . . . . . . 11·1303

Toast
Cinnamon . . . . 18·2270
Cups . . . . .6·698
French . . . . .8·962
Melba . . . . 11·1391
Milk . . . . 12·1417
Orange French . . . . .8·950
Parmesan Melba . . . . 11·1391

Toasted
Butter Pecan Cake . . . . 12·1476
Cheese Rolls . . . . .4·464
Coconut . . . . .2·224
Coconut Coffee Cake . . . . . .5·583
Coconut Ice Cream . . . . . . .5·568
Coconut Pie . . . . .6·723
Croquettes . . . . 18·2213
Croutons . . . . .6·699
Toasty Garlic Bread . . . . .8·1009
Toasty Rye Curls . . . . 15·1902
Toffee Bars . . . . 18·2271
Tokyo Turkey Toss . . . . .2·181

TOMATO . . . . 18·2273-2284
Aspic, Crab- . . . . .6·653
Aspic Soufflé . . . . .7·862
Baked . . . . 18·2279
Baked Deviled . . . . .7·771
-Bean Combo . . . . 9·1068
Bean-Stuffed . . . . 18·2277
Bouillon, Hot . . . . 18·2281
Broiled . . . . 18·2279
Broth, Herbed . . . . 17·2082
Casserole . . . . 18·2279
Catsup, Best . . . . .4·430
-Celery Aspic . . . . .1·116
-Cheese Soup, Chilled . . . . . .6·645
Cheese-Topped . . . . .4·464
Chili Stew . . . . 17·2146
Cocktail, Hot . . . . 18·2282
Cups, Stuffed . . . . 18·2190
Deviled Baked . . . . 18·2279
Dill Pickles, Green . . . . . 13·1661
Dill-Sauced . . . . 18·2276
Dilly Green . . . . 18·2278
Dressing . . . . 18·2283
Fillings . . . . 18·2278
French Dressing, with . . . . 18·2279
Fried . . . . 18·2279
Grilled . . . . 9·1075
-Gumbo Soup . . . . 9·1096
Halves, Herbed . . . . 9·1141
Ham-Stuffed . . . . 9·1114
Okra, and . . . . 12·1493
Pan-Fried . . . . 13·1559
Polenta . . . . 14·1711
Refresher . . . . 11·1319
Relish, Corn and . . . . 19·2330
-Rice Soup . . . . 18·2281
Roses . . . . 8·1012
Salad, Asparagus- . . . . .1·114
Salad, Bacon, Lettuce, and 18·2277

Tomato *continued*
Salmon-Filled .... **16**·1939
Sandwich, Oven .... **13**·1540
-Sardine Sandwiches, Egg- ...**6**·735
Sauce, Spicy .... **15**·1840
Sauerkraut .... **18**·2279
Scrambled Eggs with ..... **16**·2011
Skillet, Liver and .... **11**·1307
Soup, Cream of .... **6**·684
Soup Dressing .... **16**·1928
Soup, Savory .... **17**·2087
Spicy Whole .... **2**·167
Stuffed .... **18**·2278
Svengali .... **18**·2276
Topper .... **18**·2276
-Vermouth Cocktail ...... **20**·2457
Zip .... **5**·563
-Zucchini Scallop .... **4**·428

Tongue
Bean Skillet, and .... **18**·2285
Cheesy, on Rice .... **18**·2286
Ginger-Sauced .... **18**·2285
Spiced .... **19**·2351
-Stuffed Peppers .... **19**·2351
Tonic .... **20**·2465
Top Banana Split .... **10**·1185
Top Hat Ham and Turkey Pie . **9**·1118
Topknot Loaves .... **3**·369
Top-Notch Turkey Loaf ..... **19**·2315

Topper
Baked Potato .... **14**·1747
Cheese .... **19**·2317
Cherry .... **19**·2406
Creamy Mushroom .... **12**·1451
Orange-Sour Cream .... **8**·987
Pancake .... **13**·1553
Pastry .... **4**·424
Peanut .... **13**·1611
Tomato .... **18**·2276

Topping
Almond Fudge Delight .... **8**·1000
Butterscotch .... **5**·640
Cherry .... **4**·473
Citrus Fluff .... **9**·1030
Crumble .... **13**·1625
Minted Cocoa Fluff .... **5**·566
Mint-Fudge .... **10**·1176
Pineapple-Whipped ...... **14**·1691
Sunny Citrus-Cream ..... **18**·2286
Tropical Fruit .... **18**·2286
Topsy-Turvy Apple Pie ...... **1**·87

Torte
Almond Brittle .... **17**·2118
Almond-Peach .... **13**·1608
Black Forest-Style, Cherry . **8**·1023
Brownie .... **18**·2290

Torte *continued*
Chocolate .... **18**·2289
Chocolate Cheesecake ... **18**·2201
Chocolate-Cherry .... **18**·2288
Chocolate-Pecan .... **18**·2289
Chocolate Velvet .... **19**·2390
Coffee Chiffon .... **5**·577
Crown .... **10**·1217
Date Apple .... **1**·93
Della Robbia .... **7**·877
Easy Date Crumble .... **6**·745
Edelweiss .... **8**·1024
Forgotten Cherry .... **18**·2287
Frozen Apricot .... **8**·976
Heavenly .... **6**·763
Jiffy Butterscotch .... **3**·321
Kona Coffee .... **5**·578
Lemon Angel .... **6**·765
Lime .... **11**·1296
Mocha .... **12**·1425
Mocha Blitz .... **2**·241
Mocha-Nut .... **12**·1427
Mocha-Velvet .... **6**·768
Orange-Date .... **12**·1520
Poppy Seed .... **14**·1720
Pumpkin-Date .... **19**·2420
Sacher .... **15**·1905
Shortcut Dobos .... **7**·786
Snowy Vanilla .... **19**·2346
Strawberry .... **5**·532
Surprise Chocolate ...... **18**·2288
Swiss Cream .... **15**·1802
Twice-Chocolate .... **11**·1303
Tortilla Rolls .... **7**·840

Tortoni .... **18**·2292
Almond-Coffee .... **5**·577
Biscuit .... **2**·230
Cups, Quick .... **18**·2291
Tutti-Frutti .... **19**·2335
Tossed Green Salad .... **15**·1814
Tossed Western Salad ...... **15**·1914

Tostada
Casserole .... **11**·1407
Mexican Beef .... **18**·2292
Yankee .... **18**·2293
Tournedos of Beef
Della Casa .... **18**·2293
Tourtière (Canadian Pork Pie) ..**3**·364
Trader's Punch .... **9**·1074
Traditional Martini ...... **11**·1360
Trifle .... **18**·2294
Trifle Delight .... **6**·723
Tri-Level Brownies .... **3**·297

Tripe
Italiano .... **19**·2351
Onions, and .... **2**·190
Pepper Pot Soup .... **13**·1647

Triple
Fruit Dessert .... **8**·991
-Layered Sandwiches .... **16**·1949
Seafood Bake .... **4**·427
Strawberry Compote ..... **17**·2169
Treat Sundaes .... **11**·1302

Tropical
Apple Salad .... **19**·2419
Chiffon Cake .... **3**·338
Chocolate .... **2**·220
Fruit Topper .... **18**·2286
Ice Cream .... **10**·1173
Punch .... **15**·1807
Sundaes .... **18**·2204
Sundae Sauce .... **16**·1972
Trifle .... **18**·2295
Tropic Isle Appetizer .... **2**·232
Tropic Isle Soda .... **10**·1182

Trout
Amandine .... **7**·895
Broiled Lake .... **7**·894
Brookside Fried .... **18**·2298
Salami Topping, with .... **18**·2298
Sesame Rainbow .... **18**·2298
Truite Farcie .... **18**·2299
Tufoli Stuffed with Veal .... **2**·167

Tuna
Bake, Company .... **18**·2304
-Bean Salad .... **18**·2302
-Berry Sandwiches ..... **16**·1932
-Broccoli Casseroles .... **18**·2302
Burgers, Broiled ...... **18**·2304
-Cheese Strata .... **17**·2155
Chopstick .... **12**·1478
Chowder .... **8**·899
Company Creamed ..... **18**·2303
Croutons, and .... **18**·2302
Fruit Salad .... **18**·2303
Italian .... **7**·890
Jackstraw Bake .... **16**·2045
-Lemon Loaf .... **18**·2304
-Melon Dinner Salad ... **4**·400
Mousse .... **12**·1437
-Noodle Casserole .... **17**·2064
Omelet .... **18**·2303
Open-Facer .... **16**·1949
Pâté .... **13**·1586
Patties .... **18**·2303
Pepper Cups, in ...... **14**·1683
Pie, Rice and .... **15**·1869
-Rice Salad .... **18**·2268
Rice Soufflé, 'n .... **7**·892
Rounds .... **7**·876
Salad .... **11**·1321
Salad Bake .... **18**·2302
Salad in Iceberg Ring .... **11**·1321
Salad, Quick .... **18**·2278

Tuna *continued*
Sandwiches, Deviled Ham
  and .... **7**·773
Soufflé .... **17**·2077
-Spinach Toss .... **17**·2114
Supper Dish .... **18**·2303
Sweet and Sour .... **12**·1534
Sweet-Sour .... **18**·2218
Tangy .... **13**·1589
Toss, Apple .... **1**·86
Tugs .... **12**·1513
Turnovers .... **19**·2334
-Vegetable Pie ....**4**·426
-Waldorf Salad .... **19**·2411

TURKEY .... **19**·2307-2325
Amandine on Toast .... **1**·44
-Apple Toss .... **19**·2321
Aspic Salad .... **19**·2320
Casserole, Cantonese .... **19**·2320
Chaud-Froid of .... **4**·452
-Cheese Puff .... **19**·2317
-Cheese Sandwich .... **11**·1319
-Chip Salad .... **19**·2321
Chop Suey ....**5**·517
Cocktail .... **19**·2315
-Crab Sauce .... **14**·1776
Crepe Casserole .... **19**·2316
Croquettes, Oven .... **13**·1541
Curry, Quick .... **19**·2318
Dish, Wild Rice- .... **19**·2318
Divan, Ham and .... **19**·2316
Double-Decker .... **9**·1075
Fondue, Baked .... **19**·2317
Half Supreme .... **19**·2322
Halves or Quarters, Roast . **19**·2322
-Ham Bake, Swiss .... **14**·1776
-Ham Casserole .... **16**·2043
Hash, Oven-Style .... **6**·658
Hawaiian .... **14**·1689
Herbed, on Spit .... **19**·2311
Hickory Smoked ....**2**·151
Jambalaya .... **19**·2324
Joes .... **19**·2313
Kabobs, Fruit- ....**8**·990
-Lime Mold .... **19**·2320
Loaf, Topnotch .... **19**·2315
-Mushroom Salad .... **15**·1918
-Noodle Bake .... **14**·1767
Oven-Fried .... **19**·2322
Paella, Easy .... **19**·2318
Paprika .... **10**·1271
Parisian .... **3**·290

Turkey *continued*
Pieces, Grilled ....**2**·155
Pie, Quick .... **12**·1414
Pie, Sweet Potato- .... **19**·2320
Pie, Top Hat Ham and .... **9**·1118
-Pineapple Grill .... **14**·1772
-Potato Pancakes .... **14**·1751
-Potato Salad .... **10**·1157
-Rice Bake .... **19**·2323
-Rice Squares .... **19**·2318
Roast (Covered Pan) ..... **19**·2311
Roast (Open Pan) ...... **19**·2310
Roasts, Plum-Glazed ..... **14**·1768
Roasts, Twin .... **19**·2324
-Roni Casserole .... **19**·2316
Salad, Curry- .... **19**·2321
Salad, Holiday .... **14**·1713
Sandwiches, Apple .... **1**·87
Sandwiches, Hot .... **19**·2313
Sandwiches, Hot Curried . **19**·2313
Sandwich Supper .... **19**·2313
Sauce, Ham- .... **9**·1116
Soufflé .... **17**·2076
Sour Cream, in ...... **19**·2315
-Spaghetti Bake .... **19**·2316
-Stuffed Peppers .... **9**·1073
Swisswiches .... **19**·2313
-Taco Bake .... **19**·2317
Tetrazzini .... **18**·2265
Timbales .... **15**·1890
Toss, Tokyo ....**2**·181
-Vegetable Soup .... **19**·2317
Waldorf Salad .... **12**·1478
Turkish Zucchini Dolmas ......**7**·788

Turnip
Cheese, with .... **19**·2332
Greens Supreme .... **19**·2333
Lemon-Parslied .... **19**·2332
Lilies .... **8**·1013
Puff, Whipped .... **19**·2331
Red Dot .... **19**·2331

Turnovers
Mincemeat .... **19**·2334
Quicky .... **19**·2333
Tuna .... **19**·2334
Tutti-Frutti Tortoni .... **19**·2335
24-Hour Salad .... **15**·1917
Twice-Chocolate Torte .... **11**·1303
Twin Meat Loaves ...... **11**·1386
Twin Turkey Roasts .... **19**·2324

Two
-Berry Parfaits .... **17**·2094
-Tone Bread .... **20**·2472
-Tone Cocktail ....**2**·217
-Tone Fudge ....**3**·378
-Tone Holiday Pie ...... **15**·1805
-Way Salad Dressing ..... **13**·1637

Tyropitakia (Cheese Pastries) . **9**·1064

U

Unbaked Caramel Cookies . **15**·1798
Uncooked Frosting ....**8**·970
Uncooked Strawberry Jelly .. **10**·1213
Uppakrakakor .... **16**·2003

Upside-Down
Apple Cake ....**3**·345
Ham Loaf .... **9**·1117
Pineapple Mold .... **14**·1688

V

Vanilla
Cookie Crust .... **19**·2347
Cream Pie .... **14**·1673
Crisps .... **19**·2346
Custard Ice Cream .... **10**·1173
Dessert Sauce .... **19**·2346
Fondant .... **8**·921
Glaze .... **1**·58
Ice Cream .... **10**·1171
Ice Cream, Basic .... **6**·672
Ice Cream, Refrigerator ... **15**·1858
Nut Filling ....**5**·532
Pudding .... **15**·1796
-Raisin Pie .... **14**·1677
Sauce .... **6**·646
-Sour Cream Cake .... **19**·2346
Sugar .... **19**·2345
Taffy .... **15**·1802
Torte, Snowy .... **19**·2346
Wafer Coconut Cake ....**3**·350
Wafer Crust ....**6**·702

Variety Meat
(See *Brain, Chitterlings, Heart,
Kidney, Liver, Sweetbreads,
Tongue, Tripe.*)
Vasilopita (New Year's Bread) **9**·1064

VEAL .... **19**·2353-2365
(Listed at the end of this entry
*Chops, Cutlet, Ground, Roast,
Steak.*)
Barbecued, with Rice .... **19**·2364
Carrots, and .... **13**·1636
City Chicken ....**5**·550
Escalopes De Veau
  Flambées .... **19**·2354

Veal *continued*
Herbed Riblets and Limas . **11**·1291
-Olive Sauté . . . . **19**·2363
Parmesan with Spaghetti . **17**·2101
Patties, Pineapple- . . . . **19**·2365
Stew . . . . **19**·2363
Stew, French . . . . **8**·959
Stew 'n Dumplings . . . . . . **17**·2148
Stew with Ravioli . . . . **17**·2147
Sweet-Sour, with Rice . . . . **19**·2364

Chops
Braised . . . . **19**·2361
Italian . . . . **19**·2363
Oriental . . . . **12**·1532
Parmesan Supper . . . . **11**·1381
Veronique . . . . **9**·1050

Cutlet
Bake, Breaded . . . . **19**·2361
Bertrand . . . . **6**·729
Italian . . . . **19**·2361
Parmigiano . . . . **6**·729
Scallopine . . . . **13**·1579
Scallopine with Wine . . . . **16**·1993
Strips, Fondue . . . . **6**·729
Wiener Schnitzel . . . . **20**·2446
Wiener Schnitzel à la
Holstein . . . . **20**·2446

Ground
Chili . . . . **19**·2364
Loaf . . . . **19**·2365
Loaf, Apricot-Topped . . . . **19**·2365
Patties . . . . **19**·2365
Polish Cutlets . . . . **6**·730
Scallopine Burgers . . . . . . **20**·2460
Skillet . . . . **19**·2364
Special, Dilled . . . . **10**·1235
Tufoli Stuffed with . . . . **2**·167

Roast
Braised, Shoulder . . . . **19**·2358
Loaf, Jellied (Kalvsylta) . . . **19**·2355
Pork Roast,
Rolled, and . . . . **19**·2361
Roast . . . . **19**·2359
Sausage-Stuffed
Breast of . . . . **19**·2359
Spinach-Stuffed
Breast of . . . . **19**·2359
Swedish . . . . **19**·2359
Vitello Tonnato . . . . **19**·2355

Steak
Bake, Chopstick . . . . **4**·424
Birds . . . . **19**·2362
Cordon Bleu . . . . **19**·2354
Ham Birds, and . . . . **19**·2362
Roll-Ups . . . . **19**·2362

VEGETABLE . . . . **19**·2367-2389
(See also *Acorn Squash,
Artichoke, Asparagus, Bean, Beet,
Broccoli, Brussels Sprouts,
Cabbage, Carrot, Cauliflower,
Celery, Corn, Cucumber,
Eggplant, Green Pepper, Lettuce,
Mushroom, Okra, Onion, Parsley,
Parsnips, Pea, Potato, Pumpkin,
Radish, Rutabaga, Spinach,
Squash, Sweet Potato, Tomato,
Turnip, Yam, Zucchini Squash.*)

au Gratin . . . . **19**·2382
Bacon-Hominy Scramble . . **9**·1149
Bake, Chicken- . . . . **9**·1143
Barbecued . . . . **2**·153
Beef Brisket with . . . . **3**·288
-Beef Soup . . . . **17**·2084
Belgian Endive-Ham Rolls . . . **2**·209
Bites, French-Fried . . . . **8**·960
Bowl, Calico . . . . **14**·1682
Bowl, Garden . . . . **17**·2133
Casserole, Cheeseburger- . . **12**·1411
Celery Root Sauté . . . . **4**·437
Chicken Breasts à la . . . . **4**·499
Chowder, Chicken- . . . . **2**·174
Chow Mein . . . . **3**·327
Cocktail Soup . . . . **18**·2282
Creamed . . . . **19**·2382
Creamed Peas and New
Potatoes . . . . **6**·676
Creamy Lentil Soup . . . . . . **10**·1280
Flowers . . . . **8**·1013
Foiled . . . . **8**·919
Fritters . . . . **8**·965
Grilled, in Foil . . . . **2**·159
Hominy in Sour Cream . . . . **9**·1149
Jiffy Chili-Hominy Bake . . . **9**·1149
Kohlrabi and Ground Beef
Soup . . . . **10**·1239
Leeks with Lemon . . . . **10**·1269
-Meatball Soup . . . . **9**·1084
-Meatball Stew . . . . **17**·2147
-Meat Cups . . . . **11**·1375
-Meat Medley . . . . **9**·1069
-Meat Pie . . . . **19**·2389
Medley . . . . **6**·707; **13**·1560
Medley, Frank- . . . . **8**·935
Medley Relish . . . . **19**·2328
Molds, Calico . . . . **19**·2382
Oven-Cooked Frozen . . . . **19**·2379
Pie, Kidney . . . . **14**·1759

Vegetable *continued*
Platter, Hot . . . . **19**·2383
Rack of Lamb with . . . . **10**·1256
Roasted Sweet Peppers . . . **10**·1195
Salt Pork and Greens . . . . **1**·24
Scalloped . . . . **19**·2382
Skillet, Beef and . . . . **5**·624
Snow Peas with Water
Chestnuts . . . . **19**·2384
Soup, Easy . . . . **19**·2382
Soup, Hearty . . . . **19**·2332
Soup, Lentil- . . . . **10**·1280
Soup, Meat and . . . . **17**·2088
Soup, Quick . . . . **13**·1579
Soup, Turkey- . . . . **19**·2317
Spanish Gazpacho . . . . **8**·1014
Spitted . . . . **2**·159
Stew, Ham and . . . . **9**·1116
Stew, Short Rib- . . . . **17**·2052
Sticks, Dilled . . . . **19**·2381
Strata, Ham and . . . . **17**·2155
-Stuffed Minute Steaks . . . . **12**·1424
Summer Scramble . . . . **4**·433
Supper, Lamb- . . . . **14**·1751
Toss, Fruit- . . . . **12**·1521
Trio, Savory . . . . **17**·2131
Velouté Sauce . . . . **19**·2390
Velvety Fudge Cake . . . . **4**·509
Venison Steaks, Broiled . . . . . **8**·1004
-Vermouth Cocktail,
Tomato . . . . **20**·2457

Vichyssoise
Blender . . . . **17**·2080
French . . . . **19**·2393
Quick . . . . **19**·2393
Viennese Coffee Float . . . . **8**·908
Vinaigrette, Cauliflower . . . . . **4**·432
Vinaigrette Dressing . . . . . . **19**·2397
Vitello Tonnato . . . . **19**·2355
Volcano Potatoes . . . . **20**·2442

W

Waffles
Bacon . . . . **19**·2432
Banana . . . . **19**·2407
Belgian . . . . **19**·2409
Buttermilk . . . . **19**·2409
Cheese . . . . **11**·1314; **19**·2409
Chicken-Pecan . . . . **19**·2410
Chocolate . . . . **19**·2407
Chocolate Dot . . . . **19**·2408
Corn . . . . **19**·2409
Cornmeal . . . . **19**·2409
Date Torte . . . . **19**·2406
Dessert . . . . **19**·2407
Everyday . . . . **19**·2409
Fresh Apple . . . . **3**·273

Waffles *continued*
Gingerettes . . . . **19**·2407
Ham . . . . **19**·2409
Ham Wafflewiches . . . . . . **19**·2408
Jubilee, Dessert . . . . **19**·2406
Lobster-Cheese . . . . **11**·1314
"Oh Boy" . . . . **10**·1267
Orange . . . . **19**·2407
Orange-Sauced . . . . **19**·2406
Peanut Butter . . . . **19**·2409
Pecan . . . . **19**·2409
Perfect . . . . **19**·2410
Polka-Dot . . . . **19**·2407
Tasty Bran . . . . **3**·273
Toppers, with . . . . **19**·2407
Waikiki Muffins . . . . **12**·1441
Waikiki Sundae . . . . **8**·906

Walnut
Balls, Black . . . . **19**·2416
Cake (Karidopita) . . . . **9**·1064
Candied . . . . **19**·2416
Chicken, Chinese . . . . **19**·2424
Chocolate-Nut
   Clusters . . . . **19**·2416
Cobbler, Apple- . . . . **7**·863
Coffee . . . . **19**·2416
-Covered Chocolates . . . **19**·2416
Cream Roll . . . . **7**·878
Croutons for Salads . . . . . **19**·2419
Crunch Pudding . . . . **19**·2417
Honey-Sugared . . . . **19**·2417
Pie, Holiday . . . . **19**·2417
Salad Dressing . . . . **12**·1478
Sauce, Chocolate- . . . . . . **16**·1973
Snack . . . . **19**·2416
Toss, Tangerine- . . . . **18**·2245
Zucchini with . . . . **17**·2133
Warm Cranberry Punch . . . . **15**·1807
Warren's Glugg . . . . **20**·2464
Washington Pie . . . . **19**·2423
Wassail, Rosy . . . . **5**·524
Wassail, Spiced . . . . **19**·2423
Watercress Pinwheels . . . . . **19**·2425

Watermelon
Fruited . . . . **19**·2427
Pickles . . . . **13**·1658
Punchmelon . . . . **19**·2427
Scalloped Bowl . . . . **8**·1013
-Wine Punch . . . . **19**·2428

Wax Beans
Chili . . . . **19**·2430
Fiesta . . . . **2**·179
Mustard . . . . **1**·14
Salad, Marinated . . . . **19**·2430
Weinkraut . . . . **16**·1984
Welcome Wafers . . . . **1**·72
Welsh Rabbit . . . . **19**·2431

Western
Blue Cheese Dressing . . . . **16**·1925
Flapjacks . . . . **8**·904
Salad . . . . **15**·1854
Welsh Rarebit . . . . **19**·2432
Wheat Bread . . . . **20**·2439
Wheaten Bread . . . . **3**·281

Whipped
Butter . . . . **13**·1553
Cream Dressing . . . . **19**·2428
Cream Sauce . . . . **12**·1475
Turnip Puff . . . . **19**·2331
Whiskey Sour . . . . **20**·2444

White
Cake Supreme . . . . **3**·342
Sauce . . . . **20**·2445
Sauce, Blender . . . . **16**·1965
Stock . . . . **17**·2152
Whole Nut Fruitcake . . . . **5**·531

Whole Wheat
Biscuits . . . . **2**·228
Nut Bread . . . . **20**·2440
Rolls . . . . **9**·1045

Wiener
(See also *Frankfurter, Frank(furter).*)
-Bean Bake . . . . **2**·175
Bean Pot . . . . **8**·936
Schnitzel . . . . **20**·2446
Schnitzel à la Holstein . . . **20**·2446
Wienie-Lottas . . . . **10**·1189

Wild
Duck à la Orange . . . . **7**·812
Duck in Wine . . . . **8**·1005
Rice and Beef Loaf . . . . **9**·1045
Rice and Mushrooms . . . . **20**·2447
Rice Stuffing . . . . **20**·2447
Rice-Turkey Dish . . . . **19**·2318
Wilted Lettuce Toss . . . . . . **10**·1266
Wilted Spinach Salad . . . . . **17**·2114

Wine
(See also *Beverages, Alcoholic;
Burgundy; Champagne; Claret;
Foreign Cookery; Sauterne;
Sherry.*)
Baked Lobster Savannah . . **11**·1311
Beef à la Wellington . . . . . **20**·2459
Bordelaise Sauce . . . . **2**·250
-Broiled Chicken . . . . **16**·1987
Calico Chicken . . . . **14**·1683
Chicken Parisienne . . . . **4**·482
Clam Chowder au Vin . . . . . **5**·520
Classic Chicken Divan . . . . . **7**·782
Coq au Vin . . . . **5**·617
Crab Meat Newburg . . . . **6**·652,

Wine *continued*
-Eggs Mornay . . . . **12**·1433
Elegant Onion Soup . . . . . **12**·1511
Flounder in . . . . **8**·911
Fruit Sauce . . . . **5**·634
Glaze . . . . **7**·856
Hors d'oeuvres,
   Cranberry . . . . **20**·2459
Hot Fruit Compote . . . . . . **20**·2460
Hot Fruit Medley . . . . **14**·1740
Lobster Tails Maison . . . . . **11**·1313
Melon Medley . . . . **10**·1155
-Mushroom Sauce . . . . . . **16**·1970
Navy Bean-Stuffed
   Duck . . . . **7**·813
Orange-Port Mold . . . . . . **20**·2460
Partridge in Red . . . . **13**·1574
Punch, Watermelon- . . . . . **19**·2428
Punch, Ruby . . . . **20**·2458
Rolled Chicken
   Breasts . . . . **4**·484
Rosé Frappé . . . . **20**·2458
Rosy Wassail . . . . **5**·524
Salad, Cranberry- . . . . **14**·1740
Sauce . . . . **8**·925
Sauce, Beef with . . . . **20**·2460
-Sauced Birds . . . . **8**·1005
Sauce Diable . . . . **7**·775
Sauce, Kidney in . . . . **10**·1231
Sauce, Pheasant in . . . . . . **13**·1655
Scallopine Burgers . . . . . . **20**·2460
Shrimp de Jonghe . . . . . . **17**·2056
Soup, Onion- . . . . **20**·2459
Steak Marchand
   De Vin . . . . **15**·1895
Tomato-Vermouth
   Cocktail . . . . **20**·2457
Tripe Italiano . . . . **19**·2351
Truite Farcie . . . . **18**·2299
Veal and Ham Birds . . . . . **19**·2362
Veal Cordon Bleu . . . . . . **19**·2354
Veal Scallopine with . . . . . **16**·1993
Wild Duck in . . . . **8**·1005
Zabaglione au Madera . . . **10**·1199

WINES AND SPIRITS . **20**·2449-2468

Winter
Fruit Compote . . . . **5**·595
Fruit Medley . . . . **10**·1279
Fruit Soufflé . . . . **9**·1056
Orange Bowl . . . . **12**·1521
Preserves . . . . **14**·1781

Y

Yakamish .... 12·1531

Yam
Casserole, Polynesian .... 14·1689
Sausage Skillet, and ...... 11·1300
Skillet, Meat and .... 11·1330

Yankee
Bacon Bake ....5·637
Pot Roast .... 14·1761
Pot Roast Gravy .... 14·1761
Red-Flannel Hash .... 9·1129
Tostada .... 18·2293

Yellow
Cake ....3·342
Cake Deluxe ....3·342
Rice .... 10·1187

Yogurt
Dressing .... 11·1327; 11·1363
-Fruit Combo .... 15·1917
Salad Dressing .... 20·2475
Salad, Strawberry .... 17·2167

Z

Zabaglione au Madera ..... 10·1199

Zesty
Chicken Spread .... 17·2121
Luncheon Barbecue ....2·155
Zucchini Dip .... 11·1318
Zigzag Bowl .... 8·1013

Zippy
Beef-Olive
Spread .... 12·1497
Beet Dressing .... 11·1364
Beet Salad ....2·207
Blue Cheese
Sauce ....2·248
Butter ....3·315
Cooked Dressing .... 14·1753
Emerald Dressing .... 16·1927
Fish Fillets ....7·895
Ham Dip ....5·629
Mushrooms ....1·14
Mustard Sauce .... 12·1453
Mustard Slaw ....3·328
Pineapple Sauce ....4·482

Zucchini Squash
Chinese-Style .... 17·2133
Dip, Zesty .... 11·1318
Dolmas,
Turkish ....7·788
Florentine .... 17·2132
Fritters, Cheese-
Sauced .... 17·2132
Half Shells .... 20·2479
Parmesan .... 20·2479
Saucy .... 17·2132
Scallop,
Tomato- ....4·428
Skillet .... 17·2132
Spanish .... 20·2480
Supper,
Steak and .... 17·2134
Supreme .... 17·2133
Sweet-Sour
Medley .... 17·2131
Vinaigrette .... 18·2204
Walnuts, with .... 17·2133
Zuppa Inglese ....6·725
Zwieback
Meatballs .... 20·2480
Zwiebelfleisch (Beef with
Onions) .... 19·2395